Life in the Wilds of Central India

Life in the Wilds of Central India

By J.D. St Joseph

Published by the British Empire & Commonwealth Museum, Bristol, 2001 ©

Designed and produced by Naunton Pugh, Omnia Publicity Management, Over, Cambridge.

Set in Palatino 10.5pt on 12.5pt.

Reproduction by Matrix Pre-Press, Cottenham, Cambridge.

Printed by Rowland Digital, Bury St Edmunds, Suffolk.

ISBN 0-9530174-3-5

CONTENTS

		Page
Acknowledgements		iii
Foreword		vii
Reflections on the Account		xiii
I	A General Sketch	1
II	Camp Requisites	12
III	Early Reminiscences	16
IV	Incidents in Camp Life	61
V	Beats	107
VI	Stalking	120
VII	Still Shooting	129
VIII	Shooting	139
IX	Animal Cures for Wounds	157
X	Tiger	165
XI	Panther	224
XII	Bear	248
XIII	Sambar	261
XIV	Cheetal	282
XV	The Gaur	294
XVI	Miscellaneous Incidents	337

Appendices:

A	Working with the Bhils - Relevant Letters and Reports	367
B	A Bhil Legend, chosen from J.D.St J's collection	378
C	The Barwani State Forests	384
D	Medicinal Plants and their uses: Relevant Correspondence	397
E	Places of Interest: Extracts from The East India Company	408

Relevant documents to be found at the British Empire & Commonwealth Museum, Bristol, or at the Centre of South Asian Studies, Cambridge... 419
Glossary A: Indian words explained by the author 420
Glossary B: Indian words undefined by the author 423
British people referred to in the text 425
Finale 428

ii *Life in the Wilds of Central India*

ACKNOWLEDGEMENTS

I would like to offer my grateful thanks to everyone who has helped me to produce these century old memoirs. To everyone in the Map Room at the Cambridge University Library, to Naunton Pugh for his guidance in dealing with the text and old photographs and to Dr Gareth Griffiths of the British Empire and Commonwealth Museum for his encouragement. Above all I would like to thank Carol Pickering and Sita Narasimhan for their invaluable help. Carol for her inexhaustible patience, indefatigable energy and devoted interest in the book and its author.

And Sita, whose knowledgeable influence brought about the conviction of everyone involved that the text would prove better historically if left, unedited, in its original state.

Familiar, at different times with various areas of India, they have each written to explain their reaction to the memoirs and their reasons for leaving the text unedited.

Carol writes:

'As I have read the manuscript again its freshness has impressed me and I realise that most of the changes I made before were misleading. In fact in changing some of his expressions to those of our time it loses its contemporary character. One must remember that this is, in all ways, a period piece.

Memory has also come to my aid as I recall my late husband, Donald Hardy, a district administrative officer of the Indian Civil Service in the United Provinces (now Uttar Pradesh) during the 1930s and '40s. He spent the three cold weather months of North India almost continuously in camp, returning to his bungalow in headquarters only occasionally during that period. Earlier Forestry officers, however, must have had to spend their time always on the move, living almost entirely under canvas or in simple *dak bungalows* (government rest houses) as they went about their daily work.

Now I am able to picture John Daniel St Joseph, a very young man just out of school, with limited resources, for junior officers of many of the Indian services were on low pay, sitting alone, often feeling wretchedly ill from his "old enemy", malaria; tired after a hard day's work, contending with the discomforts of heat and stinging insects, with little companionship of his own kind, no one with whom to discuss his problems or share his thoughts.

It is likely that, as he was leading such a peripatetic life, he had with him very few books, and no dictionary to consult.

Working by the poor light of a lantern, at best an oil lamp, it is little wonder that he sometimes made mistakes in spelling, grammar and punctuation. The wonder is, rather, that he wrote so evocatively and with a freshness that brings his whole world to life for us a hundred years later. I feel now that it is a presumption to quibble with his mis-spellings, sometimes odd sentence construction or use of words, which may grate on our ears. These things matter little in comparison with his achievements. One is left with the impression of a man of remarkable intellectual gifts, of great human understanding and the ability to influence for good all those around him. In fact the very mistakes in his draft, which he himself would doubtless have corrected had he lived to do so, add to the picture I have of him sitting late at night in his tent, fighting fatigue, ill-health and various discomforts, to write a few more pages of his memoir.'

C.E.P.

Sita writes:

'When I first read the manuscript of John Daniel St. Joseph's *Life in the Wilds of Central India* I was both deeply moved and entranced.

Here was one of the men dedicated to India who are justly commemorated in Westminster Abbey who "died of the rigours of climate in India."

Born to British parents and educated in India, he worked his way up from the lowest ranks of the Forest Department. He came to England twice – the first time, in the summer of 1908, to qualify for a Diploma in Forestry at Oxford, a right he had thoroughly earned, and to get married, and then in 1914, a sick man, to die here three years later.

In temperament he is very British and also Indian, one of a now vanishing species who created, ordered, conserved and constructed modern India.

I was entranced by the idiosyncratic but precise style of this unusual but yet very familiar nineteenth century figure – pioneering, solitary, and a savant. He was a naturalist, an anthropologist, a conservationist, and a lover of wild life.

A realist, yet incurably romantic, he writes his loving, meticulous, dedicated account of the jungle and its "denizens",

where he lived a spartan life for many years, with Kipling's books for company and a small gun for finding sustenance and defending himself and others.

His main contribution was, of course, to the Forest Department: its establishment, growth, expansion into the Princely States and its professionalisation.

His work was in the Central Provinces, now Madhya Pradesh – an unwieldy wild tract of land that, down the centuries, has separated Northern and Peninsular India.

His observations touch on many issues that are of passionate national and international interest today.

For example, irrigation in the Narmada Valley; balancing the needs of man and beast in the jungle; the life-styles of tribes like the Bhils and the Gonds who helped him survive, as well as the other sometimes nameless "aborigines" who have yet to find a voice and are the stuff of politics in today's India; problems of land rights and the administration of justice in small places far from towns; the identification and classification of herbs and trees and their medicinal uses, which are now being patented in the West and in India.

There is much else that he has to offer to the student of modern India. His motto on the forest's bounty echoes the Indian sense from Vedic times of the treasures of the forest.

We owe a deep debt of gratitude to Daphne St. Joseph, who, impelled by a desire to preserve this text, has done the research necessary to make it accessible to all.

S.N.

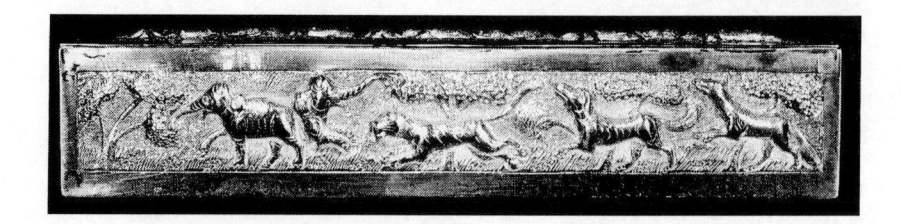

The Chase: from an Indian silver box.

vi *Life in the Wilds of Central India*

FOREWORD

The manuscript of *Life in the Wilds of Central India*, written by John Daniel St. Joseph in 1912 and originally entitled *Work and Sport in the Wilds of Central India*, was brought to England in 1914 when he had to retire from the Forestry Service to which he had devoted his life and energy for over 20 years. With the manuscript came records of his work and of relevant subjects in which he had done considerable research.

The text has been carefully treated, leaving it almost entirely as it was written; but, as owing to his early death he was unable to do the final editing himself, occasional changes have been made and recorded.

His memoirs are chiefly concerned with the country in and around the Aravalli, Satpura and Vindhya mountain ranges. They contain graphic descriptions of terraced plateaux among the hills, forest tribes whose nomadic cultivation with axe and fire was so destructive and difficult to control, wild animals and their behaviour, trees, plants and, last but not least, the climate to which everything and everyone had to adapt. His memories are clear; not only of the natural world but also of people whose character, skill or advice made a lasting impression on him.

The work is illustrated with maps, showing some of the many places mentioned in the text, and with his photographs taken in the early 1900's. No negatives remain.

No date is certain for the meticulous drawing of Lakha, an area of what is now called Jaunsar Bawar, about thirty-five miles N.N.W. of Dehra Dun. The India Office's first estimation was that it had been drawn in 1910, then, perhaps ten years earlier. Two other choices of date are possible: 1908/9 when St. Joseph was working for a Diploma in Forestry at Oxford or conceivably in 1890, for the geography examination at school in Naini Tal.

His education there may well have led to his choice of career, through interest in the country, its wildlife and the founding in 1885 in Dehra Dun of a school to train Forest Rangers.

With the growth of the Forest Service he would have become aware of the daunting tasks involved: how to protect the forests from and on behalf of the tribes who lived there, how to gain their friendship and support, how to cope with drought and famine, and how to survive.

Indian forestry and its development

In the late 18th and early 19th centuries the East India Company had provided careers in trade, medicine, engineering, administration and the Army, which sometimes led to the Forestry Service.

In the 1850's an Army officer was commended for helping to reduce the scourge of forest fires. It was a Doctor Cleghorn who drew attention to the massive destruction of teak forests, caused by the 'Kumri' method of cultivation, the burning of forests to obtain more land: a system still more disastrous in much of the world to-day.

According to St. Joseph the birth of the Indian Forest Service dates from the middle of the 19th century; for its expansion between 1848 and 1856 Lord Dalhousie was largely responsible. The aim was to preserve forests from destruction, manage and plant them to meet future demands, cover expenses, and even make a profit and to accommodate local tribes.

It was soon realised that the British had much to learn on the matter from the already expert French and Germans. In 1856 Dietrich Brandis, Professor of Botany at Bonn University was persuaded to come to India to follow up Lord Dalhousie's efforts but it was only slowly that the service expanded in spite of the fact that the richest forest areas were not unduly affected by the Mutiny.

Ten years later, because of little increase in the number of volunteers, Brandis decided to go to England to seek recruits. This venture was so successful that by 1870, after training in France or Germany, forty-four new officers were appointed.

A few, like Henry Baden Powell from the Bengal Civil Service, (and twenty years later John Daniel St. Joseph) joined with no forest training at all. When Brandis retired he was succeeded in 1881 by William Schlich, who had begun his career in Burma while the former was recruiting in England. After only four years Schlich was invited to organise the English Forest School for India at Cooper's Hill. The school was transferred in 1905 to Oxford where by 1909 Schlich had become Secretary to the Delegates for Instruction in Forestry. Two years later he was appointed the first Professor of and Reader in Forestry, a post he held until 1919, having been elected an Honorary Fellow of St. John's College, and become Sir William Schlich K.C.I.E., M.A.

Family Background in India

The 19th century members of the St. Joseph and Broadway families were born and brought up in North India where many of them worked as civil engineers or tea planters, in Forestry or the Punjab Police Force, as missionaries in the CMS or Baptist Missionary Society, or in various regiments of the British or Indian Armies: a Lieutenant-Colonel and a Major in the 5th Gurkha Rifles, a Captain in the K.O.S.B., two brothers killed in the First World War, one serving in the Royal Engineers, the other in the 2nd Lancers, and a Barrister-at-Law who became a Judge in the Punjab.

Daniel Philip Broadway, St. Joseph's grandfather, joined the CMS in 1843. He served first at Monghyr, then "after the exciting days of the Mutiny" as he put it, moved to Agra, Delhi, Patna, and then Bankipore, latterly with the Baptist Missionary Society. He retired in 1896 to Monghyr where he died aged 76.

St. Joseph's two sisters worked as missionaries in Siwan, Saran and Chanpatia, Champaran, and on retiring, lived in Dehra Dun at 8 Indar Road, a house provided by their brother.

John Daniel St. Joseph was born on June 9th 1873 in Patna, two years before Jim Corbett, author of many books about India. They were both educated at the Boys' Diocesan School, later to become Sherwood College, in Naini Tal.

Corbett was initiated into the use of a gun before he was ten years old but there is no evidence that St. Joseph owned one until he joined the Forest Service. Chapters on various aspects of shooting of which people may well disapprove nowadays have been included for historical and editorial accuracy.

To quote from *Carpet Sahib*, a biography of Corbett by Martin Booth: "In India in the second half of the nineteenth century, hunting and shooting was an accepted pastime or necessity. Royalty, maharajahs, viceroys, senior army officers and important business people attended massive shoots at which up to three dozen tigers would be shot in a day. Junior officers shot for sport and others for food. Game seemed to be universal and in continual abundance."

Shooting was also essential for self-defence, and the defence of local people.

To quote from Corbett himself: "The map of Eastern Kumaon that hangs on the wall before me is marked with a number of crosses, and below each cross is a date. These crosses indicate the

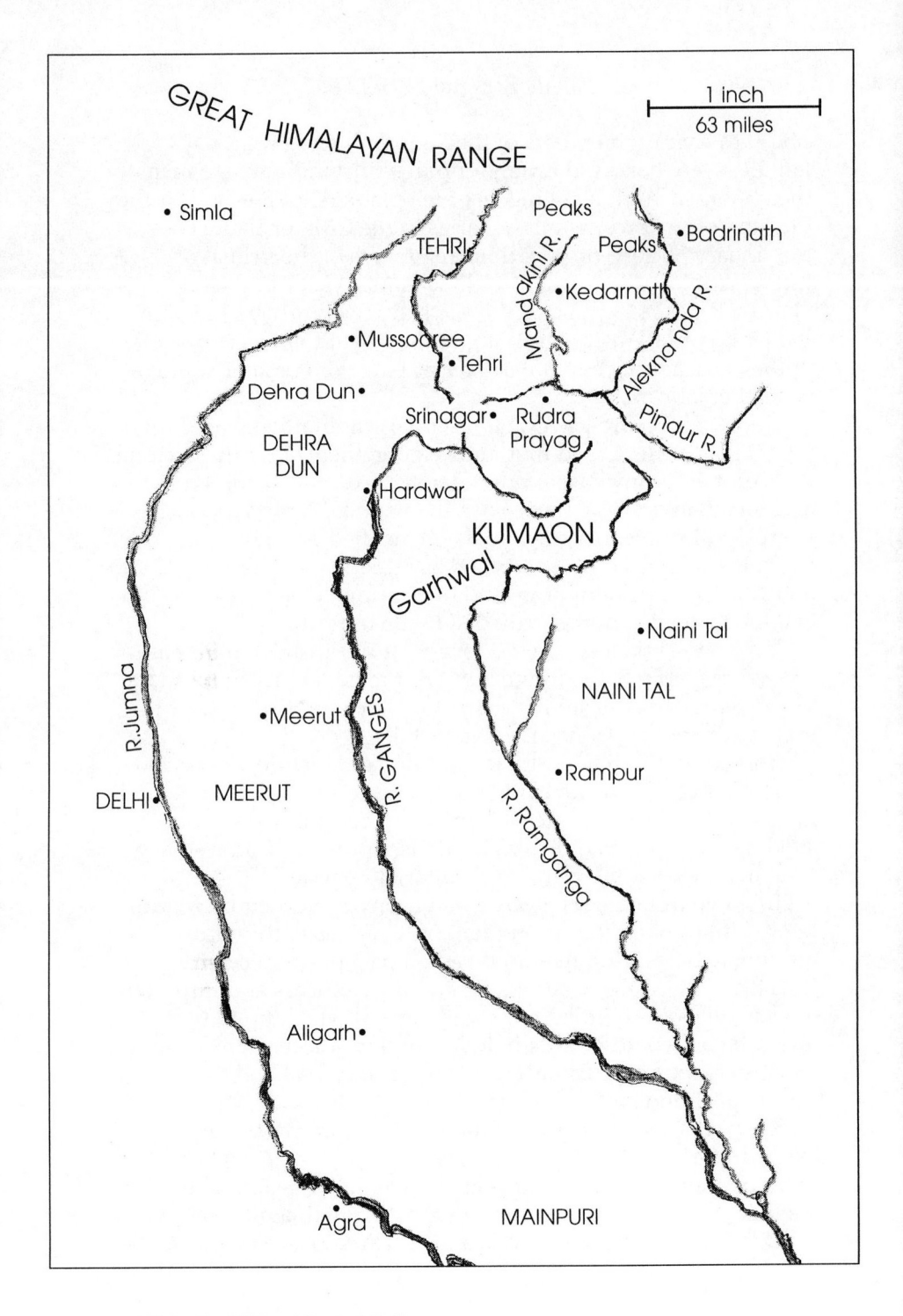

x *Life in the Wilds of Central India*

locality, and the date, of the officially recorded human victims of the man-eating tiger of Chowgarh. There are sixty-four crosses on the map. I do not claim this as being a correct tally, for the map was posted by me for two years, and during this period not all kills were reported to me; further, victims who were only mauled and who died subsequently, have not been awarded a cross and a date.

The first cross is dated 15 December 1925, and the last 21 March 1930. The distance between the extreme crosses, north to south, is fifty miles, and east to west, thirty miles, an area of 1,500 square miles of mountain and vale where the snow lies deep during winter, and the valleys are scorching hot in summer. Over this area the Chowgarh tiger had established a reign of terror."

In his *Man Eating Leopard of Rudraprayagh*, Corbett describes a similar reign of terror in the area lying between the Aleknanda and Mandkini Rivers.

Hindus in their thousands, walking barefoot from Hardwar up the pilgrim way to the age old shrines of Kadernath and Badrinath, were as vulnerable on their journey as were daily the inhabitants of the scattered villages.

Between 1918 and 1926 the leopard caused 125 tragic deaths. After months of tracking and many long nights' dangerous waiting Corbett was at long last able to kill the killer.

Of the two school contemporaries Corbett lived the longer by forty years and so had more time to adapt to the idea of conservation which had earlier on occasions attracted St. Joseph.

The latter left school in 1890, having passed the compulsory Final Examinations in English, Latin, Mathematics, Political Economy and Geography and the optional History and Urdu. The following year, aged nearly eighteen, he joined the Forestry Service and was sent to a place several miles from the tiny headquarters station of Badnur, north of the Tapti River, east of the Satpura Range and Machna River, where he spent about twelve months, some of the time at Hoshangabad officiating as a divisional forest officer. The first tribes with which he came into contact were the Gonds and the Korkus; his closest and longest association was with the Bhils, to all of whom he gave occasional medical help.

At first he travelled light, as can be understood by reading the opening paragraphs of the second chapter. To begin with the journeys in the jungle were done on foot: a horse was out of the question. For the earliest officers in the Forest Service no maps

were provided. St. Joseph described his as being only four miles to an inch and too small to be of use.

The narrative provides clues, which help to make the following timetable of his career. During the monsoons of 1894 he was quartered for a time in the Shahpura bungalow near the Machna River.

Three years later the government transferred him to the Central India Agency, which comprised the Native States in the Central Provinces. The change was defined as "deputation to foreign service". He comments in 1912 that "it is only recently that forest conservancy has attracted attention in the Native States, commencing where Government started forty years earlier".

At the turn of the century he was deeply involved in the disastrous famine which affected tribes living in the Satpura, Vindhya and Aravalli ranges. Nothing like it was known in the memory of their oldest inhabitant. St. Joseph's efforts to lessen peoples' suffering were to lead to his being awarded the *Kaisar-i-Hind* medal a few years later.

By 1900 he had been appointed Chief Forest Officer of the Bhopawar Agency in Central India, where Charles Bayley was Agent to the Governor General and Captain Barnes the Political Agent.*

As Chief Forest Officer he was able to wield an official stamp. Round its perimeter is engraved: *SI DARE VIS SILVAE PLUS TIBI CULTA FERET*, which can be translated: "If you wish to give to the forest it will yield more to you when cultivated".

In December 1901, he was in Barwani for an event written up by the correspondent of *The Pioneer*, a well-known newspaper. That and the next were years of great drought, described in Chapter XV.

Evidence of subsequent travels is to be found in the photographs. In 1903 he was in Jobat, the next year in Bhabra, Amkhut and Mandu in Dhar State. The Rana of Ali-Rajpur visited him in his camp in 1905 or 1906. The Rana was succeeded two years later by his son Pratap Singh, who ruled at least until 1935 and became His Highness Raja Sir Pratap Singh. In 1911 having made his last tour of the Bhopawar Agency (through the Jhabua State) St. Joseph was probably much taken up with the memoirs which are dated 1912.

*See Appendix A

Reflections on the account

Written nearly 90 years ago it seems surprisingly up to date, with the exception of chapters or paragraphs on stalking and shooting which today many people would find more than distasteful; but one must acknowledge the vast difference in attitudes to wildlife then and now, when the survival of so many animals is under threat.

A century ago these were far more numerous and more dangerous. Panther for example preyed on villagers and their families in the wild. When St. Joseph joined the Forest Service he was young and keen, and part of his job was to get to know and work with the local tribesmen whose sons went shooting for food as well as sport, so it was natural for him to join them. When in the jungle he depended on game for his survival.

Not only tribesmen but also the British in those days went shooting for food as well as sport. These were occasions when one met the local rulers and aristocracy as well as other British officers.

The whole book bears evidence of the author's powers of observation and interest in his work, in the people with whom he was involved, every kind of plant and tree and, especially in the last chapter, every kind of animal, bird or insect that crossed his path. He remembers the rare sighting of a peacock dance, his dogs, great companions in a nomadic existence, and his pet baboon. Chapters I - XVI are from St. Joseph's handwritten account of 1912. Appendices A - D are from his work records. I have provided a short introduction to A and D, and added Appendix E.

New friends, marriage, back to India.

By 1908 St. Joseph had met the Canadian missionary Dr. Margaret O'Hara. Aged 37e, with all the necessary medical qualifications, she had to come to Indore to work for the Canadian Presbyterian Mission in Central India where she spent most of her life until retirement, returning home to Canada in 1927.

There is no evidence of when he met William Sinclair Marris – a contemporary and friend of Rutherford - who, after being educated at Canterbury College in New Zealand and for a year at Oxford, had passed the ICS examination with flying colours (coming first by a margin of 1,000 marks). The same age as St. Joseph, he arrived in India in 1896 to work in what was later

called the United Provinces of Agra and Oudh. In 1901 he was appointed Under Secretary to the Government of India, was Governor of Assam 1921-2 and of the United Provinces 1922-7. His path must early in the century have crossed that of Dr. O'Hara.

In March 1903 William's sister Irma Robertson Marris went out from England in the S/S Himalaya to stay with her brother, we do not know for how long. She was 27, and probably took her painting things. Five years later she was back in India, again staying with her brother, through whom she met Dr. O'Hara. The story can be continued by quoting from The *Leaf of the Lotus*, a collection of letters written by Dr. O'Hara and printed in her memory by Canadian friends:

Jobat Feb. 3, 1908

"You will perhaps wonder at my present address. I had a letter from Mrs. Buchanan asking me to go to Amkhut, and am on my way, in company with Miss Marris, an English lady who is painting pictures for exhibition and has been staying with me for several weeks at Dhar. By great good fortune I learned that Mr. St. Joseph, the Chief Forest Officer, had arranged to tour in the Bhil country, so we were able to travel under his protection; in fact, we are his guests, and live very comfortably. He camps in style. Miss Marris and I have a tent, he his own personal tent, and besides there is a large dining tent, not to mention the separate accommodation for his office and clerks. There are excellent meals served in china and glass dishes. (A far cry from our missionary style of camping, you can see!) His grandfather was one of the earliest English Baptist missionaries and he is greatly interested in our work. His own lies largely in the Vindhya Hills where we are at present, wild and very ruggedly beautiful country.

Amkhut is one hundred miles from Dhar by this route, through Sirdarpur and Jobat. The only other way is by driving to Mhow entraining there for Ratlam and Dohad and then a drive of forty miles - altogether more than twice the distance.

His Highness very kindly lent us his motorcar to take us to Sirdarpur. Miss Marris and I spent the night in the very house the mission is trying to buy, so I had the opportunity of going through it thoroughly.

The following morning we started through these hills; it is difficult travelling. I have spent the morning here seeing patients, and have among other things done an operation.

Mr. St. Joseph has just come riding in to get his rifle. (We all ride over the hills, though I have not been on a horse before this since I was here in '97). He was out on inspection work and was told that a panther had killed six goats nearby, so I think I shall go to see the shooting. I have seen many panthers after they were killed, and once, years ago, I met a live one; but never have I seen the destroyer paying the penalty for his misdeeds. Many a poor Bhil mother mourns a child carried off by one of these beasts.

I go from there to Amkhut and thence to Dohad en route to Dhar and my own work, much benefited in every way by the pleasant change."

So that was how John and Irma met. They were married on August 20th, 1908 in the parish church at Cookley, near her parents' home, in Worcestershire. They went to live at 24 Beechcroft Road, Oxford, probably that autumn because he had signed on at University College to read for a Diploma in Forestry, and were still there in February 1909, as is evident from the following letter:

Oxford, 29 Banbury Road.
February 6, 1909.
From W. Schlich, Secretary to the Delegates for Instruction in Forestry.
To J.D. St. Joseph.
Sir,
I am directed to inform you that you will be considered qualified for the Diploma in Forestry after having passed the prescribed examinations in
1) General Geology 2) General Botany 3) Forest Botany 4) Forest Zoology and 5) Forestry and that your practical course in Forestry has been reduced to three months.
I am, yours faithfully
W. Schlich.

The decision conveyed in the last sentence is hardly surprising seeing that he had already had 18 years' experience. Later that year they were back in the Barwani State. There is a vivid account of the unexpectedly warm welcome given by the Bhils to his wife on their first tour together of tribal country. This must also have been a token of their respect for him, and in gratitude perhaps for his concern for their welfare and not infrequent medical advice.

Irma is mentioned on three occasions, but not by name. She was learning to shoot with her small bore .303 rifle, showed her ability to make friends with shy people like the recluse who

presented her with a pipe of peace as a memento of their visit, and with her husband braved the rapids of a river, perhaps the Nerbudda.

The first tragedy of their married life was the death of their daughter Muriel, born in January 1910, baptized in April in Christ Church, Mhow, who died before the end of the year. Because of the high mortality rate in India among the very young they thought it wise, when another child was to be born, that Irma should return to England to her parents at Cookley, even if her husband had to remain at his post as Chief Forest Officer in the Bhopawar Agency.

John Kenneth Sinclair St. Joseph was born on November 13th 1912. His father may have visited the family during the next few months, but he was certainly still in India the following year.

In 1914 alarm signals about his health reached England. So much so that when war was declared on August 4th Irma made immediate plans to go and bring her husband home, leaving for India in a troopship.

On their return they went to live in Worcester. The departure from India must have involved an immense upheaval. They took with them all available records of his work, a collection of Indian silver, treasures in stone, wood and brass, even elephant chains, books, furniture and some of Irma's paintings.

He died on March 8th, 1917 of pernicious anaemia, for which a remedy was discovered only a short time later. He was 44.

His widow and son continued to live in Worcester but moved to 60 Malvern Road, their home until 1945.

Prey to severe arthritis, Irma retired to a nursing home where she died in 1959, aged 83.

All records and relics, Indian and family, went in 1945 to Cambridge where J.K.S. St. Joseph had been an undergraduate at Selwyn College from 1931-1935, then a graduate for three years reading for a Ph.D. in Geology. He was a Fellow of the College from 1938-1994, Vice-Master 1974-1980, the year of his retirement. He became a C.B.E. in 1979, and F.B.A. in 1978. In the University he was Lecturer in Natural Sciences 1939-1962; in Operational Research with Bomber Command 1942-1945; Lecturer in Geology 1945-1948; Curator, then Director in Aerial Photography 1948-1973; Professor of Aerial Photographic Studies 1973-1980. After retirement in 1980 he was Professor Emeritus for fourteen years.

Daphne St Joseph

Déjà Vu

'I take this from my notebook, just as most of this book is transposed from notes written (in 1929) by the light of camp fires. If, in the light of later events, it may seem naïve, it at least has the veracity of being true to the time.'

Negley Farson, *Caucasian Journey*, 1951.

Chapter I

A General Sketch

These memoirs cover a period of 21 years' experience in the forests of Central India and the Central Provinces. They deal with noteworthy incidents that came under observation and were the means of gaining some insight into the manners and customs of the inhabitants.

The writer was barely eighteen when he joined the Forest department, and was straightway sent out into the jungles. The appointment placed him several miles from the tiny headquarter station of Badnur, and imposed a solitary life with duties that soon brought him under the influence of the silent forces dominating the wilds. This schooled him to the free and singular existence that is the lot of those who have to pass most of their time in the jungles.

Concomitantly, the retrospect appertains to the country of the Satpura, Vindhya and Aravalli hills which occupy the centre of the triangular continent. As the names imply, each is a self-contained group spreading over a vast tract. They vary in unity of structure but conform in general appearance in being very wild and rugged.

The principal chains as a rule comprise terraced plateaux that rise to nearly four thousand feet and tower over the adjacent features upon which their outlines look down in tiers of frowning cliffs. The lesser ranges are a series of globular hills abutting on the main chains, and are as often as not capped with massive rocks that stand out boldly in their naked ruggedness. Among these intertwine numerous watercourses which frequently find outlets through deep-seated valleys and ravines. The configuration of the surface is therefore marked by deep indentations, serried plateaux, conical tops and scarped slopes. Access accordingly is difficult and the country bold and picturesque, especially where the hillsides are studded with forest growth to soften the effects, without which they would appear a wilderness of stone and rock.

The summits and passes are dotted with the ruins of decaying fortresses that were once occupied by itinerant chiefs to overawe the surrounding country. Never quite subdued by the alien government set up by the Mohammedan Kings, they plundered and robbed with impunity, making for the hills when opposed by superior numbers at whom they could hurl defiance from their

castellated retreats. These in fact, became veritable hornets' nests from which neither friend nor foe could expect consideration. The works have long since been reduced by the elements into heaps of broken rubbish and reclaimed by trees and beasts as their original inheritance. Few instances point more forcibly to the strong arm of Britain's might, than these landmarks of unbroken struggles with the ruling powers of the time.

The rainfall is fairly copious and well distributed, but the gain this represents is counteracted by the geological characteristics. These operate to diminish the retentive capacity of rock and soil in respect of moisture and render supply entirely dependent on the seasons. Consequently, any disturbance or variation in the normal condition is more likely than not to result in a general deficiency, causing a partial or complete failure in the surface drainage.

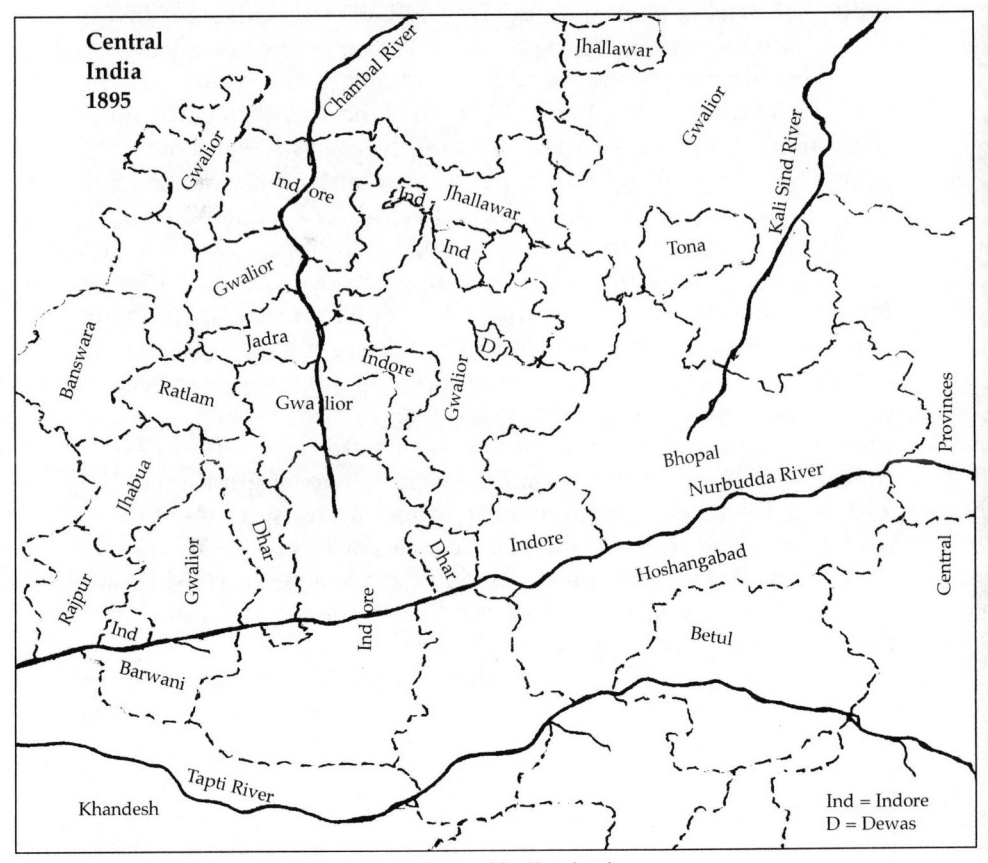

Note: Named states are those mentioned in the text.

Drought or water famine of more or less intensity is, therefore, always to be feared whenever the seasons are at all capricious.

This will show that the hilly tracts are unsuited for the practice of agriculture to advantage. They are sparsely inhabited by forest tribes who eke out an existence on jungle products supplemented by meagre harvests raised with axe and fire. On the other hand, the areas are eminently adapted for the growth of trees and despite maltreatment, forests have maintained their vitality and even flourished.

Physical considerations have, doubtless, contributed to this result. But, the lore of the jungles ascribes it to supernatural power. The legends mention the density of the stocking and the repeated failure of attempts at forming settlements over an expansive area. The habits acquired by the tribes are also proofs of the ascendancy maintained by vegetation through countless ages. These tales deal with the expulsion by disease, pestilence, or famine, or by the ravages of wild men and beasts of the settlers who ventured on an extensive slaughter of the "silent life" as exhibited by trees. They point to the displeasure of presiding deities whenever attempts have been made to dispoil [sic] of their verdant growth the "speechless life" assigned to the gigantic monuments arising as hills and plateaux. These they say were created by Nature during moments of perturbation, while she was in the process of modelling the world. Allusion is frequently made to the sanctity of dense cover as the recognised abode of spirits and demons who were allotted a separate sphere of action to prevent intercourse with man and the consequent danger of each other's extermination. It is alleged that these supernatural beings were relegated to the hills because of their greater power of resistance against the elements of Nature. Moreover, the belief is entertained that the "silent life" represented by trees was created as much to protect the weak against the strong, as to preclude interference in the undivided designs of the two ruling passions - namely, men and demons - inhabiting the earth and so forth.

Everybody knows that people constrained to live in the jungles have acquired habits peculiar to their environments. The one common to all and important from a forest point of view, is the form of nomadic cultivation with axe and fire practised by forest tribes. This primitive method of raising crops over patch clearances without the aid of bullocks, is undoubtedly the result of experience. It is based on the necessity in combining to protect

cover with the restricted cultivation needed for supplementing the exiguous requirements of indigent tribes. Isolated fellings of the type practised are obviously less harmful than wholesale clearances which would assuredly lead to erosion or intensify the evils of famine and drought.

Examples abound of the desertion of large tracts within easy approach of the hills, which has synchronized with extensive deforestation practised on the neighbouring slopes. In the writer's experience of famines and scarcities, the effects of drought have been most in evidence over hilly tracts denuded of forest growth.

This is a brief allusion to references in folklore regarding the part played by forests in the material condition of the country. However this may be, Government soon recognised the utility of forests in the internal economy of the country and took steps to preserve valuable growth as well as to reserve hill ranges where deforestation was likely to produce injurious results. The policy pursued in this respect has brought into existence the efficient service of trained officials who now control the working of all forests under the British administration. Each Province possesses a self-contained department for the management of its forests whose administrative units comprise circles, divisions, sub-divisions, ranges, sub-ranges and beats in sequence of importance. A circle is the largest charge held by an individual who is styled Conservator, while a beat comprises the smallest unit of management and is allotted to a Forest Guard. Between these are several gradations of officials, styled Deputy and Assistant Conservators at the head of divisions and sub-divisions, and Rangers and Foresters posted to ranges and sub-ranges. As may be gathered, the forest tracts in a Province include its wildest and most difficult portions, both as regards accessibility and configuration of surface. It also happens that owing to the boundaries marching with prominent features, the forests generally are the furthest removed from headquarters. Areas of administrative units vary considerably in the different provinces. But it is not uncommon for the forest area in a division to exceed one thousand square miles, while a beat is often over twenty square miles in area, from which it may be judged that individual charges are heavy.

The duties required of forest officers are essentially practical, and efficiency is best ensured by activity in the field, necessitating an outdoor existence as far as is compatible with the seasons, for

during the monsoons it is impossible for any one to remain out. The principal work consists in devising and superintending measures for protection and exploitation, that is, to safeguard the growth from injuries and to develop the capital. But, not the least important or interesting item in the programme is the expedience for observing the phenomena of plant growth with a view to effecting improvements in the composition and conditions of the forests.

Apart from the duties of a professional character, the forest officer must be able to manage the tribes who are the natural guardians of the forests so as to enlist their support, without which successful protection is both difficult and costly. Moreover he should be capable of handling the vexed questions that are constantly arising in dealings with agriculturists who draw their supplies from the forests. Practical fitness therefore, counts for more in the department, than in any other service. And considering the circumstances under which he is called upon to work, the forest officer has not only to prove himself of hard mettle, but finds himself cut off from what little society a jungle district can offer. On the other hand, he has ample opportunities for observing nature and acquiring the initiative spirit that is less easy of attainment in other services.

The above remarks apply to forest management in British India, which excludes the feudatory States. In these latter, with few exceptions, it is only recently that forest conservancy has attracted attention and so forest work is still in its initial stage. In other words, Native States generally speaking, are commencing where Government started forty years previous. Consequently, there is a good deal of leeway to make up, before their departments can be recognised as abreast of the times.

The territories occupied by the feudatory States are as a rule, in the backward parts of the country, chiefly in the hilly and mountainous portions. Many of these are still without proper roads or railways or even both, and communication is maintained by slow and antiquated methods. Administrative questions are, again, subject to a multiple of opinions prevailing at headquarters, which discounts continuity of working.

The advent of forest conservancy found some of them with excellent forests, as a result either of remote situation, or the love of *shikar* developed in the ruler. In others, the forests had been laid

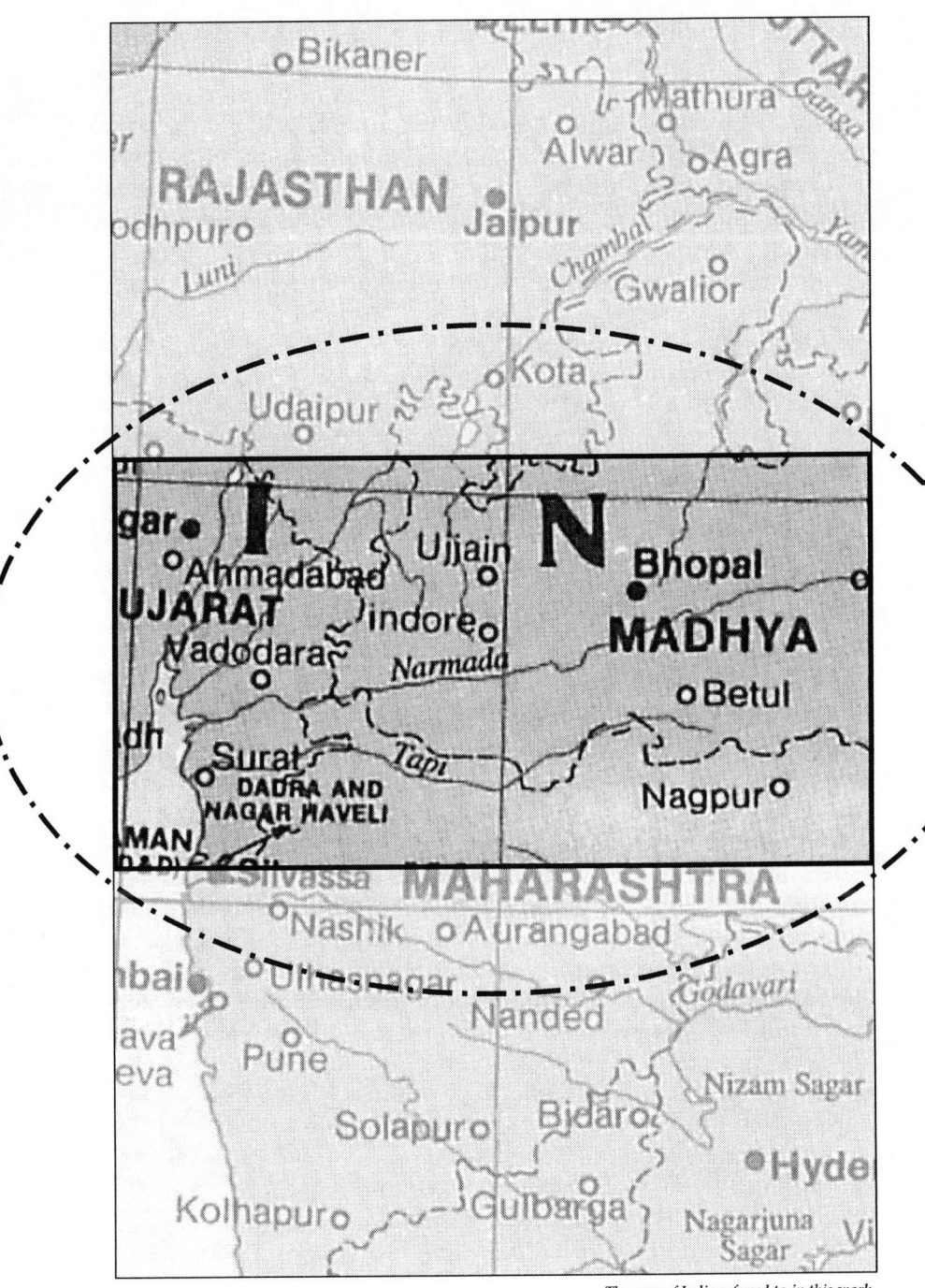

The area of India referred to in this work.

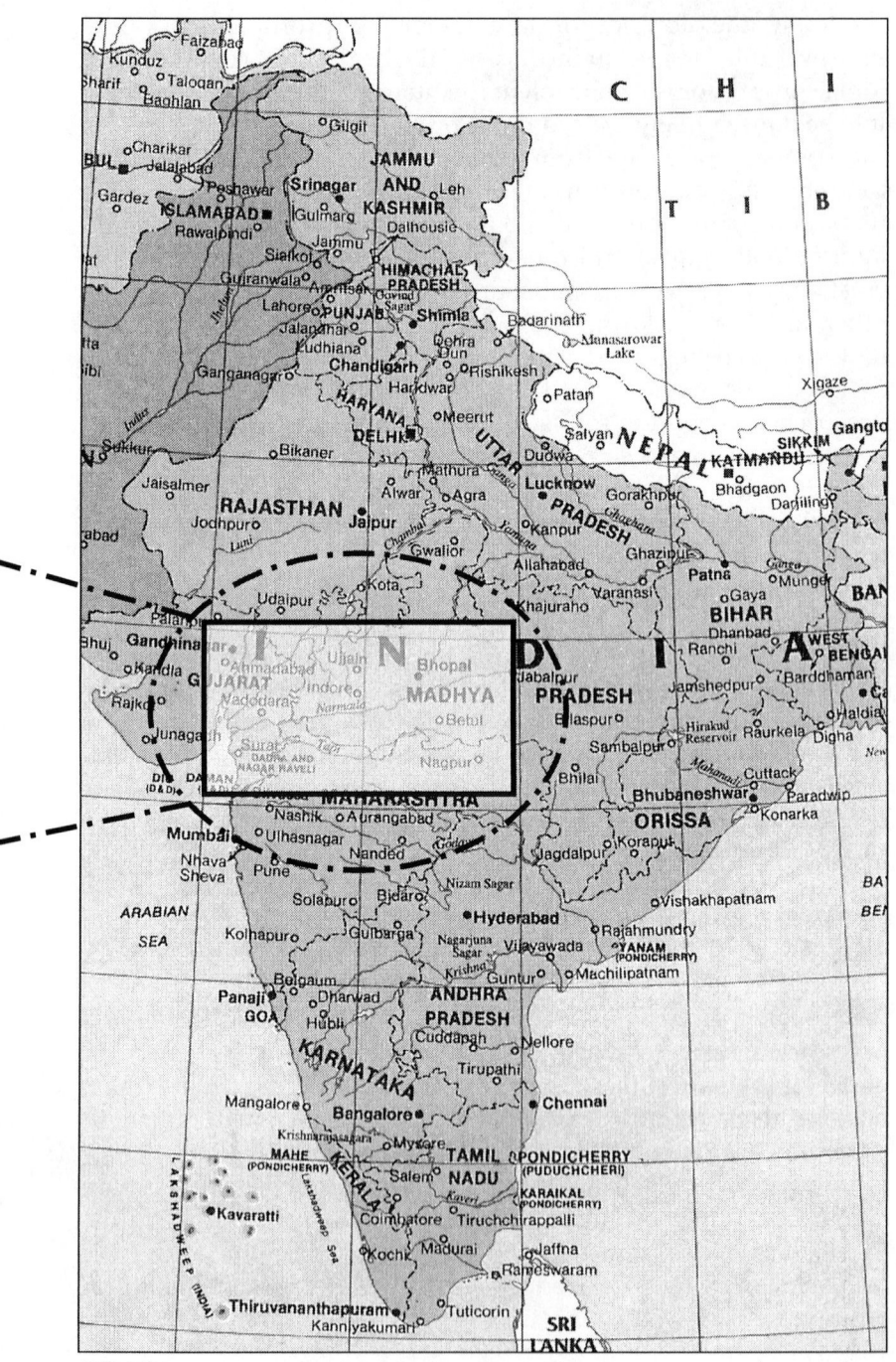

India today.

Life in the Wilds of Central India 7

waste by the absence of any means of profitable working. However this may be, in most cases, the neglect to take account of jungle growth, or the benevolent intentions of the ruler in allowing it to be utilised freely, caused forest properties to be looked upon as the common privilege from which each and all could benefit. Consequently, the constitution of a new department aiming at the reservation of forest tracts could not but be viewed in an unfriendly light by both official and non-official classes. The one saw in its creation, an end to the chief source of their perquisites, while the other, had to witness the abolition of customs and privileges that had come to be regarded as permanent.

It will be obvious that without the example of recorded precedence to point to in case of need, the State's forest officer has no easy task in framing proposals for the improvement of the growth with the view to getting them accepted. Forest administration, therefore, becomes more a question of tact and forbearance, than of technical skill in working. Concomitantly, success depends on the personality of the official entrusted with the management. The divided opinions usually prevailing in State councils without rules of procedure for guidance, render continuity of methods almost impracticable. So also, the checks afforded by the procrastinating devices, commonly adopted, cause delay in application of measures, often postponing them indefinitely. But, such discouragements provide the very stimulus needed for exertion, and the novelty of things, is in itself, an encouragement to progress. Again, the absence of rigid rules and regulations, as obtains in Government managements, gives to State administrations an elasticity for accommodating a means to an end. These differences invest the work in Native States with an interest and afford opportunities for initiative that are lacking in Government service. Hence, provided the official possesses the necessary insight to grasp matters and a conciliatory spirit for blending the issues, there is no reason why success in State forest managements should not be as great, or even greater than in Government. States who were the first to recognise the importance of forest conservancy, have established departments that compare favourably with those under Government control, so that for the others, it is chiefly a question of time to come into line with their compeers who have started ahead in the field of sylvicultural improvements.

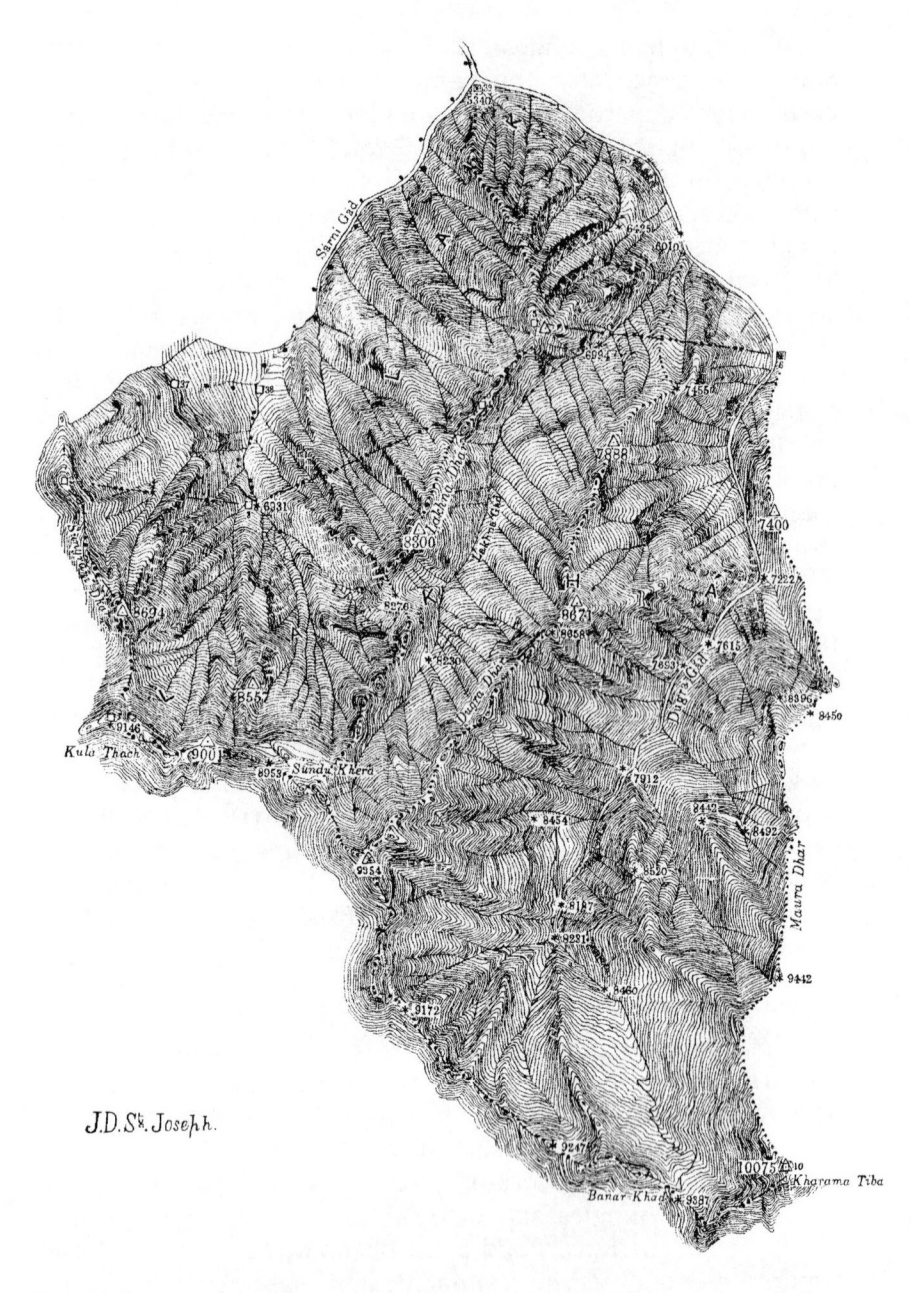

Part of India north of Kharamna Peak, 30°48'N, 77°56'E, approximately 35 miles NNW of Dehra Dun. Reproduced from map by J.D.St. Joseph, of the India Forest Service, c.1900.

Life in the Wilds of Central India 9

Administrative arrangements appertaining to forests in Native States are practically the same as those obtaining in the Government departments. Exploitation is still conducted in an improvised manner in most States. Working Plans embodying the execution of works over a series of years are hardly known in States' forest management. Nor are they very necessary during the initial stages of working when the position of forest areas that are to constitute the future reserves has not been settled or defined, and when encroachments for culturable benefit are still rife.

Adverting now to the opening paragraph of this narrative, my first appointment was to a sub-range, almost the smallest unit of management, in the wilds of the Betul district, Central Provinces. This led shortly after to the charge of two ranges constituting a sub-division. Subsequently, the Conservator claimed my services for special duty as his working plans assistant. Excepting the twelve months passed in these appointments and a brief spell as officiating divisional forest officer at Hoshungabad, my time in the Central Provinces was wholly occupied with working plans. In 1897, at the instance of the local Government, I was selected for deputation to foreign service. This meant transfer under the Central India Agency, which comprises the feudatory States in that province. Forest management was then hardly known, still less understood by the rulers, so that the work of organizing forest departments had to be commenced forthwith, and all my remaining service was passed among the Native States. This short sketch will show that the duties I was called upon to perform from time to time, took me fairly through all the phases and gradations of the service.

At the outset of my career, I had the fortune to be associated with that good old forester, naturalist and sportsman, Mr. R.H.E. Thompson, who initiated me in the ways of animal and plant life, and so stirred in me an interest in the life of the jungle, glimpses of which are only occasionally allowed to those who prefer the solitude of the wilds and are gifted with the patience to watch and observe. My duty as working plans assistant took me into the recesses of the jungles and inspired me to acquire a thorough knowledge of the forests and plant phenomena. It also gave me opportunities of observing animal life in its natural environment.

The facts set forth in the chapters that follow are chiefly the result of personal reminiscences and enquiry during rambles

through the jungles, or life among the primitive races who for centuries have made the forests their home. The witch doctors or medicine men of these tribes, as well as the adventurous spirits, are occasionally in possession of a fund of knowledge relating to the uses of products and the ways of beasts and birds that are beyond the ken of ordinary men. This advantage enables them to read the signs current, prognosticate events and work their craft with sufficient accuracy to cause them to be held in awe by their own people, just as a gifted professor of any of the sciences would be amongst ourselves.

The concomitant descriptions deal with occurrences in nature. The practical observer who has had the opportunities for witnessing these has an advantage over the technical zoologist or ethnologist. This will be obvious, for whereas the technologist bases his conclusions on a chain of hypothicated [sic] facts, the other knows them by actual experience. Thus, greater value attaches to results gained in the field, than those deduced from study in an artificial atmosphere.

Chapter II

Camp Requisites

Starting life very young, on a meagre salary, which scarcely sufficed for necessary expenses, I had my full share of rough times. During the first phase or probationership, I lived absolutely in the jungles, with only trees and the huts of Gonds and graziers to shelter me in case of rain, heat or severe cold.

My baggage at this time consisted of a few bamboo baskets made to hold the necessary pots and pans, a roll of bedding, a canvas stool and a small collapsible table, all of which could be carried by four or five men. A cot could always be made for the night by sticking four forked posts in the ground and placing saplings or bamboos between the forks to serve as frames, with thin branches or bamboo interlaced between them, and the whole covered with leaves or grass, over which the mattress could be spread. This made quite a comfortable bed. I had only one servant who cooked, as well as waited and attended to my things. A pony was out of the question and all the marches and excursions were done on foot. I never took any stores at all. Native cakes served as substitute for bread. Fowls, eggs and milk could be had for very little and often the people entirely declined payment. As for vegetables - a species of broad bean called *balhar*, which is grown on bamboo trellis at the back yard of every Gond dwelling, tomatoes of the size of large marbles, spinage and yam could always be got in the villages, while supplies of the indispensable potato were obtained from the nearest markets.

In speaking of camp dietary, drinks are perhaps of more importance than food. As a matter of fact, the less liquid taken the better it is for the internal economy of the system, while spirits should be avoided as far as practicable. Officials whose duties require them to be out for the greater part of the year, should make it a point to accustom themselves to do without liquid for long intervals. It is always necessary to boil water thoroughly before drinking and if impurities occur in suspension, a pinch of ground alum added after boiling, causes the suspended matter to settle as sediment, when the clear water can be strained off for use. During the dry period from March to June, supplies diminish rapidly and often, the only water left is in pools. These are more or less, in

stages of putrefaction owing to animal and human excretions that escape into them when visited daily for drinks and ablutions. Often also, rustics utilise deep streams and pools to submerge bundles of hemp stalks for rotting to obtain fibre. And later in the season they are the only sources of supply that escape being dried, so that the water in them being already foul, causes the most frightful irritation imaginable, when used externally. The reader will wonder how the people manage under these conditions. It is because they are sparing in the use of water, being accustomed to do without it for long intervals; also it is as often as not, taken in the form of gruel, that is, boiled with cereals to the consistency of a broth. Again, at their homes, the women folk usually manage to dribble it out into their vessels from a filtration hole scooped in the bank, close to the water's edge. I have often witnessed beaters after a hot day's work, assembled round a stagnant pool and though greatly athirst, waiting patiently for water to collect in the filtration holes scooped out hastily. They know too well what it would mean to drink from the pool direct. The importance of making sure of what one drinks is therefore obvious. In my own case, during the first seven or eight years in the jungles, I took only water. Latterly, when incessant attacks of malaria incapacitated me, a little alcohol became necessary, owing to its medicinal properties as a stimulant.

A few necessary medicines had to be carried. Quinine and an aperient, as well as an astringent comprised the stock; the former consisting of castor oil or Eno's fruit salt and the latter, of chlorodine. Besides being indispensable in camp, they were very useful for treating cases that came in spasmodically for advice. Mustard was another item, which though carried as a condiment, was as important as the others. It could be used in most ailments common to malarious tracts. Also, the wild folks believed in its efficacy, perhaps more than in any other, owing to the blister or burn resulting from its application which resembled their own crude methods of branding or cupping for almost every complaint.

My small means would not permit of owning a good rifle, and it was not till some years later that I was able to obtain a weapon suitable for all purposes, so I had to be content with a Martini rifle that I was allowed to keep as a volunteer. It was good enough to account for most game when the bullets had been indented. This was done either by slitting the tops crossways to a depth of quarter of an inch, or by boring a hole half an inch deep and inserting into

it a plug of twig or bamboo. These attempts to increase effectiveness, caused the bullet to be deflected slightly, but the result was more certain than with the ordinary hard bullet. I found that the slitting made the bullet rise somewhat, while boring caused it to go a little to the side, either right or left of the aim. Also at distances, say, of over seventy-five yards, they occasionally struck sideways or length-on making a big entrance. Once even the bullet was taken out of the animal with the slit top perfectly intact, while the thick end had flattened, showing that it had spun completely round before impact. Subsequently, when I could afford a rifle, my choice fell on a .577, as recommended by Sir Samuel Baker. This weapon has been with me ever since, and my investment was recouped within a few years' of its possession by the rewards earned for killing dangerous game. It has not been my fortune to be in very tight corners. Mr. Thompson always recommended discretion in following wounded beasts. But the rifle's tremendous stopping power certainly came in useful when matters did come to close quarters.

The question of the choice of weapons for dangerous game has been often ventilated in papers by experts and experienced hunters and I would venture to add my quota. It seems to me, then, that given accuracy of aim and more or less stationary objects, any weapon sufficiently powerful to cause penetration of a few inches is effective. The essence of the matter that really tests the value of a weapon as regards its stopping or disabling power, rests in the fact of the object being on the move, or indistinct, or it may be, a blunder in shooting ascribable to various causes any one of which will prevent the weapon producing the effect desired. This is governed more than we imagine by the vitality of the particular animal fired at. Among beasts just as among human beings, individuals of the same congener possess ratios of vitality, so that other things being equal, individual constitution or temperament has a good deal to do with the results obtained in shooting.

Again, vitality also depends on the mood of the beast when hit or wounded. An animal infuriated by pursuit or which has observed its enemy, develops in a fit of temper, an energy for mischief which it did not actually possess. When this happens, a mortal or disabling wound often only tends to cause the manufacture of vitality to impell it forward to its pursuer. In the former, the animal is constitutionally possessed of the vitality to

render it dangerous, while in the latter, it effervesces sufficiently for serious consequences. The one may be regarded as natural and the other as artificial vitality. But, whichever be the case, the impetuous career will only be checked by increased velocity combined with smashing power. This combination can in my opinion, be obtained with greater certainty from large bore express rifles, than from any other weapon. Close encounters with dangerous beasts should always be avoided, but when inevitable it is presumed the hunter is possessed of the ordinary sense of intuition and caution to take every bit of advantage that the situation affords. Many examples could be cited of wounded beasts behaving in an inexplicable way, contrary to all dictates of reason and even opposed to the laws of existence. It is these that account for by far the most accidents that occur in the pursuit of dangerous game. In short, every hunter should be always prepared for the unexpected in dealing with big game.

All sportsmen carry with them some literature to while away the time when they are inactive. But, leisure to pour [sic] over books seldom comes to officials who can, at the most, snatch a few hours to shoot in the course of their duties. With the increase of correspondence and responsibilities which must be attended to in the field, officials have little or no time for reading. The most they can do is to get through the papers and magazines to which they subscribe. However, books on adventure and sport by recognised authors are always interesting and should be carried. Books and treatises dealing with the country are even more useful to have at hand. In my own case I am indebted to the excellent accounts by Mr. Sanderson, Captain Forsyth, Sir Samuel Baker, Colonels Gordon-Cumming and Pollock and the Badminton volume on sport for hints in shooting. And to General Malcolm, Colonels Sleeman, Meadows-Taylor and Mr. Kipling for the value set on local information.

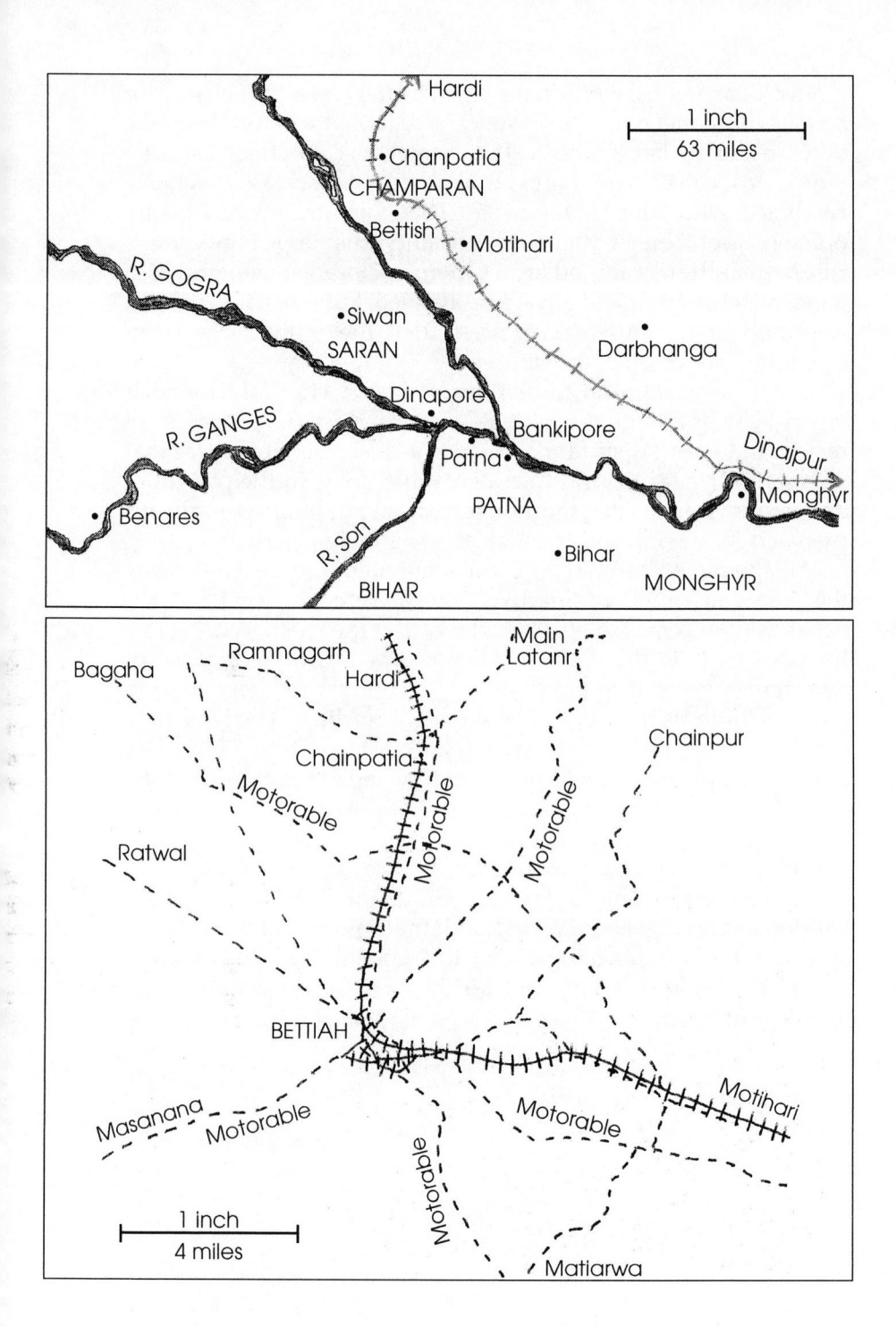

16 *Life in the Wilds of Central India*

Chapter III

Early Reminiscences

The birth of the Indian Forest Department dates practically from the early sixties of the 19th century. It heralded a new organization pure and simple, for no precedent of a similar institution existed in the country. Moreover, its scope of work embraced a continent with expansive areas under forests that became absorbed in the management. It had to start with an improvised staff contributed by other services, preference in the recruitment being shown to adventurous spirits which naturally brought in a strong military element. Accordingly, from the outset the department obtained the germs of a solid foundation for the strenuous work that life in solitary and unexplored wilds imposed on members.

In the early decades of its existence, the department donned the chrysalis stage with a reality defying comparison. While the fathers of the service were busy either evolving schemes of working or formulating proposals for recognition by an impassive Government, the staff were positively neglected. Apart from the meagre salaries allotted to the lower grades, allowances for outdoor duties were sparingly paid and in most cases not granted at all. Such things as living quarters, were unheard of and excepting in the case of high officials, tents were not provided. The wretched ranger and sub-assistant, the officers managing units, who had practically to live out of doors, found it difficult to arrange about shelter and to meet expenses of tours. They had to depend on the goodwill of rustics to help them through their dilemma by imposing freely on their compliant and hospitable nature. Shelter from sun and rain even for a brief sojourn, could always be relied upon at a moment's notice, under the thatched awning or verandah of the headman's dwelling. If there was due notice, the people erected a temporary shanty or booth of bamboos and grass with branches and leaves. Forest tribes are adept at erecting these, and I know quite substantial huts put up during the space of a few hours. During tours, they willingly saw to the removal of the light baggage to the nearest village which got it through to the next and so on till the destination was reached. There was never a demur and often the carriers would be ready without being summoned, except when the headman had

informed them of the intended departure. This was how things were when I joined, and it continued for some years after till quarters were provided and allowances sanctioned or improved.

Although these methods seemed hard on officials and people alike, they had their good points. For one thing, it brought the two into very close touch, and provided the official exercised tact, his intrusion was never resented. I have known headmen to boast about their dwellings having afforded shelter to various sahibs, while in instances that occur to me, two or more villagers would even dispute for the privilege of having the official under his roof. These old customs, excepting few Native States which keep up old traditions, have long since died out and with them the concomitant gain which Government acquired in the way of information at the expense of the official. In these days of stereotyped rules scattered broadcast, an attempt to renew the old practice, would possibly lead to trouble. The ruler, the employee and the rustic have suffered mutually by the loss in the exchange of confidences that the old methods fostered. The results are evident in the misunderstandings and frictions that have become of constant occurrence.

Englishmen regard forest tribes, who are the aborigines of India, with a feeling of interest akin to sympathy. This no doubt is owing as much to the traditions investing the name, as to the backward position to which they have been derogated in the social scale of the country. But, their crude customs and simple methods also appeal to a naturally practical mind instinct with the love of fairness. The benevolent intentions appear at first to surprise the aborigine, accustomed to be treated as vermin, while they are no less a puzzle to the races who ousted him from friendly intercourse. Both are conscious of the new sentiment which intending to advance the one, takes away nothing from the other.

The belief shared by natives in regarding the aborigine as depraved, callous and destitute of morals, cannot be sustained for a moment. His wild exterior hides a sensitive chord which is very discriminating in its choice of confidence. Though naturally reticent and distrustful, he is predisposed to be friendly and if approached with sincerity, reciprocates fellow feeling. His susceptible nature is quick to penetrate guises, enabling his intuitive mind to detect the character before him and as he shrinks from the many that he fails to understand, so he eagerly welcomes

the few whom he trusts - attaching himself to them with child-like fidelity, especially if they are intellectually and spiritually his superiors. Then the least encouragement will draw him out, causing him to recount the pettiest detail, as well as to seek advice on the smallest matters affecting his domestic life. It is sufficient for the headman or a respectable person to elect in one's favour, for the village community to adopt him as their fetish. To men who have been fortunate to command so much respect, the position is romantic and at times even embarrassing. In short, the official assumes the role of an oracle that bestows a privilege entitling him to their services on occasions of stress and trouble. The influence that such a man might exert can be better imagined than described. In these times, the supremacy he acquires is diverted to the channels of administration with a view to efficiency; and many an official owes the good results of management to the assistance of the simple folks among whom he worked. Personally speaking, their timely advice or aid has solved my difficulty in many an awkward fix.

Not so long ago, the work of administration grooved on the lines adopted by a popular personality, who had no sympathies with red-tape procedure. The old order still obtains in backward parts of the country where executive members of the service are obliged by the nature of their duties to live a more or less nomadic existence and so become identified with the people. The dwellers in the countryside are no whit behind the aborigine in expressions of goodwill and regard, therefore opportunities for ministering to the masses are many and varied. Formality and restriction disappear, and there is no lack of cordiality. Their fatalistic views and simple conceptions of events invite sympathy, which is returned by a form of idolation [sic] very like homage. The individual who succeeds in worming himself into their affections, becomes in course of time an avatar whose visits are marked as red-letter days in their monotonous calendar. During his itinerary, issues of no little consequence quite alien to his nature, come up before him for review and redress, and are cheerfully attended to and satisfactorily settled. The achievements are seldom or never given a second thought and yet, his novel ways of dealing mean setting up standards whereby he unconsciously forges links in the official chain girdling the goddess of good government. If only the methods adopted in levelling these elements of discord were

availed of for reference, what a monument of useful data could be compiled? But they pass into oblivion as soon as their part in the day's work is over.

A good instance of the form of respect officials may acquire, is afforded by the ruler of a hill district who was fortunate to pass his whole career in the one locality. His long association won such implicit obedience that a mere message from him had the force of a mandate. It was said that if trouble brewed in an outlying part of his charge, he had only to send his walking stick in a palanquin escorted by a guard, to put a stop to cavillings or riotous intentions. In fact, so reverently was he regarded by the classes that his name was construed as a household word, into that of a deified hero whose incarnation he was supposed to be. If such a fine feeling was rampant in a quiet and peaceful country, an example may equally be cited of a particularly lawless and wild district. Two officials became famed for their energy and resource in dealing with the turbulent spirits and to perpetuate them to posterity, their names were interpreted into the local language, for those of weapons used in warfare in remembrance of the intrepid character of their attacks.

The relations, however, are not always satisfactory. Cases happily very rare, occur of individuals inviting suspicion and distrust by contumely and overbearing conduct. Such a man ought never to be in executive authority and the office desk were the right place for him; in addition to undoing the work of predecessors, he leaves a troublesome legacy for successors. But the people are also very much to blame for the impairment in the good understanding. The contrary traits of the native mind preclude exposure before the mischief spreads and so the bad example stays out his time to the detriment of the common welfare. Their beliefs associate him with an evil genius to bear with whom is preferable to incurring displeasure; and they would rather put up with the bullying, than that their opposition in the course of this existence should render it possible for his spirit to also torment their souls in the next life. A tale of the great rising, for the truth of which my informant - a reverend gentleman who went through the crisis, vouched, will explain better than anything I can say, the force of what is meant. A company of sepoys stationed at an outpost mutinied and murdered the junior officers who took part in their games and pastimes and were generally popular, while the commandant who

was a martinet and very much disliked, was told he may escape as they feared harm coming to him, lest his evil spirit made it worse for them in the next world. Indeed so earnest were they, he should not risk his life in the disturbance caused by their action, that they provided an escort to see him through the danger zone. This feeling of pandering to fear is usually current in States whose rulers have had unbridled license in imposing their will on their subjects.

At the commencement of my service, there was still a good sprinkling of army officers in civil appointments. Being disciplinarians, guided by common- sense, rather than literary teachings, they were skilled at speeding up work. A certain Colonel had a smart way of disposing of petitioners who came daily to interview him. The men formed up in a parallel row by the office square, attired in spotless white, holding their petitions between the palms of the two hands in an attitude of supplication. The court-house comprised three blocks in the form of a quadrangle - a main building and two wings with an open space between. The chief offices, over which my friend presided, were accommodated in the central block facing North, while his assistants over the civil and criminal branches of the work occupied the wings. As soon as the petitioners lined up, the Colonel marched out of his office followed by his munshi that is a reader, and office peon, and stood at the head of the row. The clerk took the petitions and as he read each out, my friend drew up his hand sharply and pointed his thumb to either of the two wings or himself as the case may be, meaning the court which was to deal with the man's suit, and instantly the peon stepped forward, jerked out the petitioner from the row and shouted out the official designation of the individual before whom he had to appear for redress. The clockwork regularity about these proceedings impressed the assembly about the court with the efficacy of the system.

A propos of this, my friend was easily put out at unsightly odds and ends and the presence of even harmless refuse, like scraps of paper, occasioned stern rebuke in the responsible quarter; he was likewise particular about attire and the least speck was an eyesore; the natives compared him to an egret which frequents slimy marshes, but nevertheless keeps its plumage spotlessly clean.

The tours of provincial and divisional Governors used to be events to reckon with and needed careful thinking and planning to

get them to work smoothly. The arrivals even at remote centres were so bound up with official etiquette, that the visits assumed a ceremonial character, attended with the pomp and display befitting an Oriental ruler. For days before the arrival, the countryside was astir with the news and everything was put aside to leave the people free in setting about to make the visit welcome; while long after the departure, the great man and his doings formed the topic of conversation. The liberal scale of camp equipment allowed him a double set of living, office and audience tents that left little to be desired as regards comfort and appearance, also the retinue from the secretary to the lowest menial, wanted for nothing. The service engaged an army of servants to pitch and strike these abodes and considering the lengthy tours necessitating a formidable array of baggage and the slow means of transport by heavy country carts, camels or coolies, the train formed a moving column along the line of route from the time of starting to the last acquittance, and occupied a space of time often extending over twenty-four hours, so that in daily marches it was nothing uncommon to see the van leaving for the next stage just as the tail was arriving at the rest camp. The people repaired from far and near to witness the procession of officials and strings of transport or to gaze upon the camping grounds over which canvas settlements had sprung into existence mushroom-like, in the course of the night and presented to their eyes the scenic effect of an exotic city.

So long as the people were not put to any great inconvenience, the visits gave them pleasure; their elders and respectable men usually attended the functions and invitations were eagerly sought after. They readily furnished levies for supplies and the various odd jobs essential for the comforts of travelling. But the same could not be said of the local staff to most of whom the presence of the ruler in their midst was a matter of anxious concern. The nervousness was as much a case of guilty conscience in some who, stationed beyond reach of proper control, lent themselves to malpractices, as it was the result of excitement in others who, sensitive of their good name, could not bear the thought of failing to satisfy. The visits were therefore regarded by the majority in the light of inquisitorial parades that might deprive them of their living, and there was much searching of hearts as the time for the arrival approached. They could not escape the attention of underlings who took advantage of the state of feeling and the

protection their presence in the entourage gave them, to pester the staff for gifts on threats to humiliate them. Many a subordinate undertook the expense of offerings and prayers at the local shrines in order that they may be saved from reprimands. Often they were assiduous in their efforts to please and had recourse to auspicious expedients - the commonest of which was serving up a dish of fishes to the official's gaze as he went, so that the visits may pass without untoward incident.

But, however real or imaginary the fears, the tours stirred into active train a stream of improvements and each subordinate vied with his neighbour in rectifying the neglect of months of inattention and making the general outlook presentable. Thus, broken country tracks were put into a state of repair; offensive sights covered or removed; stagnant pools filled in; dirty villages cleaned and whitewashed. With many, the labours seldom went beyond the bare surface of things, but the deception could only pass muster with a superior unmindful of penetrating the disguises. His indifference was quickly noted and spread the incentive for scamping duties. Whereas an inquiring mind claimed the full measure of work and his progress became marked by thorough cleaning along the routes of march.

The visits were prolific of numerous incidents, for the transfer of unfamiliar elements caused surprise to people unused to the go-ahead methods associate with the sahib, while the cant of the underlings with whom they mixed, confused their thoughts. Often I have been entertained watching the dilemma of the staff who could not take in the words of a superior, or listening to the sophistry of menials to exalt themselves before the people. The developments in either case were truly too amusing, but they were regarded seriously. On an occasion, I had to meet the head of a province at the border of my district, and preceded his arrival so as to be on the spot to receive him on the following morning. The vanguard of his camp turned up during the night headed by the nazir or senior orderly mounted on an elephant. He soon made his presence felt by shouting out orders and directions that woke the whole place, and on alighting he was guided by two torch bearers to commence an inspection of the camping ground. This brought forth comments on whatever was seen - the site was too shaded to be healthy: the embankment holding up water for irrigation in the stream nearby should have been breached, as it effected [sic] the

drinking supply: the pegs were not strong enough to bear the strain of heavy tents: the village pariahs joining in the chorus set up by his loud tone, must be deported during the stay of his master. His voice flowed with invectives designed to produce sensation among the listeners and ended by finding fault with the inadequacy of supplies for a large camp. The staff responsible for the preparations were really alarmed and consulted together how to win his favour; the bag was passed round to discharge their debt, and the sequel was as effective in restoring credit, as the beginning had been baneful in lessening it, for his effusion about the pains taken over the arrangements belied his earlier complaints.

Of the variety of goods carried in the train of a Governor to ameliorate the hardships of camping, one was a large galvanised tub fixed to a rustic cart and filled with water to contain live fishes. The Province possessed few rivers where fish of a quality to suit an epicurean's palate could be obtained, and the expedient was adopted to meet the difficulty; the tub was replenished from time to time and a fresh supply of fish made available for daily use. However, the country-side looked upon the measure as evidence of the great man's authority and the tub in village gossip was enlarged into a tank, so that the uninitiated opened their eyes on hearing of a "tank" stocked with fishes being transported from place to place to satisfy his whim.

Once I was camping with the native official of a district to meet the ruler of a province. My colleague belonged to the legal profession with vague conceptions in matters affecting sport. The Governor was a keen sportsman and sent his mounted orderly in advance to ask us to arrange for small game shoots. The sowar delivered the message in the wrong quarter, and my companion wishing to steal a march over me hit upon a brilliant idea to provide the sport. He sent for men from the professional tribe of birdcatchers located on the outskirts of the village and ordered them to trap ground game; they succeeded in taking some dozen couples of quail, partridge and grouse which were brought to him in the evening. The state shikari was then summoned and told to secure the game with bits of twine among bushes in the scrub jungle skirting the fields, so that in working over the ground with the shooters, the birds would struggle to escape and draw the fire of the guns, whereupon beaters would run up and pick up the game, cutting the fastenings with penknives. Being a good

sportsman and acquainted with the ways of sahibs, the shikari pooh-poohed the proposal, which made the gentleman indignant, and they started to wrangle. Until now I was in the dark as to what had transpired, and happened to walk into my colleague's tent on a casual visit just as the scene became noisy, and seeing me the shikari appealed for support. I was surprised indeed, to hear all that had passed, and could not help bursting into a fit of laughter, which did for the plan.

But he failed to gain by the experience. A few years after the occurrence, I was camping with the head of the division who was shortly to enter that gentleman's district. He knew my friend would be glad of some shooting during his stay and to make sure, he trapped a panther, and wrote telling me of the sport he was planning. This was that my friend would be invited to the state gardens where the beast would be set free for him to shoot from the back of a shikar elephant. In answering, I tried to dissuade him from his intention, but he apparently misconstrued the purport for he had another panther caught and mentioned the fact as a piece of extremely good news in his next letter. Knowing my friend's views about shooting, I was anxious to spare him the annoyance of consenting unintentionally to the proposal and so in talking over the prospects of sport at the next camp which would be in my colleague's district, I hinted at that gentleman's enthusiasm which went to the extreme of providing caged beasts in order to leave nothing to chance. The following day we crossed into his district and after the formalities were over, he came up solemnly to request my friend to join in a panther shoot. But being forewarned he asked for details, which were no sooner related, than he declined the honour.

These incidents remind me of the great part tours play in facilitating work. Issues that appear to bristle with difficulties from the distant seat of an office chair, become shorn of their disturbing elements at being examined on the spot, at the same time the visits disclose unconsidered sources of information. The mere presence at the scene is half the battle and its practical utility may be gauged from the accounts that follow.

A part of the frontier of my old district marched with the territory of an Indian potentate whose side of the border was a thickly inhabited plain without a vestige of jungle, while a tangled chain of wooded hills sparsely populated, stretched along the

district limits. The inhabitants contained many refractory spirits who thrived by raiding the forests and selling the stolen produce to the better classes of the people. The handful of forest guards were powerless to stop the thefts, nor able to follow the raiders across the border because of native state jurisdiction, and efforts to bring the culprits to justice were frustrated by the tortuous channel of communication with the responsible authorities. The civil head of the district was fettered with rules and regulations to act independently, and withheld his support from impromptu measures designed to suppress the raids. But the disturbing reports of damage obliged him to visit the locality and study the question, and we started together on a tour of inspection. We were riding along the boundary with the forest ranger in attendance one morning when a band of raiders carrying produce unsuspectingly stepped out of the jungle a little way in front of us; without the least hesitation, the official shouted to arrest them and the ranger spurred forward to effect the capture. Notwithstanding, they crossed the dividing line before his arrival and aware of the sanctity this ensured, proceeded at a leisurely pace across country. The ranger also pulled up his pony and glanced back looking foolish at the inability to comply with the simple proposition, and although encouraged to overtake the thieves, he remained still, repeating that orders strictly forbade him to cross the line. The thieves too were flouting authority with a vengeance in affecting unconcern at our presence. The scene, to say the least, was ludicrous: here was the case in its true perspective - a high dignitary positively incapable of enforcing the laws for which he stood up. It impressed him as nothing else could have done, and on return to headquarters, he exposed the absurdity of the procedure and obtained sanction to inaugurate practical measures to cope with the raids.

Shortly after the occurrence, I was inspecting the locality with an assistant and the ranger, when we lost our way in a maze of hills and came out on the boundary, opposite to a frontier village which had an evil reputation as the abode of daring bands. The ranger said he would go and fetch a guide from the village, otherwise we could not reach camp before dark, so we waited for him by a stream. The village was a few furlongs from the site where we emerged from the jungles and our party could not have been observed, but the ranger cutting across the fields was soon

identified and seeing him approach alone, two men conspired to waylay and maltreat him because of the persistency with which he worked against their kind. He was barely gone five minutes when we were startled by his cries, and getting up the bank to investigate, we saw the stalwarts laying on to him with clubs. Not a moment was lost in rushing to the rescue and we were just in time to prevent others joining in the assault. We were four besides the ranger who was hors de combat, and we at once laid on hard and fast with the butt end of our cane walking sticks, except the forest guard who carried my empty gun, with which he kept threatening instant death as warnings to stop the fight. Fortunately, few of the new arrivals carried sticks for they had started as sightseers never expecting the development, otherwise we would have been hard put to meet the assault. Even so, the rioters were four to our one, but the presence of two sahibs - that is my assistant and I, disconcerted them and after a sharp attack they began to lose courage and retire from the fight. We succeeded though in getting hold of the ringleaders, and contrary to the extradition rules took them along with us and placed them in custody. They were tried in due course and punished and the village put under a ban restricting the freedom of the bad characters.

My circuit included an isolated charge wedged in between neighbouring territories. Though almost entirely forest, quite half of the district was rich culturable [sic] soil, but it had been greatly neglected owing to its remote situation, absolutely aloof from the estate of which it formed part and parcel. The preceding regimes had made it their chief business to get rid of the forest in order to exploit the land. With that obsession of evil bred of prejudice, peculiar to native residents of towns, they believed the existence of jungle conflicted with that of population, and so left no means untried to eradicate it root and branch, while they touted with offers of free tenures on long leases as inducements to immigration. But their efforts only resulted in dense growth of worthless scrub replacing the timber, without the gain of a desirable tenant. Fear kept them from exploring the locality, so that the rare occasion of an official's visit came to be a sham, likened to a meteoric flight, and conducted through relays of guards posted along the route of march to deter spooks and fearsome beasts from impeding the progress. In the circumstances, he was none the wiser for his experience. Knowing of the soil's fertility, they failed to make good

the deficiency of water supply which rendered vast areas unsuitable for habitation, and again, acquainted with its evil repute as a den of thieves, they made feeble attempts to oust them. On the other hand to hide their own omissions, they connived to magnify and spread accounts of its unhealthiness.

Matters continued in this state until the district passed under the administration of the newly created Forest department, and headquarters took advantage of the change to call for a report on prevailing conditions. Even at this distance of time, I seem to see the anxious faces of my men on learning of the projected tour of inspection through the locality. They were visibly perturbed; "why" they said, "the crows and kites catch fever and drop off their perches and no one is safe from the roving bands, while man-eating beasts are ever on the prowl to carry off stragglers." However, the tour was accomplished without mishap and the report went in to be soon acknowledged by orders empowering me to take repressive measures to rid the district of the evil characters, therefore I was back on the scene in six months.

Owing to its abandoned condition, marauding spirits from adjoining lands had been encouraged to make the locality their rendezvous. They found a mixed band of forest tribes with a leavening from a notorious caste of Mahommedans - cowherds in name, but thieves by profession - who inhabit outskirts of towns where there are chances of plunder. The horde made cattle lifting its chief profession for which the country offered advantages in its extensive belts of hill and dale enclosing the rich border settlements. The form of robbery appealed to the predatory instincts of the class and moreover, ran little risk of capture since herds could be waylaid on grazing grounds far from the villages, and the cow-boys easily relieved of their charges; and should succour arrive they could but disperse over the broken and wooded tracts to avoid arrest. The stolen cattle would be harboured in the district and driven by devious paths under cover of night to cantonment towns and sold to butchers who slaughtered them for the garrison and thus, removed all trace of the animals. The aboriginal element did the raiding and the others undertook to dispose of the property.

I was to have the assistance of a thuggi inspector and a squad of military police; and with the arrival of the party we moved to a central site as a base of operations. I had ascertained the robbers'

retreats on my first visit, but they maintained an efficient watch and could not be surprised without preparation. We therefore spent several days in camp, organising patrol duties in order to create the impression that the detachment had come merely for policing the district: in the meanwhile, we looked about for means that would enable us to effect a good capture, and the aid was forthcoming in the services of a tribal watchman, who had relations and friends among the gang. His prosperous condition could not fail notice and inquiries confirmed suspicions of his league with the robbers. The inspector was desirous of arresting him forthwith to force him with threats and cajolery into acting the part of an informer. But the plan was vetoed as being unsuited to the occasion, because any measure to curtail his freedom would alarm the band causing the men to disperse to their homes beyond jurisdiction, meaning no end of bother in negotiations to carry out even a single arrest. Like most of his class the turvee was interested in sport and I got him to be my guide on shooting excursions; it soon struck up a friendly spirit, making it easy to converse freely on local topics. I now had his confidence and put the matter of the gang's capture to him and he willingly consented to co-operate, provided we let him go immediately his services as a guide ended. This was only reasonable, considering his future would be imperilled were his activity to become known; it also suited our purpose.

Our plan was to operate with separate forces in different directions at the same time, employing a large body with some show of concealment to absorb attention while effecting a surprise with a few selected men. We knew that news of the detachment's movement on the rendezvous would travel like wildfire, and we supposed that long before its arrival, the place would be evacuated for a less frequented spot to which the robbers were expected to retire and where we hoped to take them unawares with the smaller force. The success of the enterprise hinged on the guide's ability to penetrate in darkness through thick jungle to the robbers' den where he was sure the band would assemble on leaving the rendezvous. Accordingly, at dawn the detachment marched out at a leisurely pace for its objective, but not a word was breathed of the next move until after dark when the picked men were quickly got together and the party stole away on its errand. By speeding up all we could, we reached the destination about twilight and halted the

men some distance from the spot, while two of us with the guide ascended a knoll to reconnoitre the position. From there we looked down into a hollow formed by the bend of a stream struggling through a knot of hillocks and saw the embers of smoldering fires, sure sign of the presence of men. All were wrapped in slumber after their enforced retreat. It took but a few minutes to deploy the party round the bivouac and then, walk up together with loaded arms trained on the sleepers and here the guide's duties ended. Our advance woke the men and though armed with muzzle-loaders and matchlocks ready for use, they were too taken aback at our close presence to offer the serious resistance of which they were capable. However, both sides indulged in some wild firing and in the ensuing mêlée, about a third of the number escaped, while two thieves and one of our men were severely wounded. But we had captured the principal leader, a fine type of his class standing eight inches over six feet, who needed the attention of half the party to disarm and secure. Subsequently, they were put on trial and sentenced to heavy terms of imprisonment; the leader on hearing his judgment calmly turned to me and ventured the remark that it was futile punishing him since he would soon regain his liberty. True to his word, after serving a year he broke out of prison by skilful use of strength and in spite of a large reward, was never recaptured. We gained our object however, in that the locality was cleared of the band's presence.

Once I was with a party tracking a gang of timber thieves who had been getting into a reserve undergoing regeneration and robbing its best stems, when a trivial incident led to the rounding up of the fugitives. The forests bordered on culturable lands sown with millets and other high crops, which in season were utilized as shelter for committing thefts. The gang had often eluded pursuit, and on the occasion we were running the trail hard, only to find the thieves had crossed the boundary into a giant millet field, and the fact of their gaining the cover before we came up expired our rising hopes. We stopped to consider and everyone inclined to think it useless continuing through the thick cover, when a pair of did-you-do-its, that is the common plover, rose out of the crops some distance ahead, uttering their familiar cry of alarm. It at once struck me that the birds had been disturbed by the gang whom we were after, and I mentioned the fact to the men, but excepting the Gond tracker they demurred to [sic] the conclusion. However,

ordering the ranger and forester who had ponies as well as I, to mount and the rest to follow as speedily as they could, we spurred forward through a round-about opening in the fields to cut off the gang's retreat and took up posts in a broken belt of scrub which stretched across the direction in which the thieves were going as indicated by the flight of the birds. We had waited barely ten minutes when the gang hove in sight, chatting and walking in Indian file, each with his axe and a choice bole of timber balanced on the shoulders. There were fourteen men and it was evident they had no suspicion of our presence. At a sign, we rode up to the line and seeing us mounted and armed with spears, they threw down their loads and axes and prepared to surrender. But one of the men, a short thickset fellow with a fiendish face, hurled his load at the ranger's pony following up the attack by flinging his axe at that official's head. In the diversion so caused, he got away shouting to the others to do likewise. But none of the others took the advice and the ranger was soon himself and able to do his part; the blow had made the pony rear, dismounting its rider and spoiling the shot aimed at him, so that the axe flew past harmlessly. Seeing he was all right, I gave chase after the runaway who had by then gained the cover of a nullah. Its windings made the going slow and very likely the culprit would have escaped, had he not run into the arms of our party coming by a short cut along the nullah's bank to join us. The gang was marched to the nearest police station and put in the lock-up. On trial they admitted to previous thefts and got exemplary punishment; he of the murderous intent, being sentenced to a longer term for having aggravated the offence.

No one who has watched a tracker following footprints, could help being struck by his fine sense of discrimination in detecting the sharpest differences about the human foot and its tread. One would think the man had made the business a life-long study and yet, with most the performance is limited to the occasions he is called upon to track. It is instructive to see him isolate the offending footprints from among numerous others along a frequented path by such trivial peculiarities, as the difference in partitions between two toes, the indentations on heel and sole which hard walkers with bare feet develop, the angular cast of the footfall or the depth of the impression, imperfections that absolutely escape the ordinary eye. Tracking thieves is a duty devolving on watchmen who are of aboriginal descent, and as the

occupation is hereditary, it is very possible that the skill is inherited.

An incident that occurs to me goes back to the early nineties. An outlying portion of my charge was exposed to frequent raids on timber and bamboos by thieves from adjoining territory. They came in bands of twenty to fifty and removed everything of value. This had gone on for years previous to my appointment with the result that the forests in the vicinity were reduced to worthless scrub, and with each season, the thefts extended further into the reserves. The country being wild and deserted and the individual charges extensive, nothing could be done to meet the situation with the available staff. The aboriginal hamlets scattered along the border either feared to assist, or connived with the raiders and so hindered rather than concerted with measures projected to cope with the raids.

The Korku tribe who lived here was subservient to a wizened old fellow who occupied the position of chief headman among the hamlets. He was reputed to be well off and his family possessed the best lands. In appearance, he was more like an evolution of the monkey, than I had yet seen. He had borne a shady character and tales were whispered of his past doings any one of which, if proved, would have meant a long detention in jail. He had three wives and a large family of grown-up sons and daughters and grandchildren. He was held in awe by the people in the neighbourhood. The subordinates feared him and even the native head officials, whether belonging to the magistracy, police or forest, treated him with respect. During my short stay in the locality, I visited the place two or three times with the hope of checking the thefts and became acquainted with the personage described. His ascendancy over the people was very marked, so that it was necessary to obtain his co-operation in any measures attempted against the raiders. But, this I failed to do by the ordinary means of persuasion, promises and threats.

At last, at my next and last visit, for I was transferred shortly after, I hit on the plan of intruding on him as a self-imposed guest, so ordering my baggage and servants to proceed to his dwelling, I made the usual detour for inspection and turned up at the hut some hours after the arrival of my things. The old fellow had come a little distance to greet me, and as his face lit up at the few words of apology I uttered for having forced myself on his hospitality, I

felt he belonged to me for the future. Arrived at the dwelling, the servant mentioned he had been supplied with everything, even with more, than what was necessary. He also insisted on entertaining my servants and subordinates in the same liberal manner. That night, seated on a charpoy or cot, under the awning of the hut, we chatted till late and fell asleep where we conversed - he by the log-fire and I on the charpoy.

In the morning, taking the old Korku, we left on a round of inspection and soon entered the area where the raids were committed. The damage that met our view was enough to gall any one. Words would have only ruffled feelings, for the Korku knew that he and his villagers were suspects. Something more was necessary which without giving offence would enlist their support. It suddenly occurred to me to feign sorrow as the best way of striking at the Korku's rough nature, so having gone over the scene of the latest exploits without a word, I sat down and gave vent to my grief. As anticipated, the fellow was completely overcome and thinking me to be in earnest, came near and begged of me to cheer up and he would promise that the thefts should be stopped. The same evening, he introduced his women folk by ordering them out to do obeisance at my feet. I noticed he had a lot to say without once alluding to the subject of our earlier excursion. Also, at the camp fire, he talked on purely domestic affairs.

In the morning, I was to go out as usual, but he would not accompany me and when I was back for breakfast, he was absent and all they could say was he had gone out. Nor was he visible again till late in the evening when I espied him coming to meet us on my return from a shoot. He was looking pleased and enquired what the bag amounted to, and joined us for the rest of the distance to his hut. Soon after, I left him to get ready for dinner while he went to the cook and ordered up my meals, telling the servant we would be going out again very shortly. On enquiring what he meant, the reply was characteristic of him, amounting to a question "whether I was not anxious to get even with the thieves."

I saw he had stolen a march on me, but the lateness of the hour seemed rather against his sudden proposition. Then, while I was having dinner, he stood by and explained his plan, which was certainly a novel one. He had some-how found out that the raiders would be coming that night, though as a rule thefts stopped when an official was on tour. He also knew the exact spot where they

would be operating. We were to go in advance and post ourselves in ambush on trees before the moon rose - she was due to rise between ten and eleven o'clock. We were to enclose the area over which the cuttings were premeditated and at a signal from him, to jump down and close on the thieves.

The scheme was in keeping with my young spirits and I readily assented, and ordering up the forester and forest guards told them to be ready to start at once for a midnight excursion to capture the raiders. Excuses and objections were overruled and we set out with a party of fourteen or fifteen men. There were only three weapons in the way of firearms, an old muzzle-loader owned by the forester, a cherished flintlock in the possession of the old Korku and my martini. The rest had axes. We had to go five or six miles over forest paths through hilly country and though we carried lanterns, we arrived at the spot just as the moon's rays began to appear on the horizon. Cautioning us not to cough and to be very still, the Korku assigned to each his post in an extended line forming a curve or semi-circle, the forester and I occupying the opposite extremities with the Korku in the centre of the curved line.

As stated, we were to get on to a branch high enough to jump from it in safety. After the lantern had been extinguished, we waited in silence and about an hour elapsed, before we heard the men coming in the distance. They walked into the enclosure and spread over it inside, each man selected his stem for cutting and soon the axes began to knock against the trees. A few minutes later, the shrill cry of the wood-owl rang out twice, in succession. This was the pre-arranged signal and we all leapt down from our branches. Although it never struck me before, I then saw at once the effect the manoeuvre produced on the thieves. Taking us to be spirits, they were absolutely terrified, and abandoning the cuttings and dropping their axes, they huddled together chattering with fear. Even when we came close upon them and were recognised as human beings, they were too disconcerted and subdued to offer resistance. However, their number was more than twice ours which offered them the incentive to attempt escape. The Korku therefore, addressed a few of them by name - apparently he knew them all - warning them that a posse of armed police under the superintendent and the forest officer were in the background and would surely fire and kill them, if they did not submit and follow quietly. Taking the hint, the forester and I walked away some paces

in opposite directions and each fired off a shot from our weapons. Lighting the lanterns and getting the forest guards to take charge of the axes, we made straight for the range headquarters, about fifteen miles from the scene of our adventure. It would not have been safe to return to the village considering its proximity to the frontier and the fear of a rescue being attempted from across the border. Arrived at our destination, it was found that eight or ten men had managed to slip away unnoticed in the dark during the journey; the rest, about 25, were punished,

A few years after this occurrence, I visited the place again when the old Korku was dead, but it was satisfactory to learn that the thefts had greatly diminished. The strangeness investing the proceedings of our previous adventure had had a salutary effect and kept the people in fear of a repetition. As an old offender poignantly remarked to me when questioned whether he was still at the game, that "who could tell, the sahib might be seated up a tree to shoot us down and have us buried in the jungle without anyone being the wiser".

Another example of the influence exerted in a similar way occurred while organising fire-protective measures. The tribes had never heard of such absurdity before and considered it a farce attempting to safeguard vast ranges of tangled hills and valleys that had been overrun with fires within the memory of the oldest inhabitants. "Why?" They told me "if the fires do not occur, we will light them ourselves", as the prevailing beliefs required that particular hilltops and topes should be burnt in the performance of certain ceremonial rites to obtain offspring. In spite of this, when once the headman was gained over by an appeal to his better feelings, it became a comparatively easy problem to keep the forests free from fires.

Once we were opposed by a stalwart Naik, a leader of a clan of Bhils, on introducing game laws in a certain district. This individual was the best shot with the bow and arrow that I have yet come across. He was known to bring down blue bull and panther with his weapon which is saying a good deal. He practically lived by the chase, which he held to have acquired as his birthright, and dared any one to stop him. The only feasible way to deal with him was to enlist him as an official to prevent poaching. The appointment, while allowing him the privilege to shoot, made it incumbent upon him to stop all others from doing so. He proved

a very useful subordinate and suppressed poaching with a strong hand, even among his own kind.

It is sad to relate he was eventually shot as a leader of dacoits. In the great famine of 1899, the police had to adopt precautionary measures to watch daring spirits. This interfered with his liberty so that he escaped and became a notorious dacoit. A large reward was set upon his head and after a long innings of robbery and murder, he was shot - swimming the Nerbudda in flood in attempting to escape from a company of military police. Though he harried the police at every opportunity, he never interfered with the forest works scattered all over the jungle. He kept out of my sight, but it was reported that on various occasions he came near my camp when I was touring in the out-landish parts. I quite believe this was to safeguard my camp, as dacoity had become rife and I went about without a guard. I cannot help thinking that with a little foresight and tact, he might have become a very useful member of the protective force.

An incident of the early attempts at forest administration in a Native State will bear relating. Before its advent, there were no taxes on minor forest produce which includes various edible, medicinal and other economic products obtained in the jungles. Local dealers trading in these, reaped a rich harvest by procuring them for a mere song from the wild tribes who bartered the produce for a few lumps of salt at the weekly markets or fairs, held on the out-skirts of the forests. But the creation of a department made it necessary to tax many of them, and a schedule was framed showing the impositions that were to be levied in future. When it came to be applied, some interested individuals worked upon the credulous minds of the tribes that the taxes were intended to deprive them of a livelihood. There was some trouble, petitions poured in and deputations waited upon me to get the schedule rescinded with the usual threats of further trouble in case it was not done. From the first, I felt it was purely a case of incitement for ulterior ends, in which the simple folks were being used as a stalking horse, and it made me eager to be even with my detractors. The deputations were therefore dismissed with promises of early redress. A day was fixed for attendance at one of the market centres and word sent to all the headmen to meet me there to discuss the matter. On the appointed date, which coincided with the local fair, I camped at the place. The headmen assembled and

the traders were summoned to attend also. When all were together, the proceedings opened with a few words from me explaining the necessity for imposing the taxes, care being taken to emphasise the fact of the profits that accrued to the salesmen from the exports of the products outside the country. The traders could not deny this nor offer a defence. But, the spokesmen of the tribes pointed out, and justly, that they received no extras above the customary values which were always low and, therefore, should not be made to pay. They were then asked to consider whether it would suit them, if the taxes were levied from the traders. There was a chorus of approval in favour of the reversal and the matter was settled to the chagrin of the salesmen. The order already issued for levying the imposition was altered to correspond with the ruling. The levy of these taxes also had the effect of making the tribes see that the State set a store by these products, for they had hitherto, been accustomed to regard them as of little or no value. In future, therefore, they asked and obtained better prices for what they bartered.

On another occasion I was asked to delineate the frontier between two States inhabited by jungle tribes. It had been the cause of serious contention and the boundary - an imaginary line - extended over a disjointed chain of hills covered with forests. Neither opponent community would accept any other line but the one that the party had determined upon for the boundary and as the respective claims overlapped and each refused to recede, the dispute gave vent to trouble. The matter had been shelved for years and the local officials seemed averse to settling it for fear of rousing the contentious spirits who appeared with their bows bent and arrows in rest, whenever an inspection of the tract was undertaken. The creation of a forest service gave the opportunity to have the settlement effected by other hands, and so it happened that the case was made over to the department whose interests the dispute chiefly concerned.

I had already been over the site and knew the bearings of the case as presented by both parties, so that when I arrived at the spot to deal with the matter it was like renewing old acquaintances. I tried by various means for the best part of a week, to make the opposing parties come to a mutual agreement about the alignment. However, each was equally obstinate in persisting in his claim and declined to have any other settlement.

I had almost despaired of settling the dispute amicably, and was hesitating between the merits of whether to lay out the boundary according to my own judgment or to leave it in view of the trouble a new line was sure to raise, when a Bhil headman from a neighbouring State arrived with an urgent letter from the Diwan or native minister. I knew the man very well, and it quite cheered me to see him. He had come upon me unawares and with the instinctive mind of the aborigine, immediately detected my state of feeling, and inquired the cause of my trouble. I told him of the dilemma in which I was placed and having listened patiently he exclaimed, "but Sir! Have you tried the rund mund faisla?", literally, "to behead", but meaning the decision by letting blood. I had never heard the phrase before, much less tried the proposition that it pointed to, in my attempts to solve the difficulty, so I asked him to explain. Whereupon he told me that the only way to get the factions to agree, would be to take a he-goat and sacrifice it to the presiding deity at the site of dispute, in presence of both parties. The two leading opponents should then be made to drag the carcass over the alignment, and the blood trail that marked the line, would constitute the boundary.

    Here was an easy solution to my difficulty, sprung upon me unexpectedly by a tribal headman and I just shook him by the hands. The next day, the advice was put into practice. After the sacrifice, the carcass was carried to the disputed site, the hind legs tied to a forked string each end of which was given to the headman of either side and they were told to drag the body. However much they pulled in opposition, there could be but one trail and along this pillars were set up, and I was glad to find that the people accepted the line without demur.

    Of other disputes I was called upon to settle a few will bear relating as being typical of the people. The examples treat of the application of rough and ready measures to obtain decisions. However distasteful the methods may appear to unpractical minds, they are nevertheless adapted to local sentiment and, exercised by one who is trusted by the people, are fruitful of good. Conciliation is the basis of the proceedings and an ignorant and easily excited people, amenable rather to the force than to the letter of the law, readily appreciate the means adopted for securing the end. Thus, no matter how the award affects interested parties, it is taken with good grace leaving no spite, which conduces to good feeling.

John Daniel St Joseph, 1901.

Ali-Rajpur Rana visiting my camp

Sir William Marris, Governor of the United Provinces,
1922 - 1927

Irma Marris at Mission bungalow, 1908

Camp: Miss O'Hara and Miss Marris, 1908

Camp: Miss O'Hara and Miss Marris, 1908.

A tiger shoot led by Sir William Marris

I was appointed with a brother officer employed by a neighbouring Durbar to assist in delineating the frontier between a State bordering an enclave of British territory wedged in among Native feudatories. The limits were shown in the old survey maps. But, with the customary aptness of native officials to profit by an undelimited boundary and to try and extend the lands of their employers, the district official had seized the opportunity to make it a moot-point for settlement. The case had been pending some years and hampered work on both borders. With the extension of forest conservancy, the jungles in the tract were added to the Forest Officer's control, and so the dispute came to be regarded as falling within the scope of his work.

By previous agreement my brother officer and I met on the border and had the representatives of each side to argue the case. The Kanungo or revenue employee in the British territory reasoned that the boundary marched with the watershed line. On the other hand, the Durbar Vakil, or agent who knew a smattering of law, said that the boundary followed the foot of the hills. In his anxiety to force his arguments on our notice, he kept expounding his views, partly in English and partly in Vernacular, using the word "summit" to describe the position of the boundary. I was at once struck by the importance of the word which he had inadvertently used in trying to magnify his debating powers. When he stopped, it was proposed and agreed that each claimant should set down his statements in writing, and I was greatly relieved to find the Vakil used the same word in his written deposition, because in cases of the kind it is extremely difficult with all the lying and perjury that are brought to bear on the issues, to arrive at a judicious finding. And here was the representative of one side himself admitting in a word the correctness of the boundary shown by his opponent.

Accordingly, I pointed out to my colleague that as there was no material difference in the opinions of opposing parties about the boundary lying along the "summit", we had better lay it out straightaway, and we proceeded to mount the hill. Our action naturally non-plussed our learned friend and he rushed up excitedly to inquire where we were going to. We explained that as he had acknowledged the boundary was on the "summit", we were on our way to mark it. He then pointed to the foot of the hills, saying that "summit" meant the bottom and not the top, as it was derived from sub meaning under, and mitto meaning to send. It

took some little time to convince him of his mistake. Indeed, he would not believe us until he had consulted a dictionary. He was intensely chagrined and said no more against our proceeding, so we were permitted to lay out the line in peace.

Once I was attached to a Border court to act as Ser-punch, meaning the president in a council of elders composed of four elected members, to assist in settling some cases involving knotty issues. Not so long ago, such courts were commonly instituted for dealing with offences against property in the backward parts of the country where it was extremely difficult to enforce legal measures. It was a rough and ready means of meting out justice among communities who were held responsible for the illicit acts of unruly members, and the system was well suited to conditions obtaining in wild tracts. It was generally during a period of scarcity that outbreaks of lawlessness occurred, and fomented and led by daring spirits, they were very difficult to suppress with the handful of poorly paid police that the States maintained. The crimes usually consisted of robberies and thefts in order to procure food or to obtain the means of a livelihood. It was seldom that anyone was seriously injured. The tribes looked upon such raids as an acquired birthright, and it was sufficient for a man of influence to dress up in the garb of a marauder and utter the kilki, or sound the call-note on the drum, for the young bloods to hasten to join him in the expedition.

The kilki or kilkai is a shrill human note rung out indefinitely and brought up sharply with a loud whoop. Uttered from a hilltop or knoll in the rolling country occupied by the tribes, the sound echoes and re-echoes through the glens, travelling far and wide. It is the tribal call to arms.

A Border court is comprised of two or more British officials, each of whom represents the interests of a group of principalities who have been called to question for the lawless acts of their subjects. It is held at a convenient spot on the border, so as to facilitate attendance of accused and witnesses who are difficult to get at. The court works on the principle of compromise based on a money transaction. On assembling, it compares notes of the reports sent in by their respective agencies of the various acts of violence committed by the people. It then proceeds to frame a sort of credit and debit account of the charges before it, showing the gains or losses to or against each State. In cases in which the

delinquencies are admitted, the necessary adjustments are made and nothing more is done. But, in those in which they are refuted or counter claims put in, the issues become involved and are consigned for settlement to councils of elders called punchayats, of whom the head or Ser is, as stated, nominated by the court. The other four men are elected by the opposing parties, two by each side. Headmen or elders are chosen for preference because of their influence, to form the council. As a rule, they are shrewd and have the commonsense to grasp the main points calling for attention, and provided the bearings of the case have been properly explained, the council is quick in arriving at a decision and makes no bones about the award. But occasionally, one has to deal with obstinate and contentious spirits who make it difficult to bring about a settlement, and the proceedings may drag on for days.

The punchayat now becomes a working entity, and moves to a retired spot, usually under a tree, to hear the Ser-punch explain the rights and wrongs of the case or cases with which it has to deal. The men then, consult together in order to fix the responsibility for the offence and to apportion the shares of the fine or compensation to be levied from individuals concerned. When they are agreed upon the finding, they inform the Ser-punch who communicates the result to the court. A statement to the effect is accordingly drawn up and signed by the council members in the court's presence. Should the punchayat disagree over details, reference is made to the Ser-punch whose casting vote is accepted without demur. Serious charges of bodily injury are dealt with by the court. The States guarantees through their representatives payment of fines imposed or value of damage assessed by the punchayats, and recoveries are made from the offending communities. Thus, numbers of cases are quickly and amicably disposed of without leaving traces of ill feeling or rancour in the minds of the people.

To proceed with my part in the business, the cases made over to me dealt with cattle lifting, highway robbery of ornaments and thefts of grain. With one exception, my colleagues of the punchayats I was assigned to as Ser-Punch, raised no difficulties and the cases made over to us were easily settled to the satisfaction of the parties concerned. The one case, related to a theft of a herd of buffaloes, valued at six hundred rupees, equivalent to forty pounds. The evidence produced showed clearly enough that the turvee or watchman of the wronged village had followed the

spoors across the border to an aboriginal settlement where the animals had been taken for shelter, and in the presence of the elders of the village had identified the buffaloes. But, my colleagues declined to consider the evidence with an unbiased mind, and wasted time in useless conjectures over irrelevant details till the best part of the day passed without result. I now thought it was time to intervene and reasoned with them on their dilatory proceedings. My remonstrances however, proved ineffective so I declared that no respite would be granted until the case was settled, which meant they would have to forego food and rest should they persist in prolonging the sitting. To enforce my orders, a guard was told off to see that they were carried out. And yet, although the men were kept on the alert throughout the night by prods from the guard's bayonet and made to sit all day in the burning sun they did not announce their findings until sunset, occupying two days and a night in futile discussion. The decision was as good as could be expected under the circumstances, even more satisfactory was the fact that it was acceptable both to the aggrieved and the offending parties. This is an instance in point in which except for the use of a little force, the punchayat would have doubtless kept parleying and prolonging the settlement indefinitely, to the great inconvenience of all concerned.

The procedure of identification on such occasions is curious. The turvee or village watchman is regarded as incapable of error in identifying goods stolen from his village. This gift or power is supposed to be inherited, so that the turvee's identification, provided the recognition has been duly carried out before elders of tribes, is seldom or never questioned. The form consists in the turvee passing his hands over the property stolen, and it is a point of honour with tribal councils to consider the theft proven if the customary formula has been observed. I have not quite succeeded in ascertaining how the form originated. But, I was told by an ancient of his race who was a humorist, that the procedure signified undoubted possession on the principle that a woman was a man's wife if he could pass his arms around her without interruption. It is doubtless a symbolical representation of the human act to denote possession and if we consider the marked preference that aboriginal races evince for everything original, the old man's version seems a probable one. That the privilege should belong to the turvee by general consent is also likely, as he is of the

clan of hereditary watchmen to the tribes. In the case before us, the kind of evidence cited was put before the punchayat, yet and in spite of the derision of on-lookers of their own people, the council demurred to be guided by it, making too much of trivialities that could not help the members in arriving at a solution.

For a short period during my career in the States, the revenue work of one of the Durbars was included among my duties. The Durbars were particularly anxious to have the numerous suits that had been accumulating for some time past, disposed of early. The best way to comply seemed to me to make a round of visits to the places from where they originated. This would enable me not only to escape the attentions of the array of council engaged by interested parties, but also to obtain facts first-hand from the people themselves.

One of the cases concerned a dispute over a strip of land stretching between the estates of two cousins. Both were well to do ryots enjoying influence in the villages around, whose parents had lived on brotherly terms. But jealousies had been started on the sons coming into their properties and fanned by evil-mongers had caused a serious split in their good relations, so that occasion was taken of every opportunity to do each other harm. The strip of land which lay between their fields had been allotted by their parents by mutual consent to afford a passage for the village cattle driven out for grazing during the rains.

It may be mentioned that the fields surrounding an agricultural village are very often rich, and every bit sown with crops. Moreover, the black cotton soil of the country becomes so sodden by rain that cattle stick and cannot move about freely. Consequently, they are taken to the gravel soils or hilly tracts on village limits where a plentiful supply of herbage sprouts up after a few showers. To get to these pastures, cattle troup out by recognised tracks called gohas, these lanes hardened by constant trampling afford easy footing.

The ownership of the track became the subject of contention, the elder claiming that it was included in his parent's rent-roll prior to the land being made over for the general convenience of the village. On the other hand, the younger relative maintained that the land had been shared equally by their parents since the gift was in the joint name of both. The case had dragged on for some years, being called up at intervals, each time only to be shelved for a

further period. In short, as sometimes happens when an administration is weak, the dispute was looked upon as a milch cow for filching the cousins who were too occupied over personal grievances to pay much heed to the treatment accorded their case at headquarters. It now came up before me and on going through the misel or file, the mass of irrelevant evidence recorded struck me as singular. However, it made me decide to camp on the spot and attempt a settlement with the aid of a punchayat.

The village lay completely off the beaten track and as anticipated, the people were surprised at my visit and to keep them ignorant, not a word was said of the dispute in question. In the afternoon I strolled out with a gun to pick up some game for the pot and by dint of questioning the village watchman carrying my gun, succeeded in getting from him a good deal of information regarding the bearings of the case. At the same time, I took the opportunity to make a cursory inspection of the land in dispute. In the morning my camp was moved to the spot and with it those of the subordinates and followers accompanying me, who were a goodly number. This was done with an object, for the cousins were called upon to make arrangements for the necessary supplies required by so large a camp. It meant therefore a tax on their resources, especially as I encouraged the belief that I would not move from the place until the dispute was settled. My men also taking the hint began to pile up requisitions for supplies.

On the case being called up, the cousins were asked whether they would not prefer to get their dispute settled by punchayet. But the assistance was declined on the plea that the matter was entrusted to vakils who would appear instead, consider the proposal, and then be dismissed. This interval was necessary to enable them to realise their obstinacy and reflect on the bother which they would be letting themselves into by protracting my stay. Again, it was as likely as not that my advent in their midst would be taken advantage of by well-wishers to exercise their influence in favour of a tolerant spirit. On the following day, the men appeared and while the elder cousin persisted in his refusal, the younger agreed to a settlement. This was something gained, though no punchayet was practicable so long as one of the parties was a dissentient, and the only thing to do was to proceed with the case.

In examining the papers, an error was discovered in the copy of

the rent-roll put in as evidence. It was such as might easily occur in copying and did not affect the issue materially, but its occurrence was fortunate in supplying the necessary stimulus for exerting pressure on the elder man in whose interests the copy had been put in and whose signature it bore, together with the patwaris who made the copy. The matter was treated as a forgery, and having enlarged on the enormity of the offence and the punishment that would follow should it be proved, I stopped the case in order to commence the hearing of the more serious charge. This was too much for my man and he pleaded for an hour's respite, which was granted. At its expiry, he appeared, full of remorse, anxious to listen to advice. So a punchayet was formed and a settlement effected to the mutual satisfaction of the cousins who were made to embrace and be friends. I subsequently learned that the occasion was celebrated by a feast and resulted in a binding friendship. The charge of forgery was of course dropped. It was never intended to be pushed, and moreover, the error was pretty evident.

Part of my role as revenue officer required me to inquire into the indebtedness of ryots, and examination disclosed some glaring instances of wrong committed by the Bunia or Sherlock class, with the acquiescence of the very functionaries whose duty it was to prevent sharp practices. I will give just one example to show how customary laws are liable to be set aside when pecuniary gains stand in the way of men sheltering under the presumed infallibility of orthodoxy.

It used to be the practice when an officer toured through the district, for village officials consisting of the patel or headman, the patwari or scribe who maintained village statistics, and the turvee or kotwal who is a village watchman, to meet him on the border and conduct him through their lands. The practice was gradually dying out and I insisted on its revival wherever I went. During the slow progress necessitated by the presence of these menials the official, if he chooses to do so, can by judicious questioning learn a good deal from them about facts relating to the locality.

It happened that at one of these entries into a village, the headman who occupies the position of the greatest importance, appeared poorly clad in torn and tattered garments which made me mistake him for a vagrant, and I asked the patwari why the headman had not come. The supposed beggar retorted that he was the patel, though merely in name, since he had been deprived of all

his substance. His sorry condition and haggard looks invited pity and I questioned the patwari about him, and gathered from his evasive replies that the case needed looking into, so he was told to be at my camp with the patel and to bring the papers relating to the case that were in his keeping.

Their examination revealed a tangled skein of jobbery. The man's father had possessed considerable lands in the village held partly free of rent for services rendered by his ancestors and partly at a nominal assessment in virtue of the family's standing as hereditary patels. The parent died during the infancy of the son, and the wife as frequently happens, indulged in lavish expenditure on feasts and charitable bequests to Brahmins, that is the priestly class, in order to perpetuate the name and high state which her deceased husband occupied during his life-time. Being without sufficient means to meet these ruinous expenses, she had recourse to borrowing at usurious terms conditional on the mortgage of the ancestral property and its subsequent foreclosure, should the debt remain unliquidated after ten years. She was an unbusinesslike woman, and the inevitable came about in the property passing entirely into the possession of the creditor, a rich bunia, residing at headquarters and in touch with the officials. He had cleverly managed to obtain the assent of the Chief courts to the transaction, consequently when the son attained majority and submitted petitions for the restoration of his ancestral lands, his appeals were dismissed with the remark that the case being barred by limitation, could not be reopened. Through no fault of his own, the son now found himself cut off from redress and reduced to poverty. To eke out an existence, he was perforce obliged to work as a common labourer in the fields of the village where some years before his parent had been courted and consulted as the influential man in the place.

The bunia remained in undisputed possession of the property for about fifteen years. Apart from skilfully manipulating the court's consent to the transfer in his favour of lands held in hereditary tenure under privileged conditions, he had also succeeded in becoming the substitute heir in getting the mutation to the deeds effected. The impostureship enabled him to enjoy the concessions in the matter of assessments and thereby to defraud the State of no small income. He was now summoned and asked if he had anything to say against making restitution of the property

to its rightful owner. He however, felt sure of his position and declined every overture, refusing even to produce the documents with him for inspection. His refusal necessitated reference to the record's office for the file, and the case was posted for the Christmas holidays which were near, and which I intended spending at headquarters.

The hearing was taken up on my return. Everything on paper was so well in trim that there was no opening to go upon in order to obtain a reversal of the previous orders. So I hit upon the fact that a woman possessed no authority to act independently in the matter of disposal of ancestral property, more so when it was immovable, during the existence in an heir of the male line. To make quite sure I consulted a Pundit and my learned friend had no hesitation in endorsing my opinion on the value set on the rule. This was a trump indeed, which I determined to use in the following day's discussion. It was Christmas day and just as I was in the middle of things who should turn up but the council of Indian officials to offer felicitous greetings as was their wont, in honour of the day. This is a form of politeness peculiar to Indians of breeding who visit relatives and friends on high-days and holidays in order to personally deliver messages of goodwill in commemoration of the day.

Welcome as their visit was, it could not have been made at a more opportune moment. I at once saw in it the means to an end by making them my coadjutors in the settlement, for in virtue of their religious, social and official position, their word could not but bring the necessary moral influence to bear on the main issue of the complicated case, as well as in overcoming so obstinate a personage as the bunia. It would also solve the difficulty of setting my opinion in favour of a reversal against previous orders. I therefore invited them to take part in the proceedings, letting them see into the merits of the case as it appeared from the documentary evidence. Having satisfied themselves regarding the position presented by the papers, their attention was called to the obvious infraction of moral law which outweighed every other evidence and which I felt sure they, as good Hindus, would not dare to confute. As expected, there was a consensus in support of my view, and it was declared to have precedence over legal technicalities contained in the documents. This was enough for my purpose, and orders were passed there and then, for the immediate restoration of the lands to their rightful owner.

It need hardly be said that the patel was almost beside himself at the turn of good luck, and overflowing with gratitude. He never forgot the event, and whenever I camped anywhere near his village, there was always a substantial basket of vegetables and fruit to greet me, while at the harvesting season he insisted on sending a cart-load of gram for the use of my pony. It was good to share in the joys of the family and of the village generally who regarded the man in spite of his misfortune as their rightful head, but the restitution of an old establishment would have compensated anyone for the part taken in its revival. The bunia of course, appealed against my finding, but the Durbar were not to be taken in a second time and his appeal was dismissed.

These few instances will show how dealings may be conducted with the backward classes. Forest administration, especially in the early years of its organisation, and in Native States more than in British India, is replete with incidents and occurrences of a character not always found in the administrative annals of other departments. Although a new creation planted on the country, Forest work has become closely allied with the welfare of the masses and plays an important role in their domestic economy.

The aim in all these cases was to get the people to take the principal part in smoothing out the differences between the opposing sides, so that while on the one hand my role in the proceedings assumed the character of a disinterested person, I took care on the other to watch them closely so as to be prepared to advise if necessary. Courts were held in the open under the spacious shelter of a banyan tree or grove as an inducement for the village elders to join in the proceedings. If they came they were shown the respect due to their years or position and invited to assist in ameliorating hostile feelings. A durrie or tent carpet was spread to accommodate them and they sat in two rows facing one another, which rendered discussion easy. Often too, a hot or cold beverage, as tea, milk or sherbet, was served up. These little attentions not only won their confidence, but brought good cheer to bear on the proceedings - an asset of no little value when jealousies and animosities are made to obscure the main issue and so defeat the ends of justice. The case opened in the local vernacular, giving a resumé of its origin and detailing the merits of rival claims. At the close of the address, the opponents were called upon to provide their punch or council, and the nomination by the

court of the Ser-punch or president followed. In ninety-nine cases out of a hundred, this led to an amicable settlement and the people went away with the feeling that the finding was entirely the result of their co-operation, while the fact of their elders having participated in the work disarmed unfriendly criticism.

Wits were not wanting to enliven the proceedings and pertinent remarks would be heard when an obstinate person turned a deaf ear to all reasoning. Thus, there would be the suggestion to harness him with the potter's ass or closet him with the village clown or to treat him as a fool convincing him of his folly by deciding the case ex parte.

I found most trouble where bunias were mixed up with agricultural interests. They were never seen to labour in the fields and being the products of the pax Britannica rule, they evaded the orthodox laws with impunity, while the courts of justice became their humble servants in enforcing the collection of scandalous debts or in the foreclosure of inflated mortgages.

Practically every forest officer comes in contact with aborigines in the course of official service. The feelings with which he was regarded by these people in the districts where they met may be fairly taken to gauge his merits as an executive officer. My own experience is that these people are valuable assets in the work of forest conservancy, provided they are properly handled. In this respect, it is necessary to differentiate between dealings direct, and through agents or subordinates acting as intermediaries. When indirect means are employed, errors of judgment that would ordinarily pass for carelessness become in the case of primitive tribes, a serious obstacle to the creation or maintenance of good feeling. Their credulous and sensitive nature is apt to intensify by the turns and twists which natives, especially subordinates, are prone to interpret the opinions of their superiors. This is usually the cause of misunderstandings that generate sullenness, instead of gaining a willing and eager response. Personally, I have found they respond more readily to originality in dealings, than to other means of treatment. This is due to their crude and simple nature, which appreciates proceedings that harmonise with their character.

In the great famine, we had to conduct forest operations for the relief of the jungle tribes who could not be got to the regular works. These forest projects were of various descriptions, but had mostly to do with the collection of jungle produce from hilly and

inaccessible tracts negotiable only by narrow paths. The operations had necessarily to be scattered over a wide area to keep them within easy reach of aboriginal settlements. On one occasion during an inspection of fodder collections, the head of a gang of aborigines came up and complained that he had been paid for a lesser quantity of grass, than the amount they had actually cut. I enquired of the subordinate in charge, in presence of the men, and he showed payments were according to the quantity received. Most of the gang-men also agreed with what he said, but the headman demurred and persisted in his accusation. The subordinate was a trusted servant who had passed his life among the tribes and was popular among them, for which reason he had been specially selected to hold charge. Thinking the headman had been mistaken, I decided against him and throwing him a couple of annas to buy sweets as a token of friendly feelings, I rode on to the next work.

My marches took me some distance from the place. A week or so passed and I forgot all about the occurrence when it was brought before me with tragic suddenness. I was camped in a different locality and had strolled out in the evening to shoot something for the pot. In stalking along a watercourse, I came upon the headman seated by the bank with his wife and two children, digging unwholesome bulbs for food. I was as much surprised to meet him as he was to see me. On enquiring, I was told that he did not care to stay on the work longer, when he was not believed. My conscience pricked me for I felt he might not have been dealt with fairly. So taking out my note book, I scribbled instructions to the official in charge and tearing out the page, gave it to him to return with it at once to the works and get the balance he claimed. This man had deliberately chosen to leave the works, rather than be disbelieved in the matter of a few annas, although his desertion practically meant starvation for him and his family. The pitiful condition, to which they had been reduced in the week or ten days that had passed since the occurrence, taught me to be more careful in dealings with the tribes in future. Examples of the sort could be multiplied, but it just shows how difficult the position is at times, and the necessity for close supervision.

The duties with which the executive was saddled were, chiefly of a detective and protective character, directly concerned with the prevention of damage to forest growth. But besides them, officials

had to settle the means for disposing of produce, as well as attend to marking and girdling operations with a view to the removal of saleable species classed as mature. Considering then, the extensive area under individual supervision, without adequate safeguards against thefts and damage, and the character of the country to be ranged over, it was only by keeping friendly with the tribes and enlisting the co-operation of the rural population, that success could be assured.

They supplied the information that led to the detection of offenders: their good-will prevented the commission of illicit acts: their regard for the official checked negligent practices: their affection for him caused them to rally from distances without summons, to put down a conflagration, or capture bands of thieves, or impound herds of almost wild cattle, let loose to graze in the reserves at nights. They were again, the best medium of information about the marketable values of products, even when the removals had no sale locally and were leased to outside contractors. Engaged in the collection, they could discern by their employee's actions whether the value of the produce at distant markets had risen or declined. Their knowledge of the forests enabled operations to be carried through quickly by dispensing with the labour that would otherwise have been necessary in selecting sites and fixing upon works, scattered over a wide area of hilly country. It will be obvious that these services meant a good deal to the official who naturally wanted good results but was hampered for want of ways and means of doing it, rather than by the friendliness of the rustics among whom he worked.

Forest Graziers
Besides the aboriginal tribes of Gonds, Korkus and Bhils inhabiting the jungles, there was a race of professional graziers of the Gaoli class who roamed over sequestered areas with large herds of buffaloes. They were supposed to be emigrants from the North, possibly from the Rakhs of the Punjab since their tales made allusion to uninhabitable expanses utilised only for pasture.

Their folklore reckoned their advent from centuries before, the exodus being attributed to a devastating famine, which drove them South in the search of pasture. They were a fine fair race, akin to the Gujars and Bharuds who are also types of professional graziers. But, the Gaolis differed from them in slimness of profile and in

having chiselled features, also in being more mindful in the observance of religious rites and ceremonies. Their women too were handsome and comparatively fair. The local people attributed these qualities to their drinking quantities of milk and doing little or no manual labour. They considered it a sin to adulterate milk and should a drop happen to fall on the ground, they would rub the spot carefully with their fingers till every sign of the same was obliterated. This was owing to the belief that any visible sign of waste would diminish the supply.

It was their custom too, when a buffalo calved to hide the newly born and for a man to take its place in the night, acting the part of the calf, till the buffalo thinking him to be her offspring, started fondling and licking the mimic. They believed this made the animals more attached to their owner. Their arrangements for protection at night in the jungle were exceedingly curious. They used to put their families and calves in the centre of a ring and the animals were made to squat in a circle facing outwards, like a Boer laager, as a protection against tigers and panthers which were then fairly numerous. On moonlight nights, especially in the hot weather months, the animals occasionally grazed at night. But, as a rule, they kept in the ring formation or laager, which I have described. When collecting the animals the grazier called in a shrill plaintive note, very much like the sound uttered by a person in pain or distress. The animals heeded the call and would often rush to the sound. Any one clad like a civilised being in the garments of contentment excited their curiosity. I have known of riders being charged - in which case the only escape lay in jumping off and letting loose the pony - and also of marriage processions being attacked that happened to be passing near by where they were grazing. But the graziers had wonderful control over their animals, and if such an outbreak occurred, one of them would rush forward and gesticulate in front of the animals, and so stop them, or else would start a shrill cry and so deviate the beasts from charging.

Often, one would come upon these men in the early morning milking their animals, and then they invariably offered one a lota full of milk to drink, which was pure and refreshing. As a rule however, they were shy but simple folk, keeping very much to themselves.

Once I happened to be passing through one of their encampments, when one of the men met me and fell into

conversation, saying that his pori meaning a little girl, was very ill with a chronic pain in her stomach, and asked if I knew of any drugs that would give relief. I asked to see the child and the father went in and fetched his daughter, but to my surprise instead of being a little girl, as I was led to expect, she was a blooming maiden of sixteen or seventeen summers. Knowing how reserved these people are regarding their women, I was rather perturbed as to what to do, especially as the father told her to show me where the pain was, which she at once did. To satisfy him, and to end the matter, I just touched the afflicted part and told him I guessed the cause, and that he must come or send to headquarters where he would get something to cure her. Knowing that these people suffered from a common complaint owing to the coarse and parched grains which they ate, I procured some worm tablets from a missionary whom I knew, and gave them to the father with a strong dose of castor oil. After a fortnight he returned with a present of ghee or clarified butter as thanks for having cured his daughter.

This was by no means the only occasion why I acquired fame as a physician. Another time when I was camping close to their shanties, I heard sounds of great distress and enquired what was the matter, and the headman himself turned up looking very mournful and said that his only son was dying of cholera. A few strong doses of chlorodine brought the boy round. Some weeks later, on my return to headquarters, the Gaoli appeared with a fine milch buffalo and calf. He could not be grateful enough for the medicine and he pressed me to accept the buffalo but I refused on the ground that no official ought to accept a present of value. The man was very hurt and would not take the buffalo back, but made it over to a local shrine in my name instead.

The grazier's buffaloes were splendid for the purpose of following up wounded tigers. But one must discriminate sharply between them and ordinary village buffaloes. When a tiger is wounded, the proposal usually made is to collect the village buffaloes to track him down. But village buffaloes unless they are many and mothers with young calves which must also be taken, will not face a tiger. As soon as they sniff him they will turn and bolt; in fact, I have seen this happen with a wounded panther. In my experience it is only the half-wild buffaloes accustomed to roam in the forests night and day, that are entirely fearless and can

be trusted to drive the wounded tiger from his hiding place.

I have only once beaten with buffaloes for a man-eating tiger. This beast inhabited very hilly country covered with extensive forests. In the interior of the hills and right in the depths of the forests, there was an old shrine near a perennial spring where formerly lived an aged fakir. He had died at an extremely old age a few years before I joined the service, leaving behind him a herd of buffaloes and cows and other wealth which was forfeited to Government, as there was no successor. The tiger, which had acquired a taste for nobler food, did not touch the hermit's cattle during his lifetime, and when he died, the countryside believed that fakir and tiger roamed the forests as companions at night. As commonly happens in such cases, an annual fair grew up in his honour, but as the actual shrine was inaccessible, except by a steep winding path passing through dense cover, the fair was held at the foot-hills three miles away. The fair lasted about a week and only the devotees actually went up to the shrine. On the fakir's death the shrine was deserted, but the fair continued to be held.

The story went that the tiger started killing human beings after the fakir's death and also, what was more extraordinary, that he never killed during the fair or at the shrine. Benighted pilgrims to the shrine swore they saw the tiger and he took no notice of them. It was believed too that he stalked in and out among the stalls every night while the fair was in progress. I had come to the fair myself when one morning my orderly woke me early in great excitement, with the news that there were tiger's pugs close by. Without stopping to dress, I got up and followed him in my sleeping suit, and sure enough, there were the pugs of what appeared to be a small tiger, about thirty yards from my camp along a shallow watercourse. All said that the tiger's object was not merely to show his respect to the dead fakir, his religious preceptor, but to keep watch and ward against robbers and other wild animals as a trustee for the departed saint in whose honour the fair was held. But he certainly did not confine himself to such commendable duties, for every year he carried off a few people who came to the jungles for forest produce or to graze cattle.

Now the country was a confused mass of hills and impossible to beat, and on the other hand the tiger would not touch a tied bait, nor lie up near anything he killed once it was discovered. Consequently all the beats for him had hitherto turned out blanks.

When Thompson came round on his annual inspection tour, I joined him as usual at the borders of the district. In the evening while seated round the campfire, he started his shikar stories and in turn, I told him the story about the tiger. His curiosity was roused and he changed his programme to take him close to the spot. He asked me to send word in advance to the villagers near the forest not to stall their cattle for the night but to let them roam about, promising that he would make good any loss. This was done for two days without a kill being reported. On the third day, a grazier came in to report that a young cow in calf had been killed at the foot of the hills and dragged away. We went to the spot. There was the kill, but the pugs were of the size of a very large panther, for which they might have been easily mistaken. However we followed the drag for about fifty yards, and found that the kill had been forced through very thick scrub growth and up a steep hillside. This feat required great strength and made it clear that the culprit could be nothing but a tiger. Thompson decided not to follow the drag further. He looked well over the country from different points of view and then we sat under the shade of a tree and arranged our plans for a beat. He suspected that the kill had been taken right up over the ridge, about three hundred feet or more, and into a depression behind it, the existence of which could be inferred from the torrent that flowed out about half a mile from where the kill had taken place. He and his daughter, whom he wanted to have the first shot, were to start at ten o'clock by a very round-about path with a few men to act as silent stops, and to take their positions at the top of the gorge dividing the outer and inner parallel chains of hills. His dispositions were conjectured, but based on his intimate knowledge of the geological formation. The only maps we then had, on a scale of four miles to the inch, were often inaccurate and too small to be of much use. Half an hour after the guns had started, I was to conduct the beat up the torrent bed. We were to be very silent and drive a herd of about sixty buffaloes before us. No noise or shouting was to be made, unless the tiger attempted to break through. We started with the buffaloes at the appointed time, and the beat went very slowly owing to the roughness and steepness of the ground and the clumsy movements of the animals. In about half an hour, we came in touch with the first silent stop on the left wing and I walked up from my position in centre of the line

of beaters, to ask what he had seen. He said that the tiger was in the beat, and that he had seen him gliding along slowly towards the lady's machan but as there had been no shot, he suspected something had gone wrong. I went back to my position to restart the beat and suddenly I heard a commotion among beaters and buffaloes on my right. In the excitement my shotgun went off and a minute or so afterward the welcome crack of a rifle rang out on my right front. The tiger had taken the course anticipated and appeared suddenly in front of the lady who had the best position, but before she could get in a shot he saw her and retreated diagonally across the front. He was checked by the silent stop on the opposite side and then, instead of going forward to the next gun as he was expected to do, he slid down the steep bank and tried to escape along a ledge at the base of the scarp, where there was hardly foot-hold for a monkey or a porcupine. Here the buffaloes winded him and began snorting and tossing their heads about, while the beaters along the ridge began to roll down stones. This turned the tiger back, and he made for the gorge and came out before Mr. Thompson who shot him. He was a fine tiger in splendid condition, about nine feet eight inches in length of a slim, wiry build, comparatively long in the body and low of stature, with quite small feet for his size.

It is worth nothing that tigers and panthers which keep to steep hills have small feet, while the tendency of the body is to be stooping and drawn out, rather than high shouldered and thick set, as is the case with animals occupying low and marshy grounds. The variation is doubtless an adaptation to environment. Obviously an animal with small feet would be more sure and quicker in steep narrow places, and mere height would be of little use to him in hunting so long as he kept to the brows and crests of the hills.

As a general rule, no firearms should be used in a beat unless of course, the animal charges. But in this particular case it happened, the shot fired unconsciously forced the tiger to decide on a course he was unwilling to take, which led him to his doom. So much for the Bhopali tiger, and strange to say, the forest people generally though not inclusive of the Gonds living among them, were not at all pleased to be relieved of his presence, but seemed inclined to resent his removal. They believed like children in the various tales of his virtues, and especially in the legend of the fakir's spirit

consorting with him. They were ashamed of the little part they had taken in his downfall: they never voluntarily alluded to it, and even if reminded of it, they preferred to turn the conversation.

This is the only beat of the kind in which I took part. What impressed me at the time was the clever way in which it was conceived, and how well the several agents co-operated. Looking back on it after twenty years, and in the light of various experiences since, I feel sure that no one else but Mr. Thompson, would have bagged that tiger, except perhaps by accident.

Axe Hunting
The early mode of life I have described brought me in very close touch with the wild tribes, Gonds and Korkus, inhabiting the forests. And being young and keen and fond of escapades, I soon made friends with the young bloods among the tribes and entered whole-heartedly into their amusements. Together we planned excursions and ran down sambar, bear, pig and antelope - at that time a rifle or gun would have been for me an expensive luxury. The form of sport we contrived for our hunts, though very simple, required nerve and athletic fitness. It depended for success on individual agility and capacity to wield an axe. The hunts were generally arranged for the middle of the day which is the hottest time when animals are not merely lazy but at a disadvantage in the matter of hearing and scenting owing to the tricks played by the breezes which usually intensify about noon, seeming to blow from all quarters. It was the practice to first mark down an animal and then manoeuvre to enclose him in a circle of hunters armed with axes. The cordon gradually drew nearer round him under cover of stumps, bushes, stems and stones. Then, when the ring had been drawn close enough, one of the men would utter a shrill cry causing the beast to get up suddenly and to charge out blindly. As a rule, he would pass within fifteen feet (five paces) of one of the men when the axe would be swung and hurled at him. Three times out of four the axe strikes home, the beast is disabled and lags behind and the men come up and finish him. If the wound is not very severe and the beast bolts, they hang on until he is exhausted, so that occasionally there is a running fight for some distance before the animal is killed.

In this way, I have been at the death of a score of animals. The hardest to despatch was the wild boar and perhaps the easiest the

sambar, owing to its being easily confused by noise. The bear is sluggish and I was surprised to find how easily he could be finished, provided the men kept their mettle they were not so much afraid of the beast himself as of the threatening language which he used. When brought to bay his clumsy movements could be easily dodged. But being tough he gave a run for his money and two or three men had always to hang on till he succumbed. His shrieks and wails sounded uncanny to inexperienced ears and even helped him to escape. Other animals were usually ended without trouble. The first time I myself struck home was at a four-horned antelope which rushed past within five or six feet of me. The axe buried itself in his ribs and as he lurched over on his side, I was quick enough to get hold of one of his hind legs. Though not a large beast, he was strong enough to struggle hard till one of the men rushed up, and was about finishing him when my Mohammedan orderly shouted to hold him for halal, that is to say, to pronounce the invocation while cutting the throat by saying bismillah, so that he may eat of the meat - believers of the prophet consider the flesh of animals not treated in this way to be taboo for food - at that, the man tried to get hold of the fore-legs to throw him, and the beast struck out with his head and pierced his cheek with his horns, causing a nasty wound which laid up the man for some months. The elders considered this affair a great feat. The only other occasion in which I myself was successful was with a young blue-bull. I have however, helped to despatch bear, boar and sambar. One boar especially, of the brown variety and comparatively small, gave a lot of trouble and nearly killed two of the men. Once a panther happened to be enclosed though his presence was not in the least suspected. He had lain up among some rocks where a boar had been marked down, and he charged out close by one of the men who in the excitement sent his axe at him. But the panther was too quick and fortunately, the axe missed striking, otherwise he would have probably mauled the men for he is too agile and aggressive to be handled with safety. Another time I remember - while arranging the cordon for a stag, we disturbed a tiger: but this incident got on to the nerves of the men, and the sport for that day was abandoned. Such escapades made me fairly active and often I could out-run or out-walk the men.

The form of axe we used was different from the ordinary one. It was like a battle-axe, only much less in weight. Its blade expanded

sharply from the head with a cutting edge twice as long as the width from head to blade and slightly concave, as sharp as a razor, indeed the men actually used it for shaving themselves. It was of light make, about five or six ounces, and was carried like a walking stick, the fork of the palm between thumb and fingers, being inserted into the hollow formed by the curve of the blade and head of the handle. The handle was light and springy of seasoned male bamboo or dhaman wood. When properly hurled, it was swung round over the head and the axe flew with a rotatory motion. Each man proved his axe to his own liking, judging of its suitability for use by the weight and length of handle which had to be of a size reaching from the individual's right palm to the ground, while he stood upright. Some men were very clever in the use of this weapon and could hit a small object, such as a hare or a peafowl, at a distance of twenty to thirty paces. I once saw a porcupine killed at a distance of twenty-four paces. It was trying to get away from the line of beaters, but one of them saw it in time and turned about and aiming his axe transfixed it in the body, which disabled it sufficiently to prevent escape.

The meat obtained from the game killed on these occasions was carefully divided among the men. Aborigines as a rule have a scrupulous regard for the exactness of shares and generally an elder is called in to make the divisions. In fact this is carried to extremes and I have known cases where the number of beaters among whom a small animal has had to be divided to be content with a few ounces of meat rather than let it be shared among a few, and the rest to wait for another opportunity. The skin usually falls to the head or leader of the party, while titbits, like the liver, kidneys or tongue, is often set aside for the headman of the village, even if he has had nothing to do with the hunt. When I happened to be of the party, they always took care before sharing to make over to my men what was needed for the kitchen.

Such a weapon as I have described may seem primitive indeed to sportsmen armed with the latest improvements in firearms. But a marvellous feat, although it may be attributed more to accident than to actual intention, will show the deadly power of even such a primitive weapon when wielded by capable hands. I am thinking of the death of a man-eating tigress which infested the Silwani reserve bordering on the Tava river.

The hero of the exploit, a Gond fire-watcher, that is a man

employed temporarily in the hot season to guard against forest fires, was in the habit of escorting his wife who used to bring his food. He usually accompanied her on her return for part of the distance which lay in his beat, through a portion of the reserve that was believed to be outside the beast's circuit - all animals have a certain range over which they roam in quest of food. One afternoon, the tigress way-laid them at a gorge through which the path lay, and as they came along in single file, it pounced out from some cover on the bank, knocked down the woman and started dragging her back along the path by which they had just come. The husband who was in front, maddened with fear, rushed up the bank to the side of the path so as to get on higher ground, and hurling his axe at the beast bolted into the nearest village four or five miles away. Here he told his tale and enlisted the help of his fellow men to accompany him the next day in his search for the remains, as it was then late in the afternoon. It happened that the axe had carried true, hitting the beast a racking blow on the right flank, cutting through three ribs and piercing the lungs and remained stuck in the side. The tigress however, had not released hold of her prey, but had dragged the woman about forty yards to the bank of the river and there dropped her under some cover: then had made for a pool in the river bed where it died.

Now the police officer happened to be camping out at some distance away, trying for a chance at this very tigress. As usual, his trackers were out in the early morning endeavouring to locate the beast, when they chanced to look down from the high bank of the river and saw it lying in the pool. Thinking it had been wallowing, as tigers often do, they sent in word that they had marked it down. The news immediately brought the police officer on the scene and from the bank he put in a couple of shots into the already dead beast. As it showed no signs of life, he supposed that it was shot through the heart, and sent his men down to get it out.

In the meantime, the Gond had also started out with his party to look for the remains of his wife, and both parties met at the pool. The police officer naturally kept the tigress while the Gonds busied themselves with the ceremonies for the dead woman. The reserve formed part of my charge, but I was right away in the opposite direction, so that it was a week or more before I heard of the occurrence. The forest men maintained stoutly that the tigress had been killed by the Gond firewatcher. As there was a big reward

offered for its destruction, I put in a claim on the man's behalf before the Deputy Commissioner who called for the proofs. An examination of the skin at once showed that the brute owed its death to the axe and not to the rifle, for the simple reason that the spot where the weapon had entered was deeply stained with blood, despite the skin having been well rubbed and cleaned, whereas there were no signs of stains around the bullet holes. Thereupon justice was done: the Gond got the reward and the skin was made over to the forest department. It was subsequently sent with the axe, to be preserved as a curiosity in the forest museum at Dehra Dun. This was a mangy tigress: the skin had bad scars of wounds which had healed, caused by firearms and sharp instruments. The uncoremonious way in which the tigress met its death, prevented a demonstration as is usual when notorious pests are brought to account. But there was a sense of relief in the countryside as the news spread that it had been killed.

Chapter IV

Incidents in Camp Life

Life in camp in the solitary wilds far removed from any habitation often palled on the men accompanying me and to enliven the long hot-weather evenings, subordinates occasionally got up shows or made sport at each other's expense. A favourite game was to mimic animals and to appear more or less unexpectedly before their dupes and frighten them out of their wits. It was easy to impose upon men who were either new to their surroundings or credulous creatures that were the butt of the camp, often too the likenesses were so thorough that it was difficult to distinguish them from the real. On such occasions I have known men who lived almost all their lives in the jungles, taken in by the forms assumed; moreover, even cattle and the writer's pony accustomed to a jungle existence, have been equally deceived on seeing the false characters, and snorted and kicked, and broke their traces, and ran. It was in the dusk of the evening or on moonlight nights that such games succeeded because in the prevailing dimness, defects in the get-up could not be easily noticed, also the imitations would appear real in the elusive light. Again, the men scattered about this time to prepare their food before retiring for the night and so were more or less isolated and easily frightened.

A man wrapped in a dark blanket with brown paper twisted into a cone resembling a dunce's cap, fixed over his face to serve for a snout, and moving on all fours uttering grunts, made an excellent device for a bear. A tiger was got up by a striped carpet wound loosely round two men, one clasping the other's waist, and keeping in a stooping position with the turban drawn over the leader's face who mimicked a tiger's growls while on the prowl. These were the favourite subjects for imitations, and a little practice made the men proficient imitators. The performers entered into the game with zest, at times carrying their jokes too far when the unsuspecting victim would retaliate in desperation resulting in the would-be animal coming off second best. An incident which occurred in this connection will bear relating.

We were camped one evening near an aboriginal hamlet called Punji surrounded by forest, in the beat of an old forest guard who had been stationed in the locality for years. It was s summer night

with a bright moon and as usual, I was seated outside the tent writing up the day's observations in my forest journal. The sound of speeding footsteps attracted my attention and looking up I saw the old forest guard come running towards me. He was breathless with excitement, and kept pointing in the direction from which he had come. I could see he was frightened and waited till he could speak, when he explained that a tiger had crept up to near where he was cooking and was about to spring on him when he had seen it and fled for his life, he asked me to hurry up with my rifle and come and shoot it.

Until now I was not aware of the men's games and knowing no better, took the man at his word and got ready to follow him after the would-be tiger. We had hardly started when my Ranger joined us and coming close up, whispered that the tiger was not real and that he would tell me all about it. Whereupon he cautioned the guard that it was not likely the beast would remain to be shot, and that rather than trouble me, he would do well to return to his cooking and he would surely find the animal already gone. The guard therefore left us and the Ranger explained how the tiger had been got up in order to test his courage since he had been boasting about his prowess in the presence of wild beasts met with during his rounds.

The Ranger had barely finished when the guard came running up again to say that the tiger was still at the spot where he had left it. This time we had to join him to save appearances; as a weapon of defence, the guard took up a burning faggot from the log fire in front of the tent and started to lead the way. On reaching the place, there was no beast to be seen for the men got up as the tiger on seeing us coming, had moved off a little distance and hidden behind a bush. Accordingly, the Ranger swore at him for causing needless trouble in bringing us to shoot a phantom tiger, he insisted on his looking to see if the tiger could not be found nearabouts. Taking him at his word, the man commenced a hunt and on passing the bush was startled by a growl. With a shriek of fear he hurled the blazing faggot that he held, at the supposed tiger and ran screaming with terror. The brand struck the leader full in the face and stunned him for the moment, and despite the covering over his face the blow caused a nasty wound and burn which took some time to heal, leaving a bad scar on the forehead.

At another time a young Forester recently joined from school

was the victim of a practical joke that might have ended seriously. We were camped at Nanda, a famous resort for game, one hot-weather night, and as usual, the men slept in a cluster in the open; the forester too retired on a charpoy - a native cot. When he was in deep slumber, four men quietly lifted his bed, carried it away some distance and placed it in a lonely spot without waking him. About midnight a panther on the prowl came by and apparently, mistaking him for a heifer owing to the white sheet with which natives are wont to wrap themselves when lying down, it sprang on him. This woke the young man, who, thinking the animal to be one of his tormentors playing him a trick, threw out his arms and tightly clasped the beast in an embrace. The competitors, however, soon discovered their mistakes, the panther freeing itself sprang aside growling while the forester equally taken aback jumped off his bed and made record time for the tents. The tumult woke the camp, and thinking from the sounds that a panther had made an attack on the camp, I rushed into my tent for my rifle. In the meanwhile, the run-away was being greeted with roars of laughter from the man, which made it evident some unfortunate was the victim of sport, the Ranger who had planned the trick, now came up and explained the situation. We laughed at the man's expense, but the blood-stained scratches about his body showed that had it not been for the sheet he was covered with and the unexpected familiarity he evinced towards the beast which doubtless disconcerted it, the wounds would have been more severe. As it was, he had to be treated to prevent blood-poisoning setting in.

The country had been the happy hunting ground of that remarkable fraternity known as the Thugs who frequented the main roads and paths and were the terror of travellers. Their proceedings have formed the subject of official accounts and numerous books, so that it will suffice to say here that the victims were decoyed or waylaid and strangled by the simple device of passing a handkerchief round the neck. A copper coin fastened to each of two opposite ends of the handkerchief facilitated the process by enabling a firm grip, as well as, in procuring the necessary purchase for the sudden twist employed in the act. The crimes were committed as much for pleasure as for gain, and practically every third halting place on the main roads was associated with some legend of thuggi outrage. It also gave rise to the usual crop of ghost stories, which deterred wayfarers from halting under trees or groves at nights.

I recollect an instance in which the village elders implored me not to camp under a banyan where thuggi victims were said to have been buried, and whose spirits were believed to have taken possession of the cover. It was an ancient tree whose aerial roots spread over half an acre of ground, the original trunk having decayed and disappeared, as is often the case with these trees. As there was no other suitable shade in the locality, I determined to risk the consequences rather than camp in the open under a broiling sun. The night was disturbed by weird sounds coming from all about the tree and though there was no mistaking them for the angry chatter of night-birds, it was easy to see how alarming they might be to superstitious people unaccustomed to hear jungle noises. In exploring the tree next morning, we found nests of two or three families of owls and as many of the Indian hornbill. Anyone knowing the language, in which these birds can indulge towards each other without the least provocation, will not be surprised at its being construed by unsophisticated persons for the incoherent speech of spooks and gnomes in the chilly stillness of the night.

On another occasion, a family of civet cats that had annexed the hollow trunk of an old mango shade-bearer, was the innocent cause of alarm to travellers seeking shelter under the tree. Apparently, as soon as darkness fell, the little beasts annoyed at the intrusion of their haunt, set up a peculiar angry murmur like the shrill breathing expressive of a monster's slumbers. But, it was interpreted for the droning of spirits during their nightly visitation to the tree.

The most unearthly sound however that I can remember hearing was uttered by the Ghorepur or large iguana lizard. The reptile lived among the surface roots of a banyan standing by a watercourse. We camped near the spot on a dismal wet day as is common during the rains. The sound we heard was a sort of moaning cry drawled out at intervals in rather a sharp key. It came from under the banyan about a hundred paces from our camp. No one could tell what it was, and in the prevailing gloom it sounded ominous giving one a creepy sensation. The men had no doubt that it was uttered by a bhut, that is a ghost, and no one was willing to go and investigate. A plucky Mohammedan lad who did odd jobs in camp now volunteered to come with me. We approached the tree cautiously so as not to disturb the creature and as the noise

ceased we kept still in the cover of a bush growing under the banyan. Then, of a sudden the cry recommenced quite close to us and we located it in a grassy patch in the bank below us. Its thickness prevented us seeing inside, so we poked the cover with a pole when a huge fat lizard about four feet, wriggled out of the grass and made for its hole, a few yards away in the roots of the tree. That night we heard the beast again, and in the dark and dripping solitude, the cry sounded if anything more gruesome than in the day.

There were some quaint beliefs about the properties of this lizard. One maintained that it was highly magnetized and could attract lightening, so that trees sheltering the lizard were sure to be struck first during a thunder-storm. A case occurred in my own recollection; lightening fell on a large neem tree standing some distance from the camp, and when the servants went to the scene out of pure curiosity, they found an iguana lying dead underneath.

Another belief made out that the flesh was a sustainer of bodily heat and vigour. Indeed, it was so common that I knew intelligent native officials to have soup prepared from the lizard's flesh and given to their riding horses or ponies in order to keep them always on their mettle.

Again, the skin was reputed to give a high tone to musical instruments in which skins are used as a sounding medium, such as drums and guitars. Then too, most people have doubtless heard tales of how burglars in former days made use of the lizard's tenacious hold to assist them in scaling walls and roofs of premises which they intended to rifle.

To return to the subject of ghostly noises, occasionally fakirs or religious devotees, who minister to the shrines of departed saints commonly met with under wayside trees or groves, practise mimicking gruesome sounds to acquire notoriety for the spot with a view to increasing their income. It enables them to strike fear into the hearts of travellers who may be passing by at night. The incident is whispered abroad and the wayside folks are alarmed. It is then hinted that evil spirits are gaining possession of the locality owing to neglect of the shrine. Offerings pour in to appease the saint and invocations are chanted when the noises cease. A deception of this sort was to my knowledge practised by the attendant of a shrine on the highway between Dudhi and Guljhara in Dhar State.

The people had inherited all manner of tales regarding the doings of thugs and could relate some thrilling adventures that would have seemed incredible were it not for the existing authenticated accounts. Their activities spread everywhere and spared neither relations, nor friends so long as the common object to secure a victim was gained. The period of tumult that preceded the advent of British authority was especially favourable for their work, and Central India in its greatly disturbed state with its tangled hills and forests, became for the Thug the country par excellence, where he could ply his trade with least fear of molestation. Here too, he could make sure of rich hauls owing to the country serving as a link on the one hand with the towns of Northern India, and on the other with the emporium port of the West, to and from which speeded emissaries of business houses with treasure.

It was during the quiet evening hours when the blazing logs gave out their cheer of warmth and welcome that the people would be induced to hold forth, and in the course of time these informal gatherings became a feature of the camps. Often very useful information bearing on the work in particular or on topics in general, could be picked up at these meetings, for listening to them was as it were feeling the pulse of village opinion on current questions. I remember a rather singular tale related by a Chowdri, that is a village agent for supplying the wants of travellers. He had been the victim of some annoyance from subordinates and to humour him he was invited to camp. Soon he had cast off his shyness, and in turn with the rest told a story of guilt and remorse as follows:-

'In a town there lived a mendicant reputed to be very rich who seeing the evil times of his day dissembled poverty in order to avoid suspicion. It was said, his wealth lay buried, and its possession would relieve the finder's descendents from anxiety for generations. One day, thugs enticed the mendicant from his home and kept him a close prisoner. But when he could not be got to disclose the whereabouts of the treasure, they married him to a sister of one of the brotherhood. The wife was warned, on pain of death to prevail on her husband within three days to reveal the hiding place. Accordingly, at night she stood over him with a sword and demanded to know about his wealth. Finding remonstrances of no avail, the man commenced to recite a series of

tales that would react in winning her over to his cause and at the same time would while away the tedious hours of the night in her company.

The first story was entitled 'The repentance of a Brahmin', who owned a beautiful parrot called Hiraman, and like himself was of the priestly class in its tribe. The bird's presence was therefore indispensable at important functions among parrots. Now there was a marriage in a section of the tribe and the country was searched for a priest to solemnise the wedding, but nowhere could they find one. At last the birds heard of Hiraman in captivity and collected at the place to petition for his release. The brahmin was surprised to see his dwelling invaded by parrots when he entered the courtyard in the morning, and asked Hiraman the meaning of the assemblage. The bird explained the purpose of the visit and its own part in the business. The brahmin was flattered at owning a bird that was held in such respect, and released Hiraman on its promising to return after the ceremony. When the marriage was over, the parrots bethought themselves that they owed the brahmin some return for promptly acceding to their request. So they scattered over the jungles in search of a suitable present, and brought the fruit of the tree of life and gave it to Hiraman to take back.

The brahmin was very pleased to see his bird again and was delighted with the fruit. It looked so tempting and luscious that he decided to make it an offering to the King. In the morning he set out for the palace and presented the fruit, mentioning how it came into his possession. The King was very pleased and rewarded him handsomely, and intending to share it with the Queen, had it placed in his room. The courtiers however, dissuaded their lord from eating of the fruit without first testing its quality. They reasoned that the bird could not be expected to distinguish between good and bad for human consumption and therefore the fruit ought not to be taken on trust. The King accepted the advice and ordered a piece to be given to his dog. But, in the interval the fruit had been poisoned by a snake which attracted by its sweet scent, had crept up the bracket where it was placed and licked it, so that the dog died soon after eating the slice. The King was exceedingly angry at the result and had the fruit flung into the remotest corner of the garden, and the brahmin was sent for and upbraided and abused. The man felt he was defamed for the rest

of his life and on returning home, took the bird out of its cage and twisted its neck.

The fruit fell on good soil and soon took root and became a plant, which rapidly grew into a tree and began to bear fruit, but the fruit was condemned as poisonous and no one would touch it. Now, the Queen's chief maid being worsted in a quarrel with her daughter-in-law, attempted suicide by eating of the fruit. To her astonishment, however, she found herself transformed into a maiden. The news soon reached the King's ears and having satisfied himself as to the truth, he ordered some of the fruit to be brought, and gave one to his courtiers. They ate it and became as young men. The King then shared one with the Queen, and they underwent the delightful experience of returning youth. The King was overjoyed at the result and summoned the brahmin to receive the honour and reward that the occasion demanded. But the unfortunate man, hearing of the marvellous virtue that the fruit possessed sorrowed over what he had done and died of remorse.

The following night the prisoner again engaged his wife's attention with a story about a hunter's repentance. The man had tamed a hawk which was his sole companion on hunting excursions. Once in pursuing game he lost his bearings and wandered about the jungle till he was overcome with thirst. Failing to find water, he laid down tired and exhausted under the shade of a large tree. Soon his ears caught the welcome sound of falling drops of water, and he looked about and saw it dripping from the trunk overhead. He rose hurriedly, took out his cup and placed it under the spot, and waited for it to fill. But no sooner the cup began to fill, the hawk would swoop down and upset it. At last exasperated at the hawk's wanton behaviour, the hunter drew his bow and let drive an arrow and killed the bird. Alone and tortured with thirst, he felt he could not do better than go to the source for his drink, so he climbed the trunk and in a hollow on the top he discovered, to his amazement, a dead python from whose putrid remains the water was oozing. The man now realized the crime he had committed in killing his hawk who had wanted to save him from drinking the poisonous liquid, fretted over what he had done and died of grief.

The last night of grace was equally employed in formulating a moral that dealt with the tragic end of a sepoy who had made a great favourite and companion of his dog. He was out one day

when the night set in before he could return home, and seeing an inn entered it to lodge for the night. Tired and weary by the day's tramping, he laid down to rest in a cot with the dog cuddled up at his feet. He woke very early when it was still dark, to prepare to leave, but each time he attempted to get out of his bed, the dog barked and tore at his clothes and stopped him. Failing to account for its savage behaviour the sepoy believed the dog must be mad and stuck his dagger into the faithful creature, which expired with a moan.

Appalled at the dog's dying yell - natives have a horror of a dog's howl believing it to presage death - he thought of his torch and lit it to go out. But as it flared up, a cobra that lay coiled up in his shoe darted out its hood to strike at him. The meaning of the dog's insistent attacks became evident and in a fit of grief the man struck the dagger into his throat and fell over dead.

Thus the mendicant beguiled the three nights allotted to his undesirable spouse for the task of extorting his secret and by moral persuasion gradually succeeded in dissuading her from the purpose. Rather than engage in a murderous attempt on his life, she consented to live with him and share his fortunes. So they planned to escape from the thugs' clutches and before daybreak, they were journeying to a far country where they lived happily ever afterwards.

These tales related by campfires were interesting as showing the trend of the people's beliefs. They told of personalities and adventures in all walks of life. Very few can be recalled to memory now and it is a matter of regret that I did not take them down at the time. One in a different vein to the foregoing, related to a personality possessing the high sounding title of Tees-mar-khan, meaning the victor in thirty deeds. I will give it with what details I can remember.

The hero of the exploits was a poor jolaha, that is a weaver, by caste who lived in an unpretentious village. The sameness of his daily life made him discontented with his lot, and he resolved on leaving his ancestral home to seek his fortunes in other lands. He therefore sought his wife and spoke to her of his intentions, telling her to get victuals ready for a long journey. Like a good wife she obeyed her lord's wishes and rose very early next morning to prepare ladus, that is balls of parched grain, flour and treacle. She took the grain roasted overnight from the oven and put it in the

mortar and pounded it with the pestle and when it was crushed, prepared thirty ladus and packed them in a bag to carry on their journey. The ass was then saddled and loaded with a few belongings; this done, the wife sat on the bundle over the donkey's back and they started on their travels.

On entering the neighbouring State, they heard of a formidable band of robbers who were plundering the countryside, and of the Chief's promise to honour and reward anyone who would destroy them. Fearing to continue his journey lest he might fall in with the gang, the man decided to retrace his steps home. But, he had not gone very far before the very band whom he was anxious to avoid, heaved in sight and began to ill-treat him, demanding to know who he was and where he was going. The jolaha trembled and pleaded for his life and escaped with a rough handling and the loss of what little he possessed. The robbers were hungry and looked about for something to eat and came upon the ladus. Coincidently [sic]they were thirty, so each had a sweet for his share. They sat and ate and soon lay down to rest.

Unknown to her, the woman had pounded up with the grain a poisonous snake that lay coiled inside the mortar and that she did not notice owing to the dim light of the early hour. Consequently, the robbers died in their sleep. The jolaha however, could not know the fate that had overtaken the robbers, and patiently waited their pleasure for permission to depart. When he saw after some hours that they did not stir, he tried to rouse them by his cries, but failing to get himself heard, he began to nudge and then, to pull them about, and so found out that they were dead. Rejoicing at his good fortune, he abandoned the idea of returning home and with a self-confidence in his importance, formed a brilliant plan of profiting by the robbers' misfortunes. With his wife's assistance, they flung the corpses about the field and taking a sword, cut and slashed at the defunct robbers and trampled the ground in order to make believe that the spot had been the scene of a hard fight. Then assuming the garb of a warrior, he hurried to the chief's palace to report his deed.

The chief could hardly credit the man's account and ordered the elephants to be saddled in order to visit the scene and make sure for himself. The nobles were also invited and joined in the cavalcade which marched to the place. Arrived there, the chief was even more surprised at the man's brilliant feat to overcome so

many stalwart and armed robbers. He praised his skill and courage and honoured him with a seat on the howda. Thus, at a stroke the jolaha found himself raised beyond his highest ambition and appointed on a handsome salary over the chief's bodyguard. As further evidence of his valiant deed, he received the title of Tees-mar-khan.

He was only a few months in office when reports reached the palace that a man-eating tiger was committing ravages in a distant part of the State and none dared to oppose the monster. The chief therefore sent for his favourite and commissioned him to slay the beast. The order sent Tees-mar-khan almost out of his senses, but he put on a brave face and made a pretence of obeying, nevertheless he resolved to return home. On the way he had to put up for the night at a village inn close to the tiger's circuit and while he was having his food, the ass broke loose and strayed away. He went in search and outside the village, came upon the tiger. Mistaking the beast in the darkness for his animal, he went up to it boldly and began abusing and trouncing it with his bludgeon for putting him to the trouble of a search. The unprovoked onslaught took the tiger by surprise and it submitted to be tied and hobbled and led to the stable to be secured. Next morning, he repaired to the stable to saddle his ass, and behold: the very tiger from which he was running away was tied up in place of the animal. He at once grasped what he had done in an impetuous moment and reflected on the renown awaiting the achievement. Its repetition moreover, assured him of the high career that was carving out for him. He accordingly gave up all thoughts of home and speeded back to announce that he had captured the tiger alive, and to ask for an escort to fetch the beast to the chief's menagerie. The chief was astounded at his tale and took a large retinue to see the beast, and the tiger was caged and brought in triumph to the palace. In honour of his prowess, Tees-mar-khan was raised to the command of the state troops.

The hero was a year in command when war broke out with a neighbouring State and the chief ordered his forces to be marshalled. He took Tees-mar-khan to the royal stables and asked him to select a horse for himself. Being an indifferent rider and with no heart for a fight, he felt he could not do better than take the bony mare with the low back which looked too ill-conditioned to be able to keep pace with other horses, so that in a charge he would

be left behind in safety. But as a matter of fact, the mare belonged to a special breed, known as Kachhu, that combined inelegance with speed.

In due course, the troops marched to the front and the nobles began testing the mettle of their horses. Tees-mar-khani could not control his mare, and she galloped off with him to the hostile ranks. He pleaded for mercy giving out that his companions had deserted him. Whereupon the commander of the hostile force declared that he had not come to fight against an individual and withdrew his forces. Tees-mar-khan however, turned the occasion to his advantage, and on his return made it known that the forces had turned back rather than face him. The chief applauded his strategic courage in dispersing the enemy single handed and raised him to the rank of a noble.

Shortly before I joined, Tantia Bhil, the Robin Hood of Indian tales, had been captured. He was very active in parts of the country where my work lay, and exciting stories of his exploits and the disguises he assumed were rife among the people. I came across a policeman in Betul whose nose had been cut off by the robber. He was on duty at one of the many out-posts established for rounding up Tantia's gangs. One morning Tantia visited the lines in the guise of a barber and the policeman took the opportunity to get himself shaved. In the course of the operation, he held forth on Tantia's wickedness and indulged in offensive language towards the robber, mentioning the straits to which they (the police) were put in having to toil in unhealthy localities and live under improvised huts. The imaginary barber listened patiently to the outflow of abuse levelled against himself, and when he had finished shaving; seeing no one about, he took hold of the man's nose and cut it off with his razor, at the same time telling him that he was Tantia. The mention of the dreaded name sufficed to make the policeman lose his wits, so that he did not even shout for help, and the robber got away without attracting notice.

Tantia was said to have hoaxed a police officer who was with the out-posts. One afternoon the official strolled out with his rifle to bag something for meat for the camp. When he was clear off the lines, a man in the garb of a village watchman came by and was asked by the officer if he knew anything of the whereabouts of game in the locality. The supposed watchman gave an

encouraging reply and the officer asked him to show the way to the places he knew. The man complied readily and on getting into the forest, asked if he might spare the officer the trouble of carrying the rifle. The unsuspecting official glad to be relieved of the weight of his weapon made it over to him. The guide shouldered it, turned about and saluted, then disclosed his identity and disappeared in the forests with the rifle.

On another occasion while being hotly pursued, Tantia hid in the branches of a tree. Some time after two women came by engaged in an earnest conversation about himself. Their mention of his name drew his attention to them, when he heard one of the women ask the other "what she would do in case they should come across the robber?" The woman addressed replied: "she would try to have him arrested and gain the reward offered for his capture." But, the questioner took a humane view expressing the opinion that rather than give him up to the police, she would ask him for a dress and ornaments. Tantia who had heard all they said, now got down the tree and told them who he was; he beat and robbed the one and rewarded the other with a fistful of silver coins, telling her to buy the dress and ornaments that her heart desired.

Officials during the course of their service have opportunities of attending various functions with which the life of the country is indelibly wound up. It was my good fortune to take part in several. An interesting function to which I was invited, was a harvest feast given by a well to do Sirvee, a class of famed agriculturists. It was to mark the close of a bumper kharif or monsoon crop, in which Ceres had been very propitious to our host... The gathering was almost purely agricultural such as I had not seen before, and everyone of note from far and near had been invited. The courses served up were exclusively of the grains grown during the monsoon rains, the Indian corn or maize the chief crop of the season forming the principal item on the menu. It alone accounted for fifteen salt and sweet dishes. A table and chair were improvised for my benefit, otherwise I tried as far as practicable to conform to my host's customs. An idea of the cosmopolitan character of the feast may be gauged from the fact that even animals were brought into the courtyard to share of the good things, and I noticed that plough oxen came in for most attention. The feast over, the maidens sang and danced before the household gods. The proceedings were impressively simple, and

the splendid bonhomie prevailing throughout the festivities and ceremonies gave the functions a friendly character.

An interesting institution in the life of the countryside is the oration of kathas, that is sermons and recitations delivered by individuals versed in the classics treating with homely virtues. As a rule, the exponent is an ancient of his class whose reverential bearing calls for close and respectful attention. It is held on the invitation of the village elders or under the patronage of a notable and is free to all who care to attend. A hall or roomy enclosure is improvised for the occasion and the people sit in circular rows while the preacher occupies the centre, so as to have easy access to the audience in moving round to impress particular points upon his hearers. The text comprises a few words or passages from a popular author, such as Kalidas, and is often simply and eloquently expounded to define a moral. The preacher is accompanied by a choir of youthful chelas or disciples who at brief intervals chant appropriate strains to the tune of music consisting of few brass or string instruments, in order to create a passionate feeling. At the close of the sermon, the reverent gentleman stands with uplifted arm and sings out benedictions attended by a chela holding a brass plate with an incense burner; the audience now file up and having embraced the preacher, drop a pice equivalent to a farthing into the plate.

It is a pretty and interesting ceremony full of sentiment that appeals to the people. I had many friends among these worthies and made it a point to attend their kathas. It struck me how much good might ensue were this means of moralising truths enlisted in the cause of the country. The pundits could so well preach on the intentions of Government as contained in official issues and notifications whose stereotyped language is apt to be misconstrued. To impress the correct versions on the minds of the people, it but needs to substitute the purport of the orders for the texts so as to render them cognisable with their tenets. I tried the experiment in my own case and had gratifying success. An unpopular measure had to be enforced for the common good, and was expected to raise a clamour. Being sure of opposition, I appealed to a friendly pundit acquainted with my views, to enlighten his audience on the subject when he again preached in the locality. My friend identified it into a text on "obedience to constituted authority", so that I had no difficulty whatever in getting the order observed.

In going about among the people, one is at times astonished at the fantastic display of ceremonial rites that would appear ludicrous were it not for the earnestness with which the proceedings are conducted. I refer to customs that are so to say, dormant and burst out before the public only when the cupidity of individuals is excited to pander to them - such are marriages between objects of affection or regard, as trees, groves, tanks and wells. The entertainments are expensive, calling for the observance of all the complicated rites attendant on a proper wedding. The celebration of lagan or consummation is gone through by mixing the waters or the twigs of the wells or trees, as the case may be. A ceremony of the sort is undertaken by a well-to-do man in business or a village functionary with means, as a headman or priest, and it serves the dual purpose of dispensing with charity and acquiring merit. A man owning a mango tree engages in its nuptials with another belonging to a friendly neighbour, or the two tanks of adjoining villages are matrimonially allied. It is considered that the union improves the value for which the objects exist, as for instance the trees will bear more fruit and of a better quality than they did before, so also the wells or tanks will have purer and sweeter water comparatively as a result of their alliance.

Apart from their spectacular character, these ceremonies have also their spiritual side for it is firmly believed that in bringing about matrimonial felicity between objects unable to negotiate themselves, the person was pleasing the deity who would reward him in due course. The differentiation of the sexes was a matter easily solved by the simple expedient of accepting the larger of the two contracting objects, as symbolical of motherhood and treating it as a female, concern if any, would be to avoid like mating like, for the people were very particular not to marry into one's own section, holding the relationship however distant, akin to brother or sister as the case may be. But, a slight variation in the produce, shape or form of the object was enough to ease their conscience and settle the difficulty.

Again, a whimsical individual would amuse himself by going to the expense of fastening silver nose-rings on fishes that he wanted let into his pond or well. I have seen a large fresh-water murrul that had on a ring, fished up from a well, the tribute of a former owner of the well. It was said that the tank at Kherla in Betul once contained fishes with gold and silver nose-rings, the fancy of a Gond Raja of olden days.

Among the many relics of a former civilization scattered about the country, perhaps the commonest are tanks and baoris. They are met with in very unlikely places in so far as one could judge of their utility from present day conditions. A baori is a sort of superior masonry well with steps leading to the water. Baoris are often spaciously designed with chambers and arched platforms where travellers may rest or partake of their food. Niches and alcoves contain idols of principal deities whom travellers may propitiate for the success of their journey. They are often works of art with decorations in raised or pierced work in stone or marble.

Most old tanks and baoris have their legends, usually connected with buried treasure. The allusion to the wealth would be ingeniously illustrated diagramatically as a puzzle, or a rhyme of few words rendered in couplet or quartette as a riddle. They were chiselled on stone or slab set up by the entrance to the steps. I heard of instances in which the key to the problem had been deciphered resulting in the treasure being found.

An incident of the sort came within my own notice. The legend declared that a Mohammedan Emperor on his departure for conquest had deposited his treasure in a vault in or near the ancient fortress of Mandu, he died on the expedition so that the wealth was never reclaimed. An old Mohammedan connected with the ancient city, persisted in the accuracy of the tale and undertook to divulge the secret, provided he was made a co-sharer in the treasure. The Durbar accepted the conditions and desired me to superintend operations. This brought me in touch with the old gentleman and I had the opportunity of listening to some curious beliefs. In the one before us however, the problem was the location of the vault. Naturally I was keen to know the procedure my colleague would adopt, especially as he was credited with second sight. But he was dilatory in getting to work and I began to doubt his bona fides. Seeing me indifferent, he confided that he needed to work through a medium and was awaiting the return of a certain youth whom he was to employ to disclose the hiding place. According to him, the youth had to be a palea, that is one born feet foremost, who only under hypnotic guidance could gain insight into hidden things under the surface. Alas! for our plans, his career was cut short by plague, which was raging at the time. His self-consciousness made him presume that he enjoyed immunity, and he took no precautions in going about among plague cases and very soon became a victim to the disease.

Numbers of these old reservoirs have been restored, but many more are regarded as inadaptable to the times and left to decay. During the great famine of 1899-1900, I took advantage of funds placed at my disposal for saving cattle, to restore several storage works occurring in the jungles on the excellent excuse that they were indispensable to water the animals daily trouping into the jungles in thousands. It was then that the importance of such works as the means of lessening mortality both among cattle and wild animals, forced itself on my attention. The jungles could always be relied upon to produce more or less fodder, but water failed beyond measure, and its difficulty could only be overcome by previous preparation, so everything possible was done to give the matter prominence before the Durbars. It was gratifying to see that Government had also taken up the question and made it part and parcel of the provisions of forest working plans.

Speaking of famines, the year of 1899-1900 was especially disastrous in aboriginal districts. The traditions of the tribes showed that nothing like it was known in the memory of their oldest inhabitant. Many schemes were devised for bringing succor [sic]to these folks who lived widely scattered among the intricate hills and dales of the Vindhyas, Satpuras and Aravallis. No wheeled traction was practicable over considerable parts of the country and often pack animals could not surmount the steep winding tracks leading to the aboriginal settlements. Their shy and restless nature made them obdurate in declining the ordinary forms of relief obtainable on public works, so the forest staff had to initiate measures of relief suitable to their case. These consisted in the collection and removal of forest products. The works had to be necessarily scattered to reach their haunts and become very popular among the people who laboured in surroundings to which they were accustomed, at the same time keeping within reach of their homes. Despite all that was done the devastating affects [sic]of the drought were very great, incomparable in my experience with the failures that came before and after 1899-1900. Animals, birds and plants suffered equally if not more, than human life.

The train of evils that a famine of any magnitude leaves in its wake is truly astonishing and cannot be realised by those who have not been through the mill. Nowhere more than in travels through rural tracts is one confronted with distressing sights. Of the many resulting disorders, a unique complaint is paralysis of the lower

limbs. The direct cause is from eating a variety of the chickpea. Indirectly, the pulse ordinarily given to cattle is consumed by the classes during hard times. Being a hardy plant requiring little or no moisture, it thrives in a year of drought and so is largely cultivated. The consequence is that numbers of otherwise able-bodied men drag themselves about in the villages.

With the return of normal conditions it becomes necessary to restart families who have lost their very all with the means of subsistence in order to tide over the months of field-work before the crops are harvested. The success of the measure depends on close personal supervision because of the inducements afforded for fraudulent practices. This necessitates impromptu visits to homesteads so as to get at the really deserving cases, and to find out their requirements. As a famine officer, this form of village to village relief occupied me the greater part of the monsoon season and notwithstanding the numbers that had to be dealt with and the straightened [sic] condition of the times, there were only two instances of petty offences which will speak for the truthfulness of the people. These will bear relating.

In one case a widow with a large family of children had received an allowance for their support. When she got back to the village, the headman's son made her believe that she owed the money to his good offices and so induced her to part with half the sum. The woman's dwelling stood on the track of my next visit, and seeing her as I rode past, I inquired casually if the money would suffice to see her through the difficult times. Her answer showed the trick practised on her unsuspecting nature. A sowar, that is a mounted orderly, was sent off to fetch the scamp and on arrival, he was tied to the flagstaff post in the market square and publicly caned. The punishment made him the laughing-stock in the countryside and deterred venturesome youths from repeating the offence.

The other case occurred in another part of the country and this time a headman was the sinner. Owing to his age and position the rod could not very well be administered, so he received correction by being placed for a few hours in the stocks in front of the market. The result was equally effective, and none dared to molest the helpless whom the Sircar had befriended.

Attempts at helping the people were not always successful. A brother official working in the adjoining district to mine had a disappointing experience. He came across many famished Bhils

during his rounds, so he opened a field kitchen with the laudable object of providing a square meal daily to every individual who came. Finding the people reluctant to invite themselves, he went out and collected the bad cases and lodged them in huts till they should recover to be able to work. The plan worked very well for a time, and others began coming in freely. One evening however, a pernicious subordinate employed on the kitchen while speaking to an inmate of the huts, jokingly said that it was not for nothing that they were being housed and fed, but because the Sahib intended transporting them to populate distant lands. The effect of the lie was magical, by next morning not a single person remained of the several hundreds in the place. Nor could they be got to come again and the kitchen had to be abandoned. My friend never found out the sudden cause of the unpopularity that ruined his scheme. But long afterwards, I heard of it from a native who was there and who knew. He brought it up accidentally as an example to show the infidelity of the wild tribes.

It is astonishing how ignorant forest tribes are or rather were, regarding the value of money. In the early years of my service, they transacted practically all business by barter, the custom being to attend the weekly fairs or markets held at fixed centres. To these they brought their loads of grain or forest products and exchanged them for necessaries. The bargain was altogether one-sided for the jungle man had no means of knowing the value of his produce and had to rest content with whatever he could get. It was only in the event of a split in the market cliques, that he got anything like a fair return. I have known valuable logs of timber that had been obtained by barter for a few shillings' worth of goods, subsequently sold for two pounds and more. Many a trader enterprising enough to hawk about his wares in aboriginal settlements accumulated a fortune by trading on the ignorance of these simple people. I knew a good few personally who told me they had commenced with a few shillings, uncertain about the next meal, and who had amassed thousands of pounds in two or three decades.

In one of my earliest excursions into the forests, I gave the aborigine who acted as guide a four anna piece for his trouble. He looked at it disdainfully and remarked - "What will I do with this, had you given a few coppers instead I would have bought sweets and taken them to my children". I told him that the coin was worth several coppers - a copper piece in India is equal to a farthing at

home, but he was not satisfied. However, it was the only coin with me at the time and he had to be content. We met again after some time and on adverting to the subject it was apparent from the man's statement that he had been cheated of half the value of the silver coin by the sweetmeat seller to whom he went for his purchase.

A more striking example of the ignorance of money than the following could hardly be found. A Bhil while wandering at the foot of the Mandu hill which contains the ancient fortress, came upon a lota, that is a brass vessel, showing signs of having been recently displaced by a landslip. He picked it up and found it to contain several gold pieces. Not knowing the metal, he took one to show the Kalal, that is a liquor vendor. The man saw through his customer's ignorance and told him that it was a brass coin and that he could have a drink, worth about a penny, in exchange. So the Bhil paid a coin every day in lieu of a drink.

But instead of resting content with his gain the kalal was curious to have the gold pieces valued and having secured a dozen he took them to town to dispose of them for current coin.

News of the dealing leaked out however, and got to the ears of the police. The investigation resulted in both kalal and Bhil being sent up for trial under the Treasure-trove Act, and each were sentenced to imprisonment and forfeiture of the gold coins. I saw the gold-mohurs which belonged to an early Mahommedan mintage, they were in excellent preservation and valued at about sixty rupees, or four pounds apiece.

I had an awkward experience that nearly let me in for a large sum of money. In the days to which the matter relates, postal facilities were few and far between, and the forest official was obliged to perform the part of a collector of forest receipts; he had to visit the vending stations and take the collections and pay them into treasury. I had completed one of these tours, which saddled me with a large sum, a good deal of which was in currency notes. These I stuffed into my greatcoat pocket, and being anxious to get back quickly to headquarters I also marched at night. The last stage had to be done in a thunderstorm, which brought down the torrents in flood. One of them detained us some hours and eventually I had to cross on men's shoulders. In divesting myself of the coat to lighten the weight, the notes slipped out of the pocket without any of the party noticing them fall.

It was long past midnight when we reached our destination and

my first thought was to put away the notes, but I could not find them. It was pretty evident that they had dropped out and I could only conclude that it occurred while removing my coat. I confided about the loss to my servant, he suggested going back to look for them, and started off with my Gond orderly for a companion. At dawn, a party of aborigines whom they met coming from the opposite direction, informed them that a bundle of "loose paper" was lying at the water's edge in the torrent ahead. They went on and found the notes by the same stream that had given us trouble in crossing overnight. The reader may imagine my relief at seeing the two men return safely with the money.

There is no gainsaying the fact that aboriginal tribes have a profound respect for the Sahib. The feeling practically amounts to filial admiration. Without doubt we owe this to the daring spirits who worked among them during the advent of British rule. Reckless alike in the pursuit of dangerous game and in the suppression of hordes of armed dacoits and thugs - the terror of the country - these handful of Britishers inspired affection and esteem among those with whom they came in contact and became their idols. Songs and tales of the doings of the principal characters of those times are preserved, and sung or recited at tribal gatherings. However this may be, their activity certainly made the task of those who followed easier in dealing with the tribes. For naturally shy and timid, the jungle men shrink from every display of feeling to an extent that invites aversion rather than attracts notice. But let the barrier be removed - and to this nothing contributes more, than moving freely among them - and they are frank and docile as children, prompt to show their gratitude.

The allusion to their nature recalls a little incident that occurred during an outing. A friend with his wife and two children were touring with me through the jungles one winter. Our camp on this occasion was near the village where the weekly fair of the neighbourhood was held. In the afternoon we strolled out by the jungle path and got separated for a little distance from the children who were too taken up with picking flowers to mind us. My friend's wife missing the kiddies, looked back and saw a number of Bhil stalwarts round the children who played on unconcerned at the wild figures watching them. The men were returning from the fair when the little ones drew their attention. Unkempt and armed with bows and arrows they looked fearsome indeed and the sight

was enough to frighten a mother. Seeing her anxious, I tried to assure her that the men meant well, and walking up asked the headman whom I knew, what interested them. His reply showed the feeling which animated them - "Sir, are these children of the gods?" Apparently the pretty pink cheeks and fair looks of the little ones had captivated their fancy. I translated the answer and the glad faces of the men soon reassured my friend's wife. She was herself at once and like a good lady asked after the welfare of their kiddies which the men appreciated and they parted the best of friends. Before leaving, they insisted on presenting the children with some sweets and nuts that they were taking home.

This feeling of homage permeated more or less all classes. I was once an unwilling listener to a singular conversation carried on between a mother and her son. She was a lady of high rank: the boy of twelve or thirteen, an intelligent little fellow, attended the chief's college, and was home for the summer holidays. I was putting up in a rest house during the hot month of June. An epidemic of cholera was raging in the vicinity and to avoid risks, the lady and her son had come in to stay in the vacant half of the bungalow.

Only a door separated the two small sitting rooms, so that it was impossible to avoid hearing in the one what was said in the other. The conversation started by the lady asking the boy to tell her what he had learnt at school during the term. This made him give a sketch of the times of the early Britains [sic]showing how they went about unclad and unkempt and how they worshipped idols and spirits and sacrificed to deities. The lady heard the boy's account attentively and when he had finished, inquired if he believed all that he had repeated. The boy replied affirming his statement on his teacher's assurance that the account was true. But she dissuaded him from his belief. She told him that his description reminded her of tales that she had heard as a child and that they were written only for the interest and amusement of children. She compared the English with an incarnation of the deity, saying that it was folly to suppose their ancestors were anything else, than wise and great like the descendents who had brought great blessings to the country.

A purely personal affair apropos to the feeling I have described, was the reception accorded to my wife when she came among the people. It is one of those occurrences that live in the

memory only to freshen with the lapse of time. The spontaneous greeting from young and old of both sexes was as surprising as it was unexpected. It was our first tour together and we were entering tribal country. Our camp equipment had proceeded overnight so the people knew we were coming and awaited our arrival on the border. Then, as we rode up in the early morning, they seemed to spring from all over and with shouts and whoops to the accompaniment of their wild music, they rushed up in bodies to greet her. Bedecked as on a gala day with crude adornments of leafy twigs and flowers, stuck into or twined about their hair, ears and forehead, and with bows and arrows slung over their shoulders, they looked a picturesque crowd. Taken aback at the wild scene, my wife had need to tremble, but soon reassured by their laughing faces, she replied through me to their numerous and well meant queries respecting herself. That night there was a great bonfire round which the people sang and danced till the small hours of the morning.

In general with the Indian character, the aborigine is as hospitable as any of the native classes. As a rule he lays by little or nothing for himself in the way of provisions for an ordinary mortal, but he will nevertheless manage to produce enough for a meal for the stranger who comes within his gate. Often in the course of my duties, I have been benighted or otherwise detained and unable to get back to camp, and obliged to take their fare, when they have always risen to the occasion and served up food out of the common for my benefit. Again, when called away suddenly to superintend the extinguishing of fire or to help in the detection of offences, when the carrier of the tiffen-basket had failed to appear, the men would invariably undertake to supply a meal.

On starting from home, jungle men nearly always take with them ingredients for a meal, such as a few fistfuls of flour, grains of salt and chillies, for they are never sure how long they will be away. Like all natives they are adepts at preparing impromptu meals, and the food though hastily cooked is wholesome. On expeditions or errands, it is usual to prepare littees which are a form of native cake about the size and thickness of a muffin. The flour is kneaded on a large leaf as that of a teak, or on an even surface of rock. Two or more lumps are rolled into balls between the palms and slightly flattened. Each cake is then placed between two green leaves, tough, as those of the dhak, and the whole - cake and covering -

laid in hot ashes of a small cow-dung heap which is quickly got ready while the dough is being prepared.

In a few minutes the cakes are baked, the leaves serving as a cover keeps them from getting burnt. They are eaten with a little condiment made of pounded onion and chillies and in season aonla or mango fruit is also included with the mixture: the crushing is done between two stones. Game as dove or bush-quail or hare is sometimes added to the meal. The birds abound everywhereand are easily trapped or killed with an arrow. The meat is cut up into three or four morsels and roasted on a spit of hard twig or bamboo. Well baked and hot, the cake has an agreeable flavour and eaten with condiment, and roast dove or quail gives the food a relish.

Subordinates stationed among the people often take advantage of their good nature to cadge on them and even become exacting in their requirements. Accordingly, what was an honoured custom dependent entirely on the good will of the people, has long been abused and rendered objectionable. In many places, subordinate officials have come to regard the hospitality as a matter of haq, that is a sanctioned perquisite. In the country of a big potentate the subordinates helped themselves freely to foodstuffs from the village markets, and they could hardly be blamed considering their poor pay which barely amounted to a living wage. The abuse had continued to the extent of becoming a by-word, forcibly rendered in the couplet:-

"Neemak Sirkar ka,
    Ata Bazar ka".

Literally it means:-
 Salt of the State,
    Flour of the market.

But actually, it signifies that the State intended the pay for the purchase of ingredients only, as salt, while the markets were for the free supply of foodstuffs, as flour.

In comparison with the food grains generally grown by cultivating classes, forest tribes raise few cereals which also, are almost entirely monsoon crops, consisting altogether of Indian-corn and millets. In their dietary, grain is treated more as a supplementary article than as a constituent, preference being given to jungle products. They know a great variety of these for food, but most of them are utilized only during times of scarcity or by the degenerate classes in ordinary years. Yams and bulbs known to be

poisonous are by a process of soaking, scrubbing and exposure to the sun's rays rendered harmless. They can at a pinch lay hands on an edible product of whose existence no one else would have had the least notion.

I have known them in the midst of forests far from any habitation when work has been prolonged longer than usual, to dart off as soon as a halt was called, to a tree or bush where they were sure of finding something to slake the craving of hunger or thirst. Such finds as the honeycomb of the little bee, certain gums or the sugary sap exuded in minute crystals by some grasses, would serve to allay both hunger and thirst.

There is a week in the year during which the higher classes eschew food prepared from grains raised by oxen labour when they gladly eat jungle products collected by aborigines. I believe it is to remind them of the life their heroes led before acquiring the ascendancy, which their descendents now enjoy.

As in the case of edible produce, the medicine men of the tribes have a fund of knowledge about the uses, and properties of medicinal plants with which they undertake to treat most ailments. In my recollection several bad cases have been treated successfully by these men and it may be of interest to mention a few. An infant son of an Indian lawyer whom I knew very well was attacked by a stomach complaint which brought on convulsions. The restoratives administered by the local practitioner failed to give relief. Incidentally, the parents heard of a man who had come that day to the local fair, and they called him in. He made a powder of the spongy tissue which encases the seed of the amaltas bean, mixed it with honey and gave it to the child. Relief followed and the infant recovered. To mark their gratitude the parents presented him with a pair of silver bangles.

One of my orderlies had developed phthisis and applied for long leave to go home. He looked so wasted that I fully expected not to see him again.

However, he turned up before the expiry of the leave looking practically cured. I enquired the cause of the change and he stated how he had consulted a medicine man who advised him to take a dozen drops of crude rosa or lemon grass oil morning and evening, increasing the dose gradually until he could stomach a tablespoonful. He followed the advice with considerable benefit to his health.

A forest guard, with others, was bitten by a mad dog. His people took him immediately to a medicine man who lived in the forest some distance away. The man made what appeared to be vegetable pills with directions to smoke one in a pipe at a time, thrice a day for three days, and the patient would recover. The guard carried out the directions and got well, while the others who were bitten at the same time and did not undergo the treatment, were attacked with rabies and died. A few months after the occurrence I had an opportunity of meeting this worthy whom the jungle folks accredited with being in possession of antidotes for various poisons, and tried to obtain from him the composition of the pills but he would not divulge the secret for any consideration. He said he had inherited it from his parent and never known it to fail if the smoke was properly inhaled.

I heard of another cure from a cultivator whose servant was the victim. The patient developed violent symptoms of fits that necessitated his being locked in the storeroom, which happened to contain a quantity of onions. These the man bit and chewed during his attacks through the night. In the morning he went to see how the patient fared and found him lying in a state of exhaustion. The man begged for a drink and drained a lota full of water, which refreshed him. He talked and behaved rationally and was released; the symptoms of rabies had disappeared and he recovered. My informant had no doubt that the onion juice had effected the cure.

A driver of a loaded cart slipped and fell off his seat in trying to control his bullocks. One of the cartwheels passed over his foot, crushing and splintering the bone about the calf. He was taken up unconscious and carried home. Various remedies were tried without result and the limb began to swell and show signs of gangrene. The local medico advised amputation as the only means of saving the man's life. But with the natural repugnance of natives to this method of treatment, his people declined to allow the limb to be operated. Eventually, his wife heard of a medicine man reputed to cure broken limbs, and she went and entreated him and he came and prescribed hot fomentations of a decoction prepared by boiling down leafy twigs of certain herbs. These applications soothed the pain and reduced the swelling and after a fortnight the injured man was on the mend. He was cured though not sufficiently to enable him to walk without limping.

Then, in my own case I was stung by a scorpion about the heel

and ball of the foot. It was at night in camp while getting out of bed to have a drink that I trod on the creature. I suffered excruciating pain till a medicine man whom my men had fetched, applied a vegetable preparation to the afflicted part. This with the massage he performed deadened the pain and in about five minutes I was quite restored. Though I promised him a reward to tell me what the application consisted of, he would not disclose the secret saying it would lose its virtue.

In a number of ailments, the treatment that these men apply, is drastic and I fear, it means cure or kill in the case of poorly constituted bodies. Branding is largely resorted to for pneumonic pains and the instrument is applied hot over the seat of pain; the flat end of a pair of tongs or the blade of a scythe is generally used in the operation. They also brand cholera patients in whose case, the brand is applied on the ball of the foot. It is believed that the sudden application of heat stimulates the nerves and stops purging and vomiting. Cupping and blistering are also common forms of treatment in cases of nervous prostration, like headache or neuralgia, as well as in those of poisonous bites or infections. The horny scute of a bullock or buffalo horn serves the purpose of a cupping receptacle.

Branding is a favourite remedy for most cattle diseases and for severe injuries, as dislocation of a limb by a fall. On the other hand, rinderpest and foot and mouth disease of which the people have a perfect horror, are treated differently. They are believed to be due to visitations of evil spirits who had to be exorcised by witchcraft before medicines could be given. Rinderpest was treated with balls of pounded sulphur sweetened with gur or Indian sugar and met with some success if administered in an early stage of the disease. In the other, a decoction of vegetable drugs was poured down the throat of the stricken beast and when the foot began to fester and gangrene, it was often made to stand for a while in water of a stream or pond to let little fishes clean the sore of maggots, after which the foot was thickly plastered with cow-dung.

Lingering diseases, such as phthisis, cancer, and also cases of sudden deaths, as from heart-disease or haemorrhage, are believed to be the work of witches who must be conciliated or their existence terminated before any medicine will act properly. It is incumbent therefore to either propitiate the witch or have the evil eye averted by a master-hand in the craft and failing them to destroy the

sorceress. This is deemed expedient as much for the efficacy of the cure, as for preventing recurrence of the malady in the family.

I will mention what happened to me during a prolonged attack of malaria. The fever had hold of me for some months before I attempted to have it treated. My neglect had brought on the attendant ailments of jaundice, spleen and dysentery. The Gonds were desirous I should try their remedy, but I preferred to be treated by a countryman and came in to headquarters for the purpose. Quinine and diaphoretic mixtures seemed to afford little or no relief and the attacks continued as bad as ever. After some time, I felt the usual foreboding common to long illnesses, as to whether I should ever get well under the treatment. In the meanwhile, the men renewed their offers to cure me and persuaded me to attempt the venture. It meant returning to the jungles and trusting myself to the tender mercies of their medicine men who seldom or never went beyond their haunts. No sooner I had decided, than some of the stalwarts carried me to their settlement a few days' journey from headquarters, and when I got in the witch-doctor was sent for to pronounce on my condition.

The day after my arrival in the jungle village a wizened old creature appeared in camp. He was the witch doctor and it was evident from the behaviour of those present that they regarded him with respect amounting to a feeling of awe. However, he was an inoffensive little man and knew his business. He came and stood by my bed and peered into my features for a minute or so, and proceeded to examine my eyes, mouth, nose and ears, then looking very solemn he declared his verdict. It was that I was under the spells of a witch who must be exorcised before medicines could do good, whereupon my attendants gave him permission to deal with the witchery, and dispersed to allow him liberty of action or rather I should say to avoid contamination with the evil spirit. Left alone with me, the wizard shut out all the light in the tent, covered me with a relay of blankets, and took measures to fortify the spot with enchantments against inimical influences. He proceeded by placing coals of fire in an earthenware pan and sprinkling it with incense. This over, he took the pan in one hand and a rod in the other and made three circuits round the outside of the tent, stooping low and muttering a chant all the while. Then he came in and repeated the performance, and after passing the burning pan as many times over my prostrate body, he placed it under the bed.

His craft enjoined the precaution to deter evil spirits coming to the aid of the one about to be expelled.

The measures as it were, prepared the way for his own spells, and his next move was to take a knotted cord from his waist to chastise the evil spirit and force it to leave me. He entered upon this with an agility that no one seeing him would have thought him capable. He skipped all over the tent whirling the cord and laying it about hard on me and everything else that stood in his way, and with every stroke shouting at the top of his voice "there she goes", meaning the witch's spirit. The thick covering warded off the blows, else I would have been badly bruised. His frantic exertions were however, enough to try anyone in bad health. Consequently, I was in a tremor of excitement and bathed in perspiration by the time it was over.

The whole - preliminaries and performance - had lasted about half an hour, before the wizard was assured that the evil afflicting me had departed and he put away the cord, opened the tent doors and came and stood by me. His calm features showed no signs of his recent agitation, and he held my hand gently to take my pulse and asked how I felt. He was satisfied with the result and assured me that I would soon mend.

He lightened the covering and made me change into dry things, and when I was again in bed, massaged my aching limbs, giving infinite relief. A professional could not have done it better, and the transformation into the solicitous attendant was so complete that one would not have credited him with the antics of some minutes earlier. The soothing effects of the massage sent me into a deep and long slumber which I had not enjoyed for many a day. When I woke he was ready with his medicines. Over the spleen, he applied a mashed vegetable plaster that produced a burning sensation like mustard application, and it was to be repeated morning and evening for a fortnight. He also gave me an emetic that brought on a violent fit of vomiting. The diet for a fortnight was to consist of milk, bread and eggs and I had to eat a slice of raw papaya fruit, dried in the sun, after each meal. In a fortnight, I felt well enough to resume my tour of inspection, and enjoyed a long respite before the malaria reappeared. I daresay had I rested and continued the treatment in the first instance longer than I did, I might have derived substantial benefit. As it was I was cured of spleen and jaundice and the dysentery also stopped.

The people have great faith in the efficacy of massage as a cure, and perhaps no other treatment is more sedulously employed in all manner of ailments. Although most natives profess to know something of the art, the exponents of the science are the barber caste with whom it is a hereditary occupation. The masseur aims at putting the patient to sleep as well as causing him to perspire freely. The treatment is undoubtedly efficacious in painful complaints and is often resorted to when other remedies fail. In cases of cholera, I have known patients brought round purely by a course of massage. Two or three men would take charge of the case, each of a separate section, but working in harmony to equalise pressure and distribution of energy until the patient recovered.

Hot fomentations are also commonly applied as remedy for pains accompanied by swellings. The lotion is usually in the form of decoction prepared from herbs, saline or earthy ingredients and animal excretions. The result sought after in the composition are properties of either a balm to relieve pain, a sedative to dispel irritation, an absorbent to draw injurious matter or an antidote to neutralise poison. A brown clay occurring near concretionary lime deposits is kneaded with powdered turmeric and ginger into the consistency of a paste and applied in cases of severe pains in the joints of arms and legs. It is put on in a thick plaster, about an eighth of an inch, over a wide surface and the patient made to sit or stand near a slow fire to heat the afflicted part gradually until the coating dries and cakes, it is then bandaged and allowed to cool. The remedy is said to relieve rheumatic pains. Similarly, a paste is prepared of vegetable extracts with cattle excretions and applied to boils and festering sores on human beings or animals, in order to allay pain, as well as to bring the affection to a head.

My long association with the country and the itinerant character of my duties, which kept me constantly among the people, strengthened the ties of amity in our dealings. Their co-operation and sympathy became assets in carrying through unpopular measures. An occasional feast to mark the close of an important event always brought good cheer to bear on the proceedings. Their wants were so few and simple that the outlay in catering for them barely exceeded a crown. Little acts of attention were sure to be appreciated and they were immensely pleased to see notice taken of their children. On visiting headquarters, I made it a point to take

back a basket of trinkets. Inexpensive little gifts of glass and lacquer ware, bangles and bead necklaces for the children, nicknacks to hold snuff or tobacco for the men and little fancy mirrors for the women's toilet, always gladdened their hearts.

One of these presentations embroiled me in a curious experience. I had brought a few things to give away to a shikari's family. He had been very obliging in taking me out and showing game. Among his children I noticed a blushing maiden of fifteen or sixteen years and being at a loss for something to say, enquired whether she were engaged or married. The father replied that he had not been successful in finding a suitor of his choice for her hand. It then occurred to me that I had seen a lad whose appearance impressed me at the time and who might fulfil the conditions. He was a bright, sturdy youth the son of the headman in a distant village where I had camped in the previous month. But though the head of the village, the parent was badly in debt and could no more hold up his head, nor provide for the son's future. The youth, however, went cheerfully about his father's duties trying to keep up the prestige of the office. I therefore spoke of the lad's qualities and ventured the suggestion that he would be just such a match as the parent desired.

After a year I again visited the shikari's home and to my surprise saw the youth at the man's house. It was evident he had taken seriously a few words dropped by way of pleasantry and secured the lad of whom I had spoken, for his adopted son-in-law. Seeing me perplexed at the situation, the man explained that he had considered my remark and had inquiries instituted, and finding the youth eligible he had brought the lad to serve the apprenticeship for his daughter's hand. This practice obtains among the tribes in the case of unendowed youths who are required to fulfil the recognised period of service at the future bride's home before they can claim them in marriage. The custom is parallel with that prevailing among the ancient Jews of which we have the account in the Bible of Jacob's servitude for Rachael. The period of service varies from one to five years, as a rule it is three, and during the time, the Lamjhana as he is called, is in all respects treated as a member of the family, sharing in the joys and sorrows of his future father-in-law's home.

This was not the only occasion when I became unwittingly involved in a domestic affair; the people took the remarks in good

part and even used them as a merry diversion of their feelings. An incident of the kind marked the change of a name and came about during a palaver with village elders who had come to greet my arrival in their village. A child accompanied them and interested in his youth, I inquired about him. I was told he was the headman and being a minor his uncle did the duties of the office. They said his name was Tumrea, meaning a pumkin. Opprobrious names are frequently given to children when the earlier issues die in infancy. They think that the mere fact of a contemptible name will convince the demon of death that the parents do not favour the child and so he will disregard it during his visitation.

I knew the boy's father had been a well-known character in the village and very naturally expressed disapproval of the name. Whereupon the uncle asked what would I have it as. For choice, I gave the name of a well-known hunter called Sambat Singh. The men acclaimed it with delight and to render the alteration valid, desired me to take the initiative in proclaiming the change. This was purely a formula necessitating my attendance at the village shrine and getting the priest to pronounce the new name in the presence of the deity, moreover I had to stand the customary feast in honour of the occasion. I readily consented and the alteration was duly carried out. But, the matter did not rest there for the boy was headman of a big settlement and changes had to be effected in the village register and rent-roll, so it had to go before the court who recognised it legally on the people's representation.

In the winter following the great famine, I was distributing blankets to the needy in a Native State. Many of the women and children were literally in rags and the funds at my disposal would not allow of providing both blankets and clothing, so I suggested to a Mahommedan cloth merchant with benevolent inclinations, who took an interest in the distribution, that the occasion offered an excellent opportunity for the exercise of his beneficence. Were he now to provide the needful clothing, it would surely count in his favour before the Almighty. He was well to do, passed middle age and without an heir which was a great grievance with him. The remark took his fancy and in a magnanimous spirit he undertook to supply clothing to all the needy in the neighbourhood. His generosity meant the free gift of cotton stuffs valued at about five hundred rupees, or thirty pounds. After a year, I had a letter from him saying that in accordance with my prediction, he had been blest with a son and heir.

In getting about the jungles, we sometimes came across fakirs living in secluded abodes. They were generally selected spots with an atmosphere of romance and comprised such resorts as hollowed niches or natural recesses by overhanging rocks or by waterfalls. The devotees also annexed cells or alcoves that had escaped destruction in ruined temples marking the sites of early habitations. Here was obtained the peace and repose essential for their meditations. As a rule, they were genuine examples of unselfish devotion who had forsaken comfortable homes and the love and esteem of relatives and friends in order to be in touch with the spiritual world. They were ever ready to discourse on religious topics, and it was not uncommon to meet an educated individual with wide experience of worldly affairs, whom it was a pleasure to hear on public questions of the day. As true fakirs, they never kept to one place, but came and went among the retreats; these movements were conducted with secrecy and dispatch which made them appear uncanny and set about wild rumours of their doings. They were hospitable and attracted visitors by their geniality and solicitude for the traveller. Most fakirs were gurus, that is religious preceptors, of a group of chelas, meaning followers, among members of the upper classes of native society.

I came upon a fakir in the act of burying himself underground with a view to enter into close communion with his god. The pit was about five feet deep and led into a recess spacious enough to hold a man seated with his legs crossed. His intention was to keep buried for a fortnight without food or drink to speak of, for he took some raisins. When he entered the cell, the villagers filled in the pit from which the cloister was shut off by a bamboo mat. The man remained inside during the three days I visited the spot. I then left to continue my tour and heard subsequently that he came out when the fortnight expired.

On another occasion, I witnessed a fakir go through a trial or test of the furnace before a large crowd. An open level space near a well on the outskirts of the village was selected for the performance, and here a few thousand cow-dung pats were heaped up. After worshipping at the local shrine, the fakir came and sat in a ringed enclosure where a dedication ceremony to hallow the spot had just before been performed. He was practically nude, wearing only a loin-cloth and daubed with a thick coat of ashes. He sat in the centre with his legs crossed in an attitude of meditation, and the

people arranged the cow-dung pats in a fence round him, raising it to a height of four feet after allowing the enclosure a diameter of five feet. The fire was applied simultaneously at several apertures, and soon converted the fence into a blazing wall which took about fifteen minutes to burn. The fakir kept like a statue, the only movement discernible being the twitching of the thumb and forefinger in telling his beads. He stood the ordeal with nonchalance and except for being bathed in perspiration and very red about the eyes, he appeared none the worse for the experience. When it was over the crowd eagerly besieged him to pay homage and obtain his benediction.

The recluse is naturally unobtrusive, but nevertheless quick to resent the least affront, that will often evoke harsh words; their evil portent acquires importance if misfortune overtakes the offending person, and of course the superstitious masses at once attribute it to the fakir's curse. In my experience two very sad events followed the imprecations of such men. In the one case the compound of an official's residence happened to contain the burial place of a local worthy. A fakir who lived near by ministered to the tomb on Sabbath days and his visits drew a musical retinue with offerings for the shrine. The drumming and clashing of cymbals made it a noisy procession which was a source of perpetual annoyance to the inmates of the residency. On one occasion, the official's wife who was ill in bed and could not bear the noise, asked that it might cease or the procession leave the place. But apparently the message was delivered flauntingly by the underling entrusted with the errand, for the people chose to retire, the fakir shouting out an imprecation against the author of the order. That night the lady was seized with an attack of cholera which ended fatally.

In the other case, I was camping with the district magnate on an island in a sacred river. It was mid-winter and the place was frequented by devotees. A fakir came into the camp and begged for a blanket and the official's wife gave the equivalent in money to enable the man to buy one. But the officer was incensed at what he considered the man's impudence to invade the privacy of his camp, and ordered that he should be expelled from the place. The fakir uttered an imprecation and left the island without any opposition. Some months later, the lady was taken ill and died.

I made the acquaintance of a recluse who had taken up his

abode in a niche of what was once a pleasure retreat in a famous fortress that had lapsed into jungle by centuries of neglect. The ruins came into prominence for their archaeological treasures which invited visits from high personages. On the very first occasion they unwittingly invaded the fakir's sanctum, which so exasperated the man that he swore and ordered them off the premises. And yet, he was of a peaceful and confiding disposition, glad to see and talk to people. A few years after the event I took my wife to see the ruins and the retreat was included in the itinerary of our inspection. Knowing of the man's sensitiveness I had cautioned my wife to forbear going near his chamber. But to my surprise he came out and met us on our arrival and guided us to the interesting relics about the place, including his own niche which possessed historical importance owing to a table let into the alcove mentioning a great event. Then, seeing my wife interested in the little collection in his sacristy [sic], he presented her with an old pipe of peace mounted on copper wire as a memento of our visit.

It is surprising what a number of deserted shrines are to be seen in jungles. Many occur in spots that seem impossible as human resorts, some even where no approach or barely foothold exists to reach them. The face of a cliff, an equally inaccessible hilltop or a subterranean vault, each has its niche for accommodating the deity of the time. I have often driven out wild animals from such ruins. Panthers especially, have a fancy for making use of them as nurseries for their young. In the Shahpur district of Betul I came upon one occupied by a pack of wolves. Another, in the Dharampuri district of Dhar, housed a family of hyenas.

I also made a chance discovery of the remains of what must have once been a miniature temple of whose existence the people of the neighbourhood had no knowledge whatever. It was wedged in the trunk of an old banyan whose aerial roots had dislodged and enveloped the shrine in their ambit round the main stem. The tree marked the site of a deserted village in the midst of forests and the spot was selected for my camp. To employ myself while the tent was being got ready, I took up an axe and began to hack at the roots entwining the trunk. Suddenly it clashed against stone, which made me eager to expose the obstacle. I therefore cut away carefully and from among some stones extricated an exquisite little image of the god Vishnu chiselled out from a block of basalt rock.

I felt entitled to keep the idol and put it away among my things. But some of the men had seen it and news of the find got abroad. My camp now became the scene of daily visits from the better classes who came to make inquiries about the image. They were desirous to celebrate the occasion and dedicate the idol to one of their temples. Not knowing exactly what to do under the circumstances, I consulted the deputy commissioner who advised me to hand it over to the chief priest in the neighbourhood. I consented, and on a day appointed he came with a following and took over the image. It was bathed and purified and placed on a platform bedecked with flowers and garlands, and carried away on men's shoulders to be deposited in a temple.

Officials who have had much to do with the native of India cannot have failed to notice his remarkable gift of ascertaining events that occur far from his midst. It is not merely fakirs whom the accepted theory accuses of possessing the intelligence, but the people generally that are able to gauge more or less accurately the signs of the times. The startling rapidity with which news of the Mutiny travelled through the length and breadth of the land, has become an historical fact. But the life of the country is full of instances where owing either to the secret nature of the proceedings, or their remote origin, it seemed impossible for people to obtain an inkling into what was being contemplated or done at the time. And yet, the news has been common property without those in authority being aware of it. If the bearer is asked to account how he came by it, the answer will usually be that it was conveyed by wind. To the onlooker it appears clearly a case of coincidence or guessing or even inspiration. But, this form of intelligence bureau is so frequent a dispenser of news which too, is often so very precise that the matter cannot be dismissed with a comment. There can be little doubt that it belongs to the range of air-currents as a medium of news developed by the inventor of wireless telegraphy. The difference in the methods would seem to be that in the one case the news is obtained by mechanical means and in the other, the acquirement is correlative with the deep sentiment pervading the masses. The proposition is supported by the knowledge that emotional natures respond more readily to the concerns of life, than matter-of-fact constitutions. I am purely assuming this, but the question is deserving of investigation by the physiologist.

In my own recollection there have been instances which puzzled me at the time how certain news treated as confidential was known to those whom it did not concern or who were the least expected to hear it. The first time the matter attracted my attention, I was working in the Bori forests of Hoshangabad. They were in an isolated corner of the district and the only habitation consisted of a few aboriginal dwellings. We were marking a coupe some distance from camp and at noon adjourned as usual to the Sonbhadra river which bounded the area, to let the workers have their mid-day meal. A fakir whom I had never seen before, was passing just then and the men engaged him in conversation. I too walked up and spoke to him. Seeing my disorderly appearance, for I had been using the axe and billhook freely, he asked why I was taking so much trouble over work that I would soon be leaving. This made me inquire what he meant and he replied that soon I would receive orders of transfer to another Province, and in a few days they came.

I knew that a proposal had been mooted for my deputation to an adjoining province, but it had led to nothing definite. Also, six months had elapsed and I had almost forgotten about it. Moreover, the correspondence was confidential in the conservator's office at provincial headquarters, consequently the intimation came as a great surprise. I never saw or heard of him again.

Equally incomprehensible are two other instances dealing with widely different events. An official, whom I knew very well, had confidential instructions to visit a remote part of his district in order to carry out a commission in a little matter that had been causing the authorities some concern. He set out quietly without headquarters knowing neither his destination nor the business for which he was bound. On the day after his departure, his wife paid a visit to one of the ladies of rank and was promptly accosted with statements relative to her husband's mission, followed with an inquiry as to its success. Taken aback at the questions, the wife showed surprise when the Indian lady not only detailed the facts, but also assured her that the mission had been successful.

In the other case, I was camped in the wilds of Mathwar when the late King Edward died. No one in the place knew anything about his illness, less so of his death. We were about a hundred miles from the nearest telegraph office and forty miles from a post office. In the morning, just about starting on the usual round of inspection, we heard the distant boom of cannon. It came from a

place at least forty miles away and made me interested to know the cause. Seeing my dilemma, the men round me at once interpreted the salutes as meaning that a great man was dead. They knew, of course, that guns fired on important public occasions, but we had heard only a few salvos and there were half-a-dozen different events for any of which they might be firing. Nevertheless, though I reasoned to this effect, they held to their opinion, quite positive that a great personage had died. Two days later the news came by post confirming the men's statement.

Unlike the fakir, the juggler and the bhat, that is a bard, are institutions of amusement. Without them the slow monotonous existence of village life would be dull indeed. They fill in the leisure hours at mid-day and at sunset, and are a source of pleasurable excitement to old and young alike. Taking the juggler, one meets extremely clever performers who would do credit to any well found stage. Before a common assembly, their tricks are simple, intended only to amuse or enliven the spirits. But when called upon to perform in the presence of rank, they excel in feats of daring and will often hold the audience spellbound.

The bard likewise, sings obscene songs or recites offensive riddles rendered to rhyme, before village folks. But put him in the presence of nobility and his whole tenor is changed, and he will recite deeds of chivalry and romance that will thrill the audience. The occupation is hereditary in families of rank and it is wonderful how a bard will commit to memory the doings of a great many generations and recite them in genealogical sequence. They are clever at composing poetry of important episodes in the family history, and will sum up the characters of the principal actors in half-a-dozen words.

The people would often bring these men to my camp to enliven my leisure hours. A variety programme would be gone through and the performance would be witnessed by all.

Of novel tricks, I saw a man thrust a flexible steel blade down his throat. It measured fifteen inches long by three-quarters of an inch wide with the thickness of a few sheets of notepaper. Quite ten inches of the blade went into the throat. He was very quick in inserting and withdrawing it, and kept it in about two minutes during which his head was thrown back. His features looked ghastly and obviously, he was under a great strain during even this short ordeal.

A unique trick also was the chewing of live coals. The man used a gargle to rinse his mouth before giving the display. The preparation was a secret, but there was no doubt that the gargle neutralised the burning effects from the hot coals.

They could perform marvellous feats of balance, such as maintaining equilibrium in all sorts of positions over swing ropes and bars. Most of them were done with weights of empty or full chatties on their heads. I witnessed a man stand on his head at the end of a high bamboo pole with a chatty balanced on the sole of each foot: all he had for support was a cross bar fixed through the pole at about two feet from its end, this he held with his arms stretched full length.

The executive officer, whose routine of constant inspections necessitates tours through rural tracts as the essential part of his duty, has opportunities of witnessing occurrences that are denied to the common observer. Curious customs and devices that sound like myths when portrayed by others are presented to the eyes in actual display. Where the people have not been corrupted by spurious politics, they are as simple as can be imagined. Their crude methods even more than their originality, appear quaint indeed to the observer. Immersed in agricultural pursuits, they seek for signs and portents in almost every undertaking. Their implements, simple and effective to a degree, are the wonder of those accustomed to mechanical appliances. Nothing could be more pleasing than to see a family of the true cultivator toiling over the soil. The husband tends to the strenuous part of the labour while the wife and children are busy with the multifarious little jobs, which combine for the one object of making mother-earth bring forth her increase.

In the cropping periods, the people devote practically all their time to the fields, the entire family, down to the newest arrival is temporarily transported to the scene of labour. When the infant objects to being left alone in a shady corner of the field, it is lulled to sleep in a cradle of bedding slung across the plough fastened to the ends of the yoke, so that in agreement with the oxen's movement, the cradle dangles between them. In case of rain or excessive heat a shelter of leaves and twigs is rigged up under which the little folks huddle till the showers are passed or till the cool of the afternoon sets in. The various divvies [sic] for diverting the evil eye or warding off intruders or frightening animals and

birds are too funny for words. Finally, when the crop is ready for harvesting, the first fruits are a sacrifice to the deity. In fact, there are so many claims upon his bounty to which he must defer by custom that it is a marvel how a cultivator of a small holding has sufficient left for his own use.

Once during a march on a summer day, I came upon a distressing sight. The route lay over the Nerbudda river. It was about ten o'clock when I rode up to the bank to be ferried across. Many men, women and children were swimming and bathing in the river and among them I recognised a well to do Bunia whom I knew. He belonged to a neighbouring town and was enjoying a holiday outing with his family. His little daughter of seven or eight was married to a boy who lived with his parents on the opposite side of the river. Cholera had been rife there and the boy was taken ill that night and succumbed to the attack before morning, but till then the bunia was ignorant of the ill news that awaited him. He saw me standing waiting for the ferry and walked up to have a chat and had entered into conversation when the ferry with passengers from the opposite bank pulled up alongside of us. It brought a messenger from the boy's parents to announce the sad tidings to the girl's family, and no sooner [did he see] the bunia than he broke the news to him. In a few seconds, the afflicted parent was lamenting the sad event in true Indian fashion and his family at once followed suit and burst into a tumult of wailing.

In the meanwhile the child-wife, unconscious of the evil fate that had overtaken her, was playing happily with other children at the water's brink a little distance off. Her mother and aunt now ran to her and taking off her holiday attire, they removed her ornaments and broke the glass and lacquer-ware bangles which she had on. The child unable to account for the sudden outburst of roughness on the part of her loved parents, began to scream and struggle with fright, but they dragged her along with them to prepare for the departure home. The scene so full of joviality a minute before, became one of mourning. The widowed child's treatment at the hands of her parents is self-condemnation of a custom that allowed of such cruelty. Yet, not a sigh nor a sign of sympathy escaped the crowd gathered at the river bank. It is but one example of the severity and exacting calls that customs enforce which cause even the love of parents to be overset in conforming with them.

Every large village nearly has its fisher folk who belong to a class called Dhemars. But fishing is a precarious means of livelihood in a country that generally eschews meat. So they supplement their earnings by engaging in auxiliary pursuits, such as the culture of silkworms, rearing of watermelons. In fishing, they use both the net and the line. The nets are of various designs and vary from light pouch-shaped net, resembling a butterfly catcher, and the weighted net for casting, to the large fan-shaped net stretched between bamboo poles whose cross sticks pivot on the waist in working. The line is nearly always set at night baited with worms or fry or frogs to hook large fish. The twine or cord of nets and lines is treated with the sap of the gab or temsu fruit to render it waterproof. This turns it brown and tough and under constant immersion the brown changes to black.

Aborigine fishermen on the other hand, fish mostly with traps. These are either decoy pools or bamboo cages, ingeniously constructed and set to attract fishes and hold them when inside. They also kill fishes with their bows and arrows at night. A man with a flaming torch sits on a rock jutting out of the water, while another with the weapon stands at the water's edge. Attracted by the light, fishes come up to the surface of the water enabling the watcher to take aim. The close shooting seldom results in a miss.

Aborigines are confirmed poisoners of fish especially when a big haul is required as for a festive gathering. The poison used is a decoction prepared from the bark and fruit of certain trees and herbs; the liquid is then mixed with the water within a confined space as a pool or backwater. In some cases the action causes the fish to die outright, in others it makes them silly for the time being and they aimlessly float on their backs and sides, when men on the watch jump in to the water and catch them. The poisons are effective in six to twelve hours.

I met a colony of Dhemars who caught wild duck which frequented a tank in the village by an ingenious method. It was a large sheet of water and the village stretched along two sides of its banks. Apparently it afforded excellent feeding for the wader tribes which flocked in large numbers. On its surface floated a great many charred earthenware pots, the birds were accustomed to see these and seemed not the least disturbed with their proximity. I may say, cooking pots and pans of earthenware, costing a few pence at the most, are discarded for trivial reasons

Boundary inspection, Kathiwara and Ratanmal, J.D. St Joseph mounted, left

Bhabra-Amkhut cart track, Binut, Ali-Rajpur, 1904

Camp under a solitary mahua, Silvad, Barwani

Ancient banyan, supported only on aerial roots

Grinding corn

Bhil hut, Amkhut, Ali-Rajpur, 1905

In the distance, hills cleared of forest, Kathiwara

My camp at Bharandpura, Dhar, 1906

A type of Bhil hut

Bhil dacoit, Amkhut, Ali-Rajpur

Typical Bhil, Ali-Rajpur, 1905

and thrown into the rubbish heap or any convenient space from time to time. This tank served the needful purpose and became a depository for the utensils.

The sense of security acquired by the birds among the flotsam and jetsam of the village was turned to advantage in effecting their capture. A man would select a pot to cover his head, pierce two holes in the side to fit in with his eyes and then swim out stealthily with his body up to the neck immersed in water. The birds, taking the disguise for one of the floating pots that drifted about among them daily, paid no attention to it, which gave the decoy the chance to glide up to them. When he was within reach a hand would be silently extended under the water and a duck held by the feet and dragged down and thrust into a net fastened at the waist; the performance would be repeated till the birds, becoming suspicious, departed. It required skill in swimming and making the captures, but a practised hand went about it so cleverly that the birds did not penetrate the disguise till a good few had been secured. It was laughable how well the stratagem succeeded; each bird caught would disappear with a "quack", making it appear it had taken a dive. Few men could boast of catching as many as half-a-dozen in an excursion; as a rule the bag was two or three duck, but a lad pointed out to me was more skilful than the rest and seldom returned with less than four, and I heard his biggest bag was six.

Pardhees or professional game catchers, are also an interesting class. They are found in few villages and live generally on the outskirts. They are a bane to sportsmen; game disappear so completely from wherever they operate that there is no question of guessing who has been over the locality. They confine their operations to ground game and field antelope, for though clever in working over open country, they are at sea in the jungle. They make excellent guides and beaters in ground game shooting, knowing instinctively where to find it.

Their methods consist chiefly in netting and trapping. The net is not unlike a fishing net with small meshes, and made to compress into a bag when pulled or subjected to tension. It is cleverly fixed so as to collapse on the object at the least attempt at resistance; this is the favourite method employed for catching birds that go about collectively, and hare and antelope. I have also known panthers to be caught in nets when they were too cunning to be destroyed by other means.

The traps are ingenious contrivances, simple and effective. They vary in design according to the victim's value, for instance songsters and birds of plumage intended for sale to bird-fanciers, have to be caught with care to prevent them struggling and hurting or damaging themselves. For these an elaborate cage of bamboo or reed lattice-work is constructed and equipped on the sides with little partitions which contain the traps that are on the drop principle. A perch is kept in position by horse-hair entanglement and bars the entrance to a spread of seed-grain, so that in trying to get at the grain, the bird steps on to the perch which drops by its weight, freeing a lattice that claps the bird into the partition. A call-bird is kept in the cage to attract wild ones.

Ground birds, such as grouse that scrape their feet in walking, are generally snared in horsehair nooses laid flat on the ground and concealed by a sprinkling of earth or gravel.

A strangling device on the principle of a jaw trap is used occasionally to catch pigeon, dove or partridge. It consists of two parts, a curved piece of elastic, wood or buffalo horn, tapering at both ends to act as a block, and a strip of the male bamboo to serve as the spring. Their ends are drawn taut by horsehair entanglement causing the spring to rest tightly on the block and giving the fixture a crescent shape. To set the trap a semi-circular scoop to fit the block is made in the ground in which it is partially embedded. The spring is then drawn out to the opposite extreme and kept in position by a hook and pin attachment connecting with a bamboo spike having a thick end fixed in the centre of the block and the other projecting into the arc. The snare now resembles somewhat a jaw trap when set. A grain of seed is glued to the detached end of the spike and a few grains dropped near about. The bird as it feeds on the ground, is gradually directed towards the snare by stealthy movements of the trapper. Seeing the grains, it hurries to peck them and eventually pecks at the glued seed and immediately displaces the fastening which causes the pin to start back, freeing the spring. This reverts to the block with a sharp blow and severely jerks the victim's neck. The bird struggles, the trapper rushes up and secures it. More often than not, the bird is held by the neck as the grain lies near the block. The trap is a toy in size measuring six to eight inches across its diameter. Moreover, it is very light and, but for the embedding, a strong bird would get away with it. Boys use it more than men do, as they expose

themselves less in guiding the birds. The bag is often three to six couples in a day.

The men also use birdlime, generally for catching birds on trees. It is applied to forked strips of bamboo cut at one end of a long bamboo pole and the fowler fixes the bird between the fork by cleverly manipulating the staff from below. A very simple birdlime snare is made of two thin strips of bamboo tied at the centre crossways and bent semi-circularly in the shape of a skeleton bowl. The strips are smeared with birdlime and a live worm suspended on a piece of thread from the joint. It is then placed on the ground with the ends down. A bird sees the worm dangling and swoops down to take it and is enmeshed in the lime and unable to fly. The Indian roller, mynas, starlings and minivets are caught by this device.

As in the case of fishing, bird catching is a precarious means of obtaining a living, more so since restrictions were placed on the export of plumage. The extension of game laws has also limited their activity. Consequently, the men labour in the fields and even rent plots for cultivation.

The traps employed by wild tribes are not quite the same as those used by bird catchers. Horsehair nooses are the favourite form of snare and are largely in use for catching jungle fowl and peafowl. The nooses are fixed at intervals of eight or nine inches, to a strong chord five or six yards in length. The chord is loosely stretched about a foot over the ground under cover of bushes with the loops of the nooses hanging downwards. These are partially hidden by bunching up fallen leaves between loops. A few men now drive the birds slowly towards the line of nooses and as they pass hurriedly from cover to cover craning their necks through every little opening, one or more birds stick their heads into the loops and get noosed by the neck.

Large game, as pig and porcupine, is taken in figure four traps whose drops are weighted with heavy stones for crushing the animal. Children use bamboo trays with high sides of two or three inches in the same way to catch quail and sparrows.

The best birdlime is prepared from the gum of the pepal (fiscus religiosa). A tree in full vigour is selected for preference and a few deep incisions made on the stem. The sap exudes and coagulates on the surface and is fit to remove in ten or twelve hours when it is collected, washed and cleansed in mustard oil. It is then placed in

an iron cup with a little oil and heated over a slow fire, after which it is put in the sun to cool gradually. The lime now congeals and is ready for use. It is a tenacious and powerful adherent: strong birds as raven, kite and eagle-hawk are easily caught with the lime.

At one of my camps, I came upon an interesting settlement of Mahommedan weavers. The place was once a famous stronghold of a Rajput chief, but he had been defeated and his domains annexed by an Indian potentate, and as usually happens, with the fall of the ruler, the busy life of the capital city had departed. It had been more or less deserted for a century, so that the works were fast crumbling into ruins. The former owner had imported the colony to establish a mart for muslins which the weavers excelled in manufacturing, and the men had stuck to the place through its long adversity, plying their trade with scant means and trusting in forlorn hopes of better times. Owing to the cheap imported cloths, the value of their manufactures had depreciated, so much so that they were reduced to a state verging on beggary. The colony had dwindled to a remnant of its original strength and every family was in the clutches of an usurer, who took care to appropriate the fabrics at his own valuation. Moreover, the locality being in a little known corner of the jungles, far from the railway and badly served by communications, the weavers were helpless to act independently in placing their goods on the market. Their only salvation seemed to lie in State aid whenever that would be forthcoming to lift them out of misery.

These people lived in stable-like dwellings different from the common native house. A fourth of the space would be screened off for the living room and the rest used as the weaving hall, which had the crudest fittings imaginable for the manufacture of such fine work as they turned out. Also, the apartment was partly sunk in the ground and practically buried in darkness to mitigate the dust nuisance from soiling the muslin while in the warp.

A curious feature of the trade was the need for soft hands so as to work the delicate threads, and the men went to some trouble to acquire the perfection. They would keep the hands bound in a layer of dough during leisure hours, or on retiring to rest, which rendered them smooth and light of touch and as soft as those of an infant. They used common thread, but it was worked to a silken texture by a process of soaking and boiling in starch prepared from the wild onion and then carefully carded with a fine wooden comb.

I spent several hours watching them at work and it was a marvel with what patience and skill they manipulated the shuttle in order to keep the fine delicate threads intact. They were also clever in working designs in gold or silver thread into the muslins, and showed good taste in their patterns. They had a standing annual order for a sari to robe a great potentate's wife, which took eight or ten men a year to prepare. The quality of the material may be gathered from the fact that it could be packed in a bamboo tube of an inch diameter which would be sealed and dispatched to the owner.

Chapter V

Beats

It may seem a truism to say that beats should be slowly and quietly conducted. But the warning should be well instilled into the men before starting, even with threats and strong words if necessary: though indeed the strongest admonitions are often useless. Beaters are sure to shout and scramble at the first token of alarm that may be caused by some inoffensive thing, such as a four-horned antelope, porcupine or peafowl getting up suddenly in their front. At the same time it is extremely difficult to keep the men from shouting. It appeals to them as a natural form of self-defence. They are practically unarmed, except for an axe or club and most of them without shoes, and their body and limbs are almost bare. Undrilled and undisciplined, it is not surprising, if they should show fear at any little thing that starts their imagination. On such occasions the beaters do not always turn and run as is generally assumed, nor unite as they might be expected to do, but the desire seems to be to get into some sort of cover, either by huddling behind rocks, stones or bushes, or getting up branches. This is as much owing to experience in the one case as they know they stand a poor chance against the swifter beasts, as to lack of unity in the other, considering the rank and file are usually made up by contributions from two or more villages. Moreover an animal breaking back, however dangerous, seldom troubles to molest anyone not in its line and even when this occurs, the beast more often than not avoids an encounter. Indeed, the same tendency seems to govern most beasts even when they are wounded.

A beat should never be too long or too spread out; in my opinion, it should not exceed five hundred yards in length and about half this in width. Animals hate to be driven and if the unpleasantness is unnecessarily prolonged, however carefully the beat may be conducted, they are sure to stampede, owing usually to one of the young beasts getting impatient or panic-stricken and frightening the rest. This occasions a general stampede which nothing will stop, and in the general disorder, the gun has just to chance his luck at an animal charging by in his direction.

I remember a tiger escaping in this manner when he was going

straight for the gun. The beat extended over half a mile or so, and among other animals enclosed were a herd of cheetal. These walked along quietly for some distance in front of the tiger, when a hind either saw or winded one of the stops on the flank and started off like lightning in the opposite direction, taking the rest with her as well as a few pig which joined in between. The tiger stopped and watched them go and then walked up after them and escaped between two stops of whom I was one. As we were stops, we had no weapons and all our efforts to turn it were in vain.

The most common faults in beating are noise and over-numerous beaters. The cause for shouting has already been mentioned. It may be useful for bear whose sense of hearing is defective, or even in places where there is flat expansion of surface for miles around, and allows the sound to flow in one direction. Too much noise is not only worrying to animals, but renders their movements uncertain and impetuous. Sambar for instance, will invariably charge through beats if there is any shouting, while other animals lose their heads and sit tight under cover till the beaters come right up, when they will jump up and spring right through them. I have known pig, four-horned antelope and even tiger and panther do this.

In hilly country where game usually resorts noisy beats are more often than not disastrous. The sound strikes the slopes in front and in flank and is hurled back, echoed and re-echoed, with more or less force - according to the character of the slopes, indentations in the surface and the density of its forest covering. Thus, it vibrates from so many different points till the beast is fairly crazy, either as to its object, or its source.

I have often observed this sitting up in a machan and wondering when the noise of the beat began, whether the shikaris had not changed its direction without letting me know. In two or three instances I have known guns actually change their position thinking the beat was coming to them from the back or sideways. It can easily be imagined, then, what effect a confused noise must have upon an animal, especially if it is the creature's first experience. It is puzzled what to do. Should it be a tiger, it will as a rule move out of cover and listen attentively and try and fix the direction from which the noise comes, and suit its movements to avoid the trouble threatening. Acting as a stop, I have twice watched tigers do this. Other animals are affected in different

ways, but most of them cower and hide as if expecting their doom, until the beaters are actually on them and then they spring through and escape, rather than face the uncertain blank in their front, that is, the space between the game and the guns, doubtless on the principle: "better bear the ills we have, than fly to others that we know not of."

This accounts for the many good chances that are spoilt, when one wonders what could have become of the game. It is very rarely that the men can be got to say what animals escaped through the line of beaters; usually they will make out that it was a pig, hind, sambar or some other equally worthless beast which they know you would not even have cared to see. It is only when your temper has cooled and the beaters are disbanded, that one of the shikaris or elders having had his fill of spirits round the camp fire, will tell you in a quiet confidential way, that "the tiger was in the beat all right, but had escaped through the beaters". I have known this to happen over and over again. But this is not the only mischief of a badly managed beat. A noisy beat disturbs the jungles for miles and miles, so that animals leave their haunts in the disturbed area for the time being. And the sportsman might as well say good-bye to shooting for the next few days.

Another fallacy is to suppose that large numbers of beaters are required to ensure success. Of course everyone, from the staff of officials and experienced shikaris down to the village elders, will urge the contrary. Their anxiety is natural if we consider the risk to the individual. But numbers stir up the mass by infusing confidence in the individual, and apart from this they are a sheer encumbrance and more often than not, the beat becomes unmanageable. In my experience the most successful beats have been those where few men were employed.

The worst excess as regards numbers is in the case of high officials, and I have known as many as five hundred men employed to drive a small tract of jungle. On such occasions, beats assume a quasi-ceremonial character. District officials who can be spared are concentrated at the site, and the gathering is so large and their wants in the matter of provisions so varied that it requires some skill especially in out of the way tracts, to cater for the camps. The showy character of such shoots accords with the customs of the country and are common sights in Native States. The people enter into their spirit with zest, while to officials they afford pleasant

recreations after the ceaseless work. Everyone is anxious to provide good sport, and opinions and plans multiply, with the result that things are overdone and often lead to disappointment.

At the commencement of my service I happened to be in charge of forests that adjoined a famous reserve where a big shoot was organised for a great man. I heard about the preparations through subordinates and being anxious to know how it was worked, I camped on a plateau along the border overlooking the reserve which lay in a huge trough shut in by hills and watered by perennial streams - an ideal game resort. Ordinarily the tract was deserted of human beings, except for a straggling settlement of Gonds and few forest subordinates quartered in the locality. The shoot caused a large influx of people which daily increased as the heads of services marched into camp.

The shoot was under the management of an experienced sportsman who was powerless to prevent the overcrowding, but trusted to his knowledge of the jungle and habits of animals to provide sport. He was sure the tract possessed too great an attraction for game to be readily effected by temporary disturbance. The arrivals, who were mostly aborigines from neighbouring tracts and accustomed to wander, soon spread over the reserve to collect supplies of fuel, fodder and various sundries required for a camp on a grand scale, and to gather honey, fruits, nuts and bulbs for themselves. Their presence in all parts of the jungle, the noise and smell carried from the gathering of beaters and baggage animals and the sight through the gloom of the night of huddled groups by the numerous camp fires, alarmed the game that were accustomed only to the peace and seclusion that the reserve enjoyed. The beasts were properly scared and began rapidly to vacate their haunts. Often and often in my rambles about the plateau, I watched the herds of deer and bison moving over the slopes. Tigers and bears followed during the night until very little of the nobler game remained. Eventually, the great man also arrived and stayed for the best part of a week, but in spite of all efforts to provide him with sport, nothing worth shooting could be turned out, and the camp broke up in great disappointment for everyone.

In Native States shoots of the kind are more successful owing to the permanency maintained about the arrangements by liberal use of money and labour. In most cases for instance, the State keeps up

a shikar department controlled by an experienced official with shikaris at the head of disciplined bodies of men to act as beaters: a useful system of roads and paths lead into the game preserves and allow of rapid concentration of guns and beaters, so that camps can be pitched at long distances from shooting grounds and disturbance avoided: elaborate chains of posts and shooting towers easily accessible traverse the grounds and prevent beaters and stops straying into the closed area. Therefore, there is nothing surprising in their reputation for success. At the same time, it is poor sport since the gun has all the advantages, while the methods often degenerate into a form of forcing game from a trap to be shot with little or no chance of escape.

Sportsmen as a class, who are mostly of moderate means, usually make their own shikar arrangements. Their purse will not admit of very liberal expenditure, so they have to depend either on their own skill to mark down game and organise beats, or to employ local trackers or shikaris to aid them. The true sportsman considers his trouble well rewarded if he is fortunate to bag even a single good specimen of the game he is after.

The choice of sites for beats requires good deal of consideration and is not the easy matter regarded by people who leave its management to others. The nature of the game that the gun is after, the season in which the shooting is undertaken and the conditions obtaining in the locality are points that chiefly influence the selection of places for drives. The tendency of animals to foregather is mutual and resorts become common favourites according as to whether or not, the places offer the advantages of cover to all. The desire to be discriminating and retire to quiet nooks develops with age and accounts for the absence of good trophies in the general turn outs of beats. So again, in the hot weather most animals and especially tiger keep near water whereas in winter they seek dry ground and therefore high positions, while in the rains they scatter to wherever they can procure shelter from inclemencies of the weather. As to prevailing conditions, the best of sites is often spoilt by its invasion by man and cattle.

A sportsman who has studied the habits of game will know where to look for the quarry he is after. But as a rule, the majority of men seeking sport know very little of the ways of beasts and trust entirely for success to luck which more often than not spells

disappointment. For those with whom time is no object, it is well if the first few days at the shooting camp are employed in learning about the locality where it is proposed to shoot. It means inspecting the ground, forbearing to empty the rifle and setting about to obtain information from local sources. The possession of facts encourages self-reliance and paves the way to success. It is useful to work with a topographical map, but the essential thing is to get in personal touch with conditions obtaining in the locality.

In each beat the limits of the ground to be covered have to be decided before proceeding to the next step of fixing the direction of drive. As a rule, beaters work over ground in a fan-tail or triangle, or in a pear-shape or ellipse. The formation is governed by the lie of the tract as also, by the number of guns taking part in the shoot. Over a valley or level stretch with one or two guns, the easiest extension is a triangle, while over undulating ground or slope as with three or more guns, the drive deploys in an ellipse. In either case the guns are posted at the apex or extremity opposite to the beaters. These are the simplest and best controlled beats. But the sportsman is not always fortunate as to ground, and difficulties are presented that require dispositions suitable to the locality. A fair example is a radiating surface whose forked gullies furnish equally good covers between which there is no choice. In such a case, the gun takes position about a common centre, while groups of beaters working in unison, though independently, through the several covers, converge on the point fixed for shooting. The beat necessarily takes up more ground, than either of the simpler forms and is moreover difficult to arrange and manage, its success depends on the men allotted to control the bodies of beaters, working so as to emerge together at the goal.

In the matter of numbers, I consider seventy-five men ample to drive the biggest and thickest of covers in any locality. Quite half of these are disposed of on special duties as stops, so that only two score or less comprise the actual beaters. Therefore, in an extension just exceeding a furlong, each beater controls a space of less than half the length of a cricket pitch, or about twelve feet on either side of him. The shikari stays in the centre of the line to exercise general supervision and reliable persons are needed to man each of the two flanks. Insistence should be put on the men to carry weapons, such as axe, spear or club, and shikaris permitted to have their firearms. The mere fact of their possession instills confidence, and men will

go without hesitation through cover that otherwise unarmed they would avoid.

Stops are men who line the sides extending from the guns to the beaters, and so complete the enclosure. They keep animals from breaking through the sides and are a persuasive means of diverting the quarry to the guns. They are essential to success in beating for big game and according to the part they perform, are classed as silent and active stops.

The arranging of the stops is the most important part of a beat and a work that should be attended to personally, or entrusted to only reliable and trained men. Intelligent men among the beaters are selected for stops, care being taken that none have colds or coughs, because in the best managed beats failure has often been traced to an individual with a chill having turned back the game from the gun by a fit of coughing or sneezing. Considering also, how apt the ordinary native is to relieve his solitude by a vociferous use of his throat, the need for withholding audible utterances cannot be too forcibly impressed upon the stops.

To enable them to obtain a clear view of the ground they guard, stops take up positions on trees, stumps, rocks or mounds. The distances between individuals depend on the thickness of cover and on the irregularity of the ground; rank undergrowth would require to be as closely watched, as a depression or cutting would call for the individual attention of a single man. With silent stops, it is usual to allow twenty-five paces between consecutive men, so that an individual guards about twelve paces on either side of him. Active stops are placed further apart.

About half a dozen men are enough for silent stops and they are usually disposed equally on both sides of the gun. Their duty is to keep very quiet and work only if the quarry attempts to pass by them; the man who is nearest to the animal, then taps lightly on a stem or utters the least audible groan or cough and the warning suffices to cause the needful diversion, edging the beast on towards the gun. Active stops on the other hand, commence to rap as soon as the beat begins and keep at it till the line moves up, and as each meets the advancing beaters, he joins them in driving. If the full complement of men is not forthcoming, a way to make up the deficiency is to increase distances between stops and mark the lines with strips of paper suspended on boughs and bushes growing between the intervals. The device is effective in preventing game

breaking through unguarded cover, for strange as it may seem, the boldest animal is deterred by this simple expedient. Any showy thing will do, but strips of paper that flutter with the wind and catch the eye soonest, are the best.

To complete arrangements two or three men are posted at distances behind the gun, as it often happens that animals even when mortally wounded dash forward past the gun and do not stop until they have gone some distance. The back stops now come in useful in seeing or marking the spot where the creature drops, and if its impetuosity has carried it beyond observation, the men's opinion as to the nature of the wound, and any noticeable change in the beast's conduct in passing, aids in forming an estimate of the damage inflicted, and in organising the hunt. Dangerous beasts are thus located and retrieved without incurring undue risks of accidents.

Stops line up between the gun and beaters. The men picked for the work go with the sportsman, making a wide detour for the spot to be occupied by the gun who takes up a post on the ground or in a machan, whichever promises the surest position in view of aim and safety. There must be no loitering and any work to be done should be accomplished as speedily and noiselessly as possible, otherwise the site becomes suspect to animal instinct and is avoided. No sooner the gun is seated [sic], the stops divide and while one party follows the shikari, the other goes with his confreres to take up places for screening the exposed sides of the drive. They must move rapidly and noiselessly to their positions in Indian file which should always be the order of march in doing these errands, as it is the quickest and quietest way of moving through undergrowth.

In the meanwhile the beaters remain halted at some distance off the place from where they are to commence driving, and deploy into line on the shikari's return. The extension is always a bow or curve concaved towards the gun, which allows of more scope of action, than a straight line. With tiger, panther and bear, the start off should be preceded by a shout, in order to rouse the beast out of its lair. Thereafter, beaters proceed at an easy pace, talking, throwing stones into bits of cover and rattling clubs and axes against stumps and stems. These noises will drive out the most obstinate animal, and should not be exceeded. Sambar and cheetal are easily urged forward by a noiseless advance, and no shouting, talking or hammering ought to be permitted.

Beats for sambar, cheetal, pig and bear should proceed with the wind as they are very sensitive to smell, and the mere fact of the breeze blowing from the men to the game, will drive them out. But scent is of less consequence in the case of tiger and panther with whom the choice of locality is of more consideration, and their one aim is to gain admittance speedily into the next best cover. Therefore, beats should follow the direction of the shortest course that leads to the resort for which they will make, and nothing could be better if the drive chances to be in line with the prevailing wind. Moreover, the direction in which a tiger drags its kill practically indicates the line along which the beat should be taken.

In fixing beats, some thought ought also to be given to the nature of the cover ahead, as unless it is suitable, game will hesitate to move and try to break out. The sportsman has to consider the retreat that is adapted to the habits of the quarry, and not the sort he fancies will do. Deer as well as bear prefer high ground and do not care so much whether it is thickly or sparsely wooded, as that it is rocky. A tiger needs a cool spot with pretty thick cover. And all animals endeavour to gain places where they will feel secure against further disturbance.

At almost every sign of activity in the enclosure, beaters imagine they have put up the quarry and call or shout to attract attention. This is due to fear as much as to excitement and no amount of warning will stop the clamour from arising. There are however, occasions when it is necessary for the gun or a stop to speak to the line, and the best way to convey instructions quickly to the noisy ranks, is to establish whistle signals between the gun, stops and beaters. This is less likely to startle bewildered game in hiding, or wounded beasts lying up and unwilling to move, than words shouted out for the men to hear. A simple code of a few words to correspond with numerical notes of a whistle can be always devised for the men to understand. For instance, a single or double note would mean to stop or proceed while a string of three or four would denote safety or danger, and so on. The gun and shikari should each possess one and also a few distributed among stops; penny whistles do as well as any.

It is usual to beat during the middle of the day when animals have settled down for their siesta. If the programme includes three or more drives, it is well to start an hour before noon, continuing to the close of the afternoon. But if there is to be one or two beats, it is best to commence soon after the mid-hour.

The gun ought to be accoutred in material that will blend with the surroundings. Personally, I prefer heather mixture to other shikar clothes. Stops should on no account be allowed to wear white or fabrics of glaring colour.

The question of paying beaters deserves careful attention; its slightest neglect leads to misuse of money that may as easily mulct the gun into defraying excess, as deprive unfortunates of their dues rendering the sportsman an unwitting cause of offence among the simple folks. The easiest way of preventing fraud is to have the men lined up in camp before starting and issue gun wads or cardboard tickets to each and all present. At the close of the shoot the beaters again reassemble to hand in their billets and as each steps forward he receives his wage. The shikari is not counted among beaters and, besides daily rations, is rewarded according to previous arrangement. Any one or more of the men singled out for special mention ought to be rewarded in addition to the pay earned. Little attentions of the kind make the men keen to exert themselves. The customary wage is four annas for a day of six hours and less for half the time, but it is usual to grant increases should the bag exceed expectations.

As a rule, aboriginal tribes furnish the beaters, so that they come of a class of men intimate with game and even interested in sport. Therefore with forbearance and tact they are easy to manage and will willingly tackle the worst covers. Once their goodwill has been secured, it needs only to send word and they come streaming in from distances of their own accord. Success always elates their spirits and events comprising unexpected feats or marking the downfall of a notorious beast, captures their imagination so much so as to gladden them into feeling they contributed to the incident. For a time it becomes the theme of village gossip and is recalled for the entertainment of subsequent visitors as well as treasured up for the benefit of their children. It is more reason why sportsmen should be generous on occasions of a turn of extra good luck, making it a point to celebrate the event by a feast in addition to the wages paid the men. Again, these men are always glad to have meat and whenever the bag is sufficiently large to be distributed, it should be shared among the beaters. It is a matter requiring careful seeing into otherwise servants and village elders are prone to annex the meat regardless of those more entitled to it. Indeed, I have known instances in which the shikari or the sportsman's

orderly sold the meat to the beaters. Such an abuse of custom ought never to occur.

Most animals when disturbed conform to rules in choosing their lines of retreat and will not be easily diverted. In withdrawing the quarry is guided partly by instinct and partly by characteristics peculiar to the tribe in taking routes least likely to contain danger. Covers and galleries along paths that appear to the human eye as inviting the best means of escape, are often avoided by fleeing animals because of the very reason of their tempting feature for harbouring foes. Consequently, in selecting position for the gun, it is important to discard advantages about the approach as the eye sees them, and only bear in mind the instinctive traits of the beast and consider whether under the circumstances, the path would be acceptable. Success is said to be assured if arrangements for beating are in accord with the ways of the quarry.

Taking the tiger for example, it will be driven in the direction in which it is willing to go and only those with an experience of tiger craft can surely forestall its line of retreat. But unless this is done, a driven tiger will in nine cases out of ten, effect its escape. The standing rule is that a tiger will go in a direction towards which it has dragged its kill and that will usually be in the bed or on the bank of a shady stream that is either flowing or contains a pool of water nearby - and here comes the rub - its choice of direction may lie along any radius of a semi-circle whose diameter intersects at right angles the line of the drag. To fix the position of the gun correctly, one must not only have some knowledge of the habits of the tiger, but also some idea of the topography of the surrounding country, for which the tiger is expected to make.

In a well-known beat in the Banka-Bharda reserve of the Betul district, the tiger always struck off at a tangent from the bank where it had dragged its kill, up a steep slope and over the plateau, into a depression about four miles from the beat. Such a journey required great energy, especially in the hot weather with the temperature anything over 110 degrees; yet for some reason the tiger seemed to prefer the heat and discomfort of it, rather than to follow the shady banks of the stream that wound through thick jungle. In my recollection five tigers were shot here at different times. They all took the same line of retreat and fell within a few paces of each other.

I questioned the old Gond who managed the beats: he was a

forest guard and headman of his village, as well as a well known shikari. He told me that he had had several failures before he discovered the right position for the gun, which he was only able to fix after having tracked two or three tigers that had escaped from previous beats. He said that they invariably made for the same lair. This excited my curiosity and one morning I went with him to see the spot. As I have said, it lay in a depression high up on the hillside, with a north-westerly aspect such as is occasionally met with on the terraced slopes of the Satpura mountains. Giant trees and clumps of bamboo overhung the spot, sheltering it from the sun and hot winds, while rocks cropped out all over the slopes and afforded good cover. As I saw it in May, there was no sign of water, but it was nevertheless damp and cool, and the dry moss clinging in the crevices showed that water continued to trickle down till late after the rains. It was an ideal place to rest after fatigue and, though there were no signs of a tiger having been there for some time, it was easy to understand why they showed such determination in making for the spot.

But it does not follow that a tiger will retire to the same lair at all seasons of the year. I believe that they fix on different places to suit the seasons, that is winter and summer, although from the beast's movements it may seem that it makes always for one or the same place.

In a frequented area in the Nanda reserve, the beats were taken in a different course according to the time of year. In winter the direction was up the stream, the gun being posted on the bank below which the tiger came; while in summer the beat was taken obliquely to the stream, though in the same direction, and the tiger at once mounting the bank, cut across a glade to get into some low hills, the gun being placed where the glade ended and the rise commenced. The local men could not explain the cause, but doubtless in summer the animal declined the winter route for the simple reason, that the limestone boulders in the dry bed of the stream would be baked by the sun's rays and blister its pads.

As a rule a driven tiger avoids going through a depression, such as a valley, the bed of a stream or a marsh. It will make by the shortest cut possible for high ground. Apparently, instinct warns it that to gain on its pursuers it must top them as quickly as possible and this is more necessary in summer when cover is open than in winter when the jungles are thick. This doubtless, explains why

the greater number of beats prove to be failures, although by many the cause is put down as a matter of luck due to the eccentric movements of the tiger or the incompetence of the shikari.

In most cases of success it will be found that the tiger has been shot at a higher elevation than the spot where the beast originally lay up. This instinct is a common one with animals. Even when one comes on them suddenly from above and they charge down for a short distance they will really turn and rush up the slope and, if possible, get above the height from which they were disturbed.

A tiger driven out of a favourite haunt and wounded will often, if it survives, return to the spot after a few days. Most people I have met are surprised at this, as they imagine that the beast would avoid the place for the rest of its existence, but considered rightly, the habit is natural enough. The wounded tiger comes back directly the creature feels it safe to return, notwithstanding that there may be other places equally good in human eyes nearby. But having returned, it will be shy and careful not to show itself too soon. I have known this to happen on five or six occasions, and the interval varied from a week to a fortnight. In two cases, the tiger was bagged on its return, though from different positions from the first attempts. In one instance it was shot from the back of an elephant, having walked almost up to it in the open, rather than pass under the tree from which the beast had been previously wounded and where lay the track that it usually took. In both these cases, the old wounds were still raw. In a third instance, a tiger was twice within a fortnight, driven out of the same locality where it had been wounded just a week before, escaping each time through the active stops. The cause of this persistence probably lies in the tiger's thorough knowledge of the locality. It can turn just where it likes to obtain its food which, in its disabled condition, is an all-important matter: and it knows all the various nooks and corners where it can hide in its restlessness, and so avoid observation not merely from forest denizens, but also from the midges and flies that are attracted by the festering sores. After all it is only following the example of man who longs to be at home when lying wounded or sick elsewhere.

Chapter VI

Stalking

Following game on foot is a test of bodily endurance as well as of skill in employing the senses, or a combination of exercise with instinct. It is only sportsmen who develop these in common, that are masters of the craft. Civilising tendencies are apt more or less to blunt the instinctive faculties and so individuals aspiring to be hunters, find themselves handicapped in the chase after the nobler quarry. But the hindrance is removed directly the latent senses are converted to use, and in stalking especially, the readiness to utilise them counts for success and leads to excellence on acquiring the intuition to determine the temperaments of the types of game.

At the outset a word may be said about tracking as it is liable to be confused with stalking. They are distinct forms of pursuit, but co-operate to assure success. As a rule, tracking is resorted to in marking down wounded quarry, or to obtain clues to the whereabouts of game and as such plays a subordinate though decisive part in all shoots. To discuss it separately therefore, would be repeating statements recorded under various chapters whose narratives are best calculated to show the relative importance of tracking in the field of sport, and the need to treat it exclusively does not arise.

In walking up animals there is always the possibility of meeting a formidable beast whose opposition may lead to serious consequences. We know all creatures do not submit tamely to being shot and a good few will sell their lives dearly. But the desire to die hard is as strictly restricted to particular types, as it is intensified in individuals of the same group. Thus it is that while an element of fear attaches to an encounter with a tiger or panther, there is no hesitation in meeting a bear or bull gaur, or that guns accustomed to dealing with these beasts are chary to tackle individuals whose behaviour fills them with misgiving. As a matter of fact, it is not uncommon to see the fierce tiger display the cowardice of the hyena or the timid gaur develop the fury of a panther. So it will be evident that the stalker needs to combine resources with knowledge of the ways of beasts. In the absence of provocation, the fiercest creatures practically speaking, are harmless and danger is to be feared only if they are wounded.

Then, their propensities for mischief are very great and regarded from this standpoint, game tribes acquire notoriety by the ferocious attitudes to which they are liable in fits of temper. Accordingly, they may be classed as dangerous or harmless; for example, among carnivora, only the tiger and panther come in the former category; the deer and antelope are inoffensive; while in the bovine race, the wild buffalo and gaur occupy a mid-position by their tendency to be malicious on occasions.

It is only seldom that one hears of a tiger or panther being stalked, although the annals of sport abound with instances showing they have been bagged on foot. Most of them, however, are of the class of lucky incidents in which more by accident than purpose while stalking for other game or during a casual excursion, the animal has been seen and shot. But I have known sportsmen who followed tiger and panther on foot with indifference: they knew the craft and were confident of foiling the great cat at its own game as surely, as walking up an inoffensive creature.

Stalking tiger is not the difficult business that it is imagined to be. For one thing there is less expenditure of time and labour, than in following a stag or gaur, for another its habit of retiring into shaded covers close by streams or pools enables the gun to pick up tracks without much difficulty. On the other hand, the element of danger makes the task hazardous. Most aborigine shikaris I met, could mark down a tiger to its lair, but very few indeed attempted to disturb it or risk a shot from the ground. The aborigine is probably without an equal in locating the great cat. With bare feet and divested of garments likely to hinder his progress, and with actions adapted to a beast on the prowl, his approach is noiseless, so that even the tiger's acute senses fail at times to perceive his presence. The hunter who can copy the aborigine's methods, is assured of a close and steady shot, very few however, compare with him and the many have to rest content with shooting the beast in drives.

Wind is about the most important factor in the well being of game tribes. It is the principal channel of communication that announces the intruder long before he is visible. It is again the means that enables them to fix the character of the foe whose presence has been detected by sound or sight, but whose identity could not be established merely by hearing or seeing. I have

observed animals dozing or feeding peaceably, start up, spin round sniffing the air and dart away before they had heard or seen the cause of their alarm. What more striking proof could there be, than the behaviour of animals in stopping short to gaze at the stalker heading towards them against the wind! In crawling after stags ringed in by hinds that detected the move, but were uncertain what to make of my recumbent position, I noticed they always stood for a good few minutes and left only when the tell-tale whiff disclosed my identity. So disagreeable is wind in opposing the stalker that he needs indeed, to be sensible of its changes and shifts of current to avoid discovery.

It is necessary before commencing a stalk to note the prevailing direction in which the breeze is blowing and thereafter endeavour to work up or across the current. The plan of conduct is exactly opposite to that adopted in beating which requires the drive to proceed with the wind. The reasons for the contrary methods will be apparent for, in the one, the aim is to drive the quarry from cover and in the other to avoid every means of disturbing it. It often happens that the gun has to contend with an adverse wind at the start and is obliged to veer around and work from an opposite direction from his line of quickest approach, and if that cannot be to postpone the stalk. At the same time, it is well to remember that animals prefer to deflect and inflect in their marches, rather than keep to a straight course and the probabilities are that tracks pointing to particular directions at the beginning of the stalk, will show a different course after going a few hundred paces. Consequently, it is as likely as not that before setting out, the game had moved into positions to which the tracks at the earlier stages of the stalk run counter. This works both ways, to aid the stalker where the deflection is across the wind or to defeat him should it join issue with the current. In practice, it will be found that on cold and windy days animals avoid breezes as much as possible whereas during spells of sultry weather, they conform with the current so as to obtain whatever benefit its dullness offers. The right course to follow in these circumstances, depends a good deal on the gun's or his guide's knowledge of the locality and its resorts and the habits of the quarry. The custom of meandering is common among big game and doubtless owes its habituation to a sense of caution in the matter of self-protection. An animal that moves by devious paths is without doubt better prepared to guard against

ambush from foes, than one which adopts more or less a beeline route of march.

The constant fear of detection by one's own effluvia is embarrassing to the stalker; so that it is worth considering whether no remedy can be found to counteract its effect. The contaminating odour of aborigine shikaris is an asset that enables them to get very near their victims, and with this fact in mind it is possible to disarm suspicion of one's presence by making use of strongly scented grasses and herbs growing in jungle tracts. Personally speaking, I have found the oil of lemon grass and the juice of an aromatic annual efficacious. They need to be rubbed over the clothes and exposed parts of the body, as hands and face. The plants are easily identified in bloom by the strong smell of the flowers, so much so that in walking through the growth, the clothes become scented by their exuberance.

I have read accounts of sport in Africa in which it was stated that smoking during a stalk had no effect on the quarry and it was argued that if the animal could detect the tobacco smoke it was equally certain to wind the sportsman. While admitting that on occasions this may be true, as for instance while heading a stiff breeze in approaching the quarry, the same will not apply generally, and my experience with game in India shows quite the contrary result. I could recount many good chances spoilt during stalks and beats simply because the gun would smoke. This is as true of stalks conducted against or across wind current, as of those working windward, so that exceptions in which the smoke does not scare the beast must be rare. Any doubt the reader has on the point can be easily set at rest by a simple experiment. Supposing we take paper or cloth, the least scented of substances, and burn it, the odour can be detected at some distance. From this it may be imagined what must be the effect of a stronger smelling substance like tobacco.

A good guide is necessary for stalking and if he combines the gift with that of tracking, the gun is fortunate in his possession. An aborigine interested in sport and belonging to the locality is without an equal for the work. A man with a quiet and reserved disposition and unspoiled by attention, is to be preferred to a garrulous and obtrusive individual who accosts the sportsman and makes believe he is indispensable.

Two is the right number for stalking, but guns who keep out for

long or take a spare weapon, need to have an attendant to free the guide from carrying the extra kit in the way of provisions, water bottle and firearms. As a rule, the third man is a body servant charged with looking after the battery, who knows his master's whims and can be relied on in an emergency. A shikari guide invariably carries his weapon, however antiquated and useless it may be as a means of defence, but excluding him the gun should see that the man he takes out is armed with an axe or spear or other weapon equally effective. The party always works in Indian file which is the form least likely to attract notice in moving by the narrow lanes and paths that afford means of egress through jungle cover. The guide takes the lead and the gun follows close at his heels, the attendant keeping behind his master. The stalk should not be hurried nor rendered noticeable by bodily gestures. An animal is quick to discern between the natural and assumed actions of an individual and while looking upon the approach in the one case as that of an ordinary traveller, it will be perturbed by the mannerisms displayed in the other, and become vigilant and decamp.

Animals are possessed with inquisitiveness just like human beings, and anything out of the common of whose identity they cannot make sure, catches their eye and they try to get at its reality. While detected in stalking I have found that stags either remain standing, or sit down to gaze at the passer-by: the Indian bison and wild buffalo invariably keep on their feet: tiger and panther crouch to the ground and relying on their skill at concealment to escape detection, will often allow the gun to come right up before attempting to move: bears stop short to watch. It is only when animals mark what appears to them as strange exhibitions on the part of the stalker that they turn to flee.

The best time to stalk depends on what game the hunter wants to shoot. Sambar ought invariably to be followed in the early morning when they are gorged, move slowly and are less sensitive. The dampness prevailing about dawn infects the atmosphere rendering it a bad conductor and effluvia are slowly disseminated. Again, tracks are fresh and can be picked up with less trouble, than when the day has advanced - a matter of some advantage in dealing with faint marks, often the only clue to the presence of the quarry. The barasinga deer are virtually like sambar in habits and would be stalked at dawn.

To stalk cheetal, both morning and evening are suitable, the gun should reach the haunts as early before sunrise or late after sunset as the light will permit of shooting. They are the hours when the creatures are most absorbed in feeding and stand about in ones and twos, allowing the stalker to approach the stag which at other times is seldom to be got at without the gun being detected by the hinds.

The gaur is about for good parts of the morning and afternoon, and in winter and the rains they keep on the move more or less through the day, so that unless camped far from the haunts, there is no need to hurry. I have come across them at all hours of the day in localities where they were free from disturbance. The beast is easier to approach during the few hours before and after sunrise and soon after sunset, than at other times. These remarks apply also to wild buffalo. In the hot months, while the gaur seeks the repose of shady altitudes, the wild buffalo lies fallow in a swamp or pool.

Custom has fixed the middle of the day when the tiger should be hunted. This is because its partiality for lying up in cool spots near water renders its whereabouts pretty certain. Moreover, its slow and sleepy manner during the hottest hours of the day aids the pursuer in foiling its stealthy moves. It is also apt to snore with gurgling snorts that can be heard at some distance and are a sure sign of its presence. But tiger are often met in early morning stalks, only owing to its low stature and its skill in evading attention ensures it from detection. The eye that can discover the tiger before it has slipped into hiding must be very quick and experienced in spotting jungle objects.

I was once guided to within twenty feet of a lair where three tigers - a tigress and its two pillars or full grown cubs - were stretched fast asleep in a cove inside the bank of a stream. They looked the picture of blissful peace and innocence that subdued the murderous designs with which I had come. The rising bank flanked our approach and we could look down the hollow with perfect safety. I was curious to know what the beasts would do on being aroused suddenly and much to the chagrin of my guide, I coughed gently to awake them. Immediately, the tigress was up and alert, as if it had been all the while conscious of our presence and in a moment bounded through the entrance, turned the corner of the bank and disappeared. In the meantime, the young tigers yawned and stretched, seemingly nonplussed at their parent's

abrupt exit, and prepared to follow. I was now reminded of my business and at once put in a right and left only to find both shots miss. This was not surprising considering the novelty of the scene that made me incline to watch events rather than shoot. But a minute before I had made sure they were already bagged. My experience was also dearly bought for the guide had fulfilled his part of the engagement and was entitled to his reward. The astonishing thing was the behaviour of the tigress. It could not possibly have heard us coming nor seen us, and yet the ejaculation uttered amid the deafening wind that rages during the middle of the day, sufficed to electrify the creature into activity immediately on awakening. Evidently, vigilant beasts acquire a sense of consciousness that renders them sensible, even in a state of repose, to the appearance of danger. I have experienced very much the same sort of feeling while watching over kills of tigers and panthers; having dropped off to sleep weary of the vigil, a creeping sensation has warned me of the beast's presence and I have awoke to find it tackling its meal.

Bears are about in the morning and evening and in unfrequented localities, keep on the move until quite late. They are slow creatures and make a good deal of noise, so provided the effluvia does not alarm them, the hunter can easily get up very close. They are generally met in stalks after sambar in hilly or broken ground. Trackers out to locate game find it easier to mark down bear than other animals.

Compared with the game enumerated, the lesser quarry offer poor sport and few sportsmen make it a point to follow them. However, they are usually come upon during rambles at sunrise or sunset when to court success at the beginning, or compensate for failure at the end of a stalk after nobler game, the gun shoots them to improve the chances of luck or to avoid a blank, as the case may be.

Field antelope, as the black buck, are best stalked during the middle of the day when they are sleepy, lie up in the open and are easy to approach. Panther are almost impossible to walk up, owing to the ease with which they can slip away unnoticed. As a rule, they are chanced upon and shot during casual strolls or stalks.

In the course of these memoirs there have been many occasions to tell about the aborigine tracker. It is also his business to mark down game for his employer in order that he may walk it up or

arrange to beat it out. A dozen men or so start in the small hours of the morning and take up positions of vantage from which animals can be seen retiring to the haunts for the day. The men work in twos, each party selecting a site independent of the others and on sighting the quarry, follow its movements until it has settled down when one of the men returns with the news, while the other keeps an eye on the beast to make certain that it does not shift from the spot. As will be obvious, the men's labours save the gun a good deal of unnecessary stalking as well as make sure of the locality where the quarry is lying up. At the same time, the plan is not as cut and dried as it sounds. Unless the men have taken precautions to conceal their approach, the prescience peculiar with animals soon make them conscious of the intrusion, and they will avoid the paths by and covers to which they usually resort, so that failures are not uncommon. Moreover on settling down, the quarry often gives the watcher the slip or moves on again after the man with the news had started, and the gun finds his excursion ends in a blank or takes him much further than he expected. It is nevertheless an admirable method of procuring sport, especially for the hard-worked district official who has not the leisure to devote to lengthy stalks and is obliged to take whatever chances come his way during his round of work. Most game can be marked down in the way indicated; its success depends entirely on the merits of the trackers.

As with time, the season for stalking has also to be considered; the choice varies between months when trophies are at their best and periods most suitable for the pursuit. In the case of stags, they combine the duration from the latter half of October to the end of February, for although not quite adapted for shooting owing to the prevailing cover, it is the time when all have their horns. In the remaining months, the majority of stags are either shedding their antlers or putting on new growth which are enveloped in velvet and unfitted for keeping, while the few that retain their ornaments, become very retiring and are seldom or never met with during stalks.

The Indian bison and wild buffalo are at their best in winter, but the rains afford better facilities for tracking. The season, however, is inclement and the sportsman runs risks of injuring his health. Most stalking is done in winter and the hot weather months. The pelts of tiger, panther and bear attain perfection in winter, but the

thick cover, especially in localities they haunt, discounts success. On the other hand, they are easy to locate during the hot weather when it is usual to hunt them.

In stalking dangerous game importance attaches to the relative positions which the hunter and the hunted occupy while the shot is fired. This is a matter that ought to be constantly in view, for it is easily lost sight of in the excitement of the moment making it awkward for the gun in case he has to meet an onslaught. In shooting from a height, the gun has undoubted advantages for few beasts will charge an eminence. But raised positions are not always available, and the next best is to fire from the proximity of such shelters, as a trunk, stump or bush, a rock or an ant heap. The gun should also take care in no way to attract the beasts' attention. These are necessary precautions as dangerous beasts have a predilection for charging on being thwarted or wounded, and every noticeable exhibition of the pursuer incites them to attack.

Dangerous game are usually found in hilly or undulating country where a little familiarity with the ground will enable the gun to get into suitable positions for shooting without much delay. On level sites he will have to make the best of the alternative means, such as the shelters afford, in screening his position. Before the days of fire protection when jungles were set alight periodically, stalking was comparatively easy work owing to the burning of cover. Fires were especially welcomed because of the facilities afforded in sighting the quarry and tracking its movements and many conflagrations owed their origins to the attraction of sport. Now, conditions are practically reversed; reserved forests where game mostly resort, are strictly fire-protected so that the undergrowth is preserved. Stalking is therefore exacting work. It may be said that the cover enables the gun to escape detection like it aids the game, but then, the hunter cannot utilise his senses to the same advantage as the quarry and so fails to compete with it in the chase.

Chapter VII

Still Shooting

To lie in wait for game is a form of sport that appeals to few, yet it is the most common one practised by native hunters. The modus operandi is to watch for the quarry from a prepared position dominating the spot where the beast is expected to appear, and to shoot on its drawing near. The shoot is planned for the intervals during which animals visit particular sites; more often it is set apart for the night when they are mostly astir; practically speaking, it is in the hours of twilight that bags are chiefly made.

Various devices are constructed to screen the gun. The one most common, is to build a support called a machan, on the forked trunk or branches of a tree, with sufficient space to seat one or two men, and enclose the structure with leafy twigs. Other forms are, a thorn fence or stone barricade erected over the ground; an excavation fitted with a heavy lid of wood, stone or branches and a chamber hollowed out of a cactus or a bamboo clump. The desideratum is a roomy seat prepared with a view to both concealment and comfort - precautions that not only diminish the chances of detection, but also keep the watcher from fidgeting if he has to sit up till late, especially as there is no means of timing the visits of wild beasts. It must be free from exposure and made to appear natural.

These bowers are usually set up over waterholes, salt licks and puddle pools which animals visit more or less regularly at particular seasons. They are also erected over frequented paths or crossings in the environments [sic]of trees whose flowers and fruits become sources of attraction. They are well adapted for shooting beasts of prey returning to kills or enticed to the site by a live goat or calf.

The construction and positioning of these shikar chambers requires skill and cunning to render them proof against detection. The question of comfort hardly enters into a native's calculation who is accustomed to insert himself in tight places without cramping, but room to assume an easy posture is essential to a sportsman for keeping still. Unless therefore, the work is personally superintended, most shikaris judge of the sahib's requirements by their own standard and rig up an uncomfortable

seat and even, leave the position exposed. It may for instance, be crooked or on a wrong slant, cramped and allowing no freedom for the hands and feet or insufficiently screened - causes which give the occupier a bad time as well as mar success.

In selecting a position avoid placing it on a beaten track or in the direction of wind current flowing towards the spot which is to be the proposed site of observation, or in an open space. Ground structures ought invariably to connect with exterior features such as, an outcrop of rock or soil or woody growth and a hollow or fault. Branches for fencing must be freshly cut and stones for barricading collected from over ground [sic] because their weathering would make the wall appear a fixture. A tree hollow or a cleared space in a clump of cactus or bamboo or bushy growth are excellent covers. Machans require to be stable and are set up on trees, bushes or clumps. The stems should be able to bear the structure with its human freight without shaking or bending, otherwise it will need to be propped with posts. The seat is made by laying shoots cut to size on frame poles fixed to the forked supports, and slanting slightly down the side on which the quarry is expected, in order to graduate aiming at an acute angle. A native cot, canvas or cane chair does almost as well for a seat.

A high machan is a disadvantage in shooting as the sharper angle of fire means a diminishing mark, while a low one would be within reach of tiger or panther attack; the correct height is ten feet above ground. Before occupying the seat, it should be tested to make sure that it will bear the human freight without shaking the branches and also that it does not creak. The watcher ought to edge about the enclosure to see there is ample room and effect any alterations necessary to his comfort, and try the loopholes left in the screen if they will do to look through and shoot. For late sitting there should be no overhead cover and overhanging leaves and twigs likely to shadow and interfere with aiming should be removed. A couple of fat cushions adds immensely to comfort and in night watching, a thick spread is needed to lie upon during hours that the spot is deserted. Failure to see to these little matters hinders the gun at the crucial moment and spoils the chances of success. It is difficult to imagine how the merest shift inside a machan is reflected on the twigs of unsteady branches; the vibration is sufficient to catch the eye of the approaching beast and deviate it from its course. Similarly, the least strain is liable to react

on any defective piece of wood utilised in the construction, causing it to creak and make the quarry shy. In the same way, any part of a branch dangling over the gun, quite unobtrusive by daylight will cast a shadow to affect seriously the vision at night. Some shikaris are adepts in fixing up the structures, and I have known them to be so cleverly hidden that it needed detective powers to discover their positions.

The human effluvia is the chief obstacle to this method of shooting which will show how important it is to have the bower erected in a position where it will not be disclosed by wind. The prevailing direction of the breeze during the day is no criterion for judging of its course in the night. As a matter of fact, atmospheric currents become fitful after the sun is down, and only men accustomed to experience the shifts of wind at nights, can point to a suitable spot where scent would be unavailing.

The antiquated weapons with which native shikaris are wont to shoot, compel them to prepare for very close shots and to check effluvia they resort to methods for smearing the body with various antidotes, such as mixtures of cattle dung and puddle and clay and ashes, or decoctions of scented gums and juices of aromatic plants. They say the fluids close the pores of the skin, while their smell displaces bodily odour and deceives the beast. Many instances are on record of animals shot at the muzzle's point and my own adventures recall visits to salt-licks and waterholes where sambar, cheetal, gaur and panther had been shot nearly touching the flintlocks. But the preparations are also efficacious in keeping off mosquitoes that torment the watcher. I have tried applying crude perfumes to check the effect of effluvia as well as the onslaught of biting insects, and there could be no doubt about their effect, for animals passed within a few feet of me. My remedies were the oils of lemon grass and sandalwood and the juices of aromatic plants such as the tobacco, the tulsi (ocimum) and the kara (daedalacanthus roseus).

Wild beasts are regular about their functions and marked changes in their habits alternate so precisely with the seasons, that a naturalist can make pretty sure of the localities where particular animals may be found at specified periods or even hours. But considering how much they are guided by intuition, he can never rely on their visits corresponding as to time. Waterholes are frequented during the hot weather and salt-licks and puddle pools

in winter. So also fruit trees especially the mahua, become while they are bearing resorts for the tribes of deer and antelope and bear and after them prowl the carnivora. Under the circumstances, it seems quite simple to sit still at one of the frequented sites and await their visits to obtain a bag. But those who have had experience in sitting up over game know differently. The prevision with which wild animals are gifted warns them when danger is eminent [sic], so that with astonishing acuteness they either avoid putting in an appearance while the risk is greatest, or exercise more than usual caution in approaching their haunts. Therefore, the watcher can never tell even by knowing the habits of game, how long he may be kept waiting before he sees the quarry, besides often his vigil ends in blanks.

Quite apart from sense and sensibility, a wave of heat or cold, a sudden spurt or lull in the breeze, the fall of a dry branch or heavy fruit, the shifting of a monkey or bird on a branch, the effulgent burst of the moon from a canopy of dark clouds or the luminous transit of a meteor are among the causes for delaying or postponing the visits of beasts to the resorts.

I can vouch for at least three incidents showing how game is disturbed by influences enumerated above. I was watching over the kill of a tiger; my Gond companion heard it arrive and warned me of its presence. The time was early for a tiger to come, and it crouched down by a clump of grass a few yards from its victim. In the transition of deceptive light that precedes the moon's illumination, its form appeared to me as part of the cover by which it sat, though apparently my man could distinguish it all right. A jungle was burning in the distance and with the passing of daylight, the breeze veered round in our direction and a hot blast of air from the fire spread through the valley. The tiger got up, walked across our front and disappeared. It could not possibly have scented us, otherwise it would not have waited so near, nor exposed itself by striding past the clearance which our machan overlooked.

On another occasion, the scene was a puddle pool where a solitary stag came to roll in the early morning. A few paces distant stood a stone-apple tree that has a heavy fruit with a hard shell. It was a frosty morning, which was more reason to expect the beast. In the silence of the hour, I made sure of its cautious steps as they drew nearer to the spot. Then its dark figure appeared in the dim light under the trees and I waited for it to get clear of their shade.

While in this state of expectancy, a fruit dropped on to the sheet of rock cropping up below the tree making a crackling report and at once the wary creature turned and fled.

In the other instance, I was watching for the return of a panther to its meal. The beast turned up soon after sunset, but instead of coming to eat, it got behind a bush standing near the spot and sat eyeing the kill from the shelter. To shoot through the cover would have been risking a miss, while there was every probability of its leaving the shelter sooner or later, and I was content to wait. A beautiful meteor now lit up the sky followed by a loud report. The panther immediately vanished and did not appear again. The occurrence relates to the third week of November 1910, and the meteor was the subject of notice in the daily papers.

These are purely coincident examples, nevertheless they point to the importance with which uncommon events are regarded by the game tribes. It is rare for a tiger or panther to be shot at a frequented watering or feeding resort or puddle pool. In my many watches over these sites, I only once saw a tiger drink at a waterhole. Also, while watching for other game, I once shot a panther over a saltlick. However, I know of a few cases of tigers bagged in the environs of mahua trees by native shikaris who were sitting up to shoot deer and antelope that came to feed on the flowers; moreover, an aborigine hunter shot one over a puddle pool frequented by sambar and pig. The paucity of cases does not explain that tiger and panther avoid the common resorts, but rather that owing to their habit of readily taking advantage of every bit of cover, they pass unnoticed in the dull light of the moon. At times after night watches, on looking over the sites in the morning, I have been surprised to find pugs of tiger and panther that had come and gone close to where I had sat without my knowing.

In shooting tiger and panther from enclosures, the usual practice is to sit up over a kill or a live goat or calf and watch for the beast's return to its meal, or trust to the victim attracting it. Panthers hardly take account of scent but rely on sight and sound for warnings. On the other hand, tigers utilise all their senses. A panther does not mind if its kill is handled or moved in its absence. A tiger however, will not come if it has the least suspicion on those scores. A panther is ravenous about its meal. But a tiger eats with relish. These distinguishing traits show what to expect in dealing with their respective kills.

The site over which it is proposed sitting up should be open to the sky, and if the watcher is going to keep up till late or through the night, he should consider the position of tall stems and boughs growing at the site in relation with the moon's circuit in order to form an idea how their shadows will effect [sic] the spot. This is a necessary precaution in sitting up over tiger and panther kills, as often the beasts are wary enough to appear when the spot is in shade rendering aim uncertain.

The matter of light is all-important in night shooting. Although planned with a view to close aim, it is surprising how even at the shortest range and with a bright moon, the light fails to depict the object clearly enough to present an accurate mark. Native shikaris who are clever in finding their way in the dark and who attempt very close shots, seldom commence their watch before dawn in the morning or prolong it after twilight in the evening. They are pothunters pure and simple, and without scruples as to age or sex of the quarry. As a rule, they are content with a victim and on securing it, seldom care to stop on. Their bags usually comprise females or immature males, which are generally the first to make for the resorts. Trophies worth having (e.g. tiger, panther, sambar) are discriminating about their visits and appear after the common stock have come and gone, and so are not often shot. On the other hand, sportsmen care only for the trophy so that their vigils have to extend through the night, and light becomes essential in ensuring success. Accordingly, it is necessary to select the period of the moon's greatest brilliancy, which occurs during the ten days, or so that she is from three-quarters full to one-quarter on the wane.

Various means have been devised for shooting in the dark such as, diamond and phosphorescent sights, and common and electric lamps. But with the exception of the last, the inventions do not answer in practice. To take the case of the sights, it will be obvious that the importance of vision is less a matter of seeing along the barrel and more a performance with the mark. This is why they fail, for while visible in the immediate gaze of the watcher, they do not illuminate the mark which remains obscure. The lamp in common use is a form of the hurricane lantern, and my own experience of its success is limited to a single case; the beast was a comparatively young panther and its lean condition explained its daring the light to finish its meal. I have heard of several instances of native shikaris bagging panther and even tiger and sambar, by

aid of pot-lamps, but could never find out if the victims were young or lean. A young and indiscreet beast would overcome shyness in seeing anything strange near its food, and so would one that was desperately hungry; whereas a wary or well-fed creature would fight shy of the spot.

The pot-lamp is a device for reflecting light in jets. It is a simple contrivance made out of an earthen pot bored with holes and containing a lamp inside. The radiation of light is feeble, but as it resembles somewhat the glow of a luminary such as a star, the effect succeeds better than the blaze of an exposed lamp. A lantern can be made to shed light in the same way by covering the globe with brown paper having meshes an inch or so apart. The lights are placed on the farther side of the kill facing the gun in order that, on tackling its meal, the animal comes between the lamp and the watcher and shows up in the glare.

The electric lamp is by far the most satisfactory, and is worked on the principle of a switch light. It is attached to a pole or branch over the bait and connects with a battery in the enclosure with the watcher who switches on the light when the beast is under it. The sudden burst of flame puzzles the animal and for the moment it becomes a fixed and clear target for a shot. A few sprigs bunched round the lamp keep it from being too visible, thus escaping the beasts' notice.

Many sportsmen decry this method of shooting. But I think it has as good a claim to be classed as sport if not a better one, than taking up a position in a tree and getting the beast driven past it. It offers a premium on a man's patience and self-control, as well as on his acuteness of seeing, hearing and observing, and develops all these faculties, while no such qualities are demanded of the man who sits to shoot in a beat. In my opinion as a form of sport, it comes next to stalking. It is the best that could be devised for panther and man-eating tigers. Even when adopted for other animals, no good sportsman would dream of shooting immature stags or bulls as natives do. He would naturally try for a trophy but would soon find to his cost that it is not as easy as it seems to bag an old stager seated from an enclosure, whatever the attractions of the spot. Tiger also are seldom accounted for by sitting up and among the few successes, even fewer owe their fall to prearranged effort. As a rule, the tiger's appearance on the scene is purely accidental, probably the result of a hunt or stalk of its own

after game which it expects to find at the resort where the gun has posted himself.

But these silent watches over game are useful also as a means of physiological study. No lover of Nature who has spent a night in the depths of a game haunted jungle, could have failed being impressed by the phenomenum [sic] that marks the change from day. The sounds awaking into existence as the shades of darkness spread, vibrate with a fervour so different from the medley of noises familiar to the ears. The transition from the general occupation of the day to the distinctive vitality of the night, introduces a feeling of awe and creates thoughts of a spiritual world whose dominant elements had sprung into life in the gloom. The legion of diverse notes resounding through the silence is no empty babel, but evidences of varied activity that can be construed into language. They furnish the cypher to scenes being enacted all round, so that one versed in jungle lore can picture them as clearly as if he were witnessing a performance. The blast and counterblast of baritone notes rung out by the deer express both challenge and warning, but only experience can tell to which of the causes the call may be ascribed. The tiger's roar at greeting the twilight rumbling through the distance means joy, while its resonant cough denotes contentment after a successful stalk, as well as pleasure on meeting with its spouse. The monkey in the boughs and the peacock on its perch signal by scent the approach of the larger carnivora, whereas the owl and the nightjar confirm their presence at sight by hissing shrieks of defiance and so on, a vocabulary could be prepared of the different noises and their meanings. Speaking truly, even the woods take part in the chorus by responding to the refreshing calm of the night, and indulge in lively airs which contribute mainly to the siren notes so common a feature of the night.

Quiet intervals occur that are due as much as not to a feeling of security among the game tribes. Thus, animals assume their noiseless way when they fear no disturbance, likewise on apprehending danger, they lie low and excepting the occasional note of warning that all understand, there is no stir. A stampede is caused by sudden infection of the sensitive organs and as a rule, is started by an over nervous creature.

Although the sounds appear to issue from all over the wilds, there are nevertheless parts over which the laws of the jungles have decreed neutrality, where tumult, riot and outrage are tabooed.

They are the environs of common resorts where animals slake their hunger or thirst or engage in their pastime, such as, watering holes, salt-licks, swinging floors and gymnasium grounds whose sanctity is respected by beasts of prey; excepting of course the wild dog which is a vermin and too despicable a creature to be bound by laws.

The noises are not the only fascinating part of the role. Looking upon the moonlit scenes the watcher is entertained by luminous displays that suggest a conjuror's wand rather than real effects of light and shade. He sees forms emerge from nowhere, gambol about and disappear without disclosing their origin; visions of familiar objects dance before him with annoying frequency; fixtures which he knows too well to mistake, acquire size and shape that the mind fails to credit and elusive figures chase each other with amazing regularity. He finds it hard to penetrate the guises that only eyes trained to the delusive light can determine with any certainty. He is hopelessly wrong and looses off his weapon at beasts that turn out to be phantoms, and so subjects himself to laughter and annoyance.

I have fired at the shadow of a bush in mistake for a panther, so natural a form indeed, did the imitation of light and shade assume owing to the speckled rays caused by the leaves. Once also, I shot a buffalo calf that was straying at night, believing it to be a bear. It was while returning from a benighted excursion with two Bhil guides. Our way lay through hilly country, and in descending a gorge the men noticed a dark patch on the bank above us. We waited and the beast began to feed and in pulling at the grass and herbs, dislodged lumps of earth and stones that began to roll down the slope. This made the men positively sure that it could be nothing else, but a bear digging away at a root, and induced me to shoot. Both guides were experienced shikaris, and the instance shows that even the practised eyes and ears of aborigines are liable to play false in the deceptive light appearing under forest growth.

On another occasion I was sitting up with a friend when we heard a tiger coming towards us. The brute seemed pleased and growled and grunted as it walked up slowly. We were sure of it as it had to pass by an opening a few yards from us, to get its drink. My friend, who was a novice at the sport, declared he could see the tiger before the beast had reached the opening, and fired in spite of my dissuasion. The tiger bounded away with a roar. On

examining the spot in the morning, it was found that he had aimed at what must have appeared a striped figure cast by shadows from bamboo stems growing near, while the tiger was about six yards from where the bullet had lodged.

By daylight, the watch though not quite so interesting as in the night, enables a closer inspection of the animal, so that a careful observer can mark almost every tremor of a beast that is near him and, should it be agitated, he can find out the cause of the excitement from its behaviour. Thus, a strange noise without a flow of scent will cause the creature to contract and expand its ears in the direction of the sound's origin. Again, it can discern from the intonation, whether the sound is of little or no consequence and undeserving of further notice, or that it is uncanny and requires to be investigated, or that its evil character is convincing and the listener must depart. The twitching of the tail implies an anxious moment due to uncertainty and, under the circumstances, no two beasts will act alike. The thrill of excitement that makes the body quaver as if it were charged with electricity, points to an excess of fear, such as would result by the unexpected vision of a murderous enemy at close quarters; the sight in most cases holds the beast spell-bound for a few seconds. Knocking the forefeet on the ground explains that the animal is in a temper at being foiled in its object, as would occur when it saw, or heard or scented a foe on its path while going to feed or drink; the rapping is also a signal of warning to approaching beasts to beware of the spot. Squatting or crouching by deer and carnivora in the presence of danger may mean, either that the beast is confused about how to act, or that it is unwilling to move out and accommodates itself to the surroundings in order to escape detection.

These few examples will show the kind of information that may be gathered by keeping in close touch with the denizens of a jungle. To me the attempts to unravel the mysteries in which the actions and movements of wild beasts are veiled have always been of absorbing interest. Many and many is the time that I have sat up watching through days and nights over haunts and resorts to find out something of the ways of game in the localities under my charge.

Chapter VIII

Shooting

Game shooting combines the education of the senses with the development of the physical powers and its success culminates in the aim. Everyone who can handle a weapon aspires to be a good shot and many claim the distinction, but very few indeed possess it. The accomplishment belongs to the individual and is therefore neither common property, nor the exclusive privilege of a specialized body of shooters. Nervous temperaments seem hopelessly unfitted to succeed and yet, good game shots are to be found among excitable and eccentric natures. Practice on the butts may improve aim, but often fails to prove a success on the shikar grounds; moreover the ascendancy acquired diminishes or ceases with the training. Proficiency springs from initiative so that the sportsman who can seize it at the opportune moment becomes the game shot par excellence.

Bad shooting is oftener than we imagine the result of straining at one's weapon, which springs from a sense of slowness in decision. The man whose eyes are rivetted on the prize will cover it promptly the weapon comes up to the shoulder and the mere glance over the barrel adjusts it with the desired mark, rendering the moment opportune to shoot. But should he fail to fix on the spot, rather than delay in shifting about the weapon, the sure course would be to lower it until he can fire with confidence. To keep nursing the rifle at the present, in trying to get it on to the mark, is almost sure to end in a miss or bad shot.

As a rule, perfect shots are mostly found among enterprising spirits, but the marksman at game is born and not made, so that the man who calculates on his aim and picks his mark, is seldom met with. The importance of true shooting is manifest at a time when a dangerous beast gets away wounded and has to be followed. In nine cases out of ten the gun will blame himself for not having done better. He is uncertain of the mark where the wound was inflicted and uses such epithets, as "If only I had waited another moment", or "If only I had kept steady", and so on with "ifs" and "onlys" that make his case pathetic, whereas in fact, the aim being calculated to kill or disable outright, the alternative warrants no pleas for excuses.

I can recall a discussion on the subject with the veteran sportsman, Mr. Thompson. In his opinion, a bullet that did not lodge on the mark aimed at, was a bad shot no matter how well it might be placed otherwise. He maintained that provided the sportsman knew what to do, he could always rely on the prospect of a single good chance with the game he encountered and it entirely rested with him to seize the opportunity for a sure aim. But should it slip, the gun would do well to withhold fire and try again instead of attempting pot-shots. The advice though very true, is admittedly hard to accept, especially nowadays when game shooting is restricted, while there is little or no margin in time or means to prolong the pursuit. The majority of men in search of game are naturally desirous to make a bid for success and will not be deterred from firing, however poor the chance of obtaining the prize. There is no denying the venture occasionally accounts for bags, still the fact remains that it involves risk shots and so is an inducement to promiscuous shooting which is the cause of animals getting away wounded oftener than need be. Moreover, there can be little satisfaction to oneself to feel that the bag was due to random firing, rather than to deliberate planning and aiming.

The accomplished shooter reflects on the result of his aim and however much he may be tempted, will not be hurried into committing himself by firing a mistimed shot. He has no reason to put forward excuses should the aim unexpectedly fail to bring about the desired effect. Of examples in the chapter on "animal cures for wounds", there are two that show very clearly the exceptional course of ascertained hits. In the one case of a tiger, the express bullet failed in its missive, causing a surface wound by setting up on the mark leading into the heart. In the other of a bear, the creature's tenacious vitality gave it a lease of life that seemed incredible from the terribly fatal character of the wound. In yet another instance, a panther hit by an express bullet below the cranium on the right side of the face survived, the ball set up outside cracking the skull bones and the beast got away. It was retrieved and killed two days afterwards. The gun being uncertain of the mark where he had aimed blamed himself for shooting badly though as a matter of fact, the shot was well placed.

It is necessary in pursuing dangerous game to take possession of the first position that promises a coign of vantage for shooting, as well as for defence. It is a matter that cannot be lightly regarded.

As we know the best of shots fail at times to take effect, while the vitality and power for mischief, which some beasts display, surpass any defence that the hunter can put up. The man who fires from a more or less guarded position, such as the top of a mound or rock, or the screen of a bush or clump, has less to fear, than one who remains unguarded. A height enables the gun to determine his shot, which the man on a level with the beast cannot always do owing to the intervening cover. A favourable situation moreover, inspires confidence that is an incentive to good shooting, but the same cannot be said of a position without an advantage. It creates a feeling of misgiving that reacts on the aim, and although in a moment of resolution he might shoot well at the crisis, the chances do not inveigh against taking precautions.

A successful shot is the gun's reward while one that fails to kill weighs on him as a penalty. The chase in the former leads to a satisfactory finish: the latter aggravates the occasion and may end in disappointment, or even seriously affect the issue in the case of a dangerous victim. The result becomes speculative and only an experienced sportsman can tell with any certainty whether the wound will drop the victim within a reasonable interval of its infliction, or cause the result to drag out with little hope of retrieving the creature. The gun has now to recall his visions of the creature's behaviour after being shot, for its gestures indicate the character of its injury.

Generally speaking, all victims lift their tails on the bullet's impact, varying the elevation according to the severity of the wound. In mortal injuries, the tail is usually raised above the line of the spine and almost to twenty-five degrees with it. But this by itself will not determine how far the victim will go before dropping; something more is needed to ascertain its probable fate, and the emotions started by the infliction of the shot furnish the clue. A wound in the region of the heart produces a visible shivering fit that cramps the body rendering the limbs out of control, so that the creature wobbles or dangles in its tracks. This is a sure sign of the end being near.

A shot through the lungs heaves the forequarters, in an effort at a deep breath implying the victim was winded. The flanks swell and shrink like a pair of bellows that indicate short career. Whereas in case of a lease of life or possible escape, the spasms are not noticeable, while the victim may even display exceptional vitality, attesting to a miss, except for the tail signal having recorded a hit.

The creature often vomits blood after going some distance.

In a stomach wound, the body is compressed and appears convexed and the victim dangles if it is going to drop, otherwise it tears forward. Small beasts, such as panther, chinkara and barking-deer, often bounce up from the shock like a rubber ball. Bleeding is usually checked by the intestines or their contents stopping the wound, but it continues internally and sometimes passes out through the anus. A wound in the loins through the liver or kidney causes the hindquarters to depress and is undoubtedly very painful; deer, antelope and bison nearly always squeal and tiger, panther and bear utter a moaning growl. The victim rarely stirs from the spot where it was shot.

These are the common instances of victims with mortal wounds being able to get away and though in most cases the suspense is confined to brief intervals, nevertheless it shows how good shots are open to suspicion. Excepting bear and the one painful utterance of the loin wound, beasts seldom speak to shots that end fatally within some seconds.

It will be obvious that the remarks relative to each case apply to single shots, as well as, to injuries of individual organs. The number of times an animal is hit must inevitably accelerate the end and the same is true of wounds to two or more vital parts as for example, the heart and the lung, or the stomach and the liver.

The shots that kill or effectually disable are those involving the heart, brains, neck, spinal cord, lungs, liver, kidney, intestines and the rare instance of two broken legs. Of these, fatal results follow quickly from wounds of the heart, brains, neck, liver and kidney, while in the cases of the rest, the end is more or less prolonged. A mystery usually hangs over wounds affecting only the lungs; their vitality for sustaining life even on being badly torn, places the issue in doubt up to the last. Therefore, it is difficult to express an opinion on the chances of retrieving a victim that has got away with a lung shot. Considering their function that renders them a desirable mark and their affinity to the heart - the common focus of aim whose diversion invariably affects the investing organs – it is safe to say that more animals escape with lung wounds and fewer with those inflicted elsewhere. I could name many instances of animals getting away with lungs shot through by express bullets, but a few from among cases exhibiting exceptional vitality, in order to emphasise the wounds' character, will do.

A panther shot with a .577 magnum express in the lungs, escaped some distance and made a good fight before it was killed. It was found on dissecting it that the first shot had shattered part of both lungs. A blue bull with a very similar wound, struggled to its feet and escaped into hilly jungle. It was recovered on the second day very much alive, having gone over six miles of difficult country. Once, I chanced upon a bear wounded in the lungs from an express rifle whose owner was shooting about twelve miles from my camp. Apparently, the bear had been wounded three days before and was dying when I came upon the scene.

The stomach shot is equally uncertain of effect. Sportsmen however, seldom have occasion to fire at the belly of a beast, and the question of its propriety as a desirable mark does not acquire anything like the importance of lung wounds. I may instance its effect on two tigers whose resisting powers as a class, are small in comparison with those of animals generally, so that the beast succumbs readily to mortal wounds. They were hit by soft lead bullets from .577 magnum express rifles; both went on for about two furlongs before falling. When marked down an hour later, they showed fight in spite of being scarcely able to move.

A shot in the brains very rarely stops short of immediate effect and I know but one instance of a bear managing to escape for a while with its scalp partly torn off by an express bullet. It was found on the following morning in a stupor and easily killed. The bullet hit over the ear, passing just under the scalp above the neck and exposing the brain.

It seems incredible that a beast shot through the heart should be able to move. Still, instances of victims making the effort to get away are by no means uncommon, but they invariably drop stone dead in their tracks.

Once a panther was enclosed in a beat for jungle fowl and turned up over a rise below which I waited for birds flighting down the slope. It had a clear view of my position and instead of trying to escape, became curious and sat down on its haunches like a cat to gaze at me. I was quite unprepared for big game and my rifle lay empty, and so it was my intention to let it pass on; but the creature persisted in sitting and staring until the temptation to bag it could not be resisted. I exchanged the shotgun for the rifle and all the while it never took its eyes off me. My shot in the shoulder went home, making it plunge forward and come straight for me in

the spasmodic manner already described, which made me certain that it was hard hit. I stood up to receive it with the second barrel and just then, it collapsed without so much as a quiver, within three paces of me. The ball had traversed the heart and lungs and passed out of the right side and yet the, creature struggled over the intervening space of about a hundred feet. On coming up, the beaters discovered two cubs which had been trying to follow the parent; and their presence accounted for the panther's singular behaviour.

A shot in the loin and into the kidney or liver drops the beast almost instantly, and very much the same effect follows a wound in the spine, only the victim in the first case soon expires, while in the latter, it may live for days or even months.

The neck shot is very fatal and I have never known a beast so wounded go beyond a few paces.

Wounds that deprive an animal of the use of any two feet are purely accidental. The victim is permanently incapacitated and can only tumble about and await its doom. Such occurrences are however rare and those in my recollection relate to two panthers and a cow bison. The panthers were shot by friends as they were standing broadside while returning to finish their kills, and though with identical wounds, the incidents relate to separate occasions and different men. The creatures were victims of defective elevation, for the shots intended for the shoulders had struck low below the chest and broken their forefeet above the elbows. They could do no more, than roll and tumble about the spot, and on being retrieved some hours later were full of spirits for mischief.

In the case of the cow bison, the wound was more or less intentional as the Mahommedan forest ranger who ate beef, wanted the halal performed before the creature should die. He aimed at one of the front feet and the ball - a solid one from a Snider - hit the near foreleg at about the knee-joint and passing at a slant under the body, caught the off hind-foot below the ham. The double injury rendered the victim more helpless, than the man had intended, and suited his purpose even better. But despite its unfortunate condition, none dared to hold the cow for fear of being ripped, so the ranger had poles cut and with them his stalwart aborigines pinned the beast down to the ground, enabling his Mahommedan orderly to perform the bismillah ceremony and to cut its throat.

The golden rule after firing a shot is to keep silent and still; the caution is paramount in dealing with dangerous beasts. The seconds that follow a shot are critical moments and need to be awaited in absolute quiet because of the fateful issues they involve. The least attempt at disturbance is not only likely to change the course of events, but might seriously embroil the gun in difficulties, the more so when it is a case of meeting a fierce beast on its own ground - easily an incentive for attack.

Big game do not always turn tail on the report of a rifle, nor are they disposed to fly at the mere sight of fear, and unless assured of the evil character, they disdain to depart. Not infrequently, beasts in the toils of danger will hesitate before they retire. Some persist in keeping their ground and will leave only if forced by events: others move off slowly, appearing to regard a precipitate departure as undignified: many are resourceful in assuming attitudes that accord with surroundings, trusting to escape notice by the deception. To give an instance of this, I fired at and missed a stag that disappeared so suddenly as to call for closer examination. On going up to look about the spot where it was last seen, my Bhil guide espied it seated on the ground and pointed to it repeatedly, but I could not make sure and in trying to get nearer, it sprang up and bounded off, leaving me too surprised to shoot. The beast sat with the head tilted over the shoulder presenting a figure that could hardly be distinguished from the protruding rocks about the place in colour, shape or size. Indeed, so well was it disguised that the horns gave the finishing touch in showing like dry stalks sticking out of a crack and though barely fifty feet from the creature, I could not make certain of its identity.

Animals possess a strong sense of inquisitiveness and prefer to stop and investigate the cause of the alarm rather than break away. But the tendency is only noticeable on occasions when there is an element of ambiguity to detain the beast longer than necessary, and arises from the feeling of unwillingness to be forced which is a feature of the human character. With animals however, the action is the result of illusion more than resolution, and if it were not for instinct governing the course of conduct, the habit would lead to extermination. Thus it is, that they grope into the jaws of danger with unconcern, or again, they behave so unexpectedly under fire, even when wounded, that experienced hunters are puzzled. In shooting, simple actions of beasts acquire prominence and deserve notice.

An animal shot at or disturbed will want to flee the second time from the report of a gun or at the sight of an intruder: so will one that is sensitive to excess. But unsophisticated beasts are not easily effected by either cause or those insensible to fear. For very much the same reasons, a beast that keeps on the scene after detecting its pursuer's identity, will prefer to depart on the sound of firearms, even should it not be the target of aim; because whatever inducement compelled it to remain, the report removes any doubt as the means to ensure safety. In the circumstances, a fierce beast wounded is predisposed to attack, as it naturally attributes the misfortune to the intrusion. But it is often indiscriminate in the choice of a victim, which explains why followers are attacked while sportsmen escape. A very appropriate example is an event that befell my ranger.

He was riding through a reserve guided by a Gond fire watcher and on nearing a river, they saw fresh pugs of a tiger that had left the path just before they came up. He dismounted and hitched the pony to a sapling, and with the guide went on cautiously to the stream in order to cut off the tiger's retreat. No sooner were they clear of the lane leading to the water's edge than they saw the tiger a few score paces up the bed about to cross, and seemingly unconscious of their approach. The ranger fired from the shelter of the bank without divulging his presence and mortally wounded the beast. The tiger charged back and coming out on the spot where it had turned off the path, forthwith seized and killed the pony, then went on a few paces and died. It is certain the beast had heard the sound of the riding and had slipped aside to avoid an encounter. But being overtaken and wounded without exactly knowing the direction from where the shot came, it connected the injury with the riding and returning to retaliate, saw only the pony and wreaked its fury on the poor beast.

Concomitantly, a fierce beast wounded after it has made sure of its pursuer but with no intention to attack, will be incited to do so should its notice be arrested by gestures or restlessness on the part of the gun or his attendant. The creature regards the obtrusion as in the way of adding insult to injury and is goaded to action.

I once came upon a family of three panthers on the scarped tongue of a plateau, so that except over the top by which I had come, there was no other means of escape from the spur. Only one panther was visible and at the time, I had no idea there were others,

as they lay quite hidden among rocks by the cliff. The creature I saw lay basking in the open and never stirred, but the twitching of its tail made it clear that my presence had been detected. Taking it for a solitary beast, I barred the exit by selecting a stump standing on the side of the neck to screen my position. The panther was facing me at an awkward slant and I could fix only on the right shoulder for a suitable mark. My shot found its billet, but instead of killing outright it made the beast spin round and round in trying to bite at the wound until its ambit took a sweep over the bank and it went down three hundred feet of precipice and was killed. I kept still and it never occurred to the beast to attack though it saw me seated within easy reach on a lower plane.

But the shot disturbed the two panthers lying among the rocks and I became aware of their presence now for the first time. They got up and glancing round hurriedly, stood staring at their companion. Soon its fall alarmed them, making them back away from the cliff and come nearer to me without the least suspicion of my proximity. I already had one covered with the remaining barrel and fired when it got on broadside, killing it on the spot. The other was shaken by the start, but seeing me it crouched to the ground at once and gleamed at me angrily, so that there was no mistaking it meant mischief. The last shot had left both barrels empty and I was obliged to refill the breach, but much as I tried to do it without appearing obtrusive, the panther never for a moment averted its gaze. It sat like the first panther though closer, and I again aimed for the mark that had before proved effective. The beast went over in a somersault, recovered itself and charged in my direction intent on attack. With its vision blurred by the tumble and the crushing blow from the shot it mistook the bearing and closed on another stump at the cliff's edge, a few feet from where I stood and the impetus carried it over the scarp. I was haunted by a presentiment of what was coming and did not stir, waiting to make sure at the muzzle's point, but as it turned out, a second shot was not necessary.

I had very much the same experience with a bear. We, that is my guide and I, disturbed it in digging a root on the slope of a hill which we were ascending. It turned as soon as it winded us and crouched down meaning business. We were about sixty feet directly below the creature before we saw it, so that it had the advantage in the matter of position for a charge. I hit it in the chest

within the horseshoe, and the beast crashed down the slope like a boulder. We kept positively still by the shelter of a bamboo clump and it brushed past us without attempting to turn: it stopped lower down and looked up at us angrily, then in making an effort to re-ascend the slope, it suddenly lay down, quite dead.

The gun's slightest diversion often gives a wounded beast the lead to attack. I had an experience with a bison as the result of having to move accidentally in my position. I almost walked into the creature, as it came feeding slowly on the very same path, and hearing it before it could detect me I turned off to a nullah nearby and sat in a depression on the side of its bank. The beast walked up unsuspiciously and when it was within thirty paces, I fired and dropped it. Somehow, I was not holding my rifle firmly and the shock of a heavy discharge made me reel, so that in trying to keep on the precarious foothold, my arms flung about automatically and disclosed my position. The gestures incited the creature to a supreme effort, and although hard hit and dying it struggled to its feet and dashed towards me. But faced with the formidable peril of being hurled down the nullah, it swerved off from quite close and ran along the high bank until checked by a bamboo clump growing on its side where it fell and expired.

In opposite cases in which victims have no suspicion of the gun's proximity, the sites where they were wounded often become the scenes of struggles until they expire or walk away to die a short distance off. The stop as a rule, is sufficient for rigor mortis to set in and in the case of fierce beasts, the futile raging in which they indulge, aggravates the wound and hastens exhaustion and cramp that cause collapse. One evening, Mr. Thompson and I were strolling through a reserve, when we saw a bear in the distance coming along the path in our direction. The wind was blowing from the bear to us and my experienced friend made sure it would come right on to us, so cautioning me to step aside into a thicket, he slipped off the path and stood by a bushy sapling ready to shoot. The beast walked up unsuspectingly and as soon as it was broadside on, he fired raking the lungs. We did not stir and for a few minutes, the bear howled and rolled over and over on the path until it died almost at his foot. Had the bear had the least suspicion of our presence so close to its struggles, it must surely have attacked or bolted, but unconscious of how it came by the wound, the beast ended its life on the spot.

In another instance, I was out before it was light with a Gond shikari to stalk sambar. It was too dim for shooting even after we had gone a mile and the man suggested our waiting on the bank of a stream which we were nearing, until the haze lifted. We selected a spot where the river elbowed and sat in a nook half way down its steep bank and so commanded the approaches for distances up and down its length. It was interesting to watch the effect of the elusive light on the sandy stretch with the waters rippling over a stony channel grown with rushes appearing as a streak in the centre of the wide bed. We could hear footsteps of the denizens dwelling in the reserve arrive and depart after their morning drink, and the monkeys beginning to be restless in the trees as they impatiently awaited the coming of the light, while the chorus of catcalls told that the peafowl were already awake. We sat and listened for half an hour, the last few minutes of which had ushered in daylight with the rapidity peculiar of Indian mornings. Peafowl were alighting in the river bed to disport themselves on the sand and the shrill note of a hind sambar echoed through the distance as a signal to warn the denizens, and immediately followed the roar of a tiger greeting the morning. The sound oscillated through the gorge in all its pent up force and as it rose and fell with the turns and twists marking the stream's course, the shikari made sure the beast was walking down the bed towards us. I was intensely excited; as our position was sheltered, we decided to stay there and watch for the beast, and I lay down to be ready for a steady shot. In a few minutes, we saw it appear in the distance still venting its voice in tones of pleasure; it was on the opposite side leisurely walking along the sandy bed and some time elapsed before it appeared on our front across a space of twenty-five yards, with its right flank facing us. I aimed at the shoulder while it passed slowly soliloquising on the grandeur of a summer's morning. As we found afterwards, the bullet hit very high; I had made the common mistake of shooting from a lying position, in not gripping the barrel tight enough. The tiger, with the rapidity of a machine, reared and plunged about the spot, convoluting in attempts to bite at the wound. It was unsafe to risk a shot and unmask our position as we were on the ground with a furious beast, and I waited for the scene to slow down. But the tiger slipped into a shelf of rocks at the water's brink and remained wedged in there hidden from view. It would only growl from time to time and we presumed it was hard

hit and unable to get out, so we crept up the bank to reconnoitre. The shikari made out a streak of its coat at which I fired and missed, causing the beast to growl and confirm our opinion of its condition, so we worked round to the opposite bank and climbed a tree overlooking the spot. From its top branches we could make out the forequarters and I placed a bullet in the neck and killed it. On examining the first shot we saw the ball had passed through the body under the spine, splintering both shoulder blades and grooving the backbone. The wound in itself was not such as to prevent the tiger from getting away, only its strenuous exhibition of temper rendered that impossible.

In a third instance, I was inspecting a coppice wood with the forester and guard of the beat; as no one expected to see game my rifle was omitted from the programme, but the forester brought his single barrel muzzleloader. Natives like carrying weapons more to please their vanity, than to appear valiant. Our intrusion roused a boar which got out of its straw nest to find out the cause of the disturbance. It stood aslant on a rise gazing at the cover towards our rear, and the forester who saw it first, handed me his weapon. It looked a fine specimen at a hundred feet, but the rifle - an obsolete twelve bore - was rammed with ball and slugs, and I had doubts as to its killing capacity at the range. I aimed at the shoulder and hit far back in the abdomen. The beast moved a little and sat down in thick cover, and the weapon being empty we could not follow straight away. For a while, the beast grunted and tore at the coppice shoots, then there was stillness and we walked up armed with sticks and found it alive and helpless and it was at once killed: the gaping wound from ball and slugs had bled profusely and made it too weak to move.

I have selected examples of powerful and vicious beasts because they add special force to what has been said about the need to be unobtrusive in dealing with formidable victims. At the same time they show that, if let alone, fierce victims will struggle until decease or prostration supervenes to cut short their existence, or to anchor them to the spot. Stillness counts to gain in obviating pursuits fraught with risk and chances of losing the quarry. The element of mystery about a shot that fails to kill enhances its uncertainty when the victim gets away, and impairs confidence in the work of retrieving the creature. Therefore no means that will lessen the chances of escape should be spared.

A beast missed while yet unconscious of the gun's presence, will often keep on the scene because its animal instinct no less than human logic, knows the safest course in the midst of uncertain danger is to remain where it is and except to start at the sound they occasionally display marked reluctance to quit the site. I have fired thrice at a panther missing each time and it showed no desire to depart, but on the contrary was curious to examine the holes in the ground where the bullets had struck, and paid the penalty for its obstinacy as the fourth shot killed it. Mr. Thompson related an instance in which he had fired twice at a tiger without making it move. He had come upon the beast as it lay asleep and though it woke with a start at the first shot, it did not stir from the spot and the second also failed to make it leave. The third shot struck home and the tiger expired with a few struggles on the spot where it lay.

Deer and antelope also often refuse to leave on the sound of a mere report. But bison herds will depart at any unusual noise while as a rule, solitary bulls and cows will not.

Considering their importance to shooting, I have laid some stress on influences that govern a beast's course of action under critical conditions, and drawn comparisons between avoidable and unavoidable causes inviting risks with which the sportsman must reckon to insure against accidents. The remarks are specially concerned with shooting from the ground. In beating, after a shot is fired animals whether wounded or not, nearly always increase their pace if walking, or start off if stationary. This however, has less to do with the report, and more with being driven. An animal will sometimes come to a standstill in full view of the gun after being fired at and missed, and will not move provided the sportsman does nothing to attract the beast's attention. Indeed on such occasions, I have known animals remain unmoved after they had been fired at and missed three and four times. It is owing to the beast being taken by surprise at the unexpected explosion in its front while being hunted from the rear. The double event so confuses it for the moment that rather than take a leap in the dark, the beast prefers to stop and use its senses to avoid further risk.

I have twice fired on a stag driven up in a beat, missing both shots, and watched it standing, dilating its nostrils and twitching its ears in order to obtain a clue as to the cause of the report before venturing further, until the third killed it. Again, a friend had four tries at a stag brought to a halt in the same way. Then he moved

and was immediately detected and the stag bounded away without a scratch.

This sense to make certain in a dilemma is general among game tribes, and many a noble beast owes its fall merely because habit induces it to observe the caution even in a critical situation. But the very unexpectedness (of this behaviour) often causes the gun to miss. I recollect an incident in which a stag close to the gun dropped into the long grass immediately after the shot and was so well hidden that the sportsman could not see it from his high position in a machan. On the beaters coming up it sprang out and charged through their midst and escaped. In another case, a tiger got the better of the sportsman in exactly the same manner.

The essential part that wounds play in shooting is evident. Excepting the very vital spots, it is seldom that two shots inflicting identical wounds on different animals of the same species, age and sex, will produce like results. Unless therefore, the sportsman can ensure good aim, he must be prepared for though not necessarily anticipate unexpected developments. It is the inconsistency about the effects of shots which imperils the hunt after a dangerous beast has got away wounded.

A fatal or serious injury tests the victim's vitality as well as discloses its mettle. There are other incentives to resistance which is the chief cause of accidents. Not all the units of a tribe combine the properties, but individuals possess them and according as they prevail, the race as a whole, acquires the reputation of being hardy or delicate, and with or without offensive propensities. The cementing of the physical and moral forces exerts strength that makes the possessor show remarkable endurance and capacity in facing obstacles before which others of its kind quail or succumb.

In every tribe of game, instances are found of victims turning to attack when brought to bay. Taking such inoffensive creatures as chinkara and barking deer, while lying disabled, they will be ready to prod or kick anyone who approaches them; and used dexterously the sharp point of the horn or the chisel edge of the hoof is capable of inflicting disagreeable wounds. In another chapter, I have related an incident in which a four-horned antelope caused serious injury to a native by piercing his cheek when he attempted to lay hold of it for halal. In a similar instance, a wounded cheetal stag, lying very sick, got up by a supreme effort and goaded one of the men standing by in the thigh, inflicting a

bad thrust which started blood poisoning, and he had to be treated in hospital. Trivial as the occurrences are, they none the less emphasise the need for caution in dealing with wounded beasts. But the matter really assumes importance on following victims, as tiger, panther, bison and buffalo which are more or less prone to be offensive.

Retrieving these beasts is always ticklish work because the chances are the victim will gain the better of the pursuer. It is however, a duty that the sportsman cannot avoid, he is in honour bound to employ every feasible means to secure the quarry, and in the case of a savage beast, he has to consider the folly of leaving it at large to attack any unfortunate happening to come upon it unawares. He runs little risk on ground without under-cover, otherwise tracking is hazardous and the skill to discover the victim in time to avert accidents rests more on individual instinct and less on use of the senses. This inspiration of warning springs to the aid of trackers absorbed on the work in the presence of danger and contravenes to foil animal resource, which in its plight, transcends their ordinary means of caution. The sportsman who is slow to perceive the proximity of the quarry, is unequipped for the work, as however cautiously he may go about the business, it is sure to detect his approach from its quiet retreat under cover.

The defence and attack of wounded beasts vary with the types of game. All animals are adepts in defence of concealment and will quickly gain coverts that accord with their habits. Tiger and panther have recourse to vociferous language as well, to warn off the pursuer. Of aggressive beasts, tiger and panther usually give vent to a rakish cough or growl which discloses their whereabouts, while bison and buffalo quickly launch their onslaught. Thus, in the one case the gun is more or less warned of what is coming, whereas in the other, he is unprepared if not taken aback, by the silence and swiftness of the move.

As a rule, attacks are not launched until the pursuer is within the negotiable distance for the beast to strike swiftly and with effect. With tiger and panther the measure is a spring's cast, that is eighteen to twenty feet, and about treble the length with bison and buffalo. This shows how necessary it is for the gun to discover the victim and place it hors de combat before he steps into the reach.

The movements of wounded game are apt to be delusive and differ in execution. Some lie up at once: others start off on a mad

career: a good many are careful to pick and choose their way rendering the trail difficult to follow. The differences have less to do with the character of the wound and more with the age of the victim. The habits of young creatures accord with the first two resources and especially the second; adults have recourse to all three means, though favouring the first; and old stagers resort to the first and third practice, but prefer to adopt the last.

Similarly, the effect of wounds varies in different animals; it is very marked in fierce beasts because of their ungovernable tempers. Some are cowed by the wound and move off no sooner they are conscious of being followed. Others wait until they obtain a glimpse of the pursuer and fearing to meet him flee from the scene: a good few prepare to attack and lose heart even while in the act of charging, either on seeing the gun stand firm or on hearing the report repeated, becoming intimidated at the last moment from following up the resolve. Such a sudden change can only arise from an excess of fear for which the wound is a good deal responsible. Moreover, the gun's steadiness or the weapon's report if it has been fired, serves to remind of additional punishment, which impresses some victims sufficiently to a further sense of danger and causes them to break off their attacks. The fact illustrates the need for a big bore weapon that will inflict a crushing wound and provide an effective deterrent against a charge.

I am reminded of an incident with a tigress that was shot in the abdomen. It kept steadily to a path all the way and only turned off to lie under a thicket of elephant climbers growing a few paces alongside it. The intestines had plugged the wound so that the blood trail was very faint most of the way. The beast held so straight to the course that no one suspected it would leave the path, and the trackers and I passed on. But when we could not find the least trace of its tracks, we stopped for a consultation. One of the men loitering at the back was coming up to join us and seeing pods hanging from the thicket, he stepped off the path to break them - the seeds in the beans of the climber are eaten by wild tribes. His innocent errand was however mistaken by the tigress for it sprang out with a growl; however the man was quick enough to avoid the attack. Before it could do more, I fired and disabled it with a shot in the spine and another put it out of pain. The tigress was so cowed by the first wound that it allowed three or four of us to pass actually within fifteen feet, making no attempt whatever to molest

us, and went for the man only in a half-hearted way because he nearly stepped on to it.

In following a wounded beast, the sportsman should take as few men as possible: two men are all he requires. Numbers mean noise, which lessens the chances of finding the victim. A few armed men may follow at fifty paces or so, provided they can be relied upon to keep together and not to speak. One of the two selected men should be skilled in tracking, while the other should be a man keen of sight and sound, and both ought to be armed with guns, axes or spears, whichever is most suitable for use on the track traversed.

The best men for tracking wounded beasts are the forest folks whose instinctive powers are schooled to the sights and sounds of the jungles; they possess moreover, the fine sense of distinguishing between their variations and so are able to ascertain the meanings indicated by respective visual or vocal changes. The tracker usually works in a bending position as it were, nosing the trail; the sportsman keeps immediately behind him, holding his weapon ready for use at a moment's notice prepared for every eventuality; the second man follows on the heels of the gun, keeping on the alert to observe every move or analyse every particle of sound. Interchange of opinions amongst the party should be strictly restricted to signs.

It is necessary to allow an interval of fifteen to thirty minutes to elapse before starting on the trail of a wounded beast. A respite is an incentive to the victim to lie up - a course which most creatures are disposed to follow if left undisturbed, while the pause aids in rendering the beast more or less impotent to do harm. Also, owing to the moderating effects of time, its ardour to charge if not past, is very much lessened. I have read in books on sport that in this lapse of time, the wounded beast's attention becomes diverted from the gun. This hardly seems correct, for even if the victim had no idea of how it came by its wound, it would fix the responsibility on the tracker no sooner it perceives him following on its trail. Were the reasoning true, there would be no risks in retrieving dangerous game.

In tracking wounded beasts liable to prove dangerous, avoid going hastily into depressions and thick cover and reconnoitre them well before entering. Where there are trees along the trail, a system of look-outs can be devised to co-operate with the trackers:

a few sharp-sighted and acute-eared men are told off to ascend at intervals and scan the ground before trackers go over it, so that a measure of safety is insured against sudden attack. It is very useful in following up panther which is clever in adapting itself to any little cover, and is besides very vindictive.

There is a slight though marked difference between the actions of wounded beasts essaying to escape and intending to charge. In the one, the creature's expression denotes hurry and its speed alternates from swift to slow, according to the damage or pain inflicted. In the other, its visage foreshadows mischief and the pace is calculated to strike within limits. The onsets of tiger and panther fluctuate from zigzag and bobbing rushes to series of short leaps and tumbles; whereas bison and buffalo come straight to the encounter. In either case, the movement is so swift that the charging beast appears contracted in a smaller mould than the original; at the same time the rapidity creates a dazzling target offering a deceptive mark. Therefore the gun has little difficulty in aiming at a beast running away, as compared with sighting one that is charging. In the circumstances, it is wise to reserve fire until the beast is close enough to ensure the aim striking in the right spot and immediately step aside to avoid the impetus.

But apart from the difficulty of aim at an onrushing beast, one has also to take into account the resistance to the shot from the development of muscular tissue, hide and bone concentrated in the forequarters, which often neutralise the bullet's striking power and thus, the further consideration arises to wait for an opportunity at a side shot. We know that before reaching their goal, charging beasts often divert from the course, while after passing it they seldom or never turn back for a second onset, so that the chance of getting in a broadside is by no means rare. The choice must rest with the sort of position the gun occupies, should it possess an advantage on which the gun can rely, he does well to elect for a side shot.

Shooting exacts a premium on the sportsman's self-control. It makes him self-reliant and develops a sure eye; it creates initiative and brings into use the latent senses; and it induces activity and endurance. In short, its pursuit renovates the constitution. The true sportsman aims not at making bags, but in gaining the science that will enable him to act independently and with confidence under all conditions, to secure the prize for which he sets out.

Chapter IX

Animal Cures for Wounds

Animals are their own physicians and it is interesting to hear the views of intelligent aborigines upon the treatment to which wounded beasts resort. They all maintain that unless a vital organ has been effected, the victim will cure itself in various ways. The methods commonly employed are: to nurse the wound by constant licking and sucking, to close it by the application of puddled clay or mud, to restore vitality by the use, externally or internally, of certain drugs composed of herbs or other ingredients, and lastly by what may be termed "the water cure".

Provided the shot fails to kill at once, every animal is more or less demonstrative on being hit. The tendency of carnivora is to stop short and with or without an expression of anger, to bite the wound regardless of the sound accompanying it. The reason is clear. The victim thinks that it has been stung by an uncommonly poisonous insect, and wants to crush it between the jaws exactly as we see a cat or dog do when tormented by a gadfly, only, with even more determination. On the other hand, the inclination of a wounded deer or antelope is to bolt for a short distance. Here again, one may suspect that the cause is the same as in the other case, for we know a pony or cow will run to shake off a poisonous fly that has settled on its body.

A victim's first concern on regaining its senses is to see to means for staunching the flow of blood which is only natural. Animals know as well as human beings that blood constitutes life, and are therefore conscious of resources to check the flow. This is often the reason why after some distance, the blood trail suddenly stops. Experienced trackers will sometimes exclaim when following up a wounded beast, that the victim has stopped the blood. Incredible as this may sound, it is nevertheless true. The expedient to which animals resort, is either to lick the wound constantly, or to close it with an effective plug, or to do both. I will quote a few instances.

A bear got away bleeding profusely for about three hundred yards at the end of which the blood suddenly ceased. Here over a tiny patch, the turf was torn and pulled about as if the beast had struggled desperately on the spot, clutching at the growth in its agony. The tracker, who was an experienced Gond, said at once

that the bear had halted there to plug the wound with grass. The trail however could be made out by other marks and we continued to follow. Half a mile further, we came upon the creature seated in a cavity in a nullah bank and it was immediately shot. The first ball had raked it fore and aft and both openings at the shoulder and arms were stuffed with grass which checked the flow of blood.

A similar experience occurred in another province. On this occasion, the bear was being driven up a steep slope. It was hit low in the right shoulder close to the arm, and the express bullet remained embedded. The creature fell over and lay still for a few seconds, then recovering itself, it shot downhill through the beaters and went on over very difficult country for a good three miles. I was sure the wound was severe and would prevent it going very far, so telling off a few trackers to follow on, I hurried to another beat. The men gave up the pursuit after a mile, saying they could not track further as the blood had stopped. But when they mentioned finding coagulated blood, it made me certain the beast was at the end of its tether, and they were induced by promises of higher rewards to take up the trail again the next morning. With good tracking they marked it lying under a rock too feeble to move out, and one of the men speared it. The cause for the blood ceasing to flow was that the bear had plugged the wound with tender leaves of the temru plant. It had also an old wound in the side nearly healed, from which two slugs were extracted.

Another time, an old baboon proved a great nuisance in persisting to stay up the mango tree under which the camp was pitched, and dirtying the tents. Every effort to drive it away failed and the only thing to do to rid the camp of its presence was to shoot it. As soon as the beast was hit it ran up to the very top of the tree and began to grab at the twigs seemingly in attempts to keep from falling. The density of the leaf canopy prevented us from making out what the beast was actually doing. But after a while, it sprang from the tree and was off, as we supposed, with a slight wound and its escape made the man who had fired look stupid. In the afternoon, one of the servants happening to go down the nullah, brought word that the baboon was lying dead and we went to see and found the wound stuffed with tender mango leaves.

Once a wounded bear was tracked to a puddle pool and hearing us come up, it got out and made off before a shot could be fired. The next morning, it was found dead in another pool at some

distance from the first one. But the surprising thing was that it seemed to be without a scratch. Being smeared with a thick coating of mud, the men began to wash and clean it. Even then, the body had to be examined before we could find the wound in which a plug of clay over an inch long was firmly wedged.

A panther sitting up facing the gun was shot in the shoulder. It plunged about the spot for several seconds and got away bleeding profusely. That evening, we followed it a short distance and getting dark, we had to return to camp. On the following morning we took up the blood trail which continued for two hundred paces before it ceased altogether at a mossy slope moistened with the sprays of falling water, where the beast had stopped some time. Here was a pool of blood and the moss on the bank was disordered, but thereafter no sign of blood could be detected, nor was it possible to see marks of pugs. The absence of every shred of evidence following closely upon such manifest proof of the creature's presence made its disappearance a mystery. It seemed as if the earth had opened at the spot and swallowed the panther. The men spread out and ranged over the ground all day, but failed to obtain the slightest clue, and having looked up every possible cover likely to contain the beast, the hunt had to be abandoned. The panther had absolutely disappeared and the Bhil shikaris were positive that it had stopped the wound with moss and escaped.

Mr. Thompson, who had the reputation of being an unerring shot, hit a tiger in the left shoulder but to his great surprise the beast made off, leaving a faint trail of blood. He supposed that the express bullet had exploded on a bamboo twig that protruded between his aim and the mark, so that only a fragment of lead had found its billet and caused the wound. He had been so certain of bagging the beast that the incident quite spoiled his tour: hardly a day passed that he did not allude to it in trying to account for the beast's escape as he felt sure of his aim. About nine months later, a tiger was shot by the police officer of the district close to the spot where the above incident occurred, and the beast was recovering from what must have been a very bad wound which was caked with mud. There could be no doubt that it was Mr. Thompson's tiger; the injury was on the shoulder at which he had aimed: the bullet stump extracted from the wound showed that it came form a rifle of the calibre which he always used and no one had shot in the reserve during the interval. His aim was true enough, but the

bullet after penetrating about an inch set up in the muscles, causing a superficial wound and the tiger succeeded in healing itself.

Besides licking, wild animals also constantly suck at a wound. Licking keeps the surface clean and prevents foreign matter lodging on the injured part, while sucking draws out coagulated blood which would otherwise set up and mortify. It is conceivable too, that an animal like the bear, possessing tremendous power of suction can sometimes actually draw out the bullet. Both licking and sucking are common with carnivora, but deer and antelope only lick their wounds, and in either case the nursing is possible if the wound can be reached by the mouth.

The plugging of wounds with clay or mud is a form of treatment known to most animals, but sambar and pig especially are addicted to it. Carnivora practise it when the wound is out of reach to be licked. The plug is forced in by constant rubbing and pressure of the afflicted part against the soft earth of a puddlehole or pool, and the treatment is renewed when the clay dries and falls off, until the wound heals. Plugging reduces risk of infection by maggots or foreign matter as well as improves the chances of healing. Wounded animals distinguish between qualities of earth suitable for application and will not resort to any and every puddle-hole or pool most of which contain germs of noxious insects. They select those in stiff soils or clay pits whose earth is of a consistency to bind and stick like plaster and flake off gradually in drying, such as obtains in pools where sambar wallow.

The use of herbs by animals to counteract poisonous results or to heal wounds is a common belief among natives and most of us have heard of it in connection with fables about the mongoose and the cobra; how the little beast, having killed the venomous reptile, immediately vanishes to devour some herb to neutralise the deadly effects of the bites inflicted by the cobra. If herbs are used externally the creature would have to rub the afflicted part against the growth to force it into the opening or enable the juice to run over the wound. More often however, the victim uses its mouth in applying the remedy, while animals like bear and monkey, whose fingers close over the palms, can also utilize the paws. In employing the mouth the herb is chewed and the wound daubed with the masticated ingredients. Thus the treatment is varied by the position of the wound and the character of the victim.

Animals undoubtedly know the healing properties of plants.

The knowledge is either inherited instinctively, or is the result of experience by previous test, or acquired from example as by seeing others of the tribe utilize the product. Also, the herbs taken may serve to restore vigour or to soothe pain as a balm or to act as an insecticide or combine two or all three properties. But generally speaking, it is taken as a drug to serve the purposes of a stimulant, laxative or purgative. We know that dogs swallow certain grasses when they are dyspeptic and most of the carnivora follow the practice, while ruminants similarly afflicted visit salt-pans or salt-bottoms. Again, I have watched the black antelope of the plains on a cold wet morning licking opium capsules for the exuding juice, which is a well-known stimulant.

It is only men who have opportunities of observing wild beasts in their surroundings, that can tell the plants used medicinally by animals; and it is thus that aborigine medicine men who live sequestered lives, obtain an insight into the secrets of animal and bird cures which they successfully employ in the treatment of their patients. Herbs supposed to contain efficacious properties by animals are various water plants, leaves of the wild onion, garlic, ginger and arrowroot, certain grasses and various parts of plants belonging to species of papaver, aconitum, stryshnos, argemone, andrographis, anisomeles, baliospermum, desmodium, emilia, hemidessmus, indigofira, ocimum, pimpinella, tribulus, vernonia, crocus, datura, asparagus and curculigo.

In undergoing the water cure the victim stands, sits or lies in a pool or stream to drown the maggots and clean the sore, but even more with the object of letting fishes pick out the grubs and nip off the decayed flesh about the wound. Deer, antelope, buffalo, pig and tiger commonly resort to this method of healing.

I once came upon a sambar stag on the banks of the Tava river seated in two or three feet of water among rushes and lilies at which it nibbled. The creature looked a strange object with only its head out of the stream and its horns waving about gently as it took bites of the lily and rush leaves trailing on the water. It stood up on hearing us approach, but seemed reluctant to leave the spot and walked out slowly. On being shot, it was found that the stag had an abcess high up on the right shoulder close to the neck caused by four slugs that were embedded in the flesh. It was evident the creature had been in the stream for the benefit of its wound which although with an opening large enough to hold a five shilling

piece, looked remarkably clean and fresh, and would have done credit to a surgeon's dressing. The Gonds with me said that after getting the sore clean, the stag would have probably plastered the wound with mud.

Apart from animals, I have also come across cases of wounded birds that were able to cure their injuries. A broken wing will often reset, at least sufficiently well for the bird to make short flights, but a safe retreat is essential where the creature can remain undisturbed while the healing process goes on. The rest enables the cartilage adjoining the injury to harden and form a secondary bone; at the same time, the bird keeps dressing the wound constantly with its oiled beak from the oleiferous glands in the tail, to aid recovery. Such re-settings however are never perfect for the bird is unable to draw the wing into its original position, so that it hangs by the side. I have observed this form of healing in peafowl, crow, wild geese and duck and scavenger vulture that being disabled by gun-shot wounds, were able to fly after five or six weeks.

I bagged a peacock whose left wing had been shot away leaving two inches of bony stump and its wound was quite healed. The bird lived a solitary existence under some thick scrub growing below the bund of a tank and as if to make up for its loss, was amazingly fleet-footed, which enabled it to escape from its many enemies. Struck by its strange appearance, I was curious to know the cause of its disfigurement and set about shooting it. But at the time I little guessed the chase it would lead me: the rapidity with which the bird dodged in and out of cover was enough to make one lose patience in trying for so trifling a bag, for it took me and a dozen beaters some hours to beat about the cover before it was shot. Evidently the wing was blown off by a charge of shot fired from close and the naked and splintered bone though healed, showed that the injury must have been very severe. The Bhil beaters were positive that the bird had cured itself by dressing the wound with the clayey soil of the tank.

I also shot a tailless partridge which sent out a disgusting odour and on examining it the tail was found to have a festering sore plastered with cow dung. The bird was accordingly made over to the sweeper who dressed it for his meal. He told me that the abscess was due to a previous gunshot wound which contained some pellets, and which was on the mend. Besides cases of healing

personally witnessed, I have heard of some marvellous cures effected by both animals and birds from intelligent aborigines whose veracity there was no reason to doubt. It may be of interest to mention a few as they only confirm what has been said of the wild fauna being gifted with the means of remedy no less than human beings.

A shikari related he had once shot a sambar hind whose under chin was missing, and he supposed the injury was due to the part of the mouth having been shot away by an express bullet. Yet, except for being somewhat lean, the creature was none the worse for the loss and had quite recovered from the wound.

A Bhil wizard gave an instance of a panther crippled by a shot in the spine. The wretched beast could only drag itself about on its forelegs and lived under a patch of thick scrub near by the man's shanty. For some years it eked out an existence from such food as it could obtain by foraging about the ground and turned up at his hut regularly after sunset to devour the offal lying about the place. Eventually, a brother shikari who was on a visit to his hut, shot the panther to gain the reward paid to those bringing in skins of such destructive beasts. The man said that the wound in the spine had quite healed, leaving the hindquarters paralysed, and the creature would have dragged out its miserable existence for years if his brother had not come across and shot it.

A Bhil tracker mentioned being in at the death of a blind bear. It went about with its mate and obtained food through its aid. In the pursuit, the creature lagged behind, which made the gun suspect something wrong with the beast and when shot it was discovered that the eyes had been blinded by a charge of buckshot.

I heard an extraordinary tale of an eagle-hawk that preyed on the poultry in a Bhil settlement. One of the young bloods sat up in ambush on the tree it frequented and as it alighted near him, he succeeded in fixing the bird with his bow and arrow. The shaft passed clean through the bird which fell to the ground, but when the man came down to pick it up the hawk suddenly recovered and flew away. For months nothing more was seen of the bird. Then, it returned and recommenced its ravages on the poultry. It had become too cute to fall again to an ambush-shot, but became a victim to a simple device. This consisted of a sling soaked in bird-lime with one end tied to a chicken and the other fastened to a pebble and left free to swing, so that as the hawk swooped up with

its prey, the cord swung round and enmeshed the feathers, arresting its flight and forcing it to alight when it was easily caught and killed. On being plucked - the Bhils use the feathers in the manufacture of arrows - the hawk was found to contain scars of arrow wounds on its back and abdomen. This left no doubt that the hawk was one and the same bird that had got away wounded some months previously.

Chapter X

The Tiger

I have referred already to the encouragement which Mr. Thompson gave me to acquire a knowledge of the jungles. His advice was to sit up over springs or salt-licks or cross paths and near the trees, such as mahua and others that produce the plums, figs, nuts and berries, where animals come to feed during the fruiting season and to observe their ways and manners as well as to note their sounds.

He was full of tales of his own experience, which seemed to me at the time almost incredible, but fascinated me and made me determined to find out for myself. Mr. Thompson suggested that I should sit up and watch a tiger kill a buffalo calf. It was generally supposed at the time that the tiger held on by the neck to throttle its victim and sucked the blood. Mr. Thompson did not believe this. He said it might be possible with a very young calf or other equally inoffensive victim, such as a goat or four-horned antelope. But, he argued the tiger, like all felines was very careful of his fur, and with a powerful victim, such as a half-grown buffalo, sambar or blue-bull, the throttling process would involve him in a hard struggle with every prospect of being badly lacerated or even ripped. He would therefore avoid that method of killing, while the idea of sucking was ridiculous as the tiger's mouth was not modelled for any such purpose.

My experience was instructive, for it disproved the theories I held of the victim being killed by a stroke from the tiger's paw or being choked by the tiger's grip. Having got my gond shikari to select a good spot in a glade near a frequented pool of water, I sat up in a tree about five o'clock in the afternoon and watched through the night, the moon being nearly full. Four nights of ceaseless watching went by without the tiger's appearing, although there were fresh marks of pugs close by and in fact, on the second night, the tiger had left the path where the calf was tied at a point from where he could not possibly have failed to see it. Every night the locality echoed with the various noises of the denizens of the jungles while on their nocturnal perambulations. Panther, bear and pig passed by the path, taking little or no notice of the calf which except for the movements of his ears, seemed deaf to all

Gatas (Bhil memorial stones), Jobat, 1902

Bhil dwellings, Ali-Rajpur, 1908

Perhaps the 'lonely spot' mentioned in the narrative?

Temples at Dharampur, on the bank of the Nerbudda River, 1906

Type of Bhil woman, Ali-Rajpur, 1905

Killers killed

sounds and lay low and very quiet, instead of struggling and moving as he did the first night. This was because his instinct dulled by living in domesticity had begun to assert itself over the animal's nature, schooling him to silence as the only means of escaping detection under his new conditions.

On the fifth night, the moon was due to rise just before eight o'clock. We had been watching for a couple of hours and from the top of the tree, could see the glade being gradually lit up by the increasing rays as she rose above the horizon, when suddenly, there was a dull sound as of a heavy weight's fall, and the Gond sitting by me grasped my arm as a sign of the tiger's presence. I looked immediately at the calf in front, barely twenty paces from the tree, to see a tangled struggling mass. The tiger was in the act of breaking the poor beast's neck with a backward wrench. This over, he backed a few paces, crouched down and watched it die; and then he walked up again, took the neck firmly in his jaws and shook it, causing a flow of blood which he carefully licked. His next business was to remove the kill which was firmly tied to the root of a tree-stump. He pulled and pulled without weakening the cord which was made of twisted bamboo cuticle. Then he tried to cut it through with his teeth, but it pricked his gums, for he let go suddenly and with a grimace, started off towards the pool.

In a few minutes he was back, making a peculiar suppressed growl which put into words would be "haun haun" that I have only once again heard under very different circumstances, rather alarming to the uninitiated. And this time, taking a firm grip of the calf by the shoulder about where it joins the neck, he lifted the forequarters of the kill and drew it in close to the peg so as to cause a loop in the cord with which it was tied, then, with a super effort he jerked the kill to his side and snapped the cuticle, while the force and suddenness of the operation unbalanced the beast and, dropping the kill he fell over. Having freed his kill, the tiger again lifted it by the shoulder where he had held it just before, and started to carry it away with the forefeet and hindquarters trailing along the ground. He dragged it nearly two hundred yards across the nullah and beyond the pool, on to the opposite bank and having eaten a few mouthfuls, he pushed it under the dense cover of some dwarf bushes.

It is strange that neither of us saw or heard the tiger and had absolutely no idea of his presence, until he sprang at the calf from

within fifteen feet of the tree on which we were seated. The crash came like a thunderbolt, with the suddenness that it made us start in the machan, and but for his being occupied with his victim, he must surely have heard us. It is difficult to say if the calf knew that his fate was on him. If he did he kept perfectly silent. In the dim light, he looked a blurred object, so we could not very well follow his motions. It is true that I was momentarily engaged in watching the effect of the light transmitted through the foliage, as the moon rose; at the same time I was facing the calf and the slightest movement could not possibly have escaped me, I cannot tell whether the calf was standing or sitting when the tiger fell on him; in any case, the crash and shock stupified [sic] the poor beast and before he had time to recover, the tiger had broken his neck. He was a full grown calf over three year's old, and could have made a good fight for life. I could have shot the tiger ten times over, and he looked a fine beast in the moonlight, but I had sat up with the express object of studying the movement and, moreover, I was not sure of my rifle which was an old Martini. Of course the shikari thought me very foolish and always remembered my abstention to my discredit.

From what I have heard, opinions differ greatly as to the character of a tiger's blow. Years ago, I read an account by Sir Samuel Baker and also in the Badminton volume on big game shooting, in which the writers compared it with a sledge-hammer blow for force and striking power, and one of them, if I remember rightly, mentioned that he had known an ox's head being smashed in by it. Now, I have seen over a hundred animals, large and small, killed by tigers, but in no single case was it evident that the victim owed its death to a blow from the paw, nor were there any signs on the head or on the body of a violent stroke. Moreover, I know personally two men who were victims of a tiger's fury and escaped with their lives. In each case, the tiger had struck with his paw, but only to scoop out big chunks of flesh. His blows were dealt on the chest and back and buttocks, and if the smashing theory were true, they ought to have crashed in and flattened the part affected, causing death immediately or shortly after. But neither man died, although both were next to death's door, owing to blood poisoning which is quite another matter. Again, I have watched a panther strike a kid and, whether it was done to amuse himself or not, the blow was barely sufficient to unbalance the little creature; certainly it left no mark upon him. I believe that a tiger cannot strike with

his paws with great force, although he has massive and very muscular arms, for the simple reason that he is not built that way. To strike a stunning and crushing blow, an animal must be able to stand or sit back and to bring his arms in such a position as to concentrate his whole power upon the substance struck and the tiger could not assume such a posture if he tried. A study of his anatomy would put any doubts at rest. Moreover, his soft pads are not constructed to deliver a crushing blow. His object is to maul. As soon as his arms are extended, the claws automatically protrude from their sockets, and give the animal a tremendous power of offence or defence, as the case may be.

I consider that the tiger's great strength is a natural acquirement for the essential purpose of existence. He has to be powerful and swift to overtake his victims in the chase and when he has done so, he must also be able to put an end to the business quickly in order to avoid endangering his own skin in tussles with strong beasts. The tiger's elongated build, like a dart or bolt, and the massive development of elastic and muscular tissue in the fore-part of his body, are designed not only to enable him to shoot forward with lightning rapidity, but also absolutely to prostrate the animals struck. We know that he has often to deal with heavy and powerful game, such as, sambar, blue-bull, bison and buffalo, as weighty as or even weightier than himself, so that without the means to place them hors de combat promptly, he would not have much chance. Moreover he needs to be strong and capable of lifting or dragging great weights in order to remove his victims with the least possible delay into cover, where he can feast in quiet and silence, aloof from the prying eyes of forest denizens. He needs to avoid giving offence to the susceptible feelings of the animal tribes. If he fed in public, he would fill them with disgust and horror, and they would leave the jungle. In other words, his obligations to his neighbours impose on him the duty of conducting his actions separately, just as a butcher does living in a Hindu town or city. Any one will appreciate my meaning. Cattle will take absolutely no notice of deaths among their number, but they hate to see the bodies being torn by vultures and dogs, and will always avoid going anywhere near the spot. This may be the reason too why game desert tracts infested by wild dogs, whereas they abound where tigers are common.

I remember seeing one feat of great strength on the part of a

tiger. This happened in the Amdhana forests, close to Shahpura in the Betul district. It was at the beginning of the rains and I was putting up in the Dâk bungalow with a Sapper lieutenant who had been forced to curtail his shooting and move in on account of the rain. One morning news was brought in of a kill in the village and we went to see for ourselves. A full-grown buffalo in calf, as fine a specimen of her kind as one would wish to see, had been killed some distance from the village, inside an enclosure such as graziers put up on the outskirts of villages for penning their cattle at night. The pen was made of stout forked posts, firmly fixed in the ground with poles stuck between the forks as rails to prevent the animals breaking out. The buffalo was in the pen with about a dozen others and some cows. The tiger had leaped the fence, about three and a half feet high, to get at her where she lay, squatted a few yards away. To get her out he had tried to force a gap in the fence by thrusting the poles apart, but failing in this he partly lifted and partly dragged the animal over the stout railing, a feat which must have required extraordinary strength of neck and jaw. Then he had dragged the victim about forty paces away under cover, and having there disembowelled her, he had decamped with the foetus. There was a partial moon, but the sky was cloudy. The villagers were sanguine that the tiger would return early and proposed to my companion that we should sit up which he readily consented to do. To get the kill out of the cover and in view of the proposed machan, it was necessary to shift it a few yards, and although there were six of us, we only just managed to get it into position which will show what a weight the victim must have been. The tiger however, never returned to the kill.

I saw another similar feat on the track between Borhna and Mowar in the same district. One of the baggage camels, a large bull, had broken loose and strayed away at night and in the early morning news came in that he had been killed by a tiger. Although the victim was out of the common, he had been thrown and his neck wrenched in the usual way; and apparently in falling he had broken one of his forelegs for the shin bone was splintered and protruded from the skin. In this case the carcass had been dragged from the track where the kill had been made to cover twenty paces away, and it required seven or eight men to move it even a few yards into the open. I sat up over the kill, and the tiger returned early but winded me and went back.

A tiger rushes to the attack at a sudden bound, or with a short run followed by a few springs like long links at the end of a chain, the strides varying in length according either to the distance, or the size of the victim. The greater the distance and the larger the animal, the more speed and striking power he develops. If he is very near his victim, as often happens when calves are tied out and he almost stumbles against them in the dark, the tiger will just pounce on them and bring them down by gripping the throat. But with game alert and on the move, he is often hard put to it to bring off his coups, and the distances from which he may launch himself will vary from ten to fifty yards or more. It would be interesting to obtain exact measurements of his rushes; but this is rarely possible owing either to the surface being hard or covered with vegetable, which prevents the marks being visible, or wobbly as a marsh or sandy bed which make equally bad negatives [sic]. Exact imprints are forthcoming only on surfaces where there has been a scene of recent fire and which are still coated with ashes, or the stiff moist beds along some riverbanks. The former is rare as tigers will avoid such areas as long as the surface remains heated, and by the time it cools the ashes will have been scattered by winds; while the other is an accident of geological conditions. The two measurements I have been lucky in getting show in the one case, that the distance of tiger from calf when sighted was one hundred and forty feet. Of this, the tiger ran for forty feet and then commenced springing and fell on the calf at the sixth bound; the lengths of these from start to finish were twelve, fourteen, sixteen, eighteen, nineteen and twenty feet respectively. In the other, the tiger started for his victim from sixty-three feet and covered the first twenty-four at a run, and the remaining distance in three springs of ten, fourteen and sixteen feet. The depth of the pugs in the last few springs showed also the greater force developed at the finale. The first onset was made upon a buffalo calf tied up at the angle of a serpentine stream with a stiff mud bed. The second was imprinted over a gravel surface sodden by the night's rain and the victim was a blue-bull browsing on aonla fruit.

To return to the question of the tiger killing his prey, breaking the neck is the common method with large animals in which the victim has been felled and stupefied by the tiger's onslaught. But I know cases of animals which have had their necks wrenched by an equally violent stroke while they were standing and grazing. This

is done by a rapid spring in which the tiger suddenly grasps his prey about the face with his mouth and one paw and forces the victim's head upwards by sheer strength as he bounces over, jerking the victim's neck and dislocating the vertebrae in his flight. The creature falls almost instantly and expires after some minutes, while the tiger keeps aside and watches it die.

I once saw this happen with a full-grown buffalo in the Nanda reserve. Here in the middle of the jungles is a circular space of rising ground which slopes away gradually all round to the edge of the reserve. It is an old culturable clearance devoid of trees and on the top of the mound are the forest huts which shelter the few forest department subordinates quartered over the reserve and excepting whom, the place is practically uninhabited. The blank is covered in the rains with a rank growth of grass which is burnt as a precaution against fires, and at the very first shower the area is carpeted with a fresh crop of grass providing excellent grazing, so that owing to its seclusion the place is a great attraction for all kinds of game from distances around. Indeed they keep in the open till quite late in the morning and come out again before sunset. It is an ideal spot to observe animals as they feed and gambol about or mingle with each other, and utter their respective notes of recognition in passing.

Being caught by an early monsoon, I was obliged to take shelter in the forest huts for a few days. One afternoon while seated listening to my clerk read out the vernacular papers, my attention was drawn to a disturbance among a colony of plovers that kept close by a shallow depression marking the course of a stream during the rains. The channel was barely two hundred yards from the huts, and my forester's buffalo was grazing by herself close to it. She was making for the huts, but moving slowly as animals do when grazing, that is, she was facing in our direction. The tiger stalked along the bed of the watercourse which was open and visible from where I was seated on the top of the rise, but as he hugged the bank, he was hidden from my view. My curiosity was however aroused, as I knew the birds would not speak for nothing: so I kept a good lookout while my clerk went on with his reading quite unsuspecting that my attention was riveted elsewhere. In a few minutes, I saw the tiger's head emerge over the bank as if to survey the ground in his front and then I at once realised what he was after. In a second, he was up the bank and lay down for an

instant as if to take rest. Then he ran or rather walked with quick long strides keeping his body as close as possible to the ground, parallel to the direction in which the buffalo was standing grazing, and coming up within ten paces on her left side, he sprang alighting within a yard of the creature's head. This was the first intimation the buffalo had of the tiger's presence, and she raised her head in astonishment, but at that very instant the tiger bounced up like a cannon ball, grasping the buffalo's cheek at the angle with his mouth and at the same time seizing her chin with his left paw, he swung round twisting the head up as he went over on the right side of her, but letting go of his hold before he had alighted.

The force practically lifted the buffalo off her forefeet, and she uttered a shrill moan sounding like the whistle from a throttle-valve, and lurched forward a few paces and fell. I was too absorbed to say a word and till then, no one else seemed to have an inkling of the tragedy that was being enacted in full view of the huts in broad daylight. But the buffalo's moan and struggles at once called the men's attention to the occurrence and despite my endeavours to pacify them, as I was anxious to see the business through, they created a tumult and rushed to the scene. This was too much for the tiger and he vanished by the way he had come. The men tried to raise the buffalo and applied cures to the wounds on her jaw, but the tiger had done his work too surely, and try as they would to revive her, she could not even sit up and expired after struggling for ten or fifteen minutes. The four canine teeth were embedded in the jaw, two just under the cheek and two just above it, that is the tiger had gripped the buffalo's face at the angle of the lower maxillary bone, while the chin bore slight marks of the tiger's claws. The distance from buffalo to bank of nullah where the tiger got up, measured twenty-six paces or about eighty feet, of this he ran about seventy feet before springing to the attack.

Graziers and Gond shikaris have given me accounts of very much the same description of tigers killing cattle. I dare say in cases where the tiger finds it convenient to stalk close up to his victim without being noticed, as would be the case more often with domesticated animals whose senses are dull, he would prefer this method of killing. I have been called hastily to sit up over cattle soon after the tiger had had them down, and in one or two instances, life was not extinct. Needless to say, the tumult usually caused on such occasions, frightens the tiger and he seldom

returns, at least it has not been my fortune to see him come back to his kill.

I have never seen a victim hamstrung or pulled down and disembowelled preparatory to its being killed or as a means of letting it die, as some authorities assert tigers occasionally do with powerful or running victims whose necks they are unable to break owing to the animal being too strong or on the move. But I have seen several with bad wounds from claws about the hindquarters and shoulders, and they were due to the tiger clutching the victim after his spring to bring it down had failed. Also in few instances, I have known a fore or hind-foot to be broken, but this again was owing to the tiger's weight bearing the beast down, causing it to trip and fall and break or dislocate its foot. Such occurrences are not uncommon when the victim is too powerful to be thrown or where it has anticipated the attack, or again, where the attack has not been delivered with sufficient force to precipitate the victim. Powerful beasts like bison and buffalo, or even a large ox or cow can and often do, withstand the first attack when the only recourse for the tiger is to cling on and force a fall.

In dealing with smaller animals such as pigs, four-horned antelope, barking deer or even cheetal, and the young of bison, buffalo, nilgai, cattle and sambar the tiger has no need to apply his athletic feats to kill his victims, as the prey is too helpless and terrified to offer any opposition, and so he has nothing to fear in the way of hurting his skin. The tiger therefore kills them by the simpler method of gripping the throat, or the nape of the neck or the head, whichever may be convenient, till death ensues by strangulation or haemorrhage. Most buffalo calves tied up as baits are killed in this manner, which is also how the panther seizes its prey.

There are thus, three distinct ways in which the tiger kills and these are varied to suit the circumstances of the occasion or the character of the victim, namely, the fall and wrench, the wrench before the fall and the grip. I have known a tiger to rush up to a large calf tied up as a bait and stop short within a few paces of him, as if uncertain whether to spring on him or not, and then to deliberately walk up and seize him by the throat.

Mr. Thompson always maintained that tigers are diurnal animals but had been forced to nocturnal habits by man. I wonder how many there are who would believe this and yet it is true. The

tiger's eyes are not formed to see for any distance in the dark; his soft tread is easier of detection at night when noises resound more than in the day when they are difficult to locate; and his scent lurks in the damp air of the night making sure of his presence, instead of being wafted away by the dry winds as in the day. Moreover the senses most developed in the tiger are those of seeing and hearing, and these combine to serve him most in the day. As regards scent, he will run like a dog with his nose close to the ground along a fresh trail, but more than this he is incapable of doing: he cannot locate the cause that produced the scent if it is wafted to him from a distance. Consequently the odds are against him when hunting by night.

Most sportsmen must have often noticed that calves tied up are nearly always killed, either in the early part of the night between six and eight o'clock, or in the early morning between four and seven o'clock, indeed in secluded localities they are often killed in the middle of the day. Of course there are kills in the night also, but only, I believe, when the tiger walks right into the animal or happens to be attracted by its sound. These are the reasons why calves are usually tied close to a frequented path and in the open and why a cattle-gong is sometimes dangled about the victim's neck.

Nowadays the ever-increasing demand for extension of cultivation, which it is the policy of Government to encourage, is lessening more and more the sizes of forest reserves and at the same time bringing them in touch with so-called civilizing agencies. The theatres of the tiger's action are therefore not only diminishing but his movements are also becoming restricted so that there are now few haunts sufficiently far from habitations of some sort or other to enable the beast to consider himself perfectly secure from prying eyes. But years ago, in the wilds of the Central Provinces and Central India, there were many such haunts; and an enterprising sportsman fond of solitude and gifted with patience had good opportunities of seeing the king of beats assume his natural manners in his own domain.

I have twice met tigers moving at their own pleasure during the day time and an enterprising sportsman fond of solitude and gifted with patience, had good opportunities of seeing the King of beasts assume his natural manners in his own domain.

Once at noon in the middle of March, I was on the way to

inspect an area in the heart of a noted reserve; the forester and Gond guard of the beat were with me. As we came upon the bank of a river, a tigress with two cubs approached on the opposite bank, she saw us as soon as we spotted her. We stopped and stared at her while she crouched down and watched us, but the slight movements of her tail showed that she was prepared for action if we attempted any liberties. The cubs, which were of the size of a dog, frolicked about their mother for a minute or so and then ran down the slope to the water's edge to drink. Having slaked their thirst, they ran up to their mother again and then she got up and quietly walked away with the cubs gamboling about her. From bank to bank the distance was about sixty yards, but the stream of water was only fifteen feet wide and a foot deep. The guard was very anxious for me to get up a tree and shoot, but I was curious to know what the tigress would do and moreover, I doubt whether the tigress would have stayed, had she seen us getting up trees.

The next time was in the Lonea forests adjoining the Silwani reserve. I had been stalking for cheetal on a December morning without seeing a good stag, and I was thinking of retracing my steps towards camp as it was past ten o'clock and so late to see them about, when we heard that peculiar call, between a bellow and a bark, uttered by stags at the rutting time. My Gond tracker faced about and noted the direction, and we started to follow. The sound seemed to come from about half a mile's distance and as it was repeated twice or thrice while we approached, it was easy to locate. The beast seemed to be in a small clearing due to sterility of soil. There are many of these in the jungle and deer and antelope usually resort to them to nip the herbage, which in such places has a distinctly brackish flavour. Coming up cautiously, we peered through the growth into the open and, instead of a stag there was a tiger crouched under a morinda bush on our left front. He had heard us coming in spite of all our care, but apparently had not been sure what we were and had waited to see. As soon as he made us out, he got up and walked away without even uttering a grunt. He lay so still that we spotted him by the merest chance owing to the twitching of his tail, which is never still while the animal is alert.

I could have fired; but the chances were in his favour, as about twenty paces separated us and the only aim would have been at the head which was held aslant, and offered a doubtful mark. Then I

remembered the call which we had followed; but there were no signs of a stag about, in fact none had been anywhere near the spot that morning. I questioned the Gond, and he said at once "Oh! But it was the tiger that was calling". This reminded me of what Mr. Thompson had said a few years before, that the tiger was an excellent mimic, and this was the first occasion I had had an opportunity of verifying it.

I have not had sufficient experience of the mimicking powers of tigers. I have given one instance of his performance in decoying a stag on to an encounter by delivering the challenge notes employed by the tribe, with the object of bagging either the male that took it up or the hind that was allured [sic] to the spot. I have however heard from aborigine shikaris that this is a fairly common practice of tigers to secure their prey. The only other instance I can recollect is hearing him utter the catcall of a peacock. This was in the morning at about eight o'clock. I had gone with the trackers whose business it was to go around in the early morning to inspect the calves tied up and to report kills or signs of tiger. We were looking down from the bank of a ravine into the stream below at a point where there was a little island, overgrown with elephant grass and dwarf bushes, then we heard a peacock call distinctly uttered several times. The calf was tied some distance up stream and had not been touched. I concluded that the bird had seen a tiger on the move and questioned the tracker, but he declared that the call had been uttered by a tiger, as there were no peafowl to be seen anywhere near the spot at the time. Besides it was too early for the birds to be in the stream. I believe the tracker was right. The same night the tiger killed, and in the beat next day the tiger and tigress came out to the guns; the former, a beauty, got away wounded while the latter was shot. The tiger was doubtless calling with the object of attracting the birds to the island on their flight to the stream, which would commence about that time.

I have been told also by jungle tribes at different times that the tiger can imitate pig, the call of sambar, cheetal and barking deer and the lowing of cattle. But I have never myself heard him do so. We all know there are excellent mimics among birds, so that there is nothing strange in animals also practising the art of mimicry. Besides actually seeing tigers on the move during the day, I have twice come across fresh kills, which must have been made within a few hours of my finding them. But the beast disturbed by the noise

of our approach had of course made off. The first time was when I was a novice, and all I could afford in the way of firearms was an old Martini rifle.

I was out after sambar with my faithful Gond in the Sarni reserve, about five o'clock in the afternoon on a day in February. We came upon a small herd and I wounded a stag who bounded off but soon pulled up and sat down. Knowing no better, I rushed up and the stag of course got up and started off again; I took one or two running shots which missed him. Again he stopped and again I chased him and this went on for some time, while the Gond kept up the chase behind me shouting to me at the top of his voice to stop. I was too excited however, to pay any heed to his shouts. The stag was making for a river about two miles from the spot where he had been wounded. I had lost my bearings and had no idea of the direction. Half an hour's pursuit brought us to the river and the stag having crossed a deep nullah which twined about the bank, mounted a knoll flanking the stream and slid down the opposite side into a deep pool. I was hot after him, and soon I too had crossed and was up the mound, when spread out before me I saw a hind cheetal which had shortly before been killed by a tiger. The tiger had been in the act of skinning his prey when we disturbed him, and he had only just retired into the very same nullah which I had crossed. In the hurry, he had tramped right over his kill leaving two big blotches of blood showing his pugs distinctly.

The sight fascinated me and I was still gazing at the kill when the Gond came quietly up. I did not hear him come and when he put his hand on my shoulder, I made [sic] certain it was the tiger's paw and quivered through and through. As tigers are apt to be furious at being disturbed on their kills, it was an anxious moment for us. For although scared from his kill by the sounds of our rushing and firing he was quite near to make us pay for our rashness, no sooner than his fear at our sudden and noisy intrusion had subsided.

The Gond realizing our danger better than I did, whispered to me to hurry from the spot and practically dragged me down into the stream and across on to the opposite bank. While we were crossing, the tiger roared and gave several angry grunts. The Gond did not think it safe to stop till we were well inside the jungle on the further side. Then he explained that he had seen vultures flying in the direction we were going which made him suspect there was

a kill, with a tiger near it. He had no doubt that if we had stayed another minute by the kill, the tiger would have attacked and probably done for one or both of us.

I came across a fresh kill the second time while taking beaters to drive for game. It was about noon and no one had the least suspicion of tiger being anywhere near. The kill, a nilgai calf, was lying under some dwarf bushes and had not been touched. It appeared to have been killed about an hour before we found it, that is about ten o'clock in the morning. The disturbance frightened the tiger right away for he did not appear in the beat, though we took special precautions in the hope of his coming out.

Yet another instance occurred in the Satsui valley through which the Lohar river wends its way. The Rajah to whom the forests belong had invited us to a shoot. Three days after our arrival a kill was reported in the valley, but it was the work of a panther, and as no one wished to go and sit up for him, the host decided to do so himself. He took my shikari and they sat up at five o'clock. The kill lay in the dry bed of the river and the machan, tied on some overhanging boughs of a tree standing on the bank, gave them a good view up and down the river. They had been in position barely a quarter of an hour, when the shikari saw a tiger some distance away coming along at the foot of the opposite bank and pointed him out to the Rajah. Apparently the tiger was quite unconscious of anything abnormal and going at the quick gliding walk which is his usual gait. Arrived opposite to the machan, he saw or winded the kill which was right in the open; and inquisitively turned and came towards it, but before he could come right up, his suspicions were aroused, doubtless by some shuffling in the machan, and he withdrew hurriedly and was soon out of sight to the great disappointment of our host.

This happened in the middle of May when the days are long and very warm. It is difficult to say what the tiger would have done had he not been disturbed. Tigers are in the habit of feeding from each other's kills, moreover they have no compunction in annexing those made by panthers, so the probability is he would have feasted on it. As a rule, tigers will not touch a kill that has been defiled by scavenger beasts or birds, such as hyena, wild dog and vulture because they scatter the contents of the stomach, which tigers and panthers are always very careful to remove intact. Among themselves, should a stronger tiger appear on the scene of

a kill made by a smaller one the latter will allow the former the precedence in feasting and himself move away snarling. But where tigers keep together they feed off each other's kills without quarrelling.

These examples will tend to show that the tiger would by choice hunt by day light if it were not for the encroachments of man on his domains, which make him perforce defer his chase till the night. I do not mean that the beast of choice would spend the night in repose, passing his hours only in ease and slumber. We know as a fact that unless he has had his fill, he is constantly on the move at night and often covers great distances.

Now how far this is attributable to human disturbance, it is difficult to say; but there is no reason to think that it is unnatural for the tiger to move by night. I think myself that his nightly perambulations, especially when there is a moon, are made with the object of exercise and acquainting himself with the geography of the locality, as well as of acquiring an idea of the habits of the local inhabitants. He can sum up by various means, such as by observing the marks and signs of acts committed during the day, what sort of people he lives among and how they comport themselves. Obviously they are an important factor in his existence living as they do on neighbourly terms with him on the outskirts of his domain so that he has need to know all he can about them, just as in the case of neighbours living next door to each other.

This would explain why tigers' pugs are often seen very close to hamlets situated inside or on the outskirts of forests, without any attempt at molesting the people; also why he is sometimes found living almost in the village precincts. I know of one case where tigers escaping from beats invariably took a path skirting the back of the village at a distance of a hundred yards or so, being assured doubtless of the safety of the route, because at the time of day the men in an aboriginal settlement are either away or within their huts. As the guns and stops prevented the tigers taking their natural route, they chose this as offering greater security in their escape. The village of course lay inside the reserve. We know also that tigers will not usually kill on moon-light nights and the reason may very well be that they are occupied with important concerns affecting their own future safety while the advantage of the light lasts, since they are prevented from doing so by day.

Tigers share the jungle haunts in common with other forest

denizens. The localities most likely to contain him are those frequented by game, that is he lives associated with the rest. Nor does his presence seem to disturb the game very much. He is tolerated by the game tribes as much for his own sake, because he is a unique specimen of brute creation, as for the fact that he is like them a creature of the wilds and so kith and kin with the game tribes. I have often seen sambar, cheetal and pig take their midday siesta within fifty or sixty yards of a spot where a tiger was lying up, without apparently the least concern, although the tiger's scent must have made them acquainted with his presence. Moreover every sportsman knows how deer, antelope and pig will turn out in a tiger beat. Their presence is so often taken to indicate that there is no tiger about, but as a matter of fact, it is often the case that the tiger was there, but had shrewdly followed the example of his keener witted neighbours and slipped through the stops. Living as these animals do among beasts of prey with whom they are no match, their senses are naturally better developed to enable them to escape from their foes. Accordingly on such occasions, the tiger is very often guided by the behaviour of his more vigilant associates, for he knows that their ability to perceive danger in the right quarter is greater than his own.

It is an astonishing fact that on being driven or disturbed, a tiger will always know exactly where to go in order to elude his pursuers. Even if forced to change his direction he will rapidly make up his mind to suit the new conditions. Now this is not done on the spur of the moment, as many people think, but his conclusions are ready in his mind as the result of previous inspection. The tiger treats the jungle as a book whose pages he can turn, to suit his pleasure. When he comes into a new locality, his first action is to explore the country. Often he will not kill for days, although he may pass close by calves or even actually sniff them, until he has made quite sure of the lie of the land for miles around.

I know no way of discriminating finely between the localities which the tiger selects for his habit, and those he avoids. Obviously his resort must have cover and must be near water, and there are few jungle tracts which satisfy both conditions. As a secondary consideration, the tiger looks for companionship and he will usually be found in the neighbourhood of game tribes on whose presence he depends not only for his food, but also for warning against danger. Then as he is essentially carnivorous, his

temperament is easily affected by extremes of heat and cold, so that he adapts his movements to conform with the seasons. In the hot weather he selects shady nooks along banks of streams or on slopes sheltered from the sun's rays and the hot winds, adjusting his position if necessary every few hours so as to escape the sun. Experience has shown me that at this time of the year, he will prefer a position with a northerly or southerly aspect. Also he usually tries to secure a spot with a commanding view.

Though he will occasionally visit water to slake his thirst and to cool his pads, he is not by any means a wader as commonly supposed, and he will avoid damp and wet localities, unless obliged to lie up in or near them temporarily, as for instance in order to watch his kill. On the other hand, in the cold weather, he will keep out of chilly and frosty localities as well as guard against biting winds. He varies his site accordingly and prefers a south-easterly or south-westerly aspect, with or without shelter from the sun. Also, he is ravenous and kills more at this season than at other times and the abundance of cover makes it difficult to locate him.

But the time when he shows greater freedom of movement than at other periods is during the rains. This is in great measure due to flooding, which transforms the surface and the appearance and activity of noxious kinds of insects, such as gadflies, so tormenting to animals; and to a lesser degree to the withdrawal from his haunts of human activity, which now becomes centered on the soil. During the rains a tiger will select rocks and crags for his repose, kill oftener in the day and make bold excursions within village precincts, killing cattle whenever the chance occurs. Indian tigers do not take to caves readily, though they will resort to them when wounded. Tigresses expecting cubs often occupy them temporarily but as soon as the progeny are able to get about the shelter is abandoned.

There seems to be no fixity about the rutting period but as far as my knowledge goes it more often falls in the spring seasons, that is from the end of February to beginning of April, than at any other season. At this time both sexes are restless and erratic in their actions.

Sometimes they will not kill, even should they almost stumble against an animal, while at others they will abandon the kill without hardly eating a morsel. During this period the males often fight, to the accompaniment of a tumult of roars, coughs and

grunts, terrifying anyone who hears them. The gestation period is reckoned by the authorities to be from fourteen to sixteen weeks but aboriginal shikaris whom I questioned maintained it lasted for about twenty-one weeks. I have also heard it said that, should the period by chance be prolonged to twenty-four weeks and the cub can also be suckled for twenty-four weeks he will, when full grown, possess the strength to kill an elephant. Mr. Sanderson mentions an instance of a tiger killing and feasting on young elephants so that is probably a distorted version of similar occurrences of tigers killing calves when elephants abounded in the forests of Central India, as they did a generation or so ago. While pregnant, the tigress goes about as usual and retires only when very near her time.

The cubs vary in number from two to six, the average I should say being three. I know of only one instances of six. The tigress was shot by a policeman in the Chirapatla forest in the Betul district and she had that number of fetuses [sic] in her, fully developed and about to be born in a week or so. I can recall three cases where there were four cubs in each litter, of which in two instances the cubs were living. In the third they were fetuses recovered after the tigress was shot. I think that a tigress can seldom rear more than three and that, even with this number, she has difficulty. While suckling her cubs – a process which usually lasts from two to three months – a tigress is very savage and will allow nothing, not even her own lord, to come near the spot. In fact, she makes intrusion difficult by retiring to an unfrequented spot to bring forth her young. But as soon as the cubs are able to accompany her and play about she has no objection to the make joining the family circle. The cubs often remain with the mother till they are full grown. They are very playful, constantly scouting and stalking each other, while the mother lies down and watches them at their games.

I was told by Ram Singh, of Panchi-Tokra, a very successful tiger shikari, that the tigress utters a shrill whine-like whistle as warning to her cubs to lie still, if she happens to be at a distance from them when she scents danger.

Natives consider tigress' milk very efficacious for certain eye diseases. Shikaris told me it was of a thick, sticky consistency and drops lost while suckling coagulated on the surface like bird-lime, and co could be scraped up and utilised days after it had been spilt.

The tiger's fat is in great demand as a cure for rheumatic pains. His claws are used as charms to keep off the evil eye, being suspended round the necks of children or worn as an amulet with other charms encased in a bag. Men and women who practice witchcraft wear them in a string round the neck or waist and arms to render themselves immune from the evil effects of spirits with whom they consort. Ascetics also wear them, doubtless for the same reason. The cartilages from the shoulders are mounted on gold or silver and used as ornaments in various devices. The ends of the tiger's whiskers are considered to be deadly. They are supposed to be useful for bringing about the death of a rival without inviting suspicion on the person who administered the poison. It is said that if the whiskers are chopped very fine and given to the victim in his food the particles will enter the liver and perforate it, causing gradual decline and death. It is because of this that natives are so intend upon burning the tops of whiskers when a tiger is shot.

A very evident fact about tigers is that the sexes are nothing like as equally represented as they should be, considering the natural conditions under which they live and breed. My own experience shows that the proportion of males to females varies in the ratio of one tiger to every four tigresses. This inequality is in a less measure the result of natural preference which aims at producing more females than males to perpetuate the race but also, in a greater degree, it is due to immature males being killed off by adult tigers either through jealousy or during fits of temper when he two have quarreled. The latter theory is what aboriginal shikaris hold to, and I think they are correct. We know that the cubs remain with the mother until they are practically full grown. Under the circumstances the tiger naturally resents the presence of another male with the tigress and tries to get rid of him in the soonest time he can. This often means the killing of the younger and weaker beast if it persists in keeping with the tigress. Again, in a quarrel over food or opposition to the tiger, the younger male would have to bear the consequences of his indiscretion. Females are seldom or never attacked by males, even if they should be the aggressors.

The tiger's dietary is very varied. Essentially he is carnivorous, but he does not distain fruit and buds which he finds palatable. In common with animals and birds he relishes the succulent corolla of the mahua flower, and jungle tribes say that he will occasionally

take the pickings of juicy fruits. I know panthers will sip the juice of the common date palm, when the crowns of the stems tapped happen to be near enough to the ground to allow them to reach the cut surface from which the sap exudes. It is therefore very likely that tigers follow their example in places such as the Deccan and Mysore, where the date palm grows in their haunts. As regards flesh, I believe he will eat of every kind under the sun. In the Bori reserve in the Hoshangabad district, I came across a python half devoured by a tiger. The reptile must have been a monstrous size, judging from the dimensions of the parts remaining. The fore-part from the head to about the middle of the body was five feet ten inches long with an average girth of seventeen inches, whilst the piece of tail discarded was eighteen inches long and eight inches in girth. The body was frightfully lacerated by the tiger's claws.

Gond and Korku shikaris have told me that the tiger enjoys a meal of frogs, crabs and fresh water shells and that he will walk along the water's edge for miles, tilting up the stones and slabs under which they are usually found, hunting for them. They declared that these creatures, with birds, form the principle food of cubs after they have been weaned. Bird is doubtless seized by various means but I know of one instance where a tigress pounced into a covey of bush quail and knocked over a few with her paws before they had time to scatter. Then most sportsmen must know of instances of vultures knocked over if they ventured on the kill while the tiger was near, although in this case it is not for food but merely to keep them off the kill. Still it affords further evidence that he is equally quick in killing birds as animals.

Like a cat the Tiger is also fond of fish and he will poach for enticing fish at night from decoy pools and drains prepared by aborigine fisher folk. I remember my surprise at hearing of this the first time I came upon these people in the early morning. To their disgust at being outdone by the tiger was added their concern at being themselves detected in the reserve. Their account interested me so much, however, that the human poachers were let off with a warning. In this case the tiger had slashed about in the artificial pool and make it very muddy, possibly with the object of blinding the fish and so rendering their capture easy. The men said that he usually bagged the sanval or fresh water murrell, and eels which are easier to capture owing to their sluggish nature.

Mr. Sanderson, in his "Wild Beasts of India", mentions hearing

from his men that a tigress fed her young with undigested meat which she brought up. I have heard this corroborated by some Gond shikaris. Ram Singh, of Panchi-Tokra, even declared that to cause her to vomit the tigress ate grass, like dogs. I believe that tiger cubs do not actually begin to fend for themselves until they are about a year old, though like cats they commence much earlier to seize rats, birds and other small creatures. I have disturbed a cub eating a mongoose near his cave, into which he rang on seeing me and my trackers and evidently he had caught and killed it himself. Again, a cub about a year old was shot by a forest officer in a teak thicket a few miles out of Badnur in the Betul district. This beast was stuck with porcupine quills all over the body and forepaws and could hardly move without pain, and looked very sick. I fancy he had lost his mother and, not being quite up to the skill of hunting, he had tackled a porcupine, which is not surprising considering the tempting bait which its slow movements invite, and were it not for its protective covering the porcupine would be an easy prey and rendered extinct years ago. A young tiger without a parent's guidance would naturally tackle such a prey on sight.

Tiger cubs begin to accompany their mother on her hunting expeditions when they are four or five months old. On game being sighted the cubs crouch and look on whilst the tigress proceeds to sieze and kill, but no sooner the prey is down they come galloping up to her and bite and tug at the victim. In the monsoons of 1894 I was quartered for a time in the Shahpura bungalow and had opportunities of witnessing a tigress and her two cubs, about five or six months old, preying on cattle, nilgai and chinkara that kept [sic] in a patch of jungle to the west of the village, stretching between it and the reserve a few miles away. The growth consisted of old pollards and shrubs. The area was traversed by the Machna river, whose banks were deeply indented and shady, affording good cover for beasts of prey. During the rains, when the fields were being ploughed and sown, the tract became the principal resort for the village cattle. Attracted by its advantages the tigress had selected a network of fissures on the right bank of the stream as a temporary haunt to bring up her young and carried on her depredations among the cattle and game that came to feed in the jungle. She had practically no opposition to contend against and her attacks became daring, and it was quite a common thing to see

her about in the day, killing in front of the graziers, despite their shouts and threats, which she utterly disregarded,

It was about the middle of the rains when I arrived at the bungalow and was soon in possession of all the news concerning the tigress. The accounts interested me and it seemed a good opportunity to obtain first-hand information of her doings, so I had machans tied up on a few trees growing about the place and offering good positions for observation. In these I sat by turn and watched for a few hours before dusk as often as I could, and saw the tigress occasionally prowling about with her cubs. Strange to say she did not once come within a hundred feet of my tree. This may have been quite accidental, but I rather think she had wind of me, though she could not locate my position for I was well hidden; but it shows the daring she had acquired to venture near even on scenting danger. Also, I never saw her actually killing, though kills were made at short distances from my tree, for again coincidentally, each time a possible chance offered of seeing the prey seized, either a depression, or trees and bushes intercepted the view. But I saw her taking the kill into cover and noticed that she always gripped it about the shoulder. If it was a calf or other equally small animal, she held it up quite on a level with her body with the hoofs or hind feet trailing along the ground. Large animals, such as a full-grown ox or cow, she dragged, pulling the carcass towards her as she backed, instead of going forward with it as commonly supposed. Once also, either scenting me or suspecting danger, she swam across with her kill - a heifer - through a deep pool about fifty yards wide, to the opposite bank of the river.

She started to feast upon a young animal as soon as she had got it into cover, either peeling off the hide gradually as she ate, or consuming the skin with the meat. On all these occasions the cubs, which were about the size of large collies, walked quietly behind the mother imitating her moves as she sat, crouched to listen, or turned to see or avoid being seen, or to withdraw if danger was suspected. When the tigress went forward to kill, the cubs remained back crouching to the ground and watching the issue. How they knew exactly when to stop is more than I can tell. They followed the mother when the kill was being removed, gripping the carcass every now and again, as if anxious to assist in its removal. They started to feed no sooner the tigress began to uncover the skin, getting furiously angry with each other over the

feeding which usually made the tigress growl at them.

My men could not understand my reasons for maintaining these watches without even an attempt at a shot. I do believe the graziers fancied that I was in league with the tigress. However during the two or three weeks of watching, six head of cattle only were killed, of which four were calves or heifers. Four kills were made within seeing and hearing distance of my positions. Twice the tigress killed nilgai and once a chinkara doe. The latter practically ran into her jaws. She was being pursued by a buck and quite unsuspicious of danger ahead, went near by where the tigress happened just then to be. The tigress had already spotted them coming, and to avoid being seen had crouched behind the shelter of a bush, and as the doe rushed up she sprang out and laid hold of her by the throat. The buck who was hot in pursuit seeing the sudden turn of events, was scared out of his wits and actually bounded over the tigress and escaped. The cubs which were near the mother at the time tried to follow her example for when she had seized the doe, they sprang out of cover, one after the other, and laid hold of the creature by the loins.

I read in the Indian Field shikar book that tigers will eat carrion, but no instance of the kind has ever come to my notice. Also every aboriginal shikari whom I know has maintained the contrary, some even going on to assert that a tiger would abandon its own kill, should it be defiled by hyena, jackals or vultures, tearing at it and scattering the contents of the intestines about. All sportsmen know that vultures alighting on a kill is a sure sign of the tiger's absence. It is quite possible though that young or sickly tigers will make no bones about eating carrion; by young, I mean tigers that are little more than cubs left to fend for themselves owing to the loss of the parent. But it is extremely improbable that the ordinary healthy tiger would demean himself to touch carrion.

The game killing tiger varies his food as much as it is possible for him to do so. He will not repeatedly kill animals of the same kind. In tracts frequented by game, where he too prefers to make his abode, he has usually a large selection - sambar, blue-bull, cheetal, four-horned antelope, barking deer, pig, porcupine, monkey, boar, wild dog, badger and peafowl and on the outskirts of the forests, chinkara and stray cattle. The tiger who has feasted on sambar, will endeavour to make his next meal of one of the others.

Blue-bull and pig are the easiest to bag, the former because it is dull of sense, and the latter because it is a gregarious animal. Sambar and cheetal are not by any means easy victims as many people suppose. Their sense of smell is highly developed and unless taken quite unawares, they are more successful than other beasts in eluding tiger. Detected by a sambar or a cheetal, a tiger will abandon the chase for the time being, because they both but especially the former, has a habit of hanging on to his tail and putting the jungle on the qui vive. A tiger will rarely tackle a boar, and he will go for wild dogs only when they are alone or in twos or threes. He avoids porcupines, but a famous old Gond shikari in the Betul district told me that he greatly relishes porcupine's flesh, though only a few tigers will attempt to tackle him, because the little beast has a way of jerking off its quills by some extraordinary manipulation of its body with such precision, that the quills stick fast in its assailant's body, and cause it such discomfort that it abandons its intentions. Apparently the porcupine possesses only few of these quills that can act like darts, for tigers with experience will first engage in feints by a few attempts at attacking the animal in order to draw off the injurious quills, when the creature becomes an easy prey.

Again, a good boar is a difficult antagonist, and tigers prefer to leave him alone. I have heard that a tiger will often stalk a boar for a long distance. He will pounce on him only when he has a chance to grip him by the nape of the neck, as a hold on any other part is nothing like as certain to render him helpless. He grips panther and bear also by the nape of the neck, and these are the only kinds of animal I have seen killed in this way. The reason is obvious. They are strong active beasts with powers of offence quite different from other animals, so that a grip elsewhere would involve a struggle, and the only way of avoiding it is to bear down the victim by gripping him by the nape of the neck. A wrench would not be practicable as their thickset bodies, with short necks, do not allow of the necessary purchase to kill.

I was once privileged to hear a great fight between a tiger and a boar at a short distance from my camp at Baretha Ghat. It was on a night in October and the noise woke the whole camp and made my forester come rushing into my tent. The combat must have started just before three o'clock and lasted till nearly five o'clock. It made a regular pandemonium of growls, coughs and snorts by the

infuriated beasts, the tiger engaging in a whir of hideous growls, broken every now and again with a loud, hoarse cough; while the boar maintained a jumble of snorts and growls. As the end came suddenly and quietly we hoped that the combat had ended by a mutual withdrawal, but when we visited the scene of the encounter, the boar was lying dead where he had fought. The tiger had driven him out of a puddle-hole in which he had been wallowing, into a little depression some distance from the bank, and there the boar took up his position. The site was like a potato patch, the thick under-growth being torn up and scattered all round. There were marks of profuse bleeding all over, and little strips of skin both of tiger and of boar. The boar was of the brown variety, not very big, just two and a half feet at the shoulder, and the tusks measured less than nine inches; but he had made a great fight. His whole body had been frightfully lacerated, and possibly he failed owing to loss of blood. He had been gripped by the nape of the neck and borne to the ground till he died. But the tiger must have been in little better case as his subsequent behaviour showed. His fury with the boar was evident from the way he had crunched the boar's head after its defeat. However he was too sick to do more, he could not even move his trophy into cover for it was dropped and left in the open, a few paces from the scene of the struggle. We beat for the tiger, but he did not appear, so that he had left the locality. I would have given much to have even just seen him. All the trackers that could be mustered were put on to locate him, but the undergrowth was much too thick for them.

Besides varying his food the tiger is a connoisseur of the quality of what he eats. He will not kill a lean, decrepit or sickly animal, still less a tough old stager, but he selects his food from those in the prime of life. He relishes the meat of half-grown animals of all species, as well as that of females carrying young, especially during their first fecundation. An incident of the kind came to my notice in a reserve in the Hoshangabad district where I had to supervise markings for fellings. One morning I had preceded the coolies and sat on a knoll with two Kurku head-men, watching the sun rise to while away the time till the men arrived, when one of the Korkus called my attention to a tiger. He was going slowly on our left front, quite unsuspicious of our presence, and passed within a few paces on the lee-side of a hind sambar who was watching us. The tiger saw her and could have brought off the coup in one spring,

but he went on. I was puzzled to account for his scrupulous conduct; the Korkus however did not appear surprised and I made enquiries.

At last, after much questioning, the elder man explained that the tiger did not attack the hind because the venison would not be worth eating as she had a young one. There is a general belief among these people that the meat of females for a week or so after they have calved has a bitterish flavour and is unsuitable for eating. Asked how he could tell, he replied that the hind had been watching us from one position ever since we got on to the knoll, and if her young had not been near she would not have stayed so long, nor been so intent in keeping us in view. We began therefore to look about in the grass and sure enough we found a little fawn a few days old. I ought to add that I had just come among these people and had not yet gained their confidence which is perhaps why they prevaricated before giving me the right explanation. Again, when the tiger attacks cattle, he generally confines himself to heifers in calf. It is difficult to say how the tiger can tell a female with young at the distance from which he usually views his victims, but perhaps the explanation lies in the instinctive qualities with which most wild animals are endowed. Aborigine shikaris have told me that the tiger fixes on the creature by scent as the effluvia from females in calf is different from the rest of her kind, and forest graziers who live among animals and whom I questioned, confirmed this. I however think it has more to do with sight; the tiger's searching glance can soon detect the female in calf.

When a tiger is on the stalk for game, he will visit the various spots where animals are likely to be. He knows them all well enough. He will look up the salt-licks and puddle-holes, or make a round of the trees which attract game on account of their fruits, buds or leaves. He knows that burnt patches in a reserve or fire traces, from which the herbage shoots out afresh as soon as the surface has been moistened by dew or winter showers, are resorts for herbivorous animals in the early morning, as well as after sunset. He haunts the pockets of clay and grit on which animals delight to roll and gambol about, or the brackish pans covered with tangled vegetation of grass, weeds and herbs. It may seem easy that the preoccupied game could be seized without difficulty in such places, but as a matter of fact it is not the case. Some species, such as bison, sambar and cheetal usually place a watch to give the

alarm and are seldom taken unawares while the wary females maintain guard. The tiger's visits are therefore more with a view to reconnoitre the ground and waylay the prey as it comes or goes from the spot, than to actually seize it. Of course if the tiger should be fortunate to come across one by itself, he carries out his coup at once, but in the majority of instances he has to wait patiently in waylaying the prey as it comes or goes from the resort.

Obeying the law of the jungles expounded by Kipling, a tiger as a rule will not kill at or near the sites of recognised drinking holes, that is where the game collect to slake their thirst, especially during the hot-weather months. He turns up at the spot usually before or after the game tribes have come or gone. His approach is as quiet as could be imagined and should any animals be drinking when he arrives, he seems to take no notice of them; while if his presence has already been discovered the game will quietly move away into cover. In case he turns up without being perceived, the animals start off with a crash. It has always puzzled me why tigers will not kill at a watering place. Perhaps it may be a matter affecting his finer feelings not to take toll of life while in the act of relieving thirst - the one craving that is common to all creatures; or it may be due to sympathy in a common suffering, for the tiger more than any other, has cause to know what thirst means. People who have lived in the arid tracts of Central India during the hot weather, know the relief that a drink affords after hours of existence in the heat of the day, and can therefore enter into the spirit of the feeling, which makes even a fierce beast like the tiger relinquish his role of butcher for the time being. Aborigines however say that the tiger abstains from killing at a watering place in order to avoid polluting the water, as an attack on the spot must surely result in a struggle and tumble in the spring. However this may be, but I have known cases in which animals have temporarily abandoned drinking holes owing to kills being made near them by panthers and wild dogs.

Experienced shikaris will never tie a calf near a common watering hole. This reminds me of what occurred in my own experience. We were a party of three shooting in one of the jungles of Central India. A week went by without a kill, although we were told almost daily that tigers had passed close to the calves. the shikaris who my friends had brought, were supposed to know their work, and consequently, nothing could have been better. But we

noticed that they had fallen out with the local men which was enough in my opinion to stamp a man as incompetent at once. Our patience was well nigh exhausted and we began to question the men more closely regarding the blanks reported day after day, and one of them said that a tiger had been drinking very close to one of the calves and was sure to kill in a day or so. I decided to go to the place with them that very afternoon and see for myself. It was a celebrated haunt of tigers seven or eight miles from the camp and we all knew it, so that as long as the shikaris were to be relied upon, there was no need of a visit to the place. But when I came on the calves, I found that they had been tied at the different water holes. This blunder was known to the local men who however, had said nothing about it to the imported shikaris, but rather laughed in their sleeves and watched the fun. I had the calves removed and tied at a distance.

When I got back, I kept my own counsel beyond saying that the calves had been changed which ought to bring good luck. Next morning sure enough, a kill was reported and a tiger came out to the guns. I then took my friends to the spot and explained the cause of our long wait. A couple of days after one of the other calves was also killed, so that in three days we had three kills as soon as the calves were removed from the common drinking holes. Another habit of the tiger is that when they go about together in two or threes and occasionally more as they often do, only one of them will actually kill while the others crouch down and look on. But the meat is shared by all. Whether they take it in turns to kill, or whether it is a question of priority, it is difficult to conjecture. My own opinion is that the one who sees the game first does the killing. But why the business should be treated as only one tiger's task, when two or more could take part and finish it more easily, is a conundrum. It may be that "too many cooks spoil the broth", or that the beasts are too sure of their mettle to require assistance, or practise against the day when they will be alone.

When a tiger has mastered his quarry, he will always endeavour to remove it into cover, screened from prying eyes. The next question is whether he will start to feed straight away, or will wait till the carcass begins to set up and to soften, offering him a more appetizing meal. His decision depends entirely on the age and size of the victim. Pork, veal and tender venison, he will commence to consume at once. In the case of the bigger animals, he will eat a few

morsels from the rump and then leave the carcass for a while to soften. Should the victim be a female with young, the fetus [sic] will be laid bare and eaten as soon as possible. The tiger's method of going about his kill differs materially from a panther's, for the latter as a rule, commences to tear and eat its victim on the spot, beginning by disembowelling the body and starting from the belly, so as to get at the heart and liver first.

It is astonishing how well the tiger can skin his prey; an operation which requires the assistance of one or two men, the tiger does unaided. But he removes the hides of only large animals whose skins are hard and tough. In the case of soft-skinned animals or young beasts, he devours the skin along with the gobbets of flesh bitten off the carcass. The tiger rips the skin under the belly as soon as possible after he has killed, to get out the stomach and so prevent the contents contaminating the meat with the evil gases that set up after life is extinct. And though the contents are contained in a ball of thin membranous tissue, he always manages in spite of his sharp claws and teeth, to remove it intact. Shikaris say that the tiger does this with his mouth and toes, the claws being retained well inside their sockets during the process. I have seen this being done, so their description is correct. The tiger starts to uncover the skin in the case of large victims when the carcass has become somewhat stale, peeling it off gradually with his mouth and paws and feeding the while, as the flesh is exposed. Any parts for which he has no liking are left with the skin on. His meal consists of gobbets of flesh bitten off and swallowed, with or without masticating: bones are treated in the same way, though he leaves the bigger and harder ones alone. When the tiger has eaten for fifteen or twenty minutes, he will stop and have a drink and to rest, either lying down or taking a short walk before going at it again. When he has had his fill, he will retire to repose. A large victim like a sambar, provides his meals for two or three days, while a small one will be eaten in a day or a few hours according to its size. The tiger does not really gorge, as is commonly supposed. If he did so, he could finish his biggest victim within twenty-four hours, but we know that even young calves take him two or three days to consume.

A tiger is not really the savage beast he is so often represented to be. Confirmed man-eaters excepted, he will always endeavour to escape from man, but should the meeting be unavoidable, he

will either try to cause a diversion by assuming a threatening attitude, expressed by growls, grunts and angry gestures, or if that fails, he will utilise his power of offence only to the extent of mauling with the intention of disabling his adversary. I have never heard of a tiger wrenching a man's neck in the way he kills animals, although there have been cases where the person attacked has provoked the beast unnecessarily and given him sufficient cause to rend him limb from limb. Generally in accidental encounters, when the tiger seizes an unarmed man, all that the unfortunate fellow usually has to show for his seizure, are a few claw impressions. Even if death occurs, it will be found that it was due to hemorrhage or blood poisoning. I am of the opinion that most tigers cannot quite comprehend man and are therefore somewhat puzzled as regards the spot where to fix his hold, with a view to incapacitate him easily, as is done in the case of animals. This would account for the erratic seizures, no two of which correspond, even when the same tiger is the aggressor.

The idea that a tiger cannot always kill a human victim outright, cannot be entertained for a minute in the light of what is known regarding his marvellous strength and still more, the tremendous power of offence with which nature has provided him. I heard a sportsman who had been badly mauled, narrate that while the tiger had him down, he felt as if a mountain had rolled over him. We may be sure that if a tiger harboured murderous intentions towards man, and supposing he could not bring off the coup by wrenching the neck, he would have no trouble and kill the victim by simply gripping the head or chest sufficiently hard to enable his fangs to penetrate into the vital organs, thereby causing almost instantaneous death. But as observed, he falls short of this. In the majority of cases all the punishment that man's rashness in attempting to compete with the king of beasts invites is a severe shaking accompanied by claw or teeth wounds, even in cases where the tiger has been wounded and so roused to his wildest passion.

I have no doubt that the tiger is really reluctant to touch man and will only do so when impelled by circumstances. It is difficult to say why he should make this difference in respect of man. I am thinking not of the well equipped and accoutred sportsman who may be presumed to present a somewhat formidable appearance, but the unarmed aborigine who except for a loin cloth, goes about

practically stripped. One is inclined to suggest that there is in man some mystic power which awes the tiger to such an extent, that even when forced to an encounter, he feels that he is committing sacrilege and is inclined to be ashamed of himself, as sportsmen who have had opportunities of witnessing such acts, may recollect by his subsequent behaviour in slinking away from the scene hurriedly, no sooner his excitement had abated. This repelling force in the gift of man is no doubt the result of his highly superior organism which invests him with a halo of dread in the eyes of all quadrupeds. I discussed this point with an intelligent old Gond - a well known character who had planned the deaths of hundreds of tigers - and I was rather struck by his explanation. According to him, human beings appeared in the tiger's eyes much as ghosts do to human beings, and he was therefore, not only afraid of them, but could not avoid a feeling of reverence for them.

Often an ascetic takes up his abode in places that are the haunt of tigers without being molested. On their first appearance the tiger probably prowls inquisitively round the booth and expresses his displeasure by growls and grunts, but in the course of time he accustoms himself to the intrusion and he takes no notice. Such occurrences are the origin of many jungle tales, for they have a supernatural appearance to the eyes of the ignorant.

I was once benighted far from camp and the Bhil guard of the beat took me to the booth hard by, where a fakir had recently taken up his quarters. The spot was in thick jungle where a gigantic rock served as a shrine to local spirits. It was at least three miles from the nearest hamlet and lay in a recess in a cleft of a hill overlooking a deep water-fall, down which tumbled the head-waters of a considerable stream on its way to the plains. Shaded by trees and overhanging rocks it commanded a picturesque and extensive view of the undulating plateau stretching in front, and, of the valley below thickly wooded with teak and bamboos, where the game from miles around resorted during the day. The spot had probably sheltered many anchorets for it had the appearance of being an old retreat. The fakir was quite hospitable and as I was tired, with the prospect of a long march over a rough path through difficult country, I decided to spend the night at the booth. So after eating some stale sweets, curd and cakes which the people brought him as offerings, we lay down to rest on grass beds by a flickering log fire. In the small hours of the morning, I was awakened by ghostly

sounds. My two men were already up and crouching near the fire, while the fakir, who was a little distance off under the rock, continued to sleep without concern; or so it appeared for I hardly think anyone could have slept undisturbed by such a noise.

I have mentioned at the commencement of this chapter the peculiar sound which I once heard made by a tiger returning to its kill. These noises were exactly like that, though conditions were different and so was the locality: but even after a lapse of over nine years, the similarity struck me at once. The beast kept up his pandemonium, prowling near the spot for about an hour, and then as he withdrew, the sound gradually died away. There was no sleep for us for the remaining hours, but the fakir seemed to sleep through it all; one of the men shouted to him without producing any effect. He was up however at the first break of dawn and in our midst before we could realise it, and when told what had passed, he remarked indifferently, that it must have been the tiger which usually came to visit him and was doubtless annoyed at our presence. Some days after, I found my camp followers had got hold of quite an exaggerated version of the occurrence from the men who had accompanied me. For they made out that the tiger had come and done obeisance at the shrine and, but for the fakir's intervention the tiger would have surely done for us instead of which the beast gave vent to his displeasure by parading about the shrine as a warning to us not to come again.

I know of a similar experience which we had with a panther years later in another province. But in this case when the noise began, the fakir got up and addressed the beast as his son and shouted out to him to stop, which in fact he did.

The audacity which a man-eating tiger will show in assailing man can only be attributed to a form of madness acquired, I believe, not by the taste of human flesh, as many suppose, but by abnormal conditions inherent in the beast which govern his actions in spite of his better judgement. Even then the attack is seldom or never from the front, but from the side or back of the victim. It is difficult to account exactly for the origin of man-eaters. Doubtless in some cases, a beast who has been rendered more or less helpless by a wound or by old age finds that man offers the least chances of a struggle, and falls an easy victim to his diminished energy. But evidently this is not the general rule. Tigers that are physically incapable could not maintain the struggle for existence. They must

either become diseased and die or lose their activity, and so fall under their human enemies' hand.

The genuine man-eater is the beast who has developed the habit during the course of its normal existence, probably owing to some defect in its cerebral equipment. Such a brute is usually extremely cunning, a clever hunter and a great rover, in fact possessing many of the traits of a human madman. The destruction of a habitual man-eater is always a difficult matter and accomplished sportsmen often fail in the attempt. It is this fallacy of confusing the real man-eater with the decrepit creature that takes toll of human lives necessitously, which led to the belief once cherished, that man-eaters are usually mangy beasts. It will be obvious that such creatures owing to the suffering they have undergone from wounds or disease must be in poor condition. The genuine man-eater on the other hand is never mangy but in as good condition as any healthy tiger.

Sportsmen who have had experience of these brutes may have observed how markedly they differ from the normal tiger in many ways. Here I may mention, that they are restless and uncertain in their movements, while they generally choose to lie up in rocks and stones on the crests and peaks of hills resembling the panther in this respect, again they are more turbulent and rapacious in their attacks at about new moon than at any other time and moreover victims snatched from their fury seldom live, being lacerated by deeper incisions of tooth and claws. Man-eaters rarely kill the larger game, such as adult buffalo, sambar, blue-bull and bison, either because their madness has engendered a fear of these powerful animals, or because they have lost through disuse the art of dealing the swift stroke which is so essential for a successful coup against a powerful victim.

A man-eater, veils its movements in a way that acquires for it a supernatural importance in the minds of ignorant folks who look upon its existence as a divine dispensation. This has less to do with the tiger's looks though naturally the brute assumes fanciful forms in the eyes of the superstitious, but chiefly because of the startling swiftness with which it attacks without the slightest indication of its presence, the people regard it with a holy dread. As an aborigine headman once put it to me, "the beast springs out of the surface and is off with its prey-like a hawk", meaning beyond the means of rescue like the bird darts up to the skies out of human reach. Shikaris ascribe the brute's cunning as acquired from human

beings on whom it feeds. This idea is no stranger than the general belief of regarding a tiger that has had opportunities of feasting on human flesh is a confirmed man-eater.

The dread inspired by a man-eater is usually so great that rather than devise measures for the beast's destruction, the people prefer to abandon their homes, looking upon the scourge as a divine visitation for the punishment of past sins. To this day one may come across culturable tracts, depopulated and wild, that date their lapse into jungle from the advent of a man-eater. But to one acquainted with the habits of the tribe, there is nothing striking, either in the way in which the brute steals upon one unawares. or the fear it inspires by leaving its victim little chance of escape. Having taken to man-hunting, the beast would naturally exercise greater caution to prevent detection than the ordinary tiger; the one is on the war-path against man and needs to take every care for fear of endangering its skin, while the other has no reason for extra precaution because rather than assume the role of hunter it considers itself to be the hunted and avoids an encounter. Moreover the change from the fearless game-killer who has no cause to be at enmity with man, to the beast who includes human victims among its prey and has therefore to fear man's vengeance, transforms the latter into an extremely cunning beast as a matter of necessity. As if fearing to face its victim, the tiger seldom or never attacks from the front, but launches on him from the back or side, more especially when it sees him preoccupied. It is doubtful if the beast would succeed against determined opposition. I have known cases of wood and grass cutters managing to escape by using their implements which they chanced to have by them when attacked. As a rule the wretched victim is so dazed and frightened that even should he recover from the suddenness of the attack, he is too feeble and helpless to offer any resistance and allows himself to be dragged away in a state of stupefaction. If the fright has not already ended his life, the tiger's grip does so sooner or later.

As far as I know, in dealing with human victims, the man-eater never attempts to wrench the neck. Shikaris say this is because the tiger fears to look into his face. The victim is rarely killed outright by the attack, but the tiger, having pounced upon him unawares, grips the shoulder and hurries with him into cover. Occasionally the neck is gripped when death is certain, but more often it is the shoulder and the victim remains alive though dazed and helpless.

The fallacy generally accepted that man-eaters are cowardly beasts would bear examination. My experience has shown that the beast is in no way more wanting in courage than the ordinary tiger. People jump to conclusions because the brute has developed more slyness and cunning in the methods of its attack and retreat. But the point lost sight of in the reckoning is to consider how the ordinary tiger behaves when dealing with its prey, and then to compare the actions of the two in ratio to the intelligence possessed by their respective victims.

A game-killer or cattle-lifter is as careful not to show itself as the tiger who takes to man-eating, only the one has less reason to be cautious, as the other has perforce to exceed it. Like all animals the man-eater knows instinctively that man of all creatures is the one being to conjure with and the means it takes to conceal its movements is purely due to self-defence and but natural, considering man's superior intelligence which enables him to circumvent his deadliest foes. Again the exceptional character of the victim evidently instills into the tiger a fear of a guilty conscience causing it to expect some form of reprisal. This would explain why the beast deviates from the habits of the tribe, such as abandoning the locality, retiring to great distances to lie up in places where tigers seldom or never resort.

Although the tiger is mad enough to kill man, it still has the sense to fear him, and the dread seems to increase in proportion with the toll of life, the effect of which is to raise the brute's suspicions. Thus an excess of cunning is assimilated which passes for cowardice. But the fear inspired by man does not make the tiger a coward by any means, and when brought to bay it shows as good a fight as the staunchest of the tribe, indeed there is more reason to fear accidents in its case than in that of an ordinary tiger. To put it briefly, the man-eater's methods of executing coups are such as to qualify it as a tactician in military parlance. It is probably because of this that the beast avoids encounters with powerful game, since the daring necessary for giving the fatal wrench diminishes in inverse ratio to the excessive caution developed.

That feasting on human flesh does not develop a passion for killing may surely be inferred from many instances in which the adult families of man-eating tigresses, accustomed to be fed on human victims, abandon the practice of killing man after the parent had been destroyed. Some sportsmen who have been fortunate

enough to bag the whole brood flatter themselves with the notion that parent and offspring alike took part in the killing, or else that if spared the young ones would have assuredly turned man-eaters having once tasted human flesh, and so they consider themselves justified in including all the bag in the number of man-eaters slain.

This fallacy has never so far as I know been attacked, perhaps because of the difficulty in proving or disproving such a proposition. Most sportsmen are merely itinerant and cannot ascertain the facts of particular cases in such completeness as to justify them in controversy: and any one who claims the laurels is likely to be left secure in their possession. I myself have very little personal experience of man-eaters, but I have at least been in very close touch with the jungle tribes among whom one occasionally finds extremely intelligent characters. I have mixed freely with them at all times and seasons of the year and have had plenty of opportunities of hearing them recount the various incidents which they had observed themselves, or which had been handed down by their elders; and I have questioned them on anything that struck me as interesting or unusual. Consequently my views are based on their beliefs and I have verified them. To come back to the subject, I think it possible that an adult cub who has seen its parent at the business, may follow suit and kill a few human beings on its own account: I am sure that he usually does not continue it, but stops soon after the parent's death. In other words, when the incentive has been removed the beast is reclaimed, and becomes the orderly tiger that nature intended him to be.

Personally I have little doubt that apart from infirmity and wounds, it is only the deranged or demented tiger who will dare to hunt man. I remember a discussion that took place on this point many years ago. A senior forest officer had had a good stroke of luck in bagging three out of a family of five reputed man-eaters. The Gonds however were positive that only the tigress killed, although her progeny as well as the lord joined in the feast. But the forest officer was of the contrary opinion and was sure that the evil would not stop until the two that had escaped, namely, an adult cub and the old tiger were also accounted for. His standing, experience and service made it impossible to contradict him: but - I can vouch for the fact - no more kills occurred, as shortly after the forests came under my charge. None the less, it took some years before people could be induced to re-occupy the deserted villages, as they too doubted the

bona fides of the two at large, believing in the adage "evil communications corrupt good manners". To judge from the pugs the old tiger must have been a very fine beast, and I tried hard to get him, but he had been beaten so often that he knew the ropes thoroughly and invariably succeeded in slipping through the stops. It needed a Thompson to devise some exceptional measure applicable to his case.

Further, in his relations with the other denizens of the jungles, a tiger will not kill for the mere lust of blood. If he has feasted or is contented with himself, he will pass by game within easy reach without attempting to molest it, and will even at times go out of his way to avoid an encounter. Consider the way in which he attacks a herd of cattle. He always selects one for his feast, although he is hungry and at his onslaught the animals stampede in all directions which of course gives him an opportunity of killing as many as he liked in detail.

A tiger will not eat putrid meat and he takes some time to get through the carcass of a large victim such as an ox or a buffalo calf, so that even supposing he had the opportunity of killing several victims with a view to stocking his larder the climatic conditions would not allow of the flesh keeping longer than a few days. There would be no object therefore, in making provision for a larger supply of meat than was necessary for the time being.

There are doubtless instances of two or three animals being killed, or in cases of calves tied out as baits near each other. But these are the exceptions rather than the rule and if means existed of judging I think we should find that his conduct was due to some provocation which caused him to deviate from his usual practice. In all my experience I have only once known of two calves being killed and then I was doubtful if the same tiger was responsible as there were a pair and the pugs showed that both had been to the calves. On the other hand I know of one instance where two calves were tied up about a hundred yards apart, one on each side of a stream. Only one was killed and it was dragged into an island in the river where the tiger lay up actually so near the living calf that the men could not go to fetch the poor beast away till after the beat for fear of disturbing the tiger.

The tiger is not always as sedate as he appears: he has his humorous side as well. Sitting up at nights, I have heard him growling under trees where monkeys had taken up their quarters for the night with the object of frightening them. This is done in

mere mischief, probably in retaliation for the annoyance they cause by giving him away during the day. This has led to a common belief among natives, that the tiger when hungry has only to growl under a tree occupied by monkeys, for one or more to fall down to his order and provide his meal. Often too when he is resting or moving and sees or hears animals that have not detected him in their proximity, he will growl or grunt to announce his presence, and scare them: or when he tries to pass through beaters, he will utter a startling cough to cause a diversion in order to enable him to break through. I have heard from jungle tribes how a tigress will play at pitch-and-toss with her cubs, and how, during the breeding season, she is capricious in her love affairs, showing partiality first to one tiger and then to another tiger, with the intention of provoking a fight.

A tiger on the prowl will often be followed for distances by sambar uttering at intervals that peculiar note of warning which has been described as resembling the first note on a trombone. This attendance is sometimes continued for miles; it seems that each sambar transfers its self-imposed duty to the next sambar met during the stalk. At night watches my attention has often been called to the incident, and by the sounds, one could follow their progress fairly well for long distances. But the interesting thing was to hear the same note pitched in different keys according to the age or sex of the attendants, as they changed watches. Sometimes the tiger would be heard to growl - the suppressed angry sound - as he went along. The sambars' calls are of course a warning to the denizens that the King of beasts is about. The tiger can only shake them off by deviating from his course and getting on the lee-side of his inquisitive attendants.

This persistency of the sambar in sticking to the tiger is natural enough if we consider his role in the life of the jungles, which I have endeavoured to explain in a separate chapter. It is what a watchman would do if he were to meet a suspicious character during his rounds.

Tigers differ in size and colour, but their variation is chiefly a matter of adaptation to local conditions. I have mentioned that long bodies and small feet are a characteristic of hill tigers. Similarly, tigers inhabiting open jungle and marshes are lightly coloured or tawny, that is showing a yellow tint on glossy coats; while those living under thick growth or in ravines, have deeper

colouring, that is the yellow gives place to dark brown of a rufous hue in bright light.

The tiger who depends for his livelihood entirely or almost entirely on game is of a wiry appearance, whereas the cattle-lifter has a thickset, sluggish look. The reasons are obvious. The one has to combine agility and strength as well as to employ his wits fully in obtaining his food - no easy matter, when the game tribes are equally well endowed with the instinct of self-preservation; whilst the other has not only less foraging to do but can easily perceive his victim and bring off his coups by no other qualities than patience and strength. An individual tiger may pass from one type to the other at some period of his existence. Thus, the game-killer would develop into the cattle-lifter were he to become less active by constant temptation to seize cattle, or when his haunts were invaded by settlers affording him opportunities to kill their animals; while in the contrary case the cattle-lifter would become the game-killer if the jungle side were deserted of settlements.

Some tigers remain small although they attain great age. I know of one shot in the Khamapur reserve in the Betul district which was barely seven feet six inches from tip of tail to point of nose, though he was very old and had lost most of his molars and incisors. Again there are tigers with a sort of rudimentary mane and correspondingly longer tufts of hair about the neck and jaws. I have seen only two shot, and as they came up to the guns they appeared higher at the shoulder than the average tiger. And in each case, though they occurred in different Provinces, the older men among the local shikaris maintained that the animal was a cross between lion and tiger. The explanation was plausible as lions did occur in the neighbouring tracts about thirty years previous. My first tigress again had the stripes under her belly interrupted with spots, while her head was smaller and more pointed than that of the average tigress, and the Gonds thought that she was a cross between a tiger and a panther. Whatever the aborigines may have to say in the matter, I believe myself that such inter-breeding is impracticable between animals so highly differentiated, although belonging to the same congener. All such slight differences are very probably survivals or reproductions of past stages in the sequence of evolution. Then of course, there are the very rare cases of black and white tigers, which can only be regarded as freaks.

There are no authentic accounts of the age attained by a tiger in his natural state. On another page I have given an instance of a tiger who was known to the people for fourteen or fifteen years before I came among them. He existed for at least another ten years of the sixteen during which the locality continued under my supervision. Supposing then, he was five years of age when he acquired his repute among the jungle tribes, it is safe to assume that the tiger attained a span of thirty years when he disappeared from the scene of his exploits. I heard that he was shot by a Khandesh official in a far away corner of the district, but there were no means of confirming the account. In the Betul district there was a tiger in the Rajgaon-Khapa reserve known to the countryside for over twenty years. He was shot by a brother officer, but I was not present at the time and only saw his skin pegged out. Judging from its dimensions, he must have been a very fine beast. He had very much the same reputation as his cousin of the Newali Satpuras.

Shikaris presume to tell the age of tigers from the number of lobes of the liver. A lobe counts for each year, while three years are added to the sum, as it is said the tiger has this number for the first year. Six to eighteen lobes have been pointed out to me in livers extracted from different tigers, and the increases agreed with other signs of age, such as a dull and ruffled coat, yellow teeth and sunken eyes, but it is difficult to accept their calculation as accurate. If this means of fixing the age of tigers could be taken as evidence I should be inclined to allow one lobe for every second or third year, commencing with the three which the tiger is said to have in the first year of its existence. I say this because I know of a few tigers about whose ages there could be little or no mistake, who had more lobes than the shikaris credited them with. In one case I had watched two cubs grow up, one of these was shot when nearly two years old and his liver had six lobes instead of the four which should have been the number according to the men. In another instance, a young tigress in cub for the first time was shot and the elders declared that she was four years old. Yet her liver had nine lobes, instead of the six which the shikari had reckoned her having. The shikaris did not know how to account for these differences except that the beasts had been in existence longer than was known.

Every sportsman doubtless knows that the pugs of a tiger can usually be distinguished from those of a tigress by their rounder

circumference, and the same is the case with individual toes. A tiger going his natural gait leaves a clearer, deeper impression than one who is on the stalk for food. Some tigers wallow more than others and prefer a pool or puddle to the clear bed of a stream: the tawny variety which haunts open forests and marshes, is especially addicted to this habit; while his darker-shaded brother who lives under dense cover, is content with a roll in pockets of clay, sand or grit found in most jungle tracts, that is he enjoys what may virtually be regarded as a mud-bath.

These forms of cleansing the body are common with most wild animals but why they should prefer a puddle pool or clayey, gritty or sandy surface, to flowing water when it is available is not very clear. It seems to me that the ticks and bugs with which the tigers get covered are more easily removed by wallowing in mire because of the incrustation of mud that forms over the body and when hardened chokes and kills a number of the vermin. On the other hand merely dipping in water barely suffices to detach - less to kill - the pests. And again, a roll over the surface would relieve irritation from bites much more than a bath and as in the case in wallowing, would kill as well as detach a good many of the vermin.

Tigers are good swimmers and I have known them to cross torrential streams in flood when the islands they happened to be occupying at the time were suddenly submerged by a spate. A grazier gave me an account of a sight he had witnessed of a tigress rescuing her cubs during such a flood. It happened in the Satsui valley on the banks of the Lonar river in which there are several little islands that always hold tiger. The grazier recounted his tale to me on the very afternoon of the event, in fact he had come with the object of getting me to go with him to capture the cubs, no doubt with the view of earning a reward and of course I would not hear of his proposal to rob the tigress.

He was out as usual with his buffaloes on the banks of the stream, when a flood came down owing to heavy rains in the hills higher up on the night before. While watching the water rise, he saw a tigress on the island in front of him come out of the growth, holding a cub in her mouth and swim rapidly for the bank on the side on which he was standing. He got up a tree through fear and saw her deposit the cub on the bank, and again swim to the island and bring back a second cub, and return a third time for her last

cub. Then after resting a while, she marched off with them to a rocky knoll a few hundred yards from his tree. As soon as he found it safe to leave, he got down and returned to his village and came on to tell me.

It is only in very exceptional circumstances that a tiger will try to go up a tree. He is a bad climber owing no doubt to his great weight which prevents him from obtaining a firm hold of the trunk, especially as cat-like he uses his claws which cannot always get the necessary grip in the soft bark or bast of the stem. He may rush up the trunk for a short height by sheer impetus and lodge in its fork, but more than this it seems he is unable to do. Cubs however are quick in getting up and down trees.

I once heard an account of a tiger being treed by wild dogs. The sight was witnessed by a young Gond who was collecting gum off a tree, and remained quietly in his seat on observing the strange event. The shikari said he could vouch for the lad's telling the truth, and he took me to see the spot. The tree was an old pollard of kalam with a thick knotty trunk about ten feet high, supporting a whorl of shoots at the apex. According to the youth, the tiger came bounding along from the direction of a stream close by, pursued by a pack of twenty or thirty dogs, and ran up the stem and lodged at the top among the nest of shoots that grew out of the head of the trunk. The dogs kept near the tree for about a quarter of an hour and then went back to the stream whence they had come, while the tiger remained up for some time longer and then slid down and trotted off in the opposite direction. It is painful to reflect that the King of beasts should have been humiliated by such vermin, and looking to the odds against him perhaps he was well advised. The dogs must have been pretty hard up to attack a tiger. My own impression was that they had either chanced upon the tiger's kill in one of their hunts, or else had killed near where he was lying up. In either case, the tiger would show his resentment at being disturbed, and the dogs being in great force would naturally endeavour to drive him away.

I remember another case told me by the Mohammedan orderly of a sportsman in the department who had left the district shortly before I joined. He declared that while acting as a silent stop in one of his master's beats, a young tiger came rushing along from the direction of the stops and ran up the trunk of a kahu tree close to where he was seated. The animal kept for a while in the uppermost

fork, fifteen feet from the ground, and then getting down slowly to the lower fork half way between, he jumped from it to the ground and made off. When I saw the place and got the man to describe the affair on the spot, it was evident the beat was one of those noisy ones that made the locality resound with shouts from all sides and so puzzled the poor beast that he did not know which side to turn, and wisely got up a tree to find out his bearings. These are the only authentic cases which I know of. During stalks and excursions, trees with deep vertical incisions have been pointed out to me as examples of the tiger's escalades, but this was mere supposition and the marks could have been caused by bears, more probably by tigers sharpening their claws.

Something like this befell me while sitting up for a tiger at Ambimata in the Debke forests of the Betul district. The kill was in a ravine some miles from camp. The ground was difficult to beat, so I decided in spite of a late moon, to sit up with my Mohammedan shikari. The machan was prepared in the fork of a pepul tree, about twelve feet from the ground, and overlooking the kill. No sooner was it dark than the tiger turned up unexpectedly from the back of us, passing under our tree to get to his kill which he commenced to tackle at once. The kill had not been disturbed in the least, and was lying just where the tiger had left it under the spreading boughs of trees growing along the nullah bank. It was so dark in the ravine that try as I would, I could not even get a glimpse of the brute, so the only thing was to wait till the moon rose at about ten o'clock. In the meanwhile the tiger continued to feast unsuspicious of our presence. About an hour passed in almost perfect stillness, broken only by the rippling of water in the stream hard by and the munching of flesh and crackling of bones. Then suddenly there was a slight rustling of leaves caused by a current of air speeding through the valley. This must have wafted our scent to the tiger, for he stopped eating, remained perfectly still for a few minutes and then as if agitated began to walk about all over sniffing the air. Having satisfied himself, he returned to the kill and continued his meal. Half an hour after there came another puff of wind and again he began perambulating further afield. He was absent quite ten minutes and ended by sitting under our tree for a third time and could have barely swallowed a few mouthfuls, when the breeze rose again with a deeper note causing the tiger to make straight for our tree in a few rapid strides. This time he

braced himself up against the trunk and began to snuff and snort, barely a foot below the machan then, having made sure of our presence he was off instantly without a sound. It may be imagined what an exciting few minutes we had in the machan. The thick cover over which we were seated made it absolutely impossible to fire vertically downwards, while a fork of the tree closer to the ground presented a veritable ladder for him to get up. But although his claw marks reached up to nine feet, he made no hostile attempt beyond using the stem as a support to enable him to stretch out to his full height and satisfy his curiosity. This experience corroborates what I have said that the ordinary tiger will always try to avoid collision with man even when the advantage rests with him.

Tigers are in the habit of constantly scraping their forepaws on hard or gravelly surfaces or against the trunk of a tree with a hard, smooth bark like that of the dhaora. This is done to sharpen the claws which are protruded during the process so that the pads hardly touch the substance. Again after feeding, they invariably clean their nails as far as is practicable by rubbing the paws in the same way on mossy or turfy soil or in wet sand. This is very necessary otherwise the bits of flesh that lodge between the hooks would set up and might cause the animal trouble, as it is despite the cleaning, minute particles manage to remain embedded in the partitions which are generally the cause of the mortification of wounds made by a tiger's claws.

I have mentioned how tigers seeking to escape often take their cue from the movements of animals. But birds as well as the jungle squirrel warn them of coming danger. The best watchmen are the common plover or did-you-do-it, the Indian magpie, raven, king-crow, the large green barbet, the mocking bird, and the golden oriel [sic]. All these utter deeper notes at the sight of anything unusual, as for instance, when they see man in places where he has no right to be. So too peafowl and parrots indicate danger by their sudden, chattering flight when disturbed, and as they often take shelter in cover near where the tiger lies up, he is quick to guess the cause and follow suit. Most of these warnings can be construed equally as omens in one's own favour, but I fancy that they are more often than not intended as warnings to the denizens of the jungles, and are the means by which the plans of the hunter are foiled, however cautiously he may have gone about the business. But apart from

this, the same birds again will utter quite different notes when they see the tiger on the move.

Jungle tribes declare that in this case the cry uttered resembles that which the birds utter when seized by animals or birds of prey. Thus, the peculiar "kaon kaon" followed by a sort of shriek of the peacock, or the raucous "yes yes" of the magpie drawn out in a series of jerky notes, finishing with a drawl, or the piercing whine of the hare, are uttered only on sighting animals and birds of prey. Again, the peculiar "cluck cluck" of the jungle fowl, uttered in a few sharp notes passing into a shrill one of terror, is a sure telltale of the beast's whereabouts. As far as I know, it is only uttered on sighting a tiger, panther or the jungle cat, and the notes are too distinctive to be mistaken.

We were once beating for jungle fowl in a patch of growth close to some aboriginal settlements scattered about the hillside. There were two positions. My friend occupied the first taking with him a boy who was keen to be in a beat, while I took the other with another friend fresh from home. Our positions were both within [a] hundred yards of the nearest hamlet. As the beat progressed and the birds came flying over, the first gun fired several shots; but very few birds came our way. When the beaters were almost up, I heard the peculiar notes which I have described in a direction between the two positions in front, and warned my friend to be ready for a panther. As he had my shotgun, I handed over my rifle to him. He was rather surprised at my abruptness and inclined to resent it at the time. However a minute after, the clear report of a rifle rang out from the other position which was barely thirty paces from where we were seated. The panther had suddenly appeared before the first position, but my friend being busy knocking over jungle fowl, had not observed it. The boy with him saw the beast though, and pointed it out. Luckily my friend also had his rifle near him as we were to try for other game after the beat. So, in spite of the delay in changing and loading weapons, he managed to get the panther. But had it not been for the boy the panther would have probably escaped, as my friend had no idea of the warning note given by the bird.

Another instance bearing on the subject occurs to me. The jungle folks maintain that the tiger is guided in his movements by the large or black-backed woodpecker, and that the peculiar note of "kir kir" which the bird utters is the precursor of evil if the warning

is neglected. They say that the bird utters these notes in the direction from which it is conscious of danger. If the tiger is on the move and hears the notes, he acknowledges them as a warning to him not to proceed in the direction from which they come. Again, should he be lying or seated when they are uttered he interprets them as a warning to him not to get up, so that he will not budge from the spot for the time being.

I remember hearing a curious tale to much the same effect about a man-eater which was wounded in a beat and took refuge in a cluster of dwarf bushes growing on the bank of a big river. After the beat, the guns and men got together and tried to dislodge him from the cover. But each time he got up, intending to swim across the river, the bird's note resounded from the opposite bank, making him withdraw into cover. This occurred three or four times: at last the animal, pressed by his pursuers, plunged into the river despite the notes of warning to escape to the opposite bank. When he was about halfway through the water he was dragged in by a crocodile. However this may be, I have seen a sambar diverted by a squirrel which was chirping in a tree as a protest against a stop sharing it with him for the while. The beast could not possibly have scented the man as the wind was in the opposite direction; moreover had that been the case, he would not have taken the trouble to walk up to within fifty feet of the stop. Also, he would not have slunk away as quietly as he did because sudden contact with a man's effluvium usually causes a hurried flight.

Cunning old tigers often succeed in baffling their pursuers by simple and bold measures. One of these beasts ranged over a wide area of country in Barwan and Khandesh Satpuras. He had run the gauntlet of the guns on more than one occasion and had always got off scot free. There were the usual jungle tales about him and he was credited with occult powers. A great point in his favour was that he despised attacking or molesting the people. He often had individuals at his mercy, but he either took no notice of their presence or uttered a low grunt as a warning to them to be off. He was a game-killing tiger, but had no compunction about seizing a fat calf should one be foolish enough to stray too near his haunts. The people said that he would never return to his kill, but as will be seen, this was not always the case.

One hot day a friend came to try for him, and brought a guest. After a week's patient waiting we decided to leave calves tied up,

but ourselves to move some miles further from his haunts so as not to disturb him while trying for other game. On the fourth or fifth day a kill was reported and we arranged to camp near the spot in order to be ready on the following morning.

The trackers now reported that the tiger had not returned to the kill during the night, which of course caused no surprise. They made certain he was lying up somewhere in the valley. It extended into the hills for about two miles and contained ideal grounds for tiger in the hot weather, all along its course, so we arranged that the two guns should be posted at the head of the valley. To reach the spot it was necessary to make a long detour through some very rough country. The plan promised every success, considering the time of the year and, above all, the confidence of the Bhil men. They belonged to the locality and knew it thoroughly, as well as the habits of this particular tiger whom they had marked down and beaten on previous occasions.

We started after breakfast. The beaters went to the spot where the kill lay, and the guns with the trackers and stops went by the route which I have described. After an hour's hard climbing we began to round a spur which would bring us over the gorge where the valley commenced. Just as we turned, and my friend and his guest with their rifle-men, who were all in front in Indian file, began to ascend the gorge, the Bhil who was following me with my rifle, bent forward and nudged me, shoving the rifle into my hands and pointing to a ledge on the hillside, hardly twenty paces distant, where lay the tiger sprawled out, watching us from under a temru tree which had bloomed into new leaf. Before I could shoot the beast gave a loud roar and got up and began walking slowly down the hillside into a ravine. His sudden explosion of wrath startled every one, and the first thing that happened was that the men holding the rifles stampeded, so that I was the only person left with a rifle. However, the men quickly rallied and we decided to cut off the beast at the head of the ravine.

The men, being well acquainted with the ground, took us helter-skelter to the spot where two machans were hurriedly rigged up for the two guns, while I returned with about twelve men for the drive. It was a comparatively easy task, for we had only to divide and to walk along the steep banks, rolling down stones. When we were about half the distance from the guns four shots rang out in a quick succession. But when we came up there were no signs of the

tiger; he had run the gauntlet and escaped. It was difficult to understand how they could possibly have missed him altogether, as he passed within fifteen to twenty feet of the guns. As a matter of fact my friend did draw blood, but apparently only from a surface wound. But there was some excuse for the bad shooting, Right in front of the guns, a bend in the nullah shut out any further view and the tiger, unconscious that he had been headed so quickly, appeared quite suddenly, walking close under the machans.

The gait and dignity of the unperturbed beast fascinated both men. Slowly and quietly he approached the guest's machan, so that the other gun naturally reserved his fire. But, being missed by a right and left, the tiger started off with a "whough whough" to the opposite side, pulling up at the back of my friend, who therefore put in a right and left also. Having to fire through some intervening bamboo shoots, however, he could not make sure of his aim and the beast got away with a mere scratch.

Two years later I tied up the bait, i.e. a goat or calf, for the same tiger, with another friend in a ravine close to the scene of our former exploit. It was in winter, soon after Christmas, when the growth is very thick. I preceded my friend by a day or so, and on my arrival I learned that the tiger had killed during the previous night, and that no one had been near the spot since for fear of disturbing him. The following morning I started with my Bhil trackers, taking a calf to tie up in case of need. The sun had been up a good two hours, but owing to its steep banks and dense growth, the ravine was still partially shrouded in darkness. I had a feeling that the tiger was near, so in spite of the Bhil's insistence I refused to go further, and we all sat down some little distance from the kill to wait until the sun should rise higher and let in more light. After an hour or more I agreed, against my better judgement, to move on because the men were confident the tiger could not be there, and, moreover, the kill was now three days old.

Taking two men, a Bhil and my Mohammedan shikari, I approached the hill very cautiously, the Bhil leading, I in the centre and the orderly in the rear. We reached the place and the Bhil began to point across the nullah to the spot where he had tied the calf, of which nothing could now be seen. We were in the act of descending to cross to examine the spot when the tiger, who had been lying all the time facing us in some reeds on the opposite

bank, began to raise himself gradually. Only the nullah intervened between us. He looked like an apparition emerging from the ground, for we had been looking all the time over and beyond him without dreaming of his presence.

We stood gazing at him, with rifles resting on our shoulders, as though we were hypnotized. The pause must have lasted a full minute when the beast at length stood up and heaved a sigh; that seemed to break the spell, for my rifle at once came up. I drew a bead on his head and should have fired in the next half-second had not the tiger, as suddenly, sprung down into the nullah with a growl. This manoeuvre made us turn and bolt up the slope, to be checked at the top by the scarp along the flank of the nullah. It was an awkward moment, for we were absolutely at the mercy of the beast. However instead of attacking us he proceeded to walk slowly up the path by which we had come, uttering low grunts of displeasure as he went along. It was plain that he had absolutely no intention of harming us, for in a couple of bounds he could have had one of us at least; moreover, he knew the ground, and the direction we took must have made it evident to him that we would be caged in by the precipitous banks. Our quickest and easiest line of retreat lay by the path which the tiger deliberately chose. I believe that the threatening attitude he assumed was entirely for the purpose of frightening us and, seeing how well he had succeeded, he just walked quietly away. When I took my friend and his wife the next day to see the place, they could hardly understand how we had managed to escape.

On this occasion at least, the tiger stayed near his kill for three nights and ate every morsel. But he would not kill again, although we kept tying up for a month. I chaffed the Bhils regarding their ignorance of his habits, in spite of the many opportunities they had to study him in the past fourteen or fifteen years in which they had known of him. The men accounted for their discomfiture as being due to the mysterious spirit which guided the tiger's movements. He was a very fine tiger and never gave me a chance again. A few years later I heard that another man had an excellent opportunity of bagging him on his kill over which he had sat up, but for some reason he hesitated to shoot and the tiger saw him and was off.

The sonorous cough with which a tiger greets the pursuer when intruded upon suddenly, or is tackled after being wounded, is demoralizing indeed. It is an explosion of fierce wrath which

barely lasts a few seconds, but it is enough to test the mettle of the stoutest heart. Ordinarily there is no more ulterior motive in the utterance than a warning to stop coming near him, but it is an asset of which the tiger knows the value and he employs it on occasions - especially when wounded - for opening the way to an attack without risk of injury to himself. This he does by bewildering his pursuer by a powerful expression of sound and so gaining the advantage to deliver his onslaught before the assailant has had time to recover from his dilemma. Those who have undergone the ordeal will at once understand what is meant. Indeed elephants, otherwise staunch after tiger, are known to quail before the sound, and even to turn and flee.

I have recollections of a painful incident of the kind during a tour with Mr. Thompson. He had wounded a tigress in a beat and proceeded to follow her up on one of his elephants which had been used after tiger several times. I kept with the trackers who showed the way, while Mr. Thompson and his daughter followed on the elephant. The jungle was mostly teak and bamboo and fairly thick, and the tigress had gone about three hundred yards and spent herself and taken shelter under a bamboo thicket covered with climbers. The trail was easy to follow and soon we were close up to the beast. The elephant winded her from fifteen or twenty paces and gave the customary warning by tapping the ground with his trunk. We, that is the trackers and I, immediately retired to the back while the driver urged his mount forward to enable Mr. Thompson to reconnoiter the cover. The tigress kept carefully concealed until the elephant was within three or four paces off her. Then she started up with the alarming cough I have described, and before Mr. Thompson could shoot the elephant turned and belted, trumpeting as he went, despite all the efforts of the driver to stop him. It may be imagined what a time the father and daughter had on his back, in dodging the branches and keeping their seats. The sharp bamboo twigs tore up their clothes and badly scratched their faces and hands, and they looked pitiful objects without their hats, their hair disheveled and blood streaming down their faces. But although the tigress had frightened the elephant out of his wits, she had, at the same time revealed her sorry plight, for the quick-eyed trackers detected her helpless condition, so that we walked her up without further ado and shot her.

Occasionally one comes across aborigines who have become

adepts in their knowledge about tigers, in fact of most animals occupying the jungles in the neighbourhood of their homes. Such men are not necessarily shikaris. As a rule they are the bhumkas or bhardwas - disease and witch doctors - who usually live sequestered lives in some remote spot, partly because screened from human eyes it is supposed they are better able to practise their craft in communion with messengers from the nether world, and partly for the very practical reason of their needing to experiment with vegetable products. As the vocation is hereditary the representative of successive generations is in possession of a vast fund of accumulated knowledge and practical experience. It is easy to understand why these men are held in respect and consulted on all matters requiring solution.

Such men are content not only with living apart, but are also careful to conceal their movements, spending most of their time under cover of the jungles, so that they appear uncanny to the ordinary eye and become invested with an importance among the ignorant folk. It will be obvious, the various roots, bulbs and other vegetable, mineral and animal products that they need in the practice of their profession have to be procured on the quiet, in order to mask their secrets. Their stealthy wandering in search of these requisites enables them also to scrutinize closely the signs and marks that are met with and that denote the presence or absence of animals and birds, as well as to read the language they import with regard to the functions of the wild life in the neighbourhood. This constant occupation puts them in possession of ways and means for drawing conclusions about the habits of beasts and birds and so acquire for them an authority about the resources of the place in the matter of shikar. They are therefore able to foretell fairly accurately what the day's sport is likely to be, provided always that the management is good and the sportsman sure of his aim. Then again, knowing every inch of the ground, they will sometimes mystify the audience by informing them whether the quarry will be actually bagged or not. There is nothing surprising in all this to one who knows the ropes. For if the positions selected are badly placed, as is sure to be the case with inexperienced or imported shikaris: or if the particular tiger has a knack of breaking through the stops or deserting his kill: or if the shikaris have failed to win the good will of the jungle folk, then the result has been from the very first a foregone conclusion. On the

other hand, favourable conditions will augur favourable results. But I will add a few concrete examples to show the reliance that may be placed on the bhardwa's predictions.

In my griffin days, after I had once been fagging hard for a tiger in a locality which was seldom without one, my orderly advised that we should consult the local oracle who lived two or three miles away in the jungles. Consequently we went to him the next morning and he asked us to come the next day. In the meantime, I was to send him a cock and about two pounds of rice for a sacrifice at the shrine of Baghdeo, the presiding spirit of the tiger tribe. The following morning he told us that there would be a kill that night and my desire would be fulfilled. I had had three calves tied up for days without result, but the next day just as he had foretold, a kill was reported in the spot most suitable for a beat, and the tiger walked up within fifteen feet of the machan and was shot. This man had a large store of information and we became great friends subsequently. I enlisted his son in the department and he proved one of the most useful men I ever had.

On another occasion, after days of unsuccessful stalks for bison in the Deosthan forests near Panchi-Tokra, I was taken by old Ram Singh, the famous Gond guard of the beat, to a similar oracle who had his residence close to the village Pat. We salaamed to the old recluse who had quite a patriarchal appearance. Ram Singh acted as spokesman since the seer could only speak a crude Gondi of which I could not make out a word. He told us to return and he would send word the next day, in the meanwhile, he asked to be supplied with a cock, about three pounds of rice, a little ghee or clarified butter and a coconut, as an offering for the jungle shrine. In the morning a lad appeared and told Ram Singh where he was to take me to obtain the object of my pursuit, and within two days I would succeed.

That evening we were out till late and sighted a fine bull within the comparatively short distance of thirty yards, but he was off before I could shoot. I think he had been watching us some few minutes and old Ram Singh's dim sight failed to see the beast before he detected us. Naturally I was disgusted, as it seemed to be the opportunity which the recluse had promised. The following morning was a blank, and my hopes sank lower still. In the evening I agreed somewhat reluctantly to have another try, and after stalking until almost dark, we sat up near a salt-lick, and had

hardly been there a quarter of an hour, when out walked a fine bull scarcely forty yards from us, and I got him with a single shot.

In another instance, a friend came to shoot with me in the Newali forests of Central India. He was staying only three days and so we had to make the most of it. There were no signs of tiger, but he was almost as keen to get a panther. Two blank days went by and we began to be anxious. My orderly suggested calling in a bhardwa and the local man was summoned. After going through various antics he declared that the sahib would be successful the following day towards the left or western quarter of the compass. The man himself by the way, dwelt on that side of the village. My friend and his wife were inclined to treat the affair rather as a joke. However a kill was reported in due time, and as it was in a thick patch close to the camp in the direction indicated, we started to beat at once. The panther walked out straight for the gun and the next minute or so would have settled him, had not my friend's shikari in his over eagerness to draw attention to the brute let himself be seen. The panther was off at once. The only chance now rested in sitting up in the hope that the beast would return to his kill. We did so and my friend bagged the panther that evening.

These examples may suffice to show that primitive folks often do have information which enables them to draw correct inferences as to the prospects of sport. More often than not, they play an important part in a shikar expeditions and the measure of success or failure may be gauged by their friendliness or opposition. Shikaris worth the name, accompanying the sportsman into new country, that is localities of which they have personally no experience, will make it a point to enlist their help, as well as that of the local folks, before commencing operations. This is very necessary to ensure success, and it is important to do it at once. Delay may wreck the chances of sport, since news of the sportsman and his entourage, whether of good or evil report, travels like wild fire, and if it is unfavourable, means are set afoot to baffle the plans. When one thinks how easily a game resort may be set astir, it is not surprising that failures are so common a feature of most excursions. A few men versed in jungle-craft, told off to points that give out an echo or where animals and birds congregate will suffice to rouse the jungle far and wide, by causing a stampede.

Sportsmen who have the patience and tact to win the confidence of the wild tribes will be regaled with many anecdotes about tigers.

They are interesting as showing the views held by these primitive people who are in closer touch with the fauna of their country and therefore, know more about the habits of the game, than an alien sportsman however curious and painstaking, can possibly expect to know during his itinerant visits to the locality. It may even be said that officials stationed in their midst can scarcely hope to compete with them with regard to such information gathered during their sojourn.

The reason for this is simple enough. How few sportsmen have the patience to watch a beast go through with its business. They hardly ever think of waiting, but open fire as soon as the game is seen and the greater the prize set on the trophy, the more impatience there is to bring it to bag. Animals are not so much the creatures of impulse as is generally supposed, but equally with human beings go about their functions in accordance with rules inherited or acquired by experience, and cannot be hurried or rushed into finishing what they are about. Moreover all actions whether fast or slow are concomitants of time and their true character cannot be gauged unless they are completed, so that when the beast's existence is cut short or the commission of its action interrupted or hurried, the result is left in uncertainty. On the other hand the native - taking him as a shikari - is not only naturally endowed with patience but he cannot afford to take risks. He waits for the most favourable moment to shoot, and more often than not this means observing the quarry for sometime which enables him to find out facts about the game that the sportsman misses by impatience. All such tales are therefore based on facts, although often their descriptive versions have been altered by being interlarded with imaginary details supplied by the reciter or handed down through distorted channels. But to one acquainted with jungle lore it is not difficult to sift the materials of the accounts and to obtain the truth. As a rule the natives have nicknames for all the important beasts in the neighbourhood of their hamlets, that is, game which have acquired importance in the minds of the people owing to some characteristic development that distinguishes them from the rest of their kind. This may be the age or size of the individual in comparison with others of its tribe; or the eccentricity in manner or temperament due to an injury or failing which distinguishes it from others of the class. Whichever be the case the idiosyncrasy of each be he tiger, panther, deer or

antelope, is carefully cherished, and should one of these favourites be unfortunate enough to be shot or to fall a prey to any other agency, the men will hang around the fallen beast and whisper to each other regarding its special qualities.

In one case, when a notorious cattle-lifting tiger was shot, the graziers of the locality started cracking cocoanuts [sic] on his head because they considered him to be an incarnation of the demon god. Similarly at the discomfiture of a cunning old stag sambar, carrying a huge pair of antlers for his size, who had led many a shikari a dance, the people began plucking bristles from his neck as keep-sakes of their old acquaintance.

Among tales, mention may be made of a few which appear to me rather striking by their singularity. The men swore they were true and named the officials, both well-known sportsmen in the Central Provinces, in whose presence the first two of these incidents occurred.

In a beat in the Jagmandal reserve of the Mandla district a tiger was being driven through a blank patch covered with rank growth of elephant grass when he was seen by the stops on trees to rise on his hind feet and walk through the grass like a human giant, looking about him. The tiger kept in this attitude until he got out of the patch which was about two hundred feet in extent. It seems strange for a tiger to assume this posture and still more so to maintain it for some distance. It was doubtless to enable him to see how the coast lay, for with the noises going on around him he needed to know his bearings to make good his escape, whereas by keeping on all fours he could not possibly see to escape through the thick cover of grass. I have known a panther do very much the same thing. It had accidentally come upon the game I had shot in an early morning stalk and left for a while to look about for other game. Seeing a meal ready to his liking, the panther had started eating during my short absence. It heard me returning but could not make out from the noise whom he had to deal with, for some thick undergrowth hid me from his view, so he stood up on his hind feet to peer over the cover. My tracker immediately spotted the beast's head and ears coming up above the growth and pointed him out, but before I could fire the panther had sat down. Apparently he was not quite satisfied with our identity, for while we waited he again stood up to look over, when I brained him.

The second account also relates to Mandla. A few miles out of

the town a tiger killed a donkey on the bank of the Nerbadda river and dragged it into a temple through a window about three feet from the ground and himself lay up inside. Two forest guards, one of whom was my informant, were on their way to headquarters on duty and, thinking the shrine to be a good place to break their fast before going on they halted, and one of them looking through the bars of the door saw the beast asleep inside. They quickly shut the window and one of the men went on at once to fetch the forest officer who got on to the roof, made a hole by removing a few tiles, and so managed to shoot the tiger.

Another story relates to a man-eater and was told by a Gond headman who was well on sixty years of age. His father - a shikari - wanted to rid the neighbourhood of a man-eating tiger. One afternoon he was stalking in quest of the brute when it pounced upon him from the back and gripping him by the shoulder bore him to the ground. Stunned and dazed by the suddenness of the attack, the man swooned away and dropped his weapon. The tiger dragged him for a short distance and then jerked him on to its back. This brought the man to his senses, and finding himself astride of the beast, he put out his arms at once and clasped the tiger round the neck. At the same time, twisting his legs under the tiger's body, he clutched it round the loins with his feet. The beast, taken aback at the man's strange proceedings took fright and, letting go of his hold started to bound off with growls and grunts while the Gond tightened his grip round its body. But being unable to retain his position for long, he let go eventually and fell off, while the brute finding itself free, increased its pace and was soon out of sight. The Gond got back to his hut and made a good recovery. The tiger, however, was so scared that he abandoned his hunting ground in the neighbourhood.

The son said his father recalled the event in his dreams on the anniversary of the occurrence, when he would shout and kick in his cot, imagining that he was riding on the tiger. The tale is not improbable if we consider the caprices to which tigers are liable on being unexpectedly opposed. An inveterate hunter who has the daring to stalk a man-eater is not one who is likely to succumb to an attack without putting up strong resistance. Though dazed for the time being by the suddenness of the attack, he would on regaining his senses naturally make a bid for life, using his hands and feet - the only means practicable - in the struggle. The tiger

being unaccustomed to opposition of the kind would also naturally be disconcerted by the victim's sudden display of vitality and take fright at the unexpected turn of events. The man seeing how well his plan had succeeded would tighten his grip until he tired and let go. I know of cases where sportsmen have had a rough and tumble with tigers, getting them off by fisticuffs and kicks, so that there is no reason to discount the tale which differs only in execution.

The elders have usually a large fund of information about sportsmen who have visited their hamlets and employed them in shikar. Their identities are kept up not by their names, which few natives can pronounce without difficulty, but by some distinguishing quality that, without the owner's knowledge, strikes their imaginations and sticks fast in their memory. Sportsmen are remembered as much for their generosity in the one case, as for their niggardliness in the other. As regards personality, stature or activity these are noted as much as a quiet demeanour or a propensity to quarrel; while daring is the cause for esteem in one, discretion is its cause in another. Again, the idol may be clean-shaven or bearded, or he may have had some permanent injury to recall him to memory. So also, habits peculiar to the individual are matters for recollection. For example, a sportsman is remembered because he went about without his coat, or because he was constantly drinking, or because he used Keating's powder before getting into bed, or because he scolded without rhyme or reason. And yet again, excesses of excitement resulting in rapid gestures, usually indulged in by a sportsman new to the job or of nervous temperament, such as striking his sides with his hands, or performing a sort of Scottish reel or skip-dance when the quarry had been bagged, or plunging to the ground to crawl and stalk every time game was sighted, are sufficiently fanciful in the eyes of tribesmen to preserve the sportsman in their memory.

The appellations adopted to characterize these various traits are tersely realistic, and an inventory of them would be both interesting and curious, as disclosing the ideas absorbed by these simple folk. For example, the cantankerous individual would be remembered by a name the equivalent of "barker", the reel dancer of "hopper", the zealous stalker of "crawler", and so on.

The Keating's powder owner caused him to be dubbed a sadhu. His servant boy was in the habit of shaking the powder freely on his master's sheets while preparing his bed in the open. One of the

elders called in to assist, observing this daily performance, questioned the boy regarding the "mud" which he sprinkled on the sheets. The youth who was at once a humorist and a man of business, explained that it was a purifying earth, manufactured from shells obtained from the ocean bed, and that only sahibs with religious qualifications could use it, whereupon the old shikari begged for some and received a half tin-full in return for various charms of which the boy stood in need.

The tin was carefully preserved and on important religious occasions a pinch of the powder would be applied to the foreheads of the male members of the family, thus completing the preparation for the ceremony. When I was camping in the village months after this occurrence the old Banjara spoke to me about it and asked if I knew of the sacred earth. I guessed from his description that he had been made the subject of a joke, and asked to see it. The son was sent to fetch the tin and when it arrived I was not a little surprised at the discovery. However, not to shake his faith entirely, I told him the powder was meant to keep the body free of animalcules and so preserve it in a purer state.

Chapter XI

The Panther

Comparatively little has been written about the panther, doubtless because he is thought to resemble in essentials his bigger cousin, the tiger. But, apart from being a distinct animal, although of the same race - the felidae - he differs from the tiger in the very particulars that are most prominent in the tiger's character. One might describe the panther in a few words by saying that he possesses all the bad points of the tiger together with those of the cat.

A comparative analysis between him and his nobler cousin would show that a panther is indifferent about the choice of site where he lies up, if caves occur in the locality he will as readily as not occupy them. He kills by gripping the prey by the head or throat or nape of the neck, or if he cannot manage this owing to the victim's size or strength, he mauls it sufficiently to cause slow and painful death. Again he is not particular as to where he feasts, it may be under cover or in the open whichever is more convenient and, moreover, he will feed on carrion. Then too he is viciously destructive, killing whatever is within reach whether he needs it for food or not. Lastly, he thieves by nature, that is he steals from another and also from tigers when chance occurs; he snatches prey seized by the lesser carnivora, like the cat, the jackal, the fox and the lynx.

Every sportsman knows how difficult it is to locate a panther. This is because he does not conform to any principle in the matter of choosing his retreat. He does not possess the sense to secure a position of comparative safety as other animals like tiger, sambar, bison which lie up where they are not only secure from intrusion, but can disconcert the pursuer should he happen to invade the sanctum. Rather than trust to his senses the panther depends on his sly and adroit movements to evade pursuit by means of his greater powers of acuteness. Any little cover that offers a screen for the time being will do, since he can easily screw his lithe and elastic frame into any shape necessary under the circumstances. This is the reason why the panther's movements are so uncertain and so puzzling to the sportsman. While he is looking for the beast in the places which seem provided by nature as a means of shelter, the

panther has lain up in some more unlikely spot, which owing to its very unsuitability as a shelter, has passed unnoticed. For this reason beats for panther are rarely a success and indeed are rarely attempted, though often a panther will turn up in other beats when he is least expected. The usual way to shoot panther is to sit up over his kill which may seem a relatively unsporting method, but is yet an exacting business in which the odds are with the panther.

Among the eccentric positions in which the beast ensconces himself, I recollect a bamboo clump standing at the edge of a field, a hollow in the trunk of a large gular tree on a nullah bank with no other cover, the fork of an isolated bur tree in a field, a deserted shanty within the village precincts, an out-crop of fissured rocks in the midst of fields, a disused well or pit and so on. In the rains, he will often take up his quarters in a field of maize or millet and carry on his depredations in the neighbouring hamlets. A sugar-cane patch will suit him even better, or he will invade gardens or orchards in and around towns, and poach dogs, goats and poultry belonging to the keepers, hiding in a hedgerow should the dawn overtake him. A good instance of his impudence occurred at Dhar. One morning it was reported to the Rajah that a panther was sitting on one of the highways barely a mile from the town. The news seemed hardly credible, as the road lay through absolutely open and frequented country and connected two palaces. However the Rajah picked up a rifle and started off in his trap and arrived in time to see the beast making off across the bare plain, where it was pursued and shot. Inspection of the site suggested that the panther had been returning to a lair when he struck the road and began indulging himself in a roll in a sand-heap collected on the roadside, regardless of the passers-by whom he was frightening.

When driven panthers will often make for caves, and they will get up trees when surrounded or frightened. Sometimes wounded panthers will run up trees when there is not sufficient undergrowth for cover, but more often they get into caves. A forest officer of my acquaintance had wounded a panther and followed him up on his elephant. As he was passing under a tree, a few drops of blood fell on his hand. Being an experienced sportsman he immediately guessed the cause and without appearing to take the slightest notice cautioned the mahawat to move on faster. When some distance away, he made the elephant stand and he looked into the tree; there was the panther flattened out on one of

the branches some height above where he had passed, and he dropped it with a shot. Had he looked up at the time the brute would have certainly pounced on to him.

Provided the under-growth is scorched or burnt, a panther if disturbed will nearly always make for a cave. In open jungles panthers take regularly to caves, staying inside most of the day and getting out at dusk to prowl about. These caves are generally surface faults which have been scoured by water or rendered habitable by burrowing animals, such as porcupine, jackals, foxes, and subsequently annexed by panthers. They are often deep with tortuous passages, and room for two or more animals. The turns and twists counteract the effect of heat and cold, so that they can be resorted to equally during warm summer days or cold winter nights. On the other hand shallow caves heat and cool rapidly and are more uncomfortable than the outside temperature, and panthers usually avoid them. But he often lies up close to one under some shade, ready to get in at the first sign of alarm. Panthers can be easily made to leave such cover, but it is practically impossible to get them to move out of a deep cave.

Of the many sportsmen who have sat up over a live goat for a panther, probably few who have seen him kill, will have observed that he holds on to the throat or head till he has killed his victim. Even if he comes rushing with a spring and throws the animal, he immediately lays hold of the throat without an attempt to do more, till the victim is practically dead from strangulation or hemorrhage and not till then does he let go and lick the blood. In the case of bigger animals, such as young kine and buffalo calves, he springs to get a firm hold on the body and seizing the nape of the neck with his jaws while his sharp claws give him a grip that defies all the victim's struggles to elude it till death ensues from the vertebrae being pierced. The tiger could not manage such a feat, but the lithe and elastic body of the panther fits him for it. As a rule, he goes for the throat near where it joins the head and grips with the force of a vice. The soft tissue of the throat is easier to penetrate and the suffocation prevents the victim from uttering any loud sound to attract assistance.

Passing through a village one evening we were attracted by the shouts of graziers returning with the village cattle. Cattle-lifting was rife in the country and thinking they had been attacked by robbers, we ran to their assistance, but soon found to our surprise

that it was a very different matter. A panther had partially mounted on a young bullock, which was charging about madly trying to shake him off. The shouting and our timely appearance decided the beast to let go and disappear quietly. But the bullock sat down almost immediately, and although the herdsmen managed to get him to walk to the village and applied remedies, he died shortly after. The claws had worked deep into both flanks and the fangs had penetrated to the vertebrae; only the bullock's size and strength had cheated the panther of his prey. I have seen a great many kills by panthers at various times and in different places, but I cannot recall a single instance where there was so much as an attempt at wrenching the neck. The panther does not know the artifice, doubtless because they have no need of it: partly because they prey on small and inoffensive creatures and partly because of their greater agility and tenacity in clinging to the prey, which not only furnishes their movements with greater rapidity, but also enables them to hang on to their victims when necessary.

The panther will usually grip young animals, as kids, fawns and pigs by the head, causing almost instantaneous death. His object may be to prevent the parents being attracted by their sounds. Birds on the other hand, he seizes by the body. I have known panthers try to play with their victims before killing them, but these are really young beasts, barely more than a year old, that are learning to fend for themselves; and their action is not play in the true sense of the word but an attempt to imitate what they have seen their parents do.

The panther is very little concerned to remove his kill. He attempts this only when he is afraid of interruption while feeding. He will then drag away the kill but whether into cover or not depends on circumstances. If he has killed by daytime or in the early hours of the morning, he will endeavour to remove the body into cover; but after sunset if the spot is frequented, he will remove it just out of sight. When the panther has killed an animal tied up as bait, he rarely makes an effort to break the cord. He will give it a few tugs because from the very fact that a beast has been made ready to his choosing the place is ominous, and instinct impels him to make at least a try to get his meal free and away. But having failed in his feeble efforts, he does not persevere and takes no precaution to escape detection. Panthers begin to devour their prey as soon as life is extinct or almost extinct. In this respect also

they differ from the tiger who allows an interval to pass between killing and feeding which varies in duration according to the age and size of the victim. I have mentioned already that they differ in the method of tackling the carcass. Panthers at once disembowel the body and separate the viscera and draw out the liver and heart and eat those first, whereas the tiger begins from the rump and goes slowly through. When there are hyena and jackal about or when he fears disturbance by villagers or dogs, the panther will hang up the remains or even the whole kill, on a tree or shrub by balancing it over a fork. His dexterity in this respect is astonishing. I have seen the body of a buck- goat, just eviscerated, hang up on the fork of a mahua tree twenty six feet from the ground, and the corpses of a donkey and a colt suspended on pollards eight or ten feet off the ground. In treeing his kill, if it is a light one, a panther springs from fork to fork holding the body in his jaws, but if the weight is heavy he crawls up the stem slowly trailing the carcass along the trunk.

Panthers will go deliberately for carrion, sometimes driving away jackals or sharing it with hyenas, if either beasts have started feeding on the carcass. When I was sitting over a dead cow once to shoot jackals, for the sake of their skins which make good rugs, I saw a panther walk deliberately up to the carcass, though there were two dead jackals lying about, and begin tearing at it. I mistook the beast for a hyena as the performance seems so unusual, and I shuffled behind my screen to frighten him away, but he sat up like a cat and then there was no mistaking him and I lost no time in putting a bullet into him. He was a fair sized beast and in excellent condition.

On another occasion a sambar got away wounded close to camp and died in a thicket not very far from where he was shot. We tried for two days to find him, looking in all the possible places except the right one, which we passed and repassed without getting into the thicket. He had a good pair of antlers and I was vexed at losing him. On the third day one of the villagers saw crows settling in the thicket, so we went to see. The dead sambar was there and the carcass was putrefying; and apparently that very morning attracted no doubt by the smell a panther had found it, and had started a meal when we disturbed him.

Panthers kill for mere lust of blood and are devoid of all conscience in this respect. Even when gorged and lazy, they will be

prepared to take life, if anything happens to come near. A panther getting into a goat-pen will do all the mischief he can. I know a case where as many as twelve goats were killed out of sixteen, although eventually only one was carried away. Another time a basket containing nineteen fowls was dragged away from close to the kitchen tent and burst open a short distance off. Before the servants could come up attracted by the noise of the birds, all had been killed although only two had been taken. I have come across dead animals, such as civet cat, mongoose, dog and badger lying before the caves of panthers which except for the teeth marks about the head or body, had not been touched. Apparently the beasts had stumbled across the creatures and taken their lives without in the least needing them for food. In one case we smoked the panther out and shot him and he was so heavily gorged that he could hardly move. The losses that villagers suffer annually from their rapacious and wanton attacks, amounts to enormous totals if all were taken into account. But it is not all panthers that raid domestic animals. Just as there are tigers which seldom go marauding within village limits so there are panthers which feed chiefly on game, only they come less to public notice.

Panthers show remarkable tenacity in retaining what they have actually seized. A dog, goat or calf rescued from a panther's clutch is in great danger of being seized again, for the panther will be so set on securing the prize which he lost before that he will even deviate from the usual practice and ignore anything else within his reach. Every one knows of cases where a panther has returned to the attack, three and four times in the night, although he had opportunities of seizing some other creature. Shikaris attribute this to the taste of the blood of the victim which is supposed to stick to the mouth until the panther has eaten the flesh. This peculiarity is especially marked in the case of man-eating panthers. Sometimes one comes across very distressing scenes when parents feel themselves unable to protect the rescued child.

A case of the kind occurred at Amkhut, a Bhil settlement in the Ali-Rajpur State in nineteen hundred. A panther had taken to killing human beings a year or so before the occurrence, and the countryside was kept in constant fear of his attacks. A large reward was offered for his destruction and various means were employed to kill him but, with that instinct which only man-eaters seem to become possessed, he had eluded all the attempts made on his life.

On this occasion he seized a girl who was going with her mother and sisters to the village pool for water in the afternoon. The woman managed to save the child and took her back to the dwelling two hundred yards away. Nevertheless the panther followed them and kept sentinel resolutely all through the night by the hut. Three times he actually got in and once even he closed upon the child although she lay by the log fire between her parents, and although there were other children also in the hut, still the panther made for the girl he had mauled. The child's parents however drove him off, but the girl mauled as well as frightened succumbed to her injuries next day.

Another case occurred at a Bhil settlement near Pitol in the Jhabua State in nineteen hundred and two. In this instance also the panther had been an addicted man-eater for a year or so, but his attacks were so frequent that the people were rapidly deserting the locality. I tried for him both by sitting and beating, but he eluded me each time. Eventually he was trapped in a very ingenious contrivance and killed with bows and arrows, but only after he had decimated the country-side killing about sixty people, mostly children, during his short career as man-eater of eighteen or twenty months. The incident I have alluded to occurred while I was camping near the site and so I had the details first-hand. One evening the panther seized the girl who was playing with other children close to the dwelling. Her cries brought out the parents, and the father pursued and hit the brute with his club to make him let go of the child. During the night the beast made no less than four attempts to seize the poor child, and eventually succeeded some time after dawn, when tired out by the night's vigil the parents closed their eyes, satisfied that there was no more a danger of molestation.

In another instance the parents finding that their wretched hut was no protection against the persistent brute's attempts, took the rescued child on a mandwa, which is a wooden platform, constructed for the purpose of watching crops on poles some height from the ground. But the panther climbed up the structure, about ten feet high, and tried to drag down the child by the foot. This child also died, probably from fright, as his actual injuries were not severe. Such occurrences are unhappily by no means rare; but the difficulty is to get a trustworthy account out of the people.

I take the origin of a man-eating panther to be much the same as

Bhil carriers cooking food, Jobat

Carting heavy timber down slope, with brushwood brake

Ruins of old fort in jungle, Bhabra, Ali-Rajpur

Adnisonia digitata near
Mandu - Nalcha road, 1906

Camels in camp, 1904

Bhils climbing toddy palms to get the juices. Note palm trunks enveloped by parasite figs.

Open air luncheon in camp, Kadwal, Kathiwara

Bhil dwelling and carrier carts, Forest Quarters, Amkhut, Ali-Rajpur

in the case of a tiger. But a demented panther is even more vicious than his bigger cousin. His peculiar inherent qualities now show themselves to a far more marked degree. Such panthers are also more difficult to circumvent by the usual method of shikar, and often their death comes about by poison or some cunning contrivance set up by the aborigines to entrap them. Of the man-eating panthers which I have been after at various times, I succeeded in shooting only three. Those only who have had experience of man-eating panthers, know what a terrible scourge the beast becomes when they take to preying on the little children of the jungle hamlets which afford little or no protection against a cunning and determined beast. Certainly every encouragement should be given to get such a beast destroyed at once, as soon as it is suspected that he has taken to killing human beings.

I was camped at Newali in May eighteen-ninety-nine when a villager arrived in haste with news that a man-eating panther of which his people lived in dread had been marked down that day and to beg of me to come and shoot him. The place was far about fourteen miles by jungle path and the day had slipped past two o'clock, moreover the country lay in the territory of another Chief, who as a body are always chary about any one shooting in their lands without permission, so I was naturally somewhat reluctant to go. But the man's harrowing accounts about the ravages committed by the beast upon the village children soon put my conscience at ease. The sun was almost setting when we arrived, and as I expected the men put on to watch the panther came up to report that he had moved away some time before, and all I could do was to have a look at the spot with the off-chance of his having returned after the men had left their post.

The country was rolling with hillocks, intersected by deep ravines and practically denuded of forest growth, also, at the season of the year it was parched and burnt with little or no ground cover. It was evident that the panther lived among the rocks and boulders banking the ravines, and it was on a rocky ledge over one of them that he had been marked down, but evidently he had seen the Bhil men watching over him and had slipped away unnoticed. Having satisfied my curiosity, we all adjourned to a stream near by to refresh ourselves after the hot march of the day. Here at the water's brink, we began to discuss ways and means of destroying the brute, when one of the men remarked that there was a shallow

cave close to where the panther had been seen. I was again curious to examine this new cover. To reach the spot, we had to go through the bed of the ravine above which the panther had lain up. We were going along noisily, dodging the boulders strewn over the course, when one of the men who had for some reason unknown to us separated from our party and was walking over the bank opposite to where the panther had been seen, whistled and on looking up we saw him sign and beckon to us to go back and come up on his side of the bank. It was clear from his manner that something unusual had occurred and we hastened from the bed and were soon on top with him. He pointed out the panther on the opposite bank sprawled out on the very same ledge of rock which we had visited a short while before. The beast lay so still with his head between his paws that against the dark blotched surface his spots showed like a jungle spider's web. It was some minutes before I could make certain of his identity and though the men were whispering and pointing at him which the brute could not have failed to notice, being only sixty or seventy feet across the chasm, he showed not the slightest sign of life. At last having made certain, I fired and he came tumbling down the bank in a heap. He was a fine male in the prime of life, and I was fortunate to get him, as the shades of evening were beginning to obscure the landscape.

The news of the panther's death soon spread, and all along the way back to camp I was besieged by the jungle folks anxious to have a look at the dreaded beast that had been the terror of the locality for the past nine or ten months. It was after midnight that I returned to my camp tired and hungry, for I had been out eleven hours and done about thirty miles on foot without practically any food. But the satisfaction of having rid the place of the monster, drove away any signs of fatigue that I might otherwise have felt, and when I sat down after a refreshing bath to a meal by the log fire in the open, with the panther in full view and the men recounting their tales of sorrow at his ravages, I felt repaid indeed for what part I had taken in his destruction. The people declared that he had killed about thirty children in the neighbouring settlements.

I may almost claim a repetition of the occurrence in another instance which took place a few years later in the same district. My old enemy - malaria - had hold of me and its attacks were aggravated by the hot sultry days which preceded the burst of the monsoon rains. I was hastening into headquarters and had

camped at Pati on the way. Feeling wretched after the march, I had retired to rest when soon after the patel's son from Semli, a village five miles distant, came in to call me to shoot a man-eater that had killed a girl just a few hours before and was lying up in a hill close to their hamlets. I had heard of the panther from the native compounder [medical]; he had been to see me on my arrival and mentioned having treated two or three cases of injuries to children by attacks from the beast who had apparently commenced killing people very recently, the last victim being his ninth. But I felt more like a worm than fit to shoot, and purely through pity for the people whom I knew very well, I determined to risk the odds. On arrival I found the people had rigged up a machan at the foot of the hill close to a pool where the victim - a girl of seven or eight - lay with her entrails torn out. The hill rose conically over the surface commanding the ground around, and it was strewn with rocks and covered with scrub growth. It was pretty evident that the panther was watching all that was going on below, so I declined to sit up for him in the machan.

Beating was out of the question also, for there was not only cover for him to break through from wherever he liked, but it was impossible to guide him to any particular spot, especially as he would be sure to have seen all that went on and be able therefore to forestall our efforts. It seemed to me that the best plan would be to gain the top of the hill and then, for the cordon of men below to shout and fire off a few shots which would rouse the beast from his lair and so enable me to see him. Having arranged the men and explained to them what they were to do, I started to climb by a steep bank where there had been a landslip carrying away all the cover over a belt of thirty or forty feet, which would also prevent the panther from lying up near. I was trudging up slowly with two faithful shikaris who elected to keep with me, and we had gone about half the distance when the soil under me gave, and before the men could hold me I had slipped below some distance. The noise of the fall and of the earth and stones loosened by my scramble clattering down, roused the panther who was lying up at the top - the very place for which I was making, and he stood up and looked down the slide. As soon as I could, I balanced myself and looked up thinking to see my men only, but at that very moment I saw the panther in the very same act of looking down at us. This was more than I had expected, and pulling myself together as well as I could

and cautioning the men not to move, I took aim and fired and made a lucky hit. The beast seemed to collapse and go over the opposite side. But being unaware at the time of the damage caused by the bullet, I shouted to the men to run to the opposite side and cut him off while I and the two shikaris hurried up to the top. The beast had hardly gone down any distance when the shouting and firing made him turn and make for the top again, so that as I came up from one side he was attempting to get up from the other and we met at the distance of a few paces, and I lost no time in putting a bullet into his shoulder. The first shot had shattered the spine just above the loins and paralysed the hindquarters making the beast almost helpless. He was a large old panther in splendid condition with rather an abnormal tail, quite six inches longer than I have seen in any other panther. The poor child, who was out with other village children feeding goats, had been attacked near the pool just before noon when the goats had come to water. The cries of the children were heard by the people in the hamlets barely a hundred yards off, and they rushed out to the rescue, but were too late to save the child. The panther had evidently come from the jungle some distance away through some open field in full view of the hamlets, and it speaks much for his daring attempting the passage in the middle of the day.

Panthers are not merely promiscuous in the matter of their food. They have no qualms about what they eat, and so nothing is too bad to be discarded. Although more agile than the tiger, they are still inclined to be lazy and will not go out of their way to hunt, so long as it can be avoided. Rather than engage in a chase, they hover round the village for pickings such as dogs, cats or other unfortunates that happen to leave the protection of the hamlets. When a panther is discomfited in his prowl, he will resort to his powers of mimicry, imitating a cat, jackal or fox and even a dog. Then the pariahs of the village start barking and perhaps one or more will rush out at the supposed intruder, and so play the game of the panther. This method of entrapping prey is usually practised by females who have cubs to feed, or by young beasts beginning to fend for themselves. Aboriginal headmen have told me that to entice dogs far away from the huts, the panther will often assume forms that the dog cannot resist and glide silently on, till the curs mistaking it in the dim light for some inoffensive creature, have been drawn out sufficiently far to prevent a rapid retreat into the

village, when the coup will be effectively made. By this means two and three dogs can be secured. However this may be, I can vouch for the rest, for I have seen panthers engaged in mimicry while I have been sitting up for them near aboriginal settlements.

On the first occasion I was hastily summoned from my tent to sit up in a cattle shed, round which the panther had been hovering and trying to get in. There was a splendid moon and I took up a position inside the pen with a goat tied just near outside. The goat would not bleat as it was too close to the huts to feel alarm, but the men assured me that the panther would soon be round again. After a quarter of an hour or so, there was the sound of a pup squealing some little distance on my left; and thinking the panther was making off with one from another settlement, I walked into the main dwelling where the men were seated round a fire and told them. In Bhil settlements, the cattle shed stands a little apart in front of the main dwelling. But the men assured me the noise was made by the coming panther, and so I hastened back to my post. In a few minutes the beast walked almost up to the goat and seized it, when she was shot.

Another time a deputation from the village waited on me soon after my arrival in camp, and begged me to free them from the depredations of some panthers which took a daily toll from their hamlets. They had removed all the scrub and growth for about four hundred yards around so that the beasts might be deterred from coming by the absence of cover. Here the villagers were a mixed lot of timid classes, who feared to undertake measures against the panthers, dreading to draw their vengeance on themselves, and rather than do this had destroyed the growth all about the village site. I went round with the headman who showed me the path by which the panthers usually came, and told me that I had only to take up a position near there to get the beasts. Though all growth had been removed, there was a hayrick standing in a threshing floor about thirty yards off which commanded the path and I decided to sit up here. There happened to be a good moon and at the appointed hour I and my Mohammedan shikari ensconced ourselves in a hollow of the stack at the very top, fourteen or fifteen feet from the ground. We did not tie up the bait because from our position we could only just peer over the top of the rick and could see nothing on the ground close by. We had sat till about nine o'clock, when there was a strange sound, as of two

kids bleating, drawn out in a sort of whirr after each note. Neither of us knew what it was, till we saw two panthers walking up to the village in a line, some distance apart, one coming by the path and the other through a field. I fired at the latter which was further away, because the path worn into a sort of trough prevented my having a clear view of the closer animal. My shot hit him rather far back and he got away for the time being. The other panther sat down on the path, as if puzzled as to the cause of the sound, and after a few minutes of silent watching, proceeded to cross the field to see what had become of her mate. Taking up the scent she started going back, presenting her broadside to me. I put a bullet into her also, but she too managed to get away for the time being. In the morning we started in search of them and found both dead. The pair were comparatively young and belonged to the same litter. The people said there was yet another, probably the old mother, but I was unable to stay as I had urgent business ahead.

A third case occurred while I was camped at Bhandara in the Barwani State. The Bhil patel of Rampura, a village four miles distant, came to ask to be rid of a pair of panthers that were destroying the dogs in the settlement. He said that a dog had been killed the previous night and hung up close to his hut, so that a kill was ready. There was a late moon, but I decided to try, and the shikari was sent to make the necessary arrangements. I followed in the evening when it was time to sit up. The shikari not finding a suitable position near the kill, selected a clump of saplings, fifty paces distant, on which he tied the machan, and having lowered the kill, trailed it along the ground to within a few paces of the position, and there fixed it to a peg. The distance seemed to me rather far to bring the kill, but the Bhils were quite sure the panthers would follow the trail. Soon after I was seated, the village herd passed over the trail on their way to be stalled, and stamped out the mark of the drag causing a break in the line for a short width. This was annoying as it lessened the chances of the panthers following the trail. The moon was to rise after eight o'clock. The kill was in a nullah with steep banks and so also was the machan where I sat, and the patel's hut was hardly hundred feet distant, above the bank. One of the panthers turned up about eight o'clock at the spot where the kill had been suspended and having climbed the vacant tree and looked about, gave up the search. He then got up the bank, and appeared at the back of the

hut, between it, and me and sat quietly for a while and then began purring like a cat. After a while he changed this purring to a harsher and louder tone, such as cats make when fighting; and this performance was too much for the only dog in the hut which began barking. In the meantime the rising moon had begun to light up the nullah bed, and the panther's mate also arrived at the tree, and climbed it and looked about; but instead of giving up the search, she walked up and down the trail, and right and left along the cattle track, and then went over the break and picked up the scent and walked right on to the kill, which it sniffed and pulled and sat down to feed. Having eaten a few morsels, she made a soft purring sound as if pleased, and this call at once brought up the other. They then sat side by side and began to feed. I fired at the new arrival, which gave me the better shot. The bullet struck him on the back and made him spin round like a top, which frightened away the other panther. The one I shot was a young male, about a year old, and the other was probably the mother.

The panther's propensity for thieving is well known, but a few examples of his daring may be worth adding. Twice after beating for tiger, I have found dead panthers close to the tigers' kills. They had apparently sneaked in to feed, either while the tiger was away or having his nap, and they had been detected unawares by the returning tigers. In both cases the panthers had been killed by being gripped by the nape of the neck. There were no signs of wrenching the neck and very few claw marks, as if the victims had been pinned to the ground and rendered helpless even for a struggle. In one case the panther had made a bolt for life, but had been caught up about twenty paces from the kill. These incidents also show the terrible swiftness of the tiger even as compared with such an agile beast as the panther. They show too how the tiger adapts his methods to circumstances, evidently he knows better than to knock over and wrench the neck of such an active beast as the panther, who would wriggle out of his grasp before he had time to effect the purchase.

I have also found a young panther dead beside the kill of a larger one. In this case there had been a good struggle. The occupants of the hamlets close by had heard the sounds of the roaring at midnight, and the dead beast was badly lacerated. He too owed his death to a strangling grip upon the nape of the neck, inflicted when he was too weak from previous maulings to elude it longer.

In another instance, a goat gave birth to kids some distance from the hamlet, and the owner went out to fetch them in. A panther lying up somewhere near was also attracted by the creature's bleats. The man forestalled the panther, and picking up the kids and driving the mother in front, hurried back towards his hut; but the panther became so insistent in his rushes to get the goat that in trying to protect her, the man let drop one of the kids, which the panther immediately seized and carried off. I have no doubt that the panther also annexes prey seized by the lesser carnivora, though for this I can only rely on the accounts of aboriginal headmen and shikaris. In this respect he would only be acting in the same way as dogs and cats.

I saw a strange sight once of a panther being forced to abandon its kill by a drove of wild pig. The kill was a calf which lay by a frequented jungle path and I had sat up chiefly with the object of finding out how the beast would proceed to skin the carcass. The panther had been at the operation - skinning and feeding as he gradually uncovered the hide - for almost an hour and I had refrained from shooting till my curiosity was satisfied feeling sure of him all the time: six or seven pigs now came quietly along the path, the panther heard them come, stopped his meal and crouched behind the carcass to which the pigs had been attracted by scent. The pigs advanced to within ten paces or so, stood for a while as if contemplating the scene, and then started grunting - a sort of hoarse sound of defiance. But receiving no challenge, they began to walk up to the kill. As they came near the panther growled which sent the pigs back a few paces grunting and snorting. Again they approached the kill, and again the panther drove them back by growling. This was repeated thrice, then at the fourth venture as if determined not to be outdone any further, the pigs rushed up in a body regardless of the panther's growls, and began tearing at the carcass, while the panther leapt to a side and sat down growling and snarling a few paces away. He was very angry at being driven from his kill, but seemed afraid of the number to even attempt a bout. I felt it was now time to shoot and fired at the panther, but the excitement through which I had passed caused the shot to just graze the beast and he was off. The pigs also bolted at the sound, but returned after a few minutes when I shot one, the rest fled and never came back again.

A panther is as nimble as a cat in getting up trees. It is rarely

that he makes for a man upon a tree, but it is always possible that he may do so and it is well therefore to be on guard against it. I personally know of five instances where it has happened, and I will mention two. Once I was sitting up with my wife over a live goat. It was her first experience and I warned her not to fire until we both were ready. I had rejected the first position prepared by the shikari because it was on a solitary tree and easily visible: and we had to prepare a second one rather hastily in a clump of saplings growing some thirty paces away. After quite a short wait, the panther rushed from some distance and bounded at the goat and had hold of it in a second. We were unprepared for anything so rapid. My wife had a better view from her seat, while I had to move a leaf in order to see clearly. The slight delay made my wife naturally think that I was waiting for her and she fired with her small bore .303 rifle, hitting the panther low in the stomach. Immediately, before I could get in a shot, the panther ran up the very tree on which the first position had been prepared, but finding no one there jumped down; and then I fired and also made a bad shot. The next instant he was up another tree which was covered with climbers, and might well have been screening his enemies.

Again I fired, but I hit the stem to which the panther was clinging, and having the extra weight of the panther upon it, it snapped at the wound, and both panther and stem crashed to the ground. Even then he started to look about in the undergrowth. I think he mistook the direction of the sounds because of there being an echo, for he never came quite our way, though it was sometime before he left the place altogether. We could not get in another shot: but he was found dead on the third or fourth day.

The other time, a panther had been driven out in a beat and wounded. He was hit in the back just below the spine and collapsed for the time being, but afterwards he got up and moved away a few paces into cover. This was about mid-day. When the beaters came up, we took the shikaris and began to look for him, by making men go up trees and make certain for the next few paces before we advanced, and so we came upon the spot at which he had fallen where there was a pool of blood proving that the wound was severe. The man on the nearest tree declared there was no sign of him anywhere, although it was absolutely certain that he could not have gone far. So I started to climb the next tree standing three or four paces further on, giving my rifle to one of the shikaris to

hold while I climbed. I had hardly got up it when out charged the panther from a little cover barely twenty feet away and I and the man who had climbed just before me, remained treed like prisoners. His charge caused a general stampede and my friend left alone by the beaters fired at close range, but missed him with both barrels. However his shots prevented the infuriated beast from closing on him and instead he retired and came and sat between the trees occupied by the native and myself. He had seen us get up from his cover and after looking up and growling at us for a while, he began to climb after the man whose tree was barely ten feet away from mine, and in spite of all the shouts and noise of the beaters around. He soon had the man by the ankle and tried to pull him down, but failing to do so, he crawled a little higher and gripped him by the knee. Even in this he did not succeed, so he got higher still seizing the unfortunate fellow by the thigh, and when this even failed, he tried to maul him by striking out at his body with his right paw.

But this fresh effort made the panther loosen his hold on the stem, which he could barely sustain owing to his wound and down he fell to the ground. Meanwhile the man kicked and howled desperately and I could only encourage him not to let go. The fall gave the wounded beast a severe shock, and he lay groaning and panting for some minutes, sprawled out where he fell. But in the rush to escape, the shikari had dropped my loaded rifle some distance from my tree, while my friend had no cartridges left and many precious minutes were wasted before my rifle could be secured. Having recovered himself sufficiently, the panther again began to look up at us and growl, as if deciding which of us to go for next and again he determined on the poor wretch on the tree who was howling with pain with the blood trickling from his wounds. Just as he was about to get up, I thought of my sola [sic] topee, the only weapon left me, and hurled it at the brute. It struck him and rolled over and held his attention for a little time. In the meantime, my rifle had been picked up, and my friend walked up with it carefully to get a full view of the beast; so that when the panther having satisfied his curiosity, was about to renew his climb, he shot him through the neck.

These instances will show what the panther can do in the way of climbing, even when partially disabled. When sitting up for him over a kill, it is therefore safer to take another man with one in

spite, I admit, of good reasons against doing so. Also it is very necessary that the position chosen should be at a good height and well enclosed among fresh branches and twigs. It should never be less than ten feet from the ground and there should be enough room to move about the feet and hands freely if necessary, as there are many little annoyances when one is trying to sit quiet and still. A couple of fat cushions should always be taken, as they reduce the chances of cramp. More than once, owing to cramped space, I have lost good chances in trying to slip the barrel out when getting the rifle in position to shoot. Panthers like all carnivora, are extremely clever at detecting moves. Especially when returning to his kill the panther is as a rule, strung up to an extraordinary degree of tension, which makes him sensitive to the slightest move or sound. Any movement in the machan, however slight, is reproduced with greater effect by all the branches and twigs, so that if the panther is looking at all in the right direction, he immediately detects it and proceeds to scrutinise the tree minutely. Usually the result is that he gives up coming or postpones till dark, when it is impossible to see to shoot. Moves within the position should be made with great reluctance and great caution, only when the breeze springs up sufficiently to ruffle the branches naturally. Birds often betray one, if the machan has been prepared in a tree where they are used to roost. The unusual sight of a human being ensconced in a tree upsets them and they will start an angry chatter just above, which is enough to attract any animal's attention. I have on many occasions lost chances simply because of the embarrassing discussion started by certain birds.

Though panthers are very cautious when returning to their kills, they seem to lose all fear when once they have approached it and eaten a few morsels. Then it is almost as difficult to make him leave, as it is in the case of a hyena. The beast sits down and proceeds with his meal caring little for noises around, and only when people come right up, will he shift a little distance away to watch what they do. As already observed, he will seldom make a real effort to break the cord or to cut through it. His attempts to do so are made only just the instant after he has killed, or after his meal, when he is loath to leave even a bone. Hyenas sometimes drive away a panther when he is eating and devour the kill themselves. This often happens in places infested with these scavengers when also they acquire boldness and take to killing

baits tied out for panthers. The thing to do then is either to fence the bait about with thorns, so that the panther can jump into the enclosure and kill and eat and leave without fear of disturbance and so return again, or to build mounds of stones packed in earth, six to eight feet high, with a flat top in the shape of a truncated cone, and to tie the bait on top of it. The panther can climb the cone which the hyena cannot.

If the sportsman watching over a kill feels that the panther has detected him and will not come, his best course is to shout for his men and to make a show of leaving by getting one of them to climb up to him and then down, and to retire talking. This stratagem is very likely to bring out the beast if he happens to be near watching. When going to sit up, especially when it is late, the party should approach the spot talking in their natural tone, and when they have got there, the men should spread out some paces apart continuing to talk, while the sportsman quietly gets into his position. When he is quite ready to begin his vigil, he should let the men know by a pre-arranged signal, such as a whistle or hoot; and they should then retire talking in the opposite direction from which they came. It often happens that the kill lies in thick growth or in a hollow or gorge, masked by bushes or hills or rocks. In such cases the men sent to prepare the position should be carefully instructed to spread out some distance from the spot selected for the machan and to engage in talking, humming or breaking sticks or leaves, while a few workers quietly get it ready. This device is necessary, as in eight cases out of ten the panther is watching from some cover. In a case that I recollect, two men were told off to sit some distance away from where the machan was being tied, as a precaution against surprise from the panther returning before he was expected. They employed their time in hacking at a stump, and soon after the men were called away, the panther walked straight up to the spot, to inspect what they had been doing before going to his kill.

In another case, the native posted as a decoy thought he could not do better than pass the time gathering plums from a zizyphus tree, and as soon as he left, the panther turned up at the tree to satisfy his curiosity before coming to the kill. Other instances could be quoted, but these will suffice to show how necessary it is to divert the beast's attention while the machan is being fixed up. Unless such precautions are carefully attended to, the sportsman

might as well give up the attempt to frustrate so cunning a beast. Their non-observance accounts for the great number of failures in this form of sport. In my own experience, the average of successes works out to one in every third try, or thirty-three per cent.

Like his bigger cousin, and for the same reasons, the panther is a diurnal animal. His size and agility and his habit of accommodating his body to almost any kind of cover, make it far easier for him to seize his prey during the day. He rarely kills at night that is from after dark to the beginning of dawn. But one thing that he will do at night is to climb trees and seize monkeys, peafowl, and other birds roosting on trees. Young panther are addicted to this form of sport.

I was privileged to witness a very strange sight one morning, about nine o'clock, while inspecting the Bhowargarh reserve in the Betul district. The place was close to the banks of the Machna where the river makes a big loop some miles south of Kantawari. We were looking for seedling plants of teak and tinas - the two principal woods in the forests - with a view to determining the conditions in the tract after a successful spell of fire-protection. It is many years to look back, but I think Jabli, a Gond shikari, was with me. Our attention was absorbed in turning over the thick matting of grass that had formed by the exclusion of fires and grazing and that hid the new plants, when we suddenly heard a great disturbance among the baboons playing about the banks. One of the men called out that it was a tiger, and we got up trees as fast as we could. Soon we saw a panther cutting across the neck of the loop holding a young baboon in his mouth with a pack of large monkeys after him, who were actually trying to rescue the victim by making combined rushes at the beast. The panther was going slowly uttering suppressed growls as if fearing an attack. I should have liked to know if the monkeys would have succeeded in their purpose. My men thought they would have, but even if they had, the victim was too badly hurt to have survived. But as it happened one of the men gave a wild whoop and that made the monkeys rush up trees and the panther bolt with his prey.

Panthers hunt for frogs, crabs and shells just as the tiger does, and often I have heard them close to camp clattering among the stones along the beds of streams and nullahs during their search. In my last tour in Central India, I was camped at Umrabara in the Jhabua State. The villagers came to ask if I would care to come out

and shoot one that was occupied in this manner in the riverbed close by the camp. It is very probable that panthers catch fish in shallow pools but I do not know of an authentic instance. Aborigines say they occasionally eat the juicy corolla of the mahua flower: and they have shown me fresh marks under date trees where a panther had sipped the juice from the pan which is used to direct it into the collecting pot. Again, I have often found a panther's pugs at salt licks.

Like the tiger, the panther is fond of night excursions, but they are nothing like so extensive as the tiger's. One may often hear him prowling about making a peculiar sound resembling a compressed grunt and snort emitted together, namely, "gurh-gon, gurh-gon" as if the notes were being pumped out of his throat through his nostrils. This puts all the animals for half a mile around on the qui vive. He is not followed like the tiger, and the animals give him a wider berth, doubtless because they suspect him and with good reason, of sly and sneaking habits. He is not particular where he drinks and for appearance sake, he will not kill at the common drinking bouts while the animals are collected together, but he has no compunction about lying up when they have dispersed, and he will seize the solitary creature that may have been delayed, or otherwise prevented from joining in at the right time, and who arrives late and alone to slake its thirst. In general game tribes are reluctant to tolerate his presence; or rather there is a mutual avoidance. They shun him and he is driven to leave his natural haunts and take up his abode close to settlements not only on the outskirts of forests, but even at distances from them, where he can more easily prey on domesticated animals that have nothing to match against his cunning.

Panthers vary in form and colour according to the localities they inhabit. In this respect the variations are just as marked as in the tiger and I need not recapitulate them. But in respect of colouring, besides the two principal markings which the tiger affects, the panther has a third dominant tinge as well, namely, a slaty-grey tint. Panthers of this class are usually met with in laterite and basalt formations, from which the soil and growth have been denuded. When seated against rocks or under dwarf scrub, they look like a jungle spider's web cast over the spot. The resemblance is enough to deceive anyone and certainly, I have found it difficult to detect them, even when pointed out by the keener-sighted aborigine.

When a panther becomes aggressive in his attacks on village hamlets, the aborigines set about to poison or to trap him. The poisons used are concoctions from the stems or roots of herbaceous annuals, known to the medicine men, which causes violent purging and spasms resulting either in death or illness for a long period. But such mixtures are bitter and unless very carefully secreted in the carcass, are sure to be detected, and the beast will abandon his meal. A more effective means of poisoning is by means of a concoction prepared from the seeds of the kodra plant (eleusine coracana) whose grains apparently secrete a narcotic poison, and the over-ripe grain is selected for the purpose. These are ground into flour and kneaded into a paste with the addition of a few eggs and a little ghi to give it a flavour. Incisions are then made in the meat of the kill, and the paste is rubbed and stuffed into the slits. This renders the meal appetizing, and the panther eats ravenously. Having gorged the beast feels dizzy; he wants to make for water, but he reels over in a drunken fit and is kept a prisoner close to the spot in a semi-conscious condition. When the day breaks, the men hurry to the scene, and to make certain that the brute is properly incapacitated, before approaching with their bows and arrows or axes or spears, they beat a drum. The hollow sound causes the poisoned panther to howl and to try to get away, but he reels over at each attempt, and the men then rush up and finish him. I have seen this done on two occasions.

The gin usually employed to trap him, is a simple contrivance on the principle of a lever. A springy sapling of teak or dhaman or equally tough and elastic wood, is balanced on a stout forked post at a height of six to eight feet from the ground. To one end a weight of from hundred to a hundred and fifty pounds is firmly attached, while a strong cord, depending in a noose is fastened at the other. The cord-end is forced down for four or five feet till the loop of the noose touches the surface, the sapling being kept in position by a slip attachment, such as the one with which we are acquainted in the figure of four trap. The loop is widened to form an opening of thirty to forty inches in circumference; and the lower part of its periphery is slightly embedded in the ground, and the top and sides are hidden in thorny branches with which the kill has been fenced round. The kill lies just inside the opening formed by the loop, so to allow the beast to step over in his efforts to get it out, and is connected with the slip. The panther having located his kill

can only get at it through the opening; in he steps 'over' and his first tug disengages the catch, causing the cord end to spring up swinging the panther by the waist. The tight noose holds him fast, dangling and struggling in the air and then the villagers rush up and belabour him with clubs till he dies. It is an ignominious but fitting end for a thievish beast.

A wounded panther is even more dangerous than a wounded tiger. This is not surprising, considering his agility and habit of concealing himself in little or no cover. If it is necessary to follow him up the sportsman should first of all allow some interval to enable the blood to congeal and so to stiffen his body more or less, according to the nature of the wound. Then, taking a few reliable men selected chiefly for their good sight and hearing, the sportsman should take up the trail, keeping next to the man who is tracking, while the others remain at the back peering around to note the least sound or movement. In spite of the untoward occurrence which I have described, the safest course is to send men up trees and to make sure of every few yards before advancing. To allow the lookout man every opportunity of seeing thoroughly once he is safe above, stones should be thrown in every cover near about. This invariably makes a wounded beast start or move. Good shikaris, if they are provided with the necessary weapons, prefer to follow a wounded beast alone, because they cannot trust an alien sportsman to move quietly enough to escape observation. In this they are right. Aborigines with their lithe limbs, springy steps and bare feet, and their senses braced, are far more fitted for the task than when they are encumbered with the company of an accoutred sportsman who finds it difficult to tread lightly, and very likely draws the attention of the beast.

It is an extraordinary fact that heavy beasts such as tiger and panther should walk so softly as not to be heard even a few paces away. The pads doubtless assist in deadening the sound but do not entirely contribute to the result, as sambar and bison, especially solitary ones, are proportionately just as quiet in their movements, notwithstanding their hard hoofs. Moreover the tread of barefooted human beings is audible enough. The real explanation doubtless lies in the springy gait which these beasts develop to perfection. At every step their muscles tend to lift the weight up instead of letting it come crashing upon the ground. This again accounts for the heavy development of muscular tissue in the

forequarters that bear the strain of the force arising from the beast's momentum. One has therefore only to consider the process repeated several thousands of times in every twenty-four hours to understand the effect of such a practice after a year. I have watched these animals from very close distances and marvelled at the silence of their movements, and it struck me that their forequarters heaved with each step, as if absorbing the weight set up by the momentum. A tiger after long confinement in a cage is a sorry spectacle compared with his forest brother; and if it were possible to obtain successive generations of caged tigers, the progeny would doubtless cease to develop the muscular expansion of the forequarters.

Chapter XII

The Bear

My personal knowledge of bears is confined to the sloth bear who inhabits the Highlands of Central India. He is essentially herbivorous, though he will feed on worms and insects and land crustacea. As regards flesh he will not disdain a meal of carrion if a carcass is lying in his path, but he will touch it only if it has already been torn and the flesh exposed, he will not meddle with a whole carcass with the skin intact. I was once sitting over a dead goat that a panther had just killed. The panther had been driven off and had failed to return, but two bears came along the track that passed close to the kill. Having winded it, they stopped and looked; then they went to the kill and started smelling it; then they turned it over, but they would not attempt to tear it. When they began to leave, I shot one, the other got away. I questioned the Gond shikari and he told me of their habits and I have had confirmation of it in another instance. On the other hand, on two occasions, while seated over a partially eaten calf and goat, I have seen bears which happened to come upon them in their nightly perambulations, begin to gorge on the flesh.

Compared with the quick-eyed denizens of the jungles, a bear is practically blind but he has a keen sense of scent to guide him. He can also hear pretty well, though nothing like so well as the tiger or panther. His shaggy coat and tough hide as well as his long claws give him an exaggerated sense of security, and so he trundles along through the forests making far more noise than it is reasonable to expect from a creature of his qualifications. He is no match for the tiger in spite of his pretensions, and his young ones fall an easy prey to panthers. A she-bear with cubs is reckless in her daring, but so is every mother beast. In her foolish rushes at the foe, a mother bear will leave her progeny unprotected and a cunning beast like a panther will swing round and be off with one of the cubs, while she goes tearing headlong forward. I have seen two or three men try and secure a bear cub while escaping in a beat. The mother charged them and they ran, but one man more nimble than the others, hooked round and caught hold of one of the cubs deserted on the ground, before she could return to them.

The deer tribe hardly take any notice of the bear, and it is

amusing to watch them when a bear comes along. The fawns will prick up their ears and look at their parents, as if to say, "Don't you think we should be off?" But the parents appear to take no notice and continue grazing. Sometimes the bear will even make the fawns start running, but they will soon pick up courage and return on seeing their parents remain unmoved.

Bears are often to be found living in colonies over a confined space provided it is rocky. I have known caves to contain five and six bears at a time, while on occasions I have seen fifteen and twenty bears occupy a rocky peak covering barely an acre of ground. Bears are not of a quarrelsome disposition and excepting during the rutting season when mature males engage in savage bouts of strength resembling a wrestling match in order to win the favour of the females, they live peaceably together. These fights are characteristic more for their tumultuous display, than for any actual damage caused to the combatants. Even when defeated, the vanquished bear seldom leaves the society of his companions.

Bears are irregular about breeding, but the course of sexual activity is most marked from end of March to beginning of April. The gestation period lasts for twenty-seven weeks, and the she-bear does not leave the society of her mate till very near her time. Two to four cubs are born at a birth. Litters with three cubs are fairly common, but those with four are rare. I know of only one case with four and heard of another from a reliable informant. The mother bear retires to a cave or a hollow or a ledge on a rocky and steep hillside to bring forth her cubs. These are blind at birth and the eyes remain closed for a fortnight or so longer. The mother is very savage for the first week after confinement, charging out of her sanctuary at the least sound prepared to attack any and everything, even inoffensive beasts such as monkey, sambar, that may happen to come near or pass by the spot. The cubs make a peculiar bubbling sound while suckling which can be heard some little way off. The she-bear is devoted to her young and mother and cubs are very human about their attachment.

The she-bear has a way of carrying her young on the back. They lie flat astride her, holding on to her shaggy coat with their feet and jaws, and are not easily shaken off. It is a comic sight, when the young are rather big; from a distance, it looks as if the mother were carrying a dhobi's bundle. I remember my chagrin the first time I saw one and shot it. I thought she was hunch-backed and when

my Gond came up, I tried to describe her as such but he looked quite surprised and failed to understand. However we went to see, as she had fallen over a bank that entirely hid her from view and to my grief, there were two cubs still holding on to her back, although she was stone dead. At the sight my man gazed at me, as if in wonder that I did not know better.

It is a pitiful business to shoot a she-bear with cubs, and should be avoided. Even when big and able to fend for themselves, the cubs will hang round the dead body, whining and every now and again giving it a nudge with their snouts, as if to say "Are you asleep? Why don't you get up and come?" They only leave the body when the men come close up.

Bears are not only very fond of their young, but the couples show much conjugal affection. Till they have arrived at the adult stage, they are inseparable. Then although foraging together, they will more often than not, lie up in separate places. A she-bear with cubs will not allow her mate to come anywhere near her lair; she fears harm to her cubs from his rough manner; he apparently means well but has an unfortunate way of showing his affection, which not unnaturally causes the mother bear to discourage his attentions, while the cubs are very young. But when she leaves them to seek food, that is when they are too young to accompany her, she will join her mate and they will forage together. I suspect that female tigers and panthers do the same, but I have not been able to get hold of an authentic case, for though on occasions, female panthers shot in company with males have had milk in their nipples, there was no knowing if the cubs were alive or dead.

Bears are naturally playful and fond of frolics, and while going about are always teasing each other for fun. In the Dhain-Bori reserve, I was out with my tracker early one morning stalking sambar. Failing to come across a good stag, we took up a position on an eminence at the foot of a high chain of hills, such as stags delight to lie up in during the day. There were several game tracks leading up the slopes, showing that they were a favourite game resort. It was still early and the position we took up commanded a wide view round-about, so that there was every likelihood of a shot at a belated stag which often keep out till late in solitary wilds. We had been seated for about half an hour during which a few hinds with an immature male, and a barking deer had gone on without detecting us showing that we were on the right side as regards

scent. Three bears then came along, grunting and snorting and playing as they walked up. We had heard them coming from some distance ahead and their noises prepared me for shooting, as it seemed certain that they would soon be passing by the foot of the knoll over which we were seated. But when they were yet a little way off, an armadillo crossed the path just in front of the bears who seeing the creature go by, ran after it. The armadillo at once rolled itself into a ball as it always does when confronted with danger. The bears apparently surprised at the creature's sudden transformation stopped short and started to sniff and grunt at the curled-up object before them. Then they took courage and went near and began striking at it with their paws, but could make no impression on the hard scaly covering, and their strokes only caused it to turn over and over.

The rolling afforded so much amusement that it took on the form of a game as with a toy, like kittens engaged in play with a worsted ball. The fun continued with such zest that the bears lost all count of time and in the twenty or thirty minutes that elapsed, the sun had risen over the hills and shone down into the valley. Also in the rolling and tumbling after the armadillo, they had got some distance off the path and had moved on close to the bank of a deep nullah which came down from the hills. Here in the excitement, they lost control of the ball and it went over the bank. This stopped the play, for the steepness prevented the bears from following of which the armadillo was quick to take advantage and escape. The disappointed bears stood and peered over the bank for a while, then realising the lateness of the hour they rapidly made a beeline for the hills. Intent as I was watching the scene and sure that the bears would return to the path and resume their course, I had not stirred from the spot. Imagine my surprise then at seeing them tearing away by quite another route. The only chance now lay in rushing up also and trying and intercept them above and this I did without a moment's hesitation. But the bears were too quick for me and had scaled the hill just before I got up, so that breathless and tired by the climb, the shots I fired at them went wide of the mark. The incident shows how wild beasts take advantage of opportunities to amuse themselves at each other's expense.

The bear cannot be described as dangerous to man. He is not vindictive and he will not attack without great provocation, and even if he does the odds are in man's favour. Occasionally a female

with cubs will charge a person who happens to go near or passes close to where she is feeding or playing with them; but more often she will endeavour to get away. Bears will not follow a man up a tree; they are slow and clumsy climbers. I have had an infuriated bear charge past under me when I drew myself up on a branch to get out of his way. This is what the aborigine commonly does, when a driven bear charges through a beat or a wounded bear makes for him. On ground the bear can always be evaded by dodging, but in country strewn with rocks, the chances of a fall are great. At close quarters the bear will often stand up on his hind legs to strike at the face and chest, which seem to fascinate him more than any other part of the human frame. With jaws bubbling, eyes flashing fire and arms gesticulating, he looks the very personification of wrath and evil.

My first introduction to the bear was in the Salimet forest of the Betul district. There is a conical hill [sic] known as Chilma-Tekri with massive rocks protruding all over its slopes and affording excellent cover. In those days it used to be infested with bear and as many as nine have been shot in a few hours. At the foot spreading out to some distance, there were plenty of zizyphus trees which yield the jujub plum, on which the bears came out to feed as soon as the sun began to sink. Accompanied by my Mohammedan orderly and a local shikar, and armed with an old Martini with a few cartridges, I stalked round the hill without seeing one, so began to perambulate again. This time we came upon four bears feeding under a tree. The noise they made scrambling about in the leaves and grass prevented their hearing us and the shikari took me to within sixty feet of them. I sat down and fired at the one that looked the biggest. He rolled over and over, trying to get at the others. They had stopped feeding and were looking at him and grunting, as much as to say, "What is all this foolery about?". A second shot missed, but it put them on the alert and they doubtless guessed the cause of their neighbour's howls. Foolishly I stood up and the bears saw me instantly. They began to come for me; I reloaded and fired, but missed each time. When almost right up two of the bears rose up on their hind legs: but even then, I missed again. Meanwhile the shikari with the loaded shotgun had climbed a tree near me, as also did the orderly, who was some distance away. Disgusted with the rifle, I put out my hand for the gun, but not receiving it, glanced round to see the shikari

motioning to me to run, which indeed was the only thing left to do. I ran and the bears followed. A deep nullah twined about at the foot of the hill, barely eighty yards from the spot, and lay across our path. I jumped down the bank, fifteen or twenty feet, which was steep here, into a pool of water, and clambered over the opposite bank by the help of hanging roots and bushes. Then getting up and looking back, I saw the bears on the spot from where I had jumped, meditating retreat. I fired my last shot, but missed. A little while after they had gone, the shikari whistled and when I replied, he and the orderly turned up smiling, to tell me the first bear was lying dead. But I was however in a very different mood for smiles and favours, and beat them both for what I considered their base desertion. I doubt whether the bears would have dared to follow me for any distance, if the men had remained on the ground. But as they were up trees, their presence was never suspected.

Bears are very quick in descending slopes, and sportsmen should be careful to take up positions above them if possible. They come shooting straight down combining a series of tumbles and rushes. In this respect they differ from the tiger or panther, which walk down rapidly in a zigzag, unless of course murderously inclined, when they will bound, or proceed in a series of leaps resembling those of the baboon when rushing along. A young friend shooting with me, was asked when the beaters came up, if he had seen anything come down the slope, he replied, "Yes! only a big monkey, and he is in that grass in front." The aborigines knowing better, withdrew smiling, and started flinging rocks into the patch, and the panther charged out and escaped. Seeing him come over the grassy descent in the manner described, my friend mistook him for a baboon.

In beating for bear in the hilly country where they usually are found, the best position to take up is one commanding a gorge situated, either on a level, or above the spot where the bear is supposed to be lying up. The gorge nearest the bear on his lee-side should be selected and approached by a roundabout way so as not to disturb him. Then, if a few men are told off to get on the windward side and walk up coughing and throwing stones, the bear will appear with a slow trundling gait allowing ample time to prepare and be an excellent mark as well. In this way between breakfast and tea time, I have had beaten out, four separate bears from different positions in the Pacham Pahars of Barwani. A bear

Life in the Wilds of Central India

can also be easily stalked in the early morning or evening, provided you keep on the lee-side of him. On beating up a ravine the position chosen should be on the side where there are most rocks.

Bears are very tenacious of life and unless the shot is placed in the right spot they will take a lot of killing. The lungs for instance, seem proof against bullet wounds and one or more shots through the organs hardly affect them. Again hits elsewhere seem to be felt only as wasp stings. I ascribe this immunity partly to his hardy nature and partly to the super-abundance of wind with which the bear is provided. I shall refer later to his tremendous powers of suction and expulsion of air. The shots that will fetch them are in the head, neck, or heart. The heart is difficult to locate owing to his podgy formation. The shaggy coat about the neck also misleads the aim, while the head by itself is a small mark. I have raked a bear from fore to aft, mistaking him for a bison at early dawn, with a hardened .577 bullet driven by eight drams of black powder. The ball traversed the lungs in its passage and still the beast made me tramp after him for fully a mile before he was overtaken and shot. A wounded bear has a way of making believe he was in extremis by rolling over and over when hit, but despite the appearances of a death-struggle, he is soon up and off faster than he is wont to go; one should therefore be quick in getting in the second shot.

I have heard and read stories of cases, where individuals pursued by bears lay down and shammed death to escape from his attentions, but none of the many intelligent aboriginal folks I have met in my rambles could substantiate this. However it does not seem inconsistent with their aversion to carcasses that have not been torn.

I have said that bears will not attack men without serious provocation unless it is a female with cubs fearing an attack. The only exception I know was an old solitary male bear that infested the Mendha forests in the Betul district and was said to charge out at individuals going along the path. A man and two women had been mauled by him, while others had been charged and escaped. During a stalk for bison, he was mistaken for one in the distance in the twilight as he walked along the crest of a slope, and was shot. He was the finest specimen of his kind I have seen and in splendid condition. He measured seven feet seven inches while his forearms taped twenty-eight inches, and the men said he weighed about five maunds, that is four hundred and ten pounds. It took four men to lift him.

Provided the branches are strong enough to support him, a bear can climb great heights on trees, though his progress is slow. He climbs chiefly to rob the bees, and at nights when the workers are more or less torpid after the toil of the day. Moreover the shades of night assist him for bees have then little inclination for a demonstration in force. I have measured heights of from forty to fifty feet, that bears have ascended on giant cottonwood, kahu and haldan trees. It seems strange that they can tell in the dark where the honey is when it is so out of reach and until not very long ago, I used to ascribe it to their scent, that is of the comb from the ground. But a Bhil collector of honey whom I met in one of my rounds, disconsolate at having the comb which he had been looking forward to appropriating, robbed by a bear during the previous night, told me that the bear located the honey by means of the excretions dropped by the bees. Again as the discharges vary during the course of the building of the hive, it also enables the bear to know if the comb is worth getting or not, that is whether the hive was full, empty or in the process of construction. Something of the sort must occur otherwise the bear's labour in ascending trees would as often as not, be futile, and considering how careful animals are to avoid risks, the explanation is very probable. The comb in question was quite forty feet and on a side branch, fifteen or twenty feet from the trunk, from which it trailed out horizontally. To attempt such feats, the bear must have a pretty firm hold, since he is not balanced like a panther or cat and could not like them, trust to falling on his feet which would be a catastrophe indeed.

The fallacy that tigers and panthers are nocturnal animals clings also to the bear. But one need not be an oculist to see that nature has not provided the bear with sight for nightly vision. The fact of his feeding almost entirely during the night is due to his sense of scent being more highly developed than either of the above animals. He forages entirely by scent, and scent is sufficiently absorbing to enable him to locate roots, bulbs and fungoid growth in the surface, even if it be hard and there are no signs of stems above ground - after the fashion of French poodles trained to hunt for truffles on the Continent. The bear prefers to feed in the daytime, and most bears leave their haunts before the sun is down. In undisturbed localities I have come on them feeding long before sunset and after sunrise. But like the tiger and panther, he is perforce obliged to forage by night wherever he fears man's intrusion in his haunts.

Apart from roots, bulbs and honey, they relish the juicy corolla of the mahua, and will occasionally eat flowers and buds of other species, as of the wood cotton tree, which they find palatable. They are very partial to fruits of wild figs, as well as plums, nuts and berries produced by various trees and shrubs. They avoid fruits with an excess of astringent properties, such as tamarind. Again, they are fond of the gums that exude from acacias and from other resiniferous trees. I have not seen a bear intoxicated, but I have often been told by the aborigine that he approaches that condition, when he feeds on the stale fermenting corolla of the mahua, such as results from the capsules remaining on damp, heated surfaces. In some of the forests that were under my charge, toddy and date palms abounded, but no authentic instance of bears drinking the juice ever came to my notice. They were however greedy to get the fruit that fell.

In their dietary are included also crabs, shells, snails and the eggs of ground birds, and so too would frogs be if the bears were quick enough to seize them. The larvae of various beetles and the mole and ground crickets, as well as the queen termites form a favourite mouthful. The bear's method of finding these is unique. When they have located their prey in the surface, they bring into play their respiratory organs and force powerful jets of air into the holes or slits where the larvae or insects happen to be lodged, until overcome by the blasts of air the prey becomes dislodged. The force is then reversed and the larvae or insect is drawn into the mouth. A bear engaged in this remarkable operation is worth hearing. He makes a noise like the blowing and puffing emitted from a powerful bellows, only with a rasping squirt different from the machine. The lungs must be especially adapted to stand the strain of reversible forces, with such power of propulsion and suction. It seems as if these organs in the bear were provided with an extra quantity of air chambers or as if they were of larger dimensions than in any other animal or individual. At the same time, the thick covering of skin over the snout or muzzle enables the bear to attempt the performance without harm to his mouth, which would assuredly occur if his face were modelled like other animals. The bear's lungs might very well be taken as an example of the efficiency of breathing space provided by nature in the animal tribes.

Bears usually lie up in sheltered nooks along the slopes of hills

and the steeper these are the better. Where there are rocks, they delight to get behind or between them: otherwise the shade of trees, shrubs or bamboo clumps suits them equally well. I have also had them driven out of thick grass with leafless sali trees overhead. They are not as is supposed partial to caves; though they will occupy them when there is little fear of molestation, as in tracts only occasionally visited by sportsmen, and also when there is room for two or more. Individual bears avoid caves, and even females about to cub do not always take to them but seem to prefer the shelter of rocks and growth on precipitous slopes.

I have spoken of the affectionate nature of the tribe towards their own kind. Sometimes it is quite pathetic in its resemblance to human emotion. Camped at Kanjitalao in the Betul district one summer, I was sleeping in the open when, about midnight, I was awakened by what seemed to be the grunts of pigs. There was a bright moon and the camp was on the bank of a nullah that contained the only pool of water for miles round, though I did not know this at the time. The noises came from three bears on their way to drink; and they had either winded or seen my bed and halted, fifteen or twenty paces distant, undecided what to do. My rifle as usual lay resting against a campstool standing near the bed with a glass of water in case of thirst at night. Consequently it was the work of a minute to take it up and fire. One bear rolled over and as she started getting up, I put the second barrel into her as well. The other two had moved off at the sound of the shot, which had also roused the servants who came rushing to know the cause. I had no more cartridges at hand and the bear was still struggling and moaning, so I ran to the tent a few paces away to get some - this took a little time as there was no light. Meanwhile the servants kept shouting that the bears were coming for us. Going out again with my rifle loaded, as I thought to put an end to the struggle, I found instead that the two unwounded bears were helping the wounded one away. They had come up while I was in the tent and when the servants had shouted, not to attack them but to remove their comrade. They held on to her just as two men would sling a helpless human being by the arm - each placing one arm on either side of her fore-arms, only instead of keeping upright as would be the case with human beings, the bears managed it by remaining on three feet, and partly supported and partly dragged her away. We ran after them shouting and I fired two more shots, but they got

into thick grass and undergrowth and we had to turn back. Next morning the she-bear was found dead about half a mile from camp.

Another time at Kadwal in the Kathiwara State where I was doing settlement work, the Thakur's uncle proposed that I should sit up one evening near a zizyphus tree for a few hours, while the moon kept fine, as bears came to feed on the plums almost every night. I had hardly been in my position an hour, when four or five bears turned up. The forests here are densely wooded. The foliage permits only streaks of light to enter and gives the surface a patchy appearance. The bears looked like phantoms as they scrambled about for the plums in and out from light to darkness. One's aim had to be more by sound than sight, but both shots took effect. Two bears rolled about under the trees, while the others seemed to disappear for the time being. It was now difficult to see at all, and some minutes were wasted while the Bhils returned with bamboo torches and lanterns from camp. When they came and we walked up, the bears were all gone. But we heard one howling in the distance and following the sound, came upon him being helped along by a second, which abandoned the attempt at rescue as soon as it saw the light come near, allowing us to settle with the wounded one. We could also hear the second wounded bear howling near us and we made for him as quickly as we could, but before we could overtake him, his friends had got him into thick cover and we had to give up the pursuit for the night. It is true that we actually did not see the second rescue party, but it was quite easy to tell by the sounds that there were others with the wounded one. Moreover when we tracked him in the morning, there were distinct marks of three bears, and the blood trail was in the centre. However he was lost for good though we tracked him for over a mile. The one which we secured in the night had the first shot through the lungs.

I can recall another case of the kind. While stalking for sambar in the Mendha forests of the Betul district, we came upon a bear feeding on a wild fig tree, about ten or twelve feet from the ground. Another bear scrambled about below, eating the figs that dropped. It was shortly after sunset, and they had no idea of our presence. I fired at the one on the tree which afforded a splendid mark, and with a few moans and struggles, he collapsed into a fork where he stuck. The sound startled the other - we could barely see him owing to the undergrowth - and he was still for a few minutes. The

Gond with me enjoined patience and said that the second bear would also climb the tree. After a short wait, he began moving rapidly round and round the tree, uttering a medley of moans and grunts. Then he started to climb and having got near his dead comrade, began to grunt and nudge at the body. The Gond now cautioned me to fire which I stupidly did, but the excitement and interest which absorbed me made me make a bad miss. The bear dropped and was off before another shot could be aimed. It would have been interesting to know if the bear would have got the body off the tree; a little more patience would have shown.

But a wounded bear does not always appreciate such offer of succour from its companion. More often the out-burst of rage that accompanies the pain renders the beast savage, so that when its companion goes up to find out the reason for its distress, it is unceremoniously attacked by the wounded creature who imagines its mate to be the cause of its misfortune. Even then the mate will not leave its unfortunate companion and though precluded from assisting because of its unwonted fury, it keeps near the wounded bear and by grunts and snorts of sympathy it encourages the creature forward. Quite a fair percentage of losses from wounds could be traced to this feeling of comradeship. This compassionate trait which compels them to stand by each other is perhaps more manifest in the bear than in other game animals, and is explained by the affectionate nature of the tribe.

A bear's howl in severe distress or pain would move the staunchest heart. It is more like a shrill piercing whine, continued half a dozen times successively, than any thing else. It is very human in poignancy; like the cry which a strong man would give if he were held down and murdered piecemeal. But in its full tone, it is uttered only, when the beast feels itself absolutely forsaken or abandoned. It may be uttered by a she-bear for the loss of her cubs, or again by a she-bear trying to ward off an attack on her cubs by a panther or a tiger; or a male defending its mate; or by a wounded bear that feels itself doomed. The sound enabled us to locate a wounded bear shot three days previous by a sportsman shooting ten miles or so from my camp at Kunkheri in the Betul district. No one in camp had the least idea of the occurrence, and our discovery was purely accidental. I was out in the early morning, about three miles from camp, inspecting a forest tract, where felling had been proposed, when we heard the wail come across the river from a

cluster of rocky peaks in the distance. It fairly stunned us for the moment. The Gonds thought that the bear had been overpowered by a tiger and we followed cautiously in the direction of the sound. As we looked about the rocks, one of the men saw some blood and we made out from the blood-trail cast on the ground that the bear was hard hit by a bullet. Following the trail we came upon the bear lying, almost listless, behind a rock in a niche or pocket of the slope. He would have died in an hour or so and was soon put out of pain. The wound was in the lungs from a heavy bullet which he had tried hard to suck out. The wound was as clean as one could wish, and the entrance of the ball was clearly visible for a few inches owing to the constant sucking.

Chapter XII

The Sambar

This magnificent beast may be regarded as the king of the deer tribes in India. My acquaintance with him is confined to the Highlands of Central India where he attains his greatest size and where the finest trophies have been obtained. He ranges over the valleys and mountains, through open and scrub jungles and dense woodlands. But he belongs essentially to the hills and nature has provided him with the requisites for a mountain home, conspicuous among which are his feet, especially adapted for mountaineering, and his thick shaggy bristles to keep him warm on the heights. At the same time he shows little or no preference, and favours equally the low country, rolling with hillocks, and the main chains which dominate them. But in either case he likes to choose a position for lying up which dominates the surroundings. He relies chiefly for safety on smelling and hearing, more especially the former. As regards seeing, his sight is better adapted for night than day. Moreover he is unable to distinguish objects at any distance, and even at close quarters, unless previously warned by scent, he has an imperfect idea of what he sees.

The sambar is a sociable deer and is found herding with all the denizens of the country over which he ranges, irrespective of class or creed. I have mentioned that he understands the tiger and is willing to show him consideration while he feels contempt for the panther and discountenances his familiarity. He is on friendly terms with the bear and has no objection to rubbing shoulders with him whenever he chooses to come round. Similarly he allows the pig and blue-bull to squat near him, so long as they are not demonstrative, but if they are, he shows his displeasure by moving away to a distance. He likes to watch the monkeys at their gambols among the branches; it seems as if their aerial feats are rather beyond his comprehension. The coquettish ways of the peacock and jungle-cock amuse and please him. He would be man's friend if he could, except for the feud started by men's ancestors and continued with relentless vigour by the unscrupulous among them. One thing he loathes, as much for its rapacity as for the degrading way in which it disposes of its prey, and that is the wild dog. If practicable he will abandon his favourite haunt as soon as he finds

that one of these vermin has set foot within it. Against their numbers, he is powerless and he is no match for their unprincipled methods of hunting. He watches with anxiety the increase in their number in modern times, which results from the gradual extinction of his neighbour and guardian of the peace - the tiger.

Sambar go about in groups of three or more, and I have counted as many as thirty-two in a heard [sic]. Hinds and young stags keep together. Mature stags associate for feeding, but otherwise keep aloof. Old stagers live in seclusion, either alone or in twos or threes, and seldom come near the others. Hinds calve almost annually, or to be precise three times in four years. The period of gestation is seven months, but the aborigines maintain that during the first fecundity the period is always two or three weeks longer. When very near her time, the hind withdraws to an unfrequented spot and selects a hollow or dip in the surface, where she brings forth her young. One or two are born at a birth, and she stays in the spot about a week or ten days, till the fawn is able to accompany her in her rambles, and then she takes it and introduces it to the others of the group to which she belongs.

The adult age varies from three to four years, and until then the young keep with the parents even if others have appeared in the meantime to supplant them in the parent's affections. Hinds are devoted to their young, and develop an abnormal caution while they are in the helpless stage. The smallest change in the normal appearance of things attracts the mother's attention and a note from her makes the fawn squat down immediately and lie flat on the ground, while the mother trots some distance off to draw the enemy. I have seen a sambar hind [to] sacrifice herself to wild dogs to save her offspring by getting up and showing herself when she heard them at some distance moving in the grass, whereas they were going in a different direction and would not have seen her had she not stirred. Again, if she is at a distance and suspects danger, she will utter a note of alarm which is a softer plaintive note than the one ordinarily uttered, to warn her offspring.

During the rutting period, which may be reckoned from the middle of February to the end of April or the middle of May, stags are restless and fierce and daring even to a fault. They will attack panther if one passes, and occasionally they will face tiger as well, though the odds are heavily against them in such an encounter. Great battles also occur among themselves and as they meet in

combat, the clashing of horns can be heard at long distances sounding like blows of heavy clubs. Sambar fights are the tamashas of the jungle. They are watched by numbers of other sambars and even of other animals, which gather to the spot attracted by the sounds, and keep a sort of ring at a safe distance to watch the sport.

I have heard tales from aborigines of men coming upon stags with their horns interlocked, unable to get them free without breaking a tine or the beam itself. Stags shot during the rutting time are often covered with bruises and have their bristles rubbed off in bunches. One that I saw had two deep wounds on the right haunch and withers, which had formed into abscesses and must have been very painful. At times, the fight ends in the death of one. I myself have not seen this actually happen with sambar, but I know of an instance in which a cheetal stag was gored by another through the lungs and died.

As a rule, the points are not sharp enough to pierce the hide; and the jungle folks maintain that it is only when a tine gets chipped or split in fight or otherwise, that it acquires a dangerous edge. When this occurs the owner has a tremendous weapon of offence and will gore every stag he fights with. The motive of these duels is of course to acquire precedence in contracting with the hinds. They are often renewed between the same combatants, even though one may have suffered defeat previously. Old stagers do not take part in them and immature stags also keep aloof.

At this season stags drop their horns, but it is difficult to say precisely whether this occurs before or after intercourse takes place. As far as I have been able to ascertain, it marks the ebb of physical activity and may be regarded as happening after intercourse.

There is no fixity about the duration of the time for which the horns are carried. Some stags drop them annually; others in alternate years; others again carry them for two or three years. It is not uncommon for a stag to be irregular in retaining and shedding its antlers; it may start by dropping them annually for a few years, then carry them successively for two or three years, and ultimately revert to its former practice. My experience has shown that the alternate rule is the commonest of all. Sometimes the horns are dropped before the full twelve months, that is in ten or eleven months, on the other hand the period may be prolonged to just

over that period, namely, thirteen or fourteen months. It seems therefore the deciding factors must be sought in the animal's own physical constitution and the surroundings where he lives.

The shedding of the horns is on the same principle as that of the leaf of a tree, that the tissues binding them at the axle gradually contract to enable a cleavage along their bases. But instead of falling to the earth by their own weight as a leaf falls, the horns are got rid of by the animal's deliberate efforts to rid himself of them, as one would of an encumbrance or obstruction. Shed horns sometimes show signs of blood around the sutures which would not otherwise be there. Occasionally also one meets with horns dangling from forks [of trees] between which they were jammed to enable them to be plucked off by force. In fact, as the time approaches for their removal, most stags take to swinging by the support of their antlers fixed tightly between forks and crooked stems or branches, as a means of gradually loosening them.

I judge that either owing to the gradual rendition [sic] of tissue along the plain at the base of the horn and the surface where it joins, the weight of the antlers becomes unbearable, or else that the severance in process was causing irritation. I am inclined to the former belief, because in the latter case instead of plucking off the horns with the aid of branches serving as a hold, the stag would naturally take to rubbing the edges of the surface round the horns against some hard object. But this he does not do because the bristles round the joints remain intact when the horn is dropped. The jungle races say that the shedding is caused by maggots eating along the plains of the joints, but if this were true the stag would certainly want to rub the joints. Again I have never come across an instance of a horn naturally shed in a blank without trees, horns are invariably picked up near some object, such as a tree, shrub, clump or bank against which they had been applied to get them off. A stag without his horns is a sorry spectacle and he seems to know it, for he is never less inclined to show himself than when he lacks these ornaments.

The new horns bud within a week or a fortnight after the old ones have been cast. The growth is quick and takes from a fortnight to a month, according to size, to attain full dimensions. At first the new horns are soft, like pulp enveloped in a thick skin or coat of soft tissue covered with hair. They are fairly brittle and the several parts cylindrical. The stag looks as if he were carrying

a frame-work of the pods of the jungle tree stereospermum xylocarpum - appropriately named by the jungle folk, sambar-singhi.

The horns take usually a month or more to harden. At this time the stags are very cautious about their movements and avoid tangled growth: indeed they even shun the company of hinds which apparently are inclined to bite off and eat the soft parts. One may say that the stags have forgotten their grievances of a month or so earlier, and unite for the common purpose of protecting their horns and so keep together, usually on precipitous slopes or in unfrequented woodlands. They join the hinds when the horns begin to harden, and as the process continues, they begin gently at first and then forcibly, to rub the antlers against stems and branches selected, as the case may be, for their smooth or rough and their soft or hard bark. This causes the velvet coating, now hard and leathery, to peal off leaving the horns with slightly indented surfaces.

It does not follow that the horns increase in dimension with each renewal, although this is certainly the case at first. But when the full size has once been attained, which may occur at the third, fourth or fifth cast, the growth ceases so far as length is concerned. Subsequent renewals show hardly any difference of length: in fact a decrease of an inch or more may even occur. The horns in velvet are considered a delicacy by aborigines and Mohammed shikaris who pronounce the flavour to be as good and sweet as marrow.

The horns of full-grown sambars vary greatly in length and thickness. In some stags, they are never very long, say under thirty-five inches: in others the length varies between forty and fifty inches and rarely exceeds fifty inches. The biggest males do not always have the longest horns, though they usually have the thickest. The longest horns will be found on stags short of stature but long of barrel. In my rambles, I have picked up a pair measuring forty-eight inches, and I have shot a few measuring between thirty-eight and forty-five inches. The finest pair recorded is with the Nawab of Bhopal and is said to measure fifty-four inches. The photograph shows the head to be small, compared with the size of the antlers. This points, though not conclusively, to a small body. I recollect another very fine horn, but unfortunately the hunter had the bad luck to lose the full trophy. A subaltern shooting in the Tapti forests of the Betul district fired at a stag

hitting him at the burr just above the base from where the brow-antler springs, breaking off the rest of the beam. The stag of course got away, but the portion of the horn broken off by the shot measured nearly fifty-two inches, so that allowing four inches for the base, the full length of the beam would have been about fifty-six inches.

To draw an analogy with an animal with which we are more familiar, I should say that the long antlered specimens are the Arabs of the tribe, while the walers or thoroughbreds are represented by the huge beasts with massive but shorter horns, while smaller stags may be compared with ponies. Some such distinction is observed by the aborigines who call the first khar or bansia, the second telia and the third gudria or tinsia. These names in their vernacular denote the descriptive characteristics peculiar to each. Thus in the first case, the distinction applies to the long slender horns, like a blade of grass or bamboo shoot; in the second, to fat and greasy [expressive of] looks; and in the third, either small, like a donkey in respect of stature or like branchlets of the tinas tree in respect of horns. Of course I am thinking only of mature stags of from five to ten years old.

The finest all-round specimen I have seen was on the Chandni plateau of the Barwani Satpuras. A friend of mine who had never seen a bison was anxious to set eyes on one. Solitary bulls occasionally ranged over the plateau, and I took him there on the chance of seeing one. Our stalk was unsuccessful and we decided that he should go with the shikari and scan the ledges along the slopes on one side while I did the same in the opposite direction. We had hardly separated, when a magnificent beast sprang up from the under growth, barely fifty paces in front of us. Being black and with the horns thrown back he looked for a minute the very picture of a bison, and I whistled to my friend to come. But the sound was also a warning to the stag who bounded off, making a fine picture as he crashed through the rank growth of elephant grass and herbaceous growth, fully six to eight feet high. He had magnificent antlers and was of exceptional length and thickness. We tracked as far as possible, but he had disappeared among the confused mass of mountains, and even the offer of large rewards to the trackers, failed to locate him.

Sambar feed in the early morning between dawn and sunrise, and in the evening from about sunset to about nine o'clock. Very

little actual feeding is done in the night time. Their food comprises all kind of herbs and grasses, as well as the flowers and fruits of most trees. Grass and herbs growing in a saline soil are especially relished, as are also, the flowers of the mahua and silk cotton tree, wild figs and plums and the fruits of the jungle plants called aonla, siwan and bahera. Some of these have astringent properties and then the sambar discriminates and selects those with a higher flavour of sweetness and the jungle folk take their cue from this when collecting the fruit for pickles. The sambar has a positive craving for salt and will travel long distances to obtain a bite from soils impregnated with saline matter. In cold weather, he seems to need more salt, for during that time he comes regularly to the salt licks. Occasionally he also consumes gravel and lime.

It is a fine sight to see a number of sambar grazing and browsing in an open woodland, especially if there are a few fawns with them. The little ones race about all the time dodging in and out between the parent's feet, absorbed in a game of hide-and-seek and uttering a soft contracted note like a bleat. Even the stags allow them to pass in and out under their bodies. There is always a wary hind or stag grazing apart as a sentry, to give the alarm on the approach of an intruder. Without this precaution, the herd would hardly be able to tell the silent approach of a tiger or panther, owing to the noises made by their movements and the games of the fawns.

Like his close associate, the tiger, the sambar indulges in night excursions and covers great distances. Old stags make their marches singly, but others go in company of two or more. Their purpose seems to be rather exercise than food, though they keep nipping herbage of any growth to which they are partial, as they pass by it in their rambles. But their senses are tense: and if they detect a tiger, they will invariably follow him at a distance and alarm the jungle.

During the day, hinds and immature stags will lie up in any site that suits their requirements, but it will nearly always be in a spot allowing of easy detection should an intruder chance upon them. Mature stags separate from the hinds and take to the slopes and prominent eminences where they usually lie up apart from each other, as a rule at the base or on the upper side, if it be on a slope, of a trunk or bamboo clump, or even in a bare patch. Old and impotent stags live practically in retirement, hardly ever joining the hinds or the mature stags. They take up positions in almost

impossible places, in ledges and nooks along precipitous hillsides. Their movements are slow and quiet and they feed usually by themselves in winter.

In winter when the ground cover is thick stags keep to the lower slopes and eminences, and during the earlier months solitary males are occasionally met with in very unlikely places, such as detached peaks and diminutive hill ranges surrounded by cultivation, into which they move soon after sun-set. The best stag I have shot was driven out from one of these patches in mistake for a boar, which the cultivators said ravaged their fields at night.

In the summer, the sambar occupies the crests and heights dominating the country, and the choice is in great measure due to the decrease of cover that causes them to seek higher positions which naturally afford greater security from attack than the low altitudes; it is also due to the refreshing breezes that prevail over heights.

In the rains he is much worried by noxious flies with which the forests swarm and he becomes very restless, moving in and out of any cover that affords him temporary relief, such as prickly bushes or tangled scrub, or fields of the tall millets, sugar cane or hemp.

Sambar are fond of wallowing and both mature and old stags are addicted to the practice. In the winter stags will often spend half the night in puddle holes or ponds, covering their bodies with a thick crust of mud which they begin to rub off as soon as the sun gets warm. The fatter the beast, the more he will indulge in the game, especially during the small hours of the morning when the chill is intense. According to the jungle folk extreme cold causes the sambar rheumatic pains and so they seek relief by a puddle bath and plaster themselves with the muddy plash. Usually they select holes of pools with a sticky mixture of clay in preference to others. Some wild tribes imitate this practice for the purpose of lessening pains in joints or hurts; and I have come across persons with a plaster of mud or cow-dung bound round some affected part to ease the pain. The relief obtained seems to be only temporary. But the device is of sufficient interest to be worth the attention of medical men.

Sambar play an important part in the life of the jungles. He is eminently the sentinel of the forests. On the one hand he warns the tiger of the approach of a foe and on the other he will rouse the game tribes to a sense of vigilance on the march of the King of

beasts. All the tribes not only look to him for a hint whether to stay or leave in the presence of danger, but also for a warning when their haunts are invaded by foes who threaten their safety. In valleys and lowlands, the hind, especially with fawn, is ever on the alert and often, unknown to the sportsman, she will detect his presence and slink away. But she may rub up against some clumsy animals, such as a pig, blue-bull or bear, which will take the hint and rush off putting all the game in the vicinity on the alert, so that it will puzzle the sportsman to understand the reason of his stalk being unsuccessful when the ground is covered with prints of all kinds of game. The stags on the heights do very much the same, and thus between them they succeed pretty well in safeguarding the interests of the game tribes.

A matter of interesting speculation is the purpose of the eye pit or sub-orbital sinus. All deer and antelope I know possess it, but the best example is that of the sambar. Nature must have provided it for some good reason, for otherwise she would not have tolerated the disfigurement which results from the pit right in the forepart of the face. The Gonds and Korkus inhabiting the forests of the Central Provinces have an interesting story of its origin. They declare that the eye-pits marked the position of former eyes; that is to say, the tribes had each four eyes instead of two. So equipped they could see so well that no beast of prey could get anywhere near them. Accordingly the carnivora appealed in a body to a fakir who dwelt in the jungle and was venerated by its denizens. He pinched together the lids of the lower pair of eyes in the ancestors of the present generations, and caused them to close permanently: and thereby deprived them of the unfair advantage they had previously enjoyed. Some say too that the eye-pit is a means of transferring scent to the nostrils by dilating it, but this does not seem probable, seeing how far above the nose the cavities are placed. The belief has doubtless arisen for their excellence of smell. But it is to be noted that bison do not possess these pits and their scent is as good as the sambar's.

I offer an opinion on the subject which concerns biologists, with some diffidence. But I believe that the eye-pit serves as a reflector, and discloses the presence of an intruder from a distance, especially if he be approaching from a height or from towards the back of the animal. When he had caught sight of the reflected image of the enemy, the beast would naturally dilate the membrane

from side to side in order to procure a better reflection. Now it is a well-known fact that the sambar's sense of seeing is imperfectly developed. They are inoffensive creatures occupying country affording every means of cover to their foes. Scent does help them considerably, but only when the breeze is in the right direction. Moreover the wind is liable to play them tricks, as when dust devils blow - a thing which often happens. Their ears again, although organs of great application, cannot detect the noiseless tread of the beasts of prey. It will be reasonable to infer therefore, that some further defence is necessary if they are to maintain the struggle against their relentless foes. So the sambar draws on his vision too, but since this by itself would avail him nothing, it has to be provided with extra equipment. A lens is impossible, and a reflector takes its place.

Before the reader condemns my suggestion as fanciful, I would ask him to remember four things. The eye pits are placed at an angle below the eyes in the form of a hollow or scoop, embedded in the face and are so posted that the animal can see into them. Again, the cavity is covered with a moist yellowish membrane which has a subdued shine, so that the eye can rest upon it without strain. Moreover as a matter of experience, I have found it impossible to stalk the stag from a higher elevation, even when favoured by wind blowing up the slope and by noises crackling all round, so that it was impossible for him to detect my presence by scent or ear. Finally when a sambar selects his positions to lie up, he is careful only about the surroundings below him or in his front. He makes no provision for danger from above or from along his flanks, which he would not do without good reason.

The last point explains the peculiar shape of the cavity or eye-pit. It is adapted so as to reflect objects approaching from an elevation or from either side, much more easily than an image coming directly from the front. It also explains why in stalks along stretches of plain or undulating country, stags and hinds will often get up - if the wind is against them - facing the sportsman and stand gazing stupidly at him, instead of fleeing. They have been warned of the approach by sound, but their noses and eyes fail to detect anything. But sound by itself is not sufficient to reveal the identity of the intruder; it may be merely a pig, a blue-bull or a bullock. His reflectors have failed to act because the danger lies ahead, and hence the animal stands at gaze. Many a fine stag has

owed his fall to this hesitation when scent and sight have failed him and sound has proved an insufficient guide. Stalking sambar is one of the finest tests imaginable of personal skill. It brings into play instincts inherent which otherwise lie dormant. It requires consummate patience; an eye which can judge country, quick to detect as well as to observe; sharp ears to note the noises; a light, quick and sure tread; endurance of bodily discomforts and above all, the faculty of rapid inference from the information his senses give him. The skilled stalker ought to make the skilled soldier under modern conditions of war. A wary stag - and those worth having are usually wary - who has detected the sportsman, will lead him, if he cares to follow, as fine a dance as he would ever wish for.

The stag's first impulse is to increase the distance between himself and his hunter. He starts by bounding off a short distance or perhaps, he trots or merely improves the paces of his walk, according as the warning has been sudden or gradual. Then he will pull up and proceed at his usual slow, springy gait, following a chain of all the difficult bits of ground in the locality. As a rule he is guided by the contours, making a spiral ascent if he has been disturbed on low ground. At last, feeling assured of having outwitted the pursuer, he will swing round and make for his favourite haunt. If the sportsman knows where this is, he will do well to follow a short distance to give the stag the impression that he is keeping up with him, and then turn and rapidly make for the spot so as to forestall his retreat. Or if he is acquainted with the configuration of the ground, he should endeavour to cut across the projecting contours and to intercept him.

It will be obvious that the fewer the number of pursuers, the better are the chances of success. The sportsman should take with him only one man, for choice an aborigine well acquainted with the locality; a quiet intelligent shikari or tracker. No other class can work as softly, nor have they such fine detective instincts. The sportsman can soon find out if he is a good man, for he will not only work by signs, but also assume an alert demeanour, unwilling either to speak or to receive suggestions. These traits are natural with most aborigines, but especially with those who practise hunting and tracking. In public they may look fools, but in the jungles no one could exhibit more intelligence.

When the quarry is spotted, a good bid should be made at the

very outset to get him. "Dodge my neighbour" tactics are unwise, sportsmen as a rule are not qualified to outwit nature's disciples. Here and there a man inured to jungle craft may become an adept at the game, but such instances are rare. The clumsiness usually displayed only arouses the stag to an increased sense of his danger, and if the stag has winded his pursuer or realised that it is a man in chase, nothing on earth will make him stop. But if he has only heard the noise of the approach, he will want to know who the intruder is. A man dodging between covers, although invisible, will make sufficient noise for tensely strained ears to catch, with the result that the stag's suspicions are aroused and he is off. Consequently if the stag has not detected his hunter, or realised him only as a vague peril, the sportsman should work with a view to give the stag the impression that he is a casual visitor on some other errand and at the same time keep an eye on the beast. This combination can be effected by adopting a leisurely gait and moving in a zigzag up the wind, till the quarry is within shooting distance. Then, as soon as you feel it is time for an effective shot, you have only to turn quickly and deliver fire. Even if the stag has shown signs of suspecting your motive, you should still simulate your actions by proceeding as described. When hinds or other animals have been disturbed during the movements which have gone in the direction of the stag, the stalk should be abandoned for it will certainly fail.

The best time is of course, the early morning, and you should start at an hour which would enable you to get to the place where the stags have been feeding or roaming, just as it is beginning to get light enough to see. In the winter this would be about six o'clock, and in summer about five. Come up very quietly and come up from the lee-side, though in the early morning scent is not quite so important as it becomes later, because the dampness of the air prevents it from travelling rapidly. Now scan each opening carefully and move slowly and cautiously from one to the next. When you spot a stag and he is unaware of your presence, but too far off for an effective shot, then decide which way the wind is blowing, so as to move on to the stag's lee-side if necessary, as quickly as possible, even if it means coming out straight in front of him.

I said just now that the stag aims at outwitting his pursuer. I was once stalking one which had been disturbed in a valley. His

trail led us for about two miles, gradually ascending until it rounded the head of the ravine from which the valley emerged. We were just about opposite our starting point, though at a higher level, when suddenly a small rock rolled down upon us. Looking up, we saw the stag about fifty yards higher up the slope, going in the direction from which he had come and he was easily bagged. The actual distance which separated the start from the finish was about five to six hundred yards, while the trail had led us over two miles and would have gone further still, if the proceedings had not been interrupted by the accident of the stone and so brought about the stag's end. If either my tracker or I had known the ground, we could have cut across the ravine and so saved ourselves a long stalk. I recall another case, when the trail led about two-thirds round the slopes of a plateau to the top over which the stag disappeared among tangled growth of dwarf trees and herbaceous plants.

I remember once a stag which I disturbed from a ledge at the crest of a precipitous slope over which rose a cliff. He slid down the steep bit and walked slowly down the ravine at its base. Then having apparently crossed, he returned by a circuitous climb to the top of the plateau from the slope of which he had been roused. This took him about two hours on a winter morning; it was ten o'clock when he was shot. But the Bhil who was the sole inhabitant of the plateau, knew the habits of the stag as well as the lie of the ground, and instead of troubling to follow the stag, he took me straight over the plain to overlook the next depression where we waited. But the stag had taken even a wider sweep than we imagined, and instead of seeing him appear where we expected, we saw him at last right on the plateau, coming quietly along the edge towards us. We allowed him to walk almost into us and his look of surprise was a study, it nearly sent him over the cliff along which he was moving, then as if realising his danger he bounded forward to cut across the plateau. But he was too near to escape and the first shot hit him mortally. His horns were thick and massive, but not very large, the beam of the longer taping a trifle over forty inches, while the other was only thirty-seven inches.

To speak of stags sliding may seem curious. But such tobogganing is a regular habit of theirs, whenever they have to descend a steep incline to escape from danger. Their method is to stretch the forefoot right forward, to draw in the hind legs, and

then to glide straight down. The weight of the body gives the necessary impetus.

The method commonly adopted to shoot this fine beast is to drive him on to the guns by a line of beaters. In comparison with stalking it is poor sport. It seldom accounts for a good stag, as the old stagers possessing the best antlers keep aloof in sequestered spots that are usually overlooked. Moreover, drives are unfortunate in their further consequences, the animals that escape warn all the neighbourhood what to expect. The other jungle creatures know how inquisitive and vigilant the sambar is and they take warning by its actions. A pig or blue-bull or any other deer or antelope does not disturb the general equanimity of the jungle half so much, as the sight of a sambar tearing past or even walking in a state of agitation. The others know the animal would not behave so without good reasons, and they grow perturbed at once and decide to quit the place for the time being.

In the chapter on beats, I mentioned that even with scores of beaters, success is difficult to ensure, that deer invariably break through. I can remember scores of cases which showed what determined attempts a sambar will make to clear a way out of a tight situation. If the line is steady and in close formation, he will push right through them, and even bound over their bodies, if any chance to fall. I know of a case where the beater who opposed a stag had to pay the extreme penalty, by being gored through the lungs.

Another method of compassing the sambar's fall - and one which is rightly condemned by true sportsmen - is to shoot him over water, when he comes to slake his thirst in the hot season, or else over a puddle hole, or at a salt-lick. Such methods are especially reprobated, because they are supposed to take the stag at a disadvantage. But, as a matter of fact, they are not much worse than taking up a position and getting the beast driven on to the gun. Owing to the extreme delicacy of the senses, the watcher over a water or puddle hole, or at a salt-lick, probably has no greater chance of success, than the sportsman waiting in a position during a beat.

In an earlier chapter, I described how some of the Gonds hunt deer with axes. An even more common method is to hunt them with dogs. All jungle tribes practise this form of sport, but the Banjara or gypsy class living on the outskirts of forests are adepts

at the game, and the Banjara breed of dog for doggedness and ferocity is well known in the countryside. The modus operandi is for a tracker to mark down the quarry in the heat of the day. Then the hunters - some of whom take dogs in leash - take up positions at short intervals apart over a stretch of country extending for half mile or so, through which the animal could be guided without much difficulty. One or two men with a few dogs quietly approach the spot where the game is lying up, and with a rush and shout and letting slip the dogs, they start the animal over the course. As the quarry passes the posts of hunters along his line of retreat, each man with his dog joins in the chase, so that the pace is not only maintained, but forced by the fresh relays of dogs that keep at the victim's heels and soon run him down to a standstill. The dogs then surround the beast and strike up a pandemonium of howls, barks and yells, and so keep the victim in a state of quandary, till the hunters can come up within close quarters and despatch him with their rude weapons. But it is seldom that a quarry is brought to account after the first run. As a rule, it is in the third or fourth course that the beast is sufficiently winded to allow the hunters to approach within killing distance. Animals held at bay by dogs always attempt to break through when they see the man coming up, for instance, deer and antelope invariably bound over their tormentors, while nilgai and pig force through them.

These hunts are always organised during the hot weather when cover is open and the chances of escape are less. The time selected is usually the middle of the day when the sun's heat is at its worst, so that it soon exhausts the quarry, while the hunters joining in as they do, at intervals along the course manage to keep fresh.

In these hunts I have known sambar, cheetal, nilgai, pig and bear to be run down and killed. The sambar is the easiest and the wild boar, the hardest to overcome. Sambar begin to tire rapidly after a hot chase of five hundred yards; over hilly, rocky or broken country he is clever in eluding his pursuers. The ideal course for sambar from the huntsman's view is a long stretch of undulating ground. In organised runs with trained men and dogs, success obtains in every seven out of ten hunts, but as in all coursings with dogs, it depends on their keeping to the one scent throughout the run. Well trained dogs can easily manage this by themselves, but most dogs once they have got far ahead of the men, strike off at a tangent for the first little creature that gets up along their path, with

the result that the chase is spoilt. To avoid such risks, experienced hunters while taking up their position shake their clubs as noiselessly as they can in every bit of cover likely to hide game, in order to clear the ground of other animals. Runs after [a] solitary beast promise more success as well as afford the best sport, so that hunters always aim at securing a quarry that is lying up by itself.

The chase is always very exciting and the men enter into it with zest. I have been in at the death of a bear that was followed by young Bhil bloods and their dogs for about eight miles through country rolling with hillocks. Eventually the beast sat down and refused to budge even when worried by the dogs, till the hunters came up and put an end to him with their bows and arrows. Adult animals rarely succumb to domesticated dogs, and so long as the hunters keep out of sight, the quarry will manage to remain at bay, in marked contrast to the helpless fear it displays when cornered by wild dogs.

A stag looks a picture of insulted pride while at bay. The yaps and howls do not seem to disconcert him. Though he will occasionally lower his head to show his tormentors that he possesses weapons of defence, he will not attempt to strike, disdaining as it were to soil his antlers with the blood of victims unworthy of his regard. It is only when they plunge in to bite or grip that the stag's annoyance can be marked, as with hackles erect he tosses his antlers at them in a menacing manner. As soon as he has proved the courage of his pursuers, he squats down and assumes a nonchalant air, as if the tumult were of ordinary daily occurrence. While following up with dogs I have tried to restrain the men from breaking upon the scene in order to obtain a view of the sight which is full of interest to one who cares to watch in patience. A hind also appears indifferent to her pursuers and is effective in keeping them off with her feet. Nilgai get flurried and snort and cut capers, and exhaust themselves so that they become an easy prey. A bear assumes a sang froid worthy of his character; he squats down in a leisurely manner when pressed, and the dogs mistaking his action for a sign of weakness, chip in to grip him when the bear is up and at them like a knife. It is only dogs with previous experience of bear hunts that can resist the temptation to keep at a safe distance from their wily antagonist. A sow growls and grunts while she is hemmed in, her threatening language being sufficient to save her from molestation. Immature beasts are easily

run down and are often torn and killed by the dogs before the hunters are up. This is because they are easily excited and collapse through exhaustion inviting an attack.

With the instinct bred of nature, game in the full possession of their senses distinguish between the domesticated dog and the bloodthirsty villain of the jungles. Thus, while in the one case, they are not afraid to oppose or parry with their pursuers, they are become in the other, panic stricken with terror at the onset of their relentless foes.

The hunter has to be quick to get in a blow with a knife; and indeed, he can do so only with the assistance of the dogs. But Banjara and jungle men, turn on the quarry with spears and axes, or else with firearms and bows and arrows which can be employed from a distance, so that the finish is a sorry business. I have heard of dogs being gored or badly cut by the hind's feet in such encounters. Domestic dogs as a rule will not attempt to touch the game, and are content with merely yapping all round it. Wild dogs on the other hand, dash in and inflict bites, driving the quarry and giving it no rest, until it drops through sheer exhaustion and is incapable of doing much, and then they literally tear it to pieces. It would be interesting to know if a sportsman has ever come across a wild dog gored to death by a stag. I have twice shot wounded dogs showing unmistakable signs of having been stabbed by sharp instruments, such as a horn or tusk, but more than that it was difficult to determine. In both cases there was a thrust and a slight rip, in one dog on the haunch, and in the other on the shoulder. Wild dogs will only attempt to run down a mature stag or hind when very hard up for food. As long as less offensive game can be had they leave the bigger and tenacious beasts severely alone.

A bear shows the most endurance and usually manages to escape, even when wounded with shot or arrow wounds. A sambar's pace is fastest, but is maintained over a short distance only, so that the pursuers gain on him rapidly towards the finale. Cheetal are seldom hunted by dogs, because the ground over which they occur is not practicable for coursing, and the deer can easily foil their pursuers in the net-work of nullahs that are so common a feature of their haunts.

Hunts on the same principle are organised by young bloods to run down peafowl, especially cock birds which are handicapped by the long streamers of tail feathers that are in full plumage in

summer, and by their length and weight impede the bird's flight very considerably. The men post themselves in relays over a stretch of bush or scrub jungle in the middle of the day while the birds are roosting under cover. A few men then creep up to the spot from the opposite side to which the relays are posted, and with a sudden burst of noise and pelting, they start the birds in the direction of the relays. The flight of tailers seldom exceeds a hundred yards, and they soon get separated from the hens which unlike the big tailers, scatter right and left while the others go soaring straightforward. As soon as the cock alights, he is set upon by the nearest man with his dog and immediately is forced to take to its wings, care being taken by shouting and pelting to keep the bird constantly on the move. The flights diminish in length of distance as the bird tires, until at the fifth or sixth attempt, it becomes winded and is able only to run a short distance, when it can easily be killed by the men or dogs. I have known three birds captured in a few hours in these hunts, but more often only one is accounted for. These hunts are organised by grown-up lads more for the pleasure of the sport, than for the pot.

Sambar sometimes take to water when pursued by dogs. I once saw one standing in four or five feet of water in a pool in the Tava riverbed, close to Gelai in the Betul district, with a pack of fourteen wild dogs howling all round at the water's brink. It was about ten o'clock in the day, and I was returning from an inspection through a jungle patch which passed a few hundred yards from the river bank. The howls of the dogs attracted our notice and we, a guard and a Gond being with me, stalked cautiously to the bank to find out the cause. The dogs formed a ring round the pool, and were trying vainly by howls and plunges to drive the hind out of her sanctuary. It was a precarious situation, but she stood her ground, and seemed quite unconcerned. The leaders would swim in a few paces and then beat a hasty retreat. Not one ventured to swim out to the hind though they had only a short distance of twenty or twenty-five feet to reach her. Armed with only a single-barrelled Martini, I could not do much; but made the two other men sneak across to the opposite bank so as to be ready to strike with their axes, if the dogs passed by their way. Then I fired at one dog, which made the rest bolt up the opposite bank close by the men who killed another as the dogs ran passed them. The hind dashed out of the water with a great splash and fled up the bed of the river.

Occasionally trained dogs will run sambar to water, and I have heard Banjara and aborigines sportsmen describe hunts in which the quarry took refuge in a pool or river when chased by their dogs. Sometimes a stag will foil the dogs by bounding up a steep slope and then toboggan down a precipitous bank and dash off into a valley containing other game. If the first run does not tire the dogs the latter dodge is sure to throw them off the scent.

Speaking of Banjara dogs reminds me of their thieving propensities, habits which their owners inculcate into them so thoroughly that they have come to acquire a hereditary tendency. Dogs from a Banjara encampment will often travel a mile or more to prowl round hamlets during the quiet part of the day, that is at noon, and seize and carry off unsuspecting fowls, kids or lambs that may happen to be outside the dwelling. Having secured the prize the dog will make a bolt by a bee-line to its owner's shanty where its master or mistress is on the lookout for the dog's coming and will take the booty and hide it away cunningly until chances of a visit from the owner are past. I have retrieved a lamb from a Banjara hut which was carried off by a dog from my kitchen tent to a Banjara hut, and twice shot others making off with my fowls.

Another curious means employed by some of the jungle folks to shoot game, is to use a decoy stag or hind, to inveigle others to approach within a shot-distance or else under its shelter to enable the hunter to get within reach of wild ones. For this purpose, a fawn is caught and tamed, and trained to keep with its owner and to obey his signs and calls. But to ensure success it is essential to establish a close attachment between the tamer and the tamed. This is very necessary as animals reared among wild surroundings are prone to desert and join their jungle friends and regain their freedom as soon as they are grown up, that is when they may be expected to have become useful for the purpose of successful decoys. To thwart this without unnecessary restraint on the creature's customary freedom, the only practical means lies in the use of drugs by getting the beast addicted to the practice. So drawing upon the example afforded by opium-eaters, the owner starts inculcating the creature with the habit from an early age by giving small doses of the drug in its food so that even if the debauched creature takes to the jungle, it invariably returns at the appointed hour for a dose of the drug. Then when it goes back, out goes the Gond with it. It may be the rutting season. If so he lies in

wait; his decoy begins to bellow and call: the stags answer and approach and he shoots them as they come. Or else using the decoy as a stalking horse, he steals right into the sanctuary under cover.

However this immoral sport is I hope uncommon. Personally I have known of only two instances of it. These men lived in remote clearings in the jungles; and it needed very close acquaintance with them to unearth their little game. In one case the owner and his neighbours were made to vacate their dwellings inside the reserve, and settle on its outskirts in a less secluded spot, nine or ten miles from their former abode, in the hope that the opium-drugged hind would return to her natural ways on losing touch with the men. But she managed to hunt out the new settlement, where she took up her quarters in the adjoining jungle, turning up at the hamlet of her owner as usual for a dose of the drug. Then there was nothing to be done but to shoot the hind to prevent the man or his friends from imposing on the animals any further.

This illustration shows that wild animals equally with human beings can become addicted to the vice. The experience accords with what is more or less common knowledge that some Indian potentates cause tiger in their preserves to be drugged by a concoction of bhang and other ingredients, by mixing it regularly in the drinking holes which he visits, so as to make certain of the quarry when the great magnate goes for his shoot.

A peculiar habit of the sambar - indeed of all deer and antelope, though more characteristic of the sambar - is its manner of striking its forefeet on the ground when it suspects danger. It raps out a series of sharp taps, usually with the right forefoot and preferably on some hard resonant substance. The stroke is made by retorting [sic] the elbow and ankle joints with the upper part of the leg held more or less taut, so as to concentrate the energy in the foot. Usually this rapping is a preliminary warning to other beasts to be quiet, while the sambar as detective, unravels the mystery of which it has obtained an inkling. On hearing the taps, all ruminants and pigs as well, should they happen to be on the move or feeding, instantly become still or squat down. Though other deer and antelope do the same thing, their raps of warning do not resound so much, nor are so effective in quieting the other animals as those of the sambar. More often than not, it is the hind that gives the signal; in fact she is an adept at it. Aborigines say that the action is also a sign of anger.

A hind will use a somewhat similar stroke with the forefoot to drive off panther, pig or other obnoxious creatures that may happen to come near her, especially when she has a helpless fawn. In this case the stroke can be delivered with such force and precision that it not only causes the beast to flee, but at times inflicts a deep cut in the body. I have myself been struck on the instep in this way by a young tame hind and, in spite of a thick sock and boot, the blow was hard enough to leave a painful bruise. The motion is slightly different from that of the signal-stroke. The whole limb is exerted for the blow. At the same time, it differs from a kick. It resembles a sort of sharp cut, such as would be caused by a heavy instrument being dropped and instantly drawn in towards the striker.

In shooting, the best spot to hit a sambar is of course, behind the shoulder; but the bullet must be placed rather low to get at the heart if fired from about the same level. It should strike the beast below the middle of the barrel. This is the surest shot, but more often than not, the stag will go a short distance before dropping. The shots that make him drop instantly are those in the neck, head, spine or kidney, that is to say in the hind-quarters just below the loins. This last shot also makes the beast utter a sharp plaintive bleat, which shows that it must be more painful than other wounds. As regards the head and neck shots, the former must be placed in the temple to be immediately effective, while the latter should never be much above the middle of the neck. I have known instances of sambar, with bullets lodged actually in their brains from frontal shots going a long distance, and the same of blue-bull and black buck. Again, a sambar with the top of its neck cut through by an explosive bullet, has led the sportsman quite a long chase before being accounted for. The spine shot is always difficult and should not be attempted because there is so great a chance of a miss if it is a little high, or of a bad wound if it is a little low. The shots affording the best mark for immediate effect are those behind the shoulder and below the loins.

Chapter XIV

The Cheetal

It may seem fanciful to liken the beautiful cheetal or spotted deer to a large butterfly, which Nature has reproduced in the animal kingdom for its edification. But for its flitting movements, bright markings and beauty, it is the butterfly among animals.

The cheetal are a gregarious deer. They go about in herds feeding together and lying up collectively and hardly ever mixing with other animals. The number in a herd varies from anything between half a dozen to fifty or more. As a rule, the herd thinks and acts en masse. They grow to rely so much on each other that even when forced to split up, they will rejoin again at the first opportunity. Single deer seem to lose their heads. They will either stand gazing stupidly or bound about for nothing. This conservatism is a marked trait in the species, and is doubtless the cause of their easy destruction both by man and beast. In my experience I can think of six haunts of cheetal which have been utterly denuded of these beautiful creatures. A few in each case possibly escaped into other sanctuaries, but the greater number without doubt fell victims to their obstinate nature to face the worst, rather than leave the locality they knew.

The haunt of the cheetal is generally a network of the depressions and knolls which are so common a feature along the foot of mountain slopes or astride the banks of mountain streams. The ideal place is one where the river happens to be a short distance, a mile or so, from the foot of the hill, with a stretch of level or rolling woodland between, or else a wooded upland forming the watershed between streams flowing at short distances on either side. This allows room for the deer to change their positions in accordance with the seasons or when pursued by foes. In the rains and the early part of the winter they keep to the higher ground, while during the rest of the year, they hug the stream or river. But if chased or molested they will move from one to the other, and will quarter themselves in one or the other, as the case may be, for the time being.

Naturally, such localities as I am describing contain good soil - for the cover afforded by the growth arrests the material brought down by the water. They are therefore coveted for agriculture by a

shortsighted people. The very nature of the indentations with their steep banks and sharp curves might convince any one who cares to look ahead that interference with the natural protection invites erosion, so that the question of soil fertility is only a matter of time. But the cultivator does not look ahead and it has been my painful duty to deforest such tracts in order to satisfy popular clamour. In one instance, a locality full of cheetal only ten years ago, now holds not a single one. In this case, the deer emigrated bodily into other territory about twenty miles distant, as a protest against the occupation; and today the principality although possessing extensive forests, is without so much as a single specimen of the deer.

Cheetal are not fond of journeys and seldom go any distance from their haunts. As a rule, they move in an orbit about the circuit of their home, feeding as they go. They invade fields sown with crops within or adjoining their haunts, and do much damage. But, they are easily frightened and any conspicuous object or scarecrow will keep them from entering. On the other hand, they do not mind hedges or fences and invariably jump them. In the Dehra Dun, I came across a cruel contrivance erected within the hedge for the purpose of destroying trespassing deer. It was a simple stake of sal sapling stuck in the ground, leaving about four feet projecting above, with the end sharpened to a point like that of a pencil. The owner of the field explained that the deer usually jumped the hedge and alighted at the same point. Consequently, as the hedge screened the stake, the deer would impale itself as it jumped over. It is a cruel device: but those who employed it were ignorant as well as needy.

The cheetal's food is practically the same as the sambar's. Differences do occur: cheetal prefer certain fruits and grasses for which the sambar has not the same relish. Cheetal however consume far more foliage than sambar, in which respect they are like goats, but their feeding does not produce the same blighting effect that is produced by the browsing of goats.

Cheetal venison is tender and palatable and natives fancy it more than sambar meat. They also consider the raw horns more appetising than sambar's. The shin and thighbones make excellent soup. The skins make pretty spreads for the floor, and when dressed into leather are used for various purposes like sambar's.

An acquired taste peculiar to the cheetal, is its almost ravenous

liking for cloth and paper. Of this I had a curious experience shortly after joining the service. I had a tame fawn which followed me all over my camps. About that time the stamp system for disposing of produce had been introduced in the Province and the headquarter's authority sent out some thousands of rupees worth of stamps in sheets for distribution among vendors. I appointed a central place for the licensed officials to meet me and to take over their shares. On the day appointed, I was busy apportioning the shares when, the fawn ran up and seizing a whole sheet in her mouth, decamped to a distance, and before it could be retrieved, she had devoured stamps of the value of eleven or twelve rupees. The matter was reported to the head-office, with a view to getting the sum written off the accounts. But the application only evoked a curt reply to the effect that the owner must make good the loss, as it was his fault for keeping a destructive beast - an example of the amenities of official life.

Cheetals seldom drink at night, their usual time for drinking is a few hours after the sun has risen. They depart from this practice only when molested or disturbed. They remain on the move until they have had their drink, and as a rule, the whole herd march together in files to the water, the hinds leading and the stags bringing up the rear. They approach the stream or pool from the windward direction. Having had their drink, they prepare for the mid-day siesta by getting under the cover of bushes and shrubs or between clumps of saplings. Where the water channels are sandy and shady, they prefer to lie in the sand.

The herd squats together; stags however sometimes sit apart. They keep very still, appearing to take no notice of the noises and movements around. Their haunts, being usually favourite grazing resorts for village cattle, are almost daily invaded by graziers and cattle. But one of the herd is always on the alert; the slightest indication of unfriendliness on the part of an intruder is immediately resented, and the whole herd get up and troop off, so very quietly, as not to give the slightest symptom of their departure, though perhaps fifty or more may have filed past at a few yards' distance from the disturber of their peace.

I have often marvelled how they manage this stealthy move with so many together, especially in the hot weather when every inch is covered with dry leaves and twigs. The fact is that they keep the paths leading into their sanctuaries clear of tell-tale

materials, like dry leaves and twigs, by brushing them aside with their feet as they move. In my novice days, I observed a stag unsuspicious of my presence, getting out of cover, and as I then imagined, playing with the leaves along his path by kicking them aside as he went. It was only years after that the true meaning of the incident dawned on me. The need for the precaution is clear enough, for timid creatures that herd together and have to manoeuvre in a limited space.

Mature stags usually keep with or near the hinds. The only time when they show a disposition to keep aloof is when their horns are budding and tender. Then they mount higher on the slopes to lie up, or else they take to an unfrequented patch of woodland tabooed for some reason by the deer tribe. Their movements however are regulated by the hinds whom they follow keeping at a safe distance at the back so as not to be observed. Apparently they fear that the hinds may damage their raw horns, indeed they actually run from the hinds during the first fortnight that the horns are very tender. Senile stags keep apart from the herds, but never at such a distance as to be separated entirely from the crowd to whose movements they also conform.

The rutting season practically corresponds with that of the sambar, and as in the case of that deer, combats among males are fairly common. But they are never conducted with the same deadly earnestness, nor does the victor cheetal show the same insistence as the sambar on separating the vanquished competitor from the hinds. He is content with the victory only and does not mind if the vanquished champion rejoins the herd. Also unlike the sambar, the defeated cheetal never attempts a second bout with the victor, any attempt on his part at renewing the battle being treated as a joke. The clash of horns resounds like a bout at quarterstaff and the encounters occasionally end fatally. I can recall an incident of this in my own experience. During a shooting camp at Sitlamata in the Nimanpur district in the spring of 1903, we were entertained while at dinner, by a cheetal combat raging on the opposite side of the river on which we were camped. In the morning one of the shikaris reported that a stag was lying dead on the scene of the night's encounter and it was found he had been gored through the lungs by his antagonist. He was a fair-sized stag in the prime of life with thirty-three inch horns.

Cheetal are as irregular in shedding their horns as sambar, and

the time which the horn takes to develop and harden, is about the same in the one case as in the other. I have known a mature stag to carry the same pair for nearly three years or to be precise for two years nine months and three weeks.

Like sambar, cheetal detach their horns by various means when the shedding season approaches. I was told by a shikari who lived among these deer and had many opportunities of observing them, that even stags who did not drop their horns, rubbed and pulled at them just the same as those who shed them. I have not heard this authenticated in the case of sambar. But it is very probable that at the appointed season all stags are infected with the shedding mania, and the few who retain their horns, attempt to dislodge them in pursuance of the common practice.

Cheetal horns are smaller in build - length and thickness - than those of sambar. But as regards appearance, there is little to distinguish between them, and if it were not for the rusty colour of the one as compared with the dark brown of the other, cheetal horns would be easily mistaken for those of a small sambar. The largest I have shot had horns a trifle less than thirty-six inches, but a friend procured one whose horns were thirty-eight inches. The finest pair of which I have recollections was carried by a stag in the Pipri forests of Nimanpur. He was a fine old stager who had been often hunted, and was an adept in slipping away at the slightest indication of danger. On one occasion we came across him while a friend was shooting with me. We marked him with a herd early one morning and felt sure of getting him as he was too occupied gallivanting with the hinds to notice our presence. The herd was slowly wending its way to a well-known cover: the breeze was in our favour so I cautioned my friend to steal a march over them by making a rapid detour for the spot, and to intercept the stag before he vanished into hiding. After my friend had left, I followed the herd with the intention of heading them to the spot, in case the deer should leave the path for another route. Our little plans fitted in splendidly and my friend had the noble beast almost in his grasp, but he was excited at the good fortune that awaited him, and he made a bad miss. The herd immediately mixed up and charged past without allowing for a free shot at the stag. How well I remember his disgust at the failure which quite spoiled the remainder of his holiday.

The gestation period in cheetal lasts about thirty weeks or seven

months, but for the first pregnancy it is usually prolonged to eight months. One and occasionally two are born at a birth, and almost every year fresh births occur. Hinds with young acquire a certain independence of action, and for the first week or ten days after birth, till the fawn is capable of keeping up with the herd, the mother remains apart looking after the fawn. As a rule, she hides her young in some cover while she herself keeps at a distance as a safeguard against surprises. She goes near the fawn only at intervals for nursing. If she has reasons to suspect danger, she will warn the fawn by a few plaintive calls and will then bound away to a distance.

The cheetal's note is very much like that of a sambar, but in a lower, sharper key. Mature stags develop a peculiar call, that may be described, as a loud bellow and bark drawled out at the same time, intermingled in delivery, and neither distinct. The call is usually prolonged to half a dozen such sounds and is uttered more often at the rutting season, and only when the deer are feeding or are on the move. The notes of fawns resemble a bleat.

Cheetal do not wallow, but they like to roll in dry sand or grit or pockets of clay. They will swim across swollen streams or pools when pursued, or to return to the sanctuary if cut off by a sudden rise in a river. I have watched herds swim across and as in other movements, the hinds always led. This is a performance which I have not seen in sambar. But strange to say, when pursued by dogs cheetal unlike sambar never take up a stand in water but rush or swim through it if it should happen to be on their path. This may be because cheetal are more easily frightened than sambar.

Although disinclined to journeys owing to their inherent conservatism, cheetal are fond of great romps resembling hide-and-seek. For their sport they choose the patchy bits of scrub and wood over a sandy or gravel plain. They are the cause of the numberless foot prints one so often sees over these patches in cheetal haunts. They race each other, several at a time, over the blanks, in and out and round the patches, performing all sorts of acrobatic feats in their headlong course - jumps, plunges, dives and bounds - very much as long-dogs do in play. These games are almost of daily occurrence, and are held either between eight or ten o'clock at night, or between three and five o'clock in the morning. Their purpose is doubtless rather exercise than mere pleasure. Fawns usually play by themselves, the only difference being that

they bleat as they race about. Their revels are a sight to see and one that lives in the memory. The spectator should come on the herd unawares from the lee-side, and should gradually and patiently reduce the distance from them, till he obtains a glimpse of the arena. More than this he should not attempt or he will spoil the show. The game can always be detected from a little distance by the noise of the scrambling that goes on, or by the bleats of the fawns.

The first time I ever saw it was when I was returning late to camp. We had been benighted in our excursions and my Gond was taking me by a short cut through cheetal country. His experienced ears caught the sounds and guessing what was going on, he asked if I cared to see a sight. I could hardly make out what he really meant, but I agreed to follow, and we approached very cautiously till we got a glimpse of the exhibition in the moonlight. Since then I have twice had opportunities of watching the sport. On all such occasions, there are a few hinds and stags standing apart as sentinels who take no part in the game.

Although not so inquisitive as his bigger cousin, the cheetal in common with most animals is of an inquiring nature. He will stop to satisfy his curiosity on observing sounds or noises to which his ears are unaccustomed, or to view sights pleasing to his fancy. I was once returning from an unsuccessful stalk after cheetal and was taking a short cut over a knoll when a lively scene in the glade below caught my eye. There was a collection of peafowl picking and scraping at the ground for food, while in their midst at short intervals apart, three cocks were giving an exhibition of dancing. They strutted about with their fans of resplendent colours displayed to perfection, executing various figures and vying with each other in rendering their actions acceptable to their unadmiring spouses; the ringing rattle emitted by the feathers as the owners twisted and turned them sharply into fantastic shapes could be heard clearly, and as my approach had not been observed, I stopped to watch the proceedings. Soon after my arrival a small herd of seven or eight cheetal came quietly upon the scene by the path skirting the foot of the knoll. The leader - a hind - stopped immediately on detecting the performance in front of her; the others did the same intuitively and then gradually edged up to the leader to witness the spectacle. The birds were so intent with their own concerns - dancing and feeding - that they apparently did not

detect the presence of the deer also. The whole scene was so peaceful and absorbing that although the object of my earlier pursuit, for there was a good stag with the herd, seemed as it were sent on purpose for my gratification I could not bring myself to shoot and spoil the picture. The dance continued for a quarter of an hour or so until the cocks seeing that the hens had wandered off some distance they stopped dancing to join them, when the cheetal resumed their march.

On another occasion, I saw a colony of monkeys watching a similar dance from the boughs of a mahua tree, and it held their attention so closely as to keep them quite still while it lasted. These are the only two instances I have personally witnessed but my tracker, an experienced Gond, told me that all animals, even tiger and panther, were fascinated by a peacock dance and invariably stopped to watch it, if they chanced upon the scene without being noticed by the birds.

As a rule, most females exhibit greater curiosity than males. This is only natural and comes of the protective instinct engendered in the sex for their young. Not the least curious is the means which female of deer and antelope employ for penetrating the identity of an object that strikes them as strange. I mention the fact here because the conservative nature of the cheetal renders them most susceptible to the practice which as often as not, aids the sportsman in his stalk after the stag. It is the habit of the hind on seeing or meeting with anything unfamiliar to strike the ground with her forefoot following it up with a short plunge forward. It matters little if the object of her regard is an animate or an inanimate thing, stationary or moving, so long as it appears uncommon to the eye. Thus it may be practised at a scarecrow set up in a field, especially on the creature's first visit, or at a charred stump or log. The action is somewhat different from the habit of warning by raps with the feet, described in the preceding chapter. It is a movement combining a stroke with the foot and a plunge with the body, with or without an utterance. The intention is an incitement to rouse the object which is the cause of suspicion from its seeming lethargy, and to disclose its identity. But if stillness is maintained for a while the creature is reassured and soon drops the game, and turns her attention elsewhere. This means of unmasking a supposed disguise is nearly always employed by individuals on watch, while the herd is resting or browsing or is

otherwise engaged. I have known hinds to approach very near the stalker by such short rushes. If he has the patience to go through the ordeal without raising the hind's suspicions, he generally succeeds in getting a shot at the stag when the reassured hind relinquishes her attention and moves away.

In the cheetal, as in the sambar, the senses of smelling and hearing are highly developed. But unlike the sambar, both these faculties in the cheetal are of the same value; I mean that scent is not of more importance than hearing. Like his bigger cousin the cheetal is shortsighted and his eyes seem to be made for seeing better by night than day. Also his eye-pits reflect impressions, but he does not make as much use of them as the sambar. Cheetal are lightly built and more nimble in their movements than the sambar; nor do they present the same variety either in respect of physique, or in the matter of the dimensions of horns as obtains in the sambar.

Stalking cheetal is nothing like so arduous as the pursuit of the bigger quarry. The method adopted for approaching the stag to get in a shot, should be the same as I have described for the sambar. In cheetal haunts there is usually more cover from shrubs and bushes or turns and twists of water channels, which promise success by inviting hide-and-seek tactics; and sportsmen very often adopt them instead of a simpler and bolder course which requires patience and skill in execution. But, in spite of the cover, a wary stag is extremely difficult to circumvent, and dodging tactics only raise his suspicions. Besides, there are often hinds and fawns about who take the pursuer to be a beast of prey and give the alarm.

A common way of shooting cheetal also is to get the stags driven to the guns in regular beats. Obviously it is poor sport as compared to the other, and besides seldom yields good results. I was once beating for a stag in a patch of forests in the Bhowergurh reserve, and took up a position on a bank overlooking a wide nullah which sloped down in front for some distance. Soon after the beat started, a panther broke cover and getting into the nullah began walking up towards me. A few seconds later the stag also appeared almost at the same spot where the panther had come out, and followed him keeping a few paces in the rear. The stag did not appear to mind the panther's being just in advance of him and they both came on slowly, the panther stopping at intervals to look back with a grimace at the stag which also stopped and shook his head as if hurling defiance at the beast, and they kept this up till within thirty

or forty feet of my position. My attention was so taken up in watching these little passages of temper that I had forgotten to shoot. But their nearness soon roused me to the fact and I decided to begin with the panther whose presence in the beat was quite unexpected. The stag moreover had not the large pair of antlers that I had imagined he possessed. So I let the panther have the first barrel of my heavy .577 which sent him spinning head over heels against the opposite bank. The stag now did a strange thing, he charged forward at the sound of the shot and got up the opposite bank some distance past me and stood for a moment, then either misjudging the direction of the panther's groans, or frightened by the noise of the beaters, he again charged down into the bed of the nullah, and rushing up the bank where I was seated, bolted past within fifteen feet of me. I was rather puzzled by his eccentric movements and fear I fired at random, for close as he was I clean missed him. This corroborates what has been said about animals of such opposite natures as the deer and the carnivora, living and moving in close proximity to each other with apparently little concern about eventualities.

Banjaras and aborigines also hunt the deer with dogs, but with less success than with sambar, because the cheetal being fleet of foot and more elusive generally manages to dodge the dogs and escape. The deer also know how to make use of the innumerable turns and twists of the nullahs which are so common a feature of cheetal haunts. It is the reason too why the deer is seldom hunted by axe-hunters - a mode of sport described in an early chapter.

Cheetal, if anything, have more vitality than sambar and are more difficult to account for when wounded. The effective shots are the same as those for the sambar. To the stalker, they present a pretty picture; as they dodge between covers, moving nimbly, now brilliant and now dim, like sly nymphs of the forest, between alternations of sunshine and shadow. Often the herd is so mixed up that it is difficult to single out the stag. Indeed I have known this pleaded as an apology by a man who shot hinds and immature stags too often for the excuse to be convincing. The best time to get a stag is in the early morning, especially about the time when he is going to call or is calling. As a rule, he stands still while delivering his challenge, and the others move on, so that he gets separated for the time being.

Mature stags and hinds do not fear the panther, but will not

stand up to him like the sambar. They will move aside and let him pass, instead of showing him defiance and making him leave the path as the sambar do. I have seen a herd stand on a bank and watch a panther as he crept along in the bed of the stream, barely thirty feet below, without appearing to care. One of the hinds kept tapping with her foot which the panther must surely have heard, but to which he paid no attention. He was a big male panther who was shot as he came upon his kill over which I was watching. Cheetal are afraid of a tiger and always try to avoid him but there is nothing approaching terror in their behaviour when seeing or escaping from him. The one beast they detest and with reason for he is a curse to their existence, is the wild dog. The coming of these vermin into a haunt means the extermination of the fawns. The adults are fleet of foot and will manage to escape at the commencement. But lack of space in their own ground deprives them of sufficient protection, and they seek salvation in scattering into adjoining woodlands. When this happens cheetal may be seen in localities which they would never otherwise enter. They will return when the wild dogs have left, but if the marauders' raids are repeated too often, they will desert the haunt in a body for all time.

There is no mistaking an animal which is being chased by wild dogs. The creature has the marks of abject terror imprinted on every lineament. I first saw this sight while I was accompanying Mr. Thompson on an elephant in a coppice-wood for the purpose of examining the growth. We were moving along slowly, talking forest matters, when a hind cheetal came dashing along from our front looking the very picture of mortal terror, such as one might imagine in a beast that knows he is doomed to death by torture. With lolling tongue and bulging eyes and a ghastly look, she tore along at a reckless gallop. My experienced companion who had divined the cause as soon as he saw the beast, asked me what it was fleeing from. I guessed that it had been chased by a panther or a tiger, or frightened by the sight of our elephant. While speaking he had snatched up his gun and loaded it with large shot, which struck me at the moment as an unusual thing to do. The hind crossed about twenty paces in front of the elephant which had been brought to a stand, and soon following about fifty yards behind her, came a pack of half a dozen wild dogs which we could not see owing to the long grass, till almost abreast of the elephant. They were not going very fast and looked spent: they were just keeping

up a steady trot, showing the chase had been a long one. With a right and left, Mr. Thompson bagged two of the dogs, which scattered the rest and delivered the hind from her inveterate pursuers. Since then, I have several times seen hunts by wild dogs: and twice in the case of a calf tied up for a tiger and once in that of a sambar hind, I have come on these poor victims being devoured piecemeal.

Cheetal are easily tamed and show greater attachment to their owners than other deer. Natives of position like to keep them as pets. Village headmen of settlements near cheetal haunts often have one. Fawns play about like kids with the village children. Wild tribes believe that cheetal have the power of perceiving invisible danger and will give warning by stamping and pointing in the direction from which it is expected. I have had no opportunity of verifying this, but it may partly account for the reason why the cheetal in particular among deer is sought after for taming by the better classes.

I have heard that unscrupulous shikaris employ adult hinds or stags for decoys to enable them to penetrate the sanctuary of wild cheetal, as is done in the case of sambar, described in the preceding chapter. But I have not myself come across an authentic instance of it.

Chapter XV

The Gaur

The Gaur or Indian bison is without doubt the most attractive species of the ox family, surpassing the other members of the group in its powerful physique, combining strength and stature, that gives it a striking appearance over its cousins. Few sportsmen have followed this magnificent beast with the object of observing it in its home, and this is an endeavour to sketch its ways and manners, as I have conceived them from a close acquaintance with the tribe lasting over two decades.

The habits of the gaur are unlike those of its cousins, the Bovinae and the Bubalus, from which it is descended and between whom it is classed in the natural system, neither do they resemble those of the true bison, whose name it has usurped. On the other hand, they conform with those of the Himalayan sheep and goats and the sambar deer, though widely separated from them in the order of classification. Turning from these connections to the attractive feature that excites the cupidity of sportsmen, it carries a handsome trophy coveted by all lovers of sport.

The gaur is typical of the Plateau country known under its familiar title of Peninsular India which was in an early geographical era an independent continent. The creature is as much a child of the mountains, as the wild buffalo is of the plain country. Its peculiar build cast in the mould of a massive tapering barrel supported on short legs easily hidden in the grassy slopes of its haunts and its dusky brown colour are well in keeping with the surroundings. The eye scanning the distance sees its form stand out like a dolmen, so suggestive of the rock exposures that are a common feature of the country, and for which it is often mistaken. It revels in the highlands of its mountain home abounding in rugged slopes and distorted valleys whose steep gradients it can mount and dismount with the greatest ease. Nothing else could explain the diminutive hooves and small compact limbs in an animal of massive build. No slope is steep enough, nor curve sharply cornered to stem its course, and it will travel as readily over a scarped ridge, as along the brink of a precipice where a false step would hurl it to instant death. The ease and facility with which it moves over these dangerous positions amaze the onlooker,

Christmas camp, Bhandara, Barwani State, 1906

Christmas Day Tamasha (celebration), Bhandara Camp, 1906

Massive isolated rock at Kadwal, Kathiwara State; favourite resort of bees and bears. (Observe the little figures of Bhils on the top.)

Bhil dancers, Ali-Rajpur, 1905

Young Bhil playing the timkini, Ali-Rajpur

Bhil beaters invoking success at local shrine

Bhil beaters being paid, Kathiwara

while the silhouette of its bulky form on the skyline fascinates his eye. The feats show that the beast is provided with the finest Alpine stalks that the ambition of a mountaineer could desire. Indeed, it is unequalled as an example of constructive model for overcoming physical obstacles characteristic of the formidable heights to which it resorts.

The gaur represents a solitary type that is intolerant of other company. The tribe keeps aloof from such amenities as are shared between animals. In order, however, to keep from breaking with its neighbours, it passes among them with an ease that excites no rivalry. In the assembly of animals, the gaur takes an isolated place; it may be approached, but may not be courted. It tolerates the sambar because of the security that its presence promises, as the deer's role in the life of the jungles is an obligation to be requited by friendship. Its visits therefore, are welcome if it chooses to come and squat with the gaur. The tribes do not fear the tiger, but acknowledge its rank as the monarch of the forests. The gaur is too tough a customer for the tiger to gain much by attempting its life, and an attack is so infrequent, as to belong in the lists of accidents or a freak of fancy; so when the beef-eater prowls round, the gaur gazes at it with mingled feelings of defiance and awe. The elephant is the only animal with whom the tribe is actually friends; they will join in rambles and feed and herd together. The gaur's striking figure is only less imposing than the elephant's, and of the two the latter is more alert to the sense of danger, so that its proximity reduces the chances of surprise. With man the tribe is ordinarily very sensitive and will always recede on his advance. On the other hand, it takes little objection to the presence of jungle folks who make their abode in its haunts.

It will be evident that the Indian bison is out and out a mountaineer, and in feats of climbing it will concede points to even the sambar. Between them, they share the triumphs in the arts and crafts of hill ranging. The gaur's diminutive feet are only less noticeable than the immense development of the shoulders that runs up the stature of males to nineteen hands and over. Marked as the contrast is, they show how organs are specially modified to suit the natural surroundings; small feet are as essential to assure firm footing on the steep inclines that the creature frequents, as the massive concentration in the fore-quarters is to enable it to haul its bulky frame swiftly over the difficult reaches encountered in its

native wilds. An example of types conforming with the environment is also afforded by comparison with the hill tiger, while the feet of both are designedly small, they differ markedly in stature which is as important in the one case for the effective use of the senses upon which the gaur relies for self-defence, as it is unnecessary or rather a hindrance to existence in the other.

Like sambar, Indian bison often leaves the heights for the foothills, but unlike the deer except in solitary instances, it never wanders far, keeping within range to mount the slopes at the first indication of alarm. The gaur as a tribe, is not fond of excurtioning [sic] and travels short distances in feeding or moving of its free will. Nevertheless, they possess abundance of sustaining energy and are extremely quick, and if disturbed will forthwith cover long distances over the roughest country imaginable. Comparing its rate of progression with man's, the ordinary sportsman is absolutely outmarched by the beast, and even the wiry aborigine of the hills finds difficulty in keeping in touch with its movements.

The gaur are pseudo-gregarious; notwithstanding the tendency to live united, they never continue in a group to form a herd in the true sense of the word. Cows and immature bulls are very much together, but they split up at intervals and rejoin off and on. Mature bulls keep more or less with the cows, though in common with the practice their movements are erratic, keeping with or away from the cows. It is not that this inconstancy is a feature of the rutting period in which case it would be easy to account for their behaviour, but the alternating changes are manifest at all seasons. At one time there will be one or more bulls with a herd of five or more cows, later on the bulls will have withdrawn to rejoin after some days interval. Thus, they combine and disperse without apparent reason, unless it be due to caprice. Away from the cows, the bulls keep either singly, or two or more together. Old bulls, passed the stage of usefulness, keep very much alone, avoiding both cows and mature bulls. The habits therefore, conform both with those of the sambar and the cheetal, without the tribe acquiring either the independence characteristic of the one, or the stability bred of the other. As a result, they lack resource and caution which causes them to blunder into difficulties on the appearance of danger. The tribe's whole nature is opposed to change and interference and the pressure of passing events seriously impairs its cohesion as a living unit, letting in the ills to

which a fretful existence is liable, and so threatening it with extinction.

Whatever doubts may exist of the gaur being domesticated in the hill-tracts east of Bengal, it is certain that in Peninsular India the creature has never been known to come under the same influence. On the contrary, no matter what the inducement, its temperament is averse to captive existence. Aborigines, who have for ages made their home among its haunts, are sure that no inter-breeding between cattle and gaur has occurred to their knowledge, and evidence of experienced observers whom I have met from all parts of the country, says the same. Nevertheless, it is strange that an animal closely allied to cattle as is the gaur should be so intolerant of domestication, as to preclude the possibility of its being put to man's use. The layman finds it difficult to account for this contradiction, but there can be little doubt that the creature belongs to one of those specialised forms which Nature sprinkles among her works to afford food for thought. The jungle fowl, plentiful in most gaur haunts, is another exception; allied very nearly to the parlour hen, it is more averse to domestication than most wild birds, and dies if held in captivity.

In the hot weather, gaur invariably keep to the plateaux which possess moderate temperatures and are swept by refreshing breezes, as compared with the lower altitudes that are sun-baked and scorched by hot winds. Moreover, the highlands offer physical difficulties that guarantee protection from enemies whom it has most to fear, whereas the foothills devoid of cover, are no longer safe-retreats. Again the summits are comparatively free from exporters and carriers of forest produce who swarm over the sub-hilly tracts in this season, disturbing game and scattering them from their resorts.

During winter, in the earlier months more than at any other period, gaur are restless and no locality will accommodate them for any length of time. Accordingly, they may be met with in places where they do not usually resort.

In the rains, they show preference for the broken stretches that cumber the foothills. This is partly, to escape the biting flies which swarm out in the season and infest exposed positions and partly, to feed on the luxuriant vegetation springing up in the deep valleys that meander through the tracts.

As a rule gaur choose a commanding situation for their resting

place. Favourite sites are the broad shelves or ledges wedged in between contiguous slopes or terraced over a rise in the hill-side, and saddles or gorges on hill tops. A herd squats fairly close together forming a fan-shaped figure pivoting on the side from which an attack is least to be feared. They lie with their heads pointing outwards, in ones, twos or threes, a yard or so apart, and the way they sit enables them to scan an extensive view as well as to get the most benefit from the breezes blowing up the slopes. An approach is therefore likely to be detected long before it is within sight. Solitary bulls are if anything, more discriminating than herds, as to choice of positions and like stag sambar, usually retire to situations on the steepest hills.

The dietary of the tribe comprises grasses, herbs and leaves of fodder plants, such as are commonly consumed by cattle. They are especially partial to leaves and succulent shoots of reeds and bamboos and tangled grass found on saline soil occurring along banks of streams or in bottoms of surface depressions. They eagerly browse on leaves and tender twigs of various jungle trees and climbers. Unlike deer, they do not relish flowers and fruit, but occasionally eat of certain juicy kinds with astringent properties. They are also partial to bark of saplings and coppice shoots containing traces of astringent matter and will eat the bast fibre for preference.

In winter, gaur evince a ravenous appetite for salt and the craving intensifies with the severity of the weather. They travel long distances to the salt-licks and are very regular in their visits. These resorts are of various origin; the salt may be impregnated with chalk which needs to be bitten off and chewed, or collected as deposits in depressions which are merely licked, or mixed with earth or saline efflorescences in salt bottoms, the soft dry mud of which is sucked into the mouth and swallowed in the same way as bran.

This craving is not a peculiarity of the gaur, but is noticeable with all wild animals. I have often wondered why it should be aggravated only in the winter, and am inclined to think that animals make a virtue of necessity in their choice of season for consuming the ingredient. We know that salt increases thirst, so that its use has to be eschewed during the hot months when the country becomes parched and dry and most streams, pools and springs fail, and water is obtainable in places, few and far between.

On the other hand, cold diminishes thirst and water is easily procurable, accordingly animals no longer require to be sparing in the use of salt, and make up for the forced restraint of the hot season, by eating largely of the ingredient. During the rains they obtain the needful salt from the new growth that springs up, and that is saltish in flavour.

Gaur are sparing in the use of water and as a rule, drink once in the twenty-four hours. In the hot weather they visit the frequented pools and water holes, going to them between the hours of seven and nine at night. They never wallow and carefully avoid wet localities. They make up for what they miss from a bath, by rolling over dew-laden grass or undergrowth of herbs and weeds. Pockets of loose clay or grit serve the same purpose in dry weather.

They feed more or less through the night, grazing during morning between the hours of four and eight and after sunset from six to nine, and browsing between. In undisturbed localities, they are often on the move long before the sun is down. They rest during the day but get up occasionally either to change positions in order to avoid the sun or to feed for a brief interval. I once came upon a bull in the early afternoon browsing an aonla tree laden with fruit. A gaur consumes a large quantity of fodder and the excretion is tinged with green.

The sheltered positions to which Indian bison retire and the precautions taken against surprise make it very difficult to get within measurable distance. It is only possible if the wind is favourable, by an approach from the protected side on which the flank is pivoted. As the obstacles along the line are greater than elsewhere, it is necessary to stalk with patience and caution. On summits, they will rest in a trough whose approaches they can command, or on top of a knoll which is equally dominating, and neither present encouraging prospects of getting near. On slopes, the recesses as it were, inserted purposely by Nature as premises for wild beasts, are the best covers. The seats invariably abut on a bank which may be the side of a ridge, the dip of a gorge or the wall of an escarpment, and in sitting the beasts dovetail on the rise which moreover, acts as a screen for the flank, and the only means of getting near is by way of this ascent. On emerging over the shelter, the sight that meets the eye is too thrilling for words.

Imagine a gaping precipice or sharp depression, starting almost from under the seat and expanding into wooded slopes that stretch

far down to the foothills: the trees looking their worst, shorn of their mantle of leaves, and their stems charred and blackened by fire that in its irresistible rush has omitted patches of odd shapes and sizes, as evidences of the changes and shifts of winds that fanned it forward: wild plantain and euphorbia, the only plants with any vestige of freshness - the one a mere stump of green, the other a striking imitation of an unwieldy chandelier in green paint - cap the spurs showing conspicuously against the dark hue of the surroundings: perhaps too, the faint though welcome ripple of a stream confined within a constricted bed and heard but not seen, is borne to the ears as it wends through the trough-like channel it has scoured out of the hard surface rock. But to return to the gaur. Immediately below the climb, the slope recedes abruptly or elbows round a spur, flattening a space by the terrace or projecting the base of a pocket, with room for animals to recline. Rocks, trees and bamboos overhang the spot on whose congested floor is collected the only visible life in the expansive scene. It is the gaur's sanctum; breezes sweep up to cool and refresh the apartment already shaded from the sun, and stillness reigns and invites slumber.

The beasts recline in various attitudes of somnolence - heads bent on shoulder, resting on the ground or pillowed on a companion's body; tails never cease to obey calls to whisk off flies and midges attracted by the fleshy odour; ears and nostrils trace their functions proving the senses are not dulled during the body's repose. At intervals, one or two of the creatures awake sufficiently to take a few turns at chewing the cud, and drop off again. A wary bull or cow is on watch and ward and stands listlessly or stoops to take a few mouthfuls of fodder; it is very much alive to the fleeting changes of sound and smell, and on indication of danger will be quick to alarm its confiding companions. Tits and warblers flit among the branches while a pair of fantail fly-catchers monopolise the ground and display familiarity in darting in and out among the recumbent forms in search of flies and ticks on which they feast, rendering their hosts signal service in ridding them of the parasitic pests. A little way from the herd and closer to the edge of the cliff, a hairy form can be made out lying motionless; it is a sambar that has been attracted by the advantages of the spot. The gaur do not mind its presence and should it care to join them, would welcome it into their midst. They are all so quiet that it would be excusable if at first sight, they are mistaken for denuded rocks - a common

occurrence on the heights. The calves rise as the afternoon closes, and tease their parents to mind them, for they are hungry. It is a sign to be up and moving, and soon the herd will be filing off by the narrow mountain path contouring around the hill side.

The sight more than repays the toil and fatigue encountered in gaining the sanctum without disturbing its occupants; it is one that the painter or lover of Nature would give a good deal to witness. The varied settings stand out boldly in their rugged character over the wild expanse of country the eyes survey; and yet, the attraction is the carefully guarded miniature on the summit. Here the monarchs of the mountains lie in blissful peace, sure that their senses and precautionary measures guarantee absolute security for their retreat. It is a sacrilege to shoot and destroy the peace of such a spot.

I have only twice succeeded in tracing herds to their mountain coverts and a few particulars will add to the information. The scenes relate to the widely separated plateaux of Asigarh and Deogar in the Betul and Barwani Satpuras and are spanned by an interval of fifteen years. The herd in the one case comprised fourteen head – three young bulls, three calves and the rest cows, of which a wary old creature did sentinel, a stag sambar lay close by and was the first to leave when evening drew near; in the other it numbered eleven – a big bull that stood guard, two young bulls, two calves and cows. Their whereabouts were discovered about noon in the hot weather and I stayed some hours at each place.

A herd of gaur makes a good deal of disturbance in feeding and tramping through jungle so that besides their sensitive organs something more is needed to discover the presence of foes likely to take advantage of the noise to endanger life. But, as in the case of resting, the chance of surprise is precluded by one or two animals keeping watch. The duty is voluntary and individuals undertaking it keep a little apart from the herd, regulating their positions with the movements of the group. A sentinel gaur is very cautious, treading softly and hardly feeding while the herd moves. Twice during a week I have noticed the same bull doing watch and each time it was the first to suspect and warned the rest by is alarm note. It would be something to know if the guard was relieved but the brief intervals for which herds can be seen mornings and evenings are inadequate to come to a conclusion. It is very tiresome to march any distance with a herd, for though the noise aids the stalker their precaution enables them to detect his presence.

The tendency of individuals to surpass their companions in susceptibility is nothing uncommon among wild animals. Human nature affords many examples of sharp-witted persons exercising influence over their communities and we have more members that excel in the use of their senses and by their instinctive superiority invite confidence and so assume the ascendency or guardianship over the rest of the community.

Aborigines who have for ages made their home among its haunts, are sure that no inter- breeding between cattle and gaur has occurred to their knowledge.

A striking instance of sentinel work that I came across was afforded by a lame stag inhabiting the Ladee forests in the Betul district. The sambar's lameness was owing no doubt to a gun shot wound; its off fore leg below the knee was withered and it could step on the foot only very lightly, making the barest impression with the point of the hoof. The stag was a bane to the local shikaris; with all their knowledge of jungle craft the aborigine huntsmen could not outwit the beast. It not only eluded their pursuit, but alarmed the game in the vicinity making shooting impossible. Its officious behaviour became a standing joke among the jungle folks in the neighbourhood, so that when its note of warning rang out clear and true, a man would be heard to make a pointed remark on the skilful use to which it put its services, in such words as "Hark! The creak of the lame creature's crutch has swayed the woody limbs meaning the branches, that will reflect it in all corners of the jungles, so good-bye to shooting." On my visits to the forest, I tried hard to bag one of the many fine stags that it contained, but the meddling beast spoilt all chances of shooting by calling the jungle's attention to our presence. The stag grounds were pretty well known and yet, not one showed itself in the many beats and stalks that were planned. Aided by extremely keen senses, this frail creature could detect every movement within reasonable distance and it was hopeless trying to outwit it. It is no wonder if simple and credulous people see in the doings of so astute a beast, the influence of mysterious working that forms the basis of their superstitious beliefs. Rare as the occurrences are, they become the origin of the many strange tales in the countryside relative to the performances of particular beasts.

The eye-pits noticed in deer and antelope are wanting in gaur, but without this special provision, as I consider, for aiding

detection, the beast is more sensitive than them though like the others it will stand and gaze stupidly at an intruder of whose approach it has no warning. The tribe do not possess the sambar's elusive cunning and are apt to become panic-stricken on meeting a foe, and rush pell-mell for the shortest cuts to the summits and do not stop until they are secure in cover on steep hill sides. The way a frightened gaur will tear over terraced uplands is truly marvellous; its way will zigzag along the hazardous footing and up and down sharp indentations that occur with annoying frequency in its haunts. It seldom heads for the foothills, except to gain a neighbouring chain with which they link. It does not slide down steep bits of slopes like the sambar and for very good reasons, apparent in its ponderous size that precludes the feat.

I have alluded to the perfection of silence to which animals can attain during their wanderings through the jungles, but nowhere is this quality so marked as in the gaur. It seems inconceivable that a hoofed and an enormously heavy beast should tread quite as lightly as the padded tiger, and it is not easy to reconcile the merit common in two animals so dissimilar as they are in proportion and build. The art of subduing noise is inherent, for no amount of practice could achieve the same excellence. Herds as we have noticed, are noisy enough in moving and feeding, and often an individual crashes over the ground with rattling sound. Only game going about singly or in pairs, have recourse to silence. Then, the largest bulls will pass without breaking the stillness, so much so that even the sharp eared dweller of the jungles fails to discover its approach. While seated watching over animal tracks, I have known gaur to come within a score of paces and not emit a sound, and only on emerging in sight, has its presence been detected. Thus, silence is the safeguard of the unit and disappears when the individual loses itself in the community.

The art of stifling sound is a necessary element in animal life and is attained by developing a springy tread which is very different from the steady human pace or the lumbering steps of domesticated beasts. The sportsman who from a close position, has watched a solitary gaur walking, cannot have failed to observe the bowing gait that it affects, and that differs again from the tiger's sliding movement. Though the two vary in style of execution, they are equally noiseless in effect; it would be as tiresome for a tall animal to turn and twist its body in getting about, as it would be

tedious for a beast of long and low stature to raise and depress its frame in walking. In treading, wild beasts affect one or other of these standards which is also influenced by build; a few combine the two and the blending subdues both characteristics, and neither is very marked.

Gaur rut during winter, the early months being the period of most activity. For weeks before the change comes on, the males engage in bouts; these are at first, playful displays with the usual goading and butting we are accustomed to see among cattle, but afterwards they take on a serious aspect and become more or less fiercely contested between companion bulls of herds in order to acquire ascendancy in the groups. The fights eventually culminate in furious combats between champion bulls of different herds that chance to meet and arouse the necessary rivalry in their leaders. As examples of brute force and fury, these contests would be hard to equal; cows and other bulls flee from the scene, leaving the competitors alone to settle the issue.

The fight opens as a rule, with notes of challenge delivered in solos of snorts and puffs prolonged in metallic hisses; the bulls keep at some distance with heads lowered and horns swung forward in the full splendour of their magnitude, and to add to their effective display, keep brandishing to the tune of the music; the eyes gleam and flash defiance as each sizes up the other's chances in the preparing struggle, while in rhythm the off forefoot paws at the ground. The sight is fearsome to say the least, and no wonder herds give the scene a wide berth. I have qualified the opening statement because, occasionally bulls attack without any demonstration whatever.

The parrying lasts a few minutes, then the beasts close with a terrific crash almost to dislodge their balance. The onlooker espies a simultaneous rush, but really there is always the start of a few steps undetected by the eye, that gives the initiator an advantage over its opponent by obliging it to accept the brunt of the blow, thereby often wresting victory at the outset. The shoulders become the targets and bear the force of the attack, and the bull that succeeds in hooking its adversary's forequarters, scores points.

A bout lasts some time, the chest and shoulders being contused by hammer strokes from head and horns. The struggle paces forwards and backwards under the strain. On tiring of pounding and pushing, they disengage and lash and thrust with their horns in

attempts to rip and prod each other. The longer the tussle lasts, the more tenaciously it is fought, keeping the bulls too occupied to know what is going on around. Not infrequently, the fight lasts for days with indefinite breaks for rest, to start again with unabated vigour, unless one of the bulls manages in the night to slink away unnoticed. Also, the fight reappears in new positions to which the beasts wander aimlessly while engaging in running bouts.

The vanquished is set upon by the victor and pursued for miles, even through strange surroundings, amidst inhabited parts which they would never otherwise enter. The anxiety to allow the victim of the defeat no respite is prompted by a vicious spark that lurks under a timid exterior; the failing blazes out when the passion is aroused, with disastrous consequences on the unfortunate lying at its mercy.

During the encounter, the bulls mumble at intervals a curious rumbling sound that combines a variation between the jumbled utterances of a bull camel and the shrill hissing of a steam whistle. It can be heard some distance and followed up cautiously, will lead to the scene; the bulls are goaded to madness and a rash attempt to break upon them would be unwise.

The rage of the beasts is too awful for words and their hammer blows are fearful to witness; the impulse is to turn away; but the demoniacal sight holds the visitor in a fascinating grip and roots him to the spot. A drama could not fit in better with the stage for which it was composed, than the surroundings in which the battle is waged; the expansive arena perched on a summit, its impressive solitude and its alternating effects as light and shade dazzle over the glade, are well in keeping with the mighty beasts at strife. These giants in the magnitude of splendour, champions of their herds surge to and fro to dispute a claim in which one must fall or be banished from its companions. To those acquainted with the folklore of the country-side, the scene suggests the combat of supernatural heroes who inhabited the woods and on whose conflicts none may dare to look for fear of being consumed in the deadly glow cast by the heat of their bodies, as they warmed to the strife.

The first occasion I saw gaur fighting was during a visit to the Teta-Bhatori jungles in the Asir range of Betul. My Gond who had been out to track and locate sambar with a view to an evening stalk, was attracted to the scene by the noises described and hurried back

with the news. I had just sat down to a late breakfast after a fagging inspection, so that another excursion was the last thing to be attempted. There was no pony in camp and a long tramp with the doubtful chance of our errand being successful, was not likely to enliven the spirit. Consequently, when the man was admitted, brimful of his good news which he knew would be sure of prompt attention, he was disappointed at my cold reception of his plan to accompany him back to the spot. However, I felt a different person after my belated meal and the Gond's glowing account and persistence to get me to go with him prevailed, and I was rewarded by a sight that soon made me forget the fatigue of the rough march.

The man had come upon the beasts about nine in the morning and we got there in the early afternoon when they were still fighting, and kept at it till we left about sunset. Once we saw them sit or rather drop down through sheer exhaustion, and they lay on their sides for half an hour panting and blowing like steam engines. No sooner one got up, the other was on its feet also which renewed the fight. Next morning there were no signs of the beasts, nor could we tell when or how the struggle ended. Quite possibly each withdrew in the darkness without attracting the other's notice. Assuming the bulls began to fight an hour or so before they were discovered, the duration of their attacks can be safely reckoned at twelve hours.

We watched from a knoll a hundred paces from where the fight was proceeding, and with the wind in our favour our presence was not suspected, though the bulls constantly changed positions in scrimmages over the ground. I gathered, their object was to obtain a throw rather than to bleed each other; the blows were always dealt as low as they could reach the chest and shoulders almost uplifting the fore-feet off the ground, but their short sturdy limbs were equal to foiling the coup by discounting the force of the strokes and maintaining their balance. The object is clear, a fall would have been a catastrophe indeed, immediately placing the unfortunate at the mercy of its adversary, whereas the thick tough hide could be relied on to resist the hardest blows and deepest thrusts.

This was my very first experience of seeing wild beasts fight and for me it had an absorbing interest; my old weapon was no match for powerful animals and I was content to watch the wild scene. Shortly after the adventure and in the same range of forests while

camped at Rajgaon-Khapa, a defeated bull with the victor at its heels, charged by our encampment near the village and through a herd of buffaloes, without paying the least attention to the shouts of the village folk and graziers.

Years after these experiences, another chance occurred of seeing a gaur fight. It was being contested on the Devasthan summit in the Saouligarh forests, and close to where I had bagged a bull in the previous year. On the occasion, I was stalking with the well-known shikari, Ram Singh of Panchi-Tokra, when the weird noises of the bulls reached us and there was no mistaking the fierce struggle going on at some distance. We crept up very cautiously as the ground was open and one could be detected in the park-like settings. However, we succeeded in getting within easy distance of the bulls without arousing suspicion, and watched from behind a screen of saplings. To get the shikari, who was reticent as usual, to disclose his views on the merits of the bulls, I proposed to toss him on the result of the fight and he took my bet with a zest of which I did not think him capable. Winning the toss to choose between the competitors, I fixed on the bigger and heavier beast of the two, while the shrewd old Gond was content with his bargain. The fight ended within a few hours of our arrival and to my surprise, the bull I had imagined would win easily, turned out to be the loser which lost me the bet.

The defeat came about in a very unexpected manner. The bulls engaged in a long bout, hotly contested with slashes and thrusts delivered with such force that it seemed a miracle neither succumbed to the onslaught. Then, they stopped to get their wind and began backing slowly, measuring the pace for a fresh onset. Soon they had reached the limits and stood for a brief moment in a threatening attitude vomiting notes of defiance; their voices dropped and in the next instant the large bull was speeding to the attack with a fury that boded ill for its opponent. We strained our ears expecting to hear the crash, but instead of closing, it brushed past its adversary, converting the charge into headlong flight. This was accepting defeat in earnest and its antagonist was not slow to take advantage and turn in pursuit of the runaway. It was an untimely and inglorious ending to a grand fight, and made me determined the beast should pay the forfeit for disgracing its fine trophy. Consequently, when they rushed past us, I let the leader have a right and left from my .577 and both shots found their billets

in the lungs, making it slow down, when a lucky hit in the loins dropped it. The firing turned the victor bull at once and it hastened out of sight.

Our adventure led me to tell Ram Singh of my previous experience which unlike the one we had witnessed, was fought on a high plateau close to the edge of its scarped face. It made me express surprise that the infuriated rushes and blind drives did not involve the bulls in disaster. Whereupon he remarked that an accident was quite within the bounds of possibility, and instanced coming upon a bull in one of his excursions, lying under a cliff of the Moran gorge through which the river of [the] same name flows. It had fallen down a height of a hundred feet or more and he gathered from the bruises on its body, that it was the victim of a fighting misadventure. He supposed that it had been either pushed over the bank in a tussle by its opponent, or inadvertently over-stepped the edge in a charge and got flung down the ravine.

A bhardwa, that is a witch doctor, living in seclusion on a plateau in the interior of the jungles where gaur abounded, and with unrivalled opportunities of knowing about them, had a fund of useful information about the temperament of these grand beasts. He said a fierce fight kept alive bitter memories which the lapse of time could not soften. Consequently, whenever the rival bulls chanced to meet, no matter whether alone or in company, they immediately attacked without provocation. He told of a case in which the bulls belonged to his neighbourhood and he knew them from close acquaintance. On the occasion, he was watching a fight between a conquering bull and another aspiring for the honour, when a third appeared on the scene quite by accident. He recognised in the newcomer, the bull defeated by the champion in the past year after a closely contested struggle waged near the ground where the fight was going on. No sooner the beast saw the others, it forthwith attacked its old rival and, opposed by two, the conqueror broke off the fight and fled. He took me over the ground which was a wide stretch of upland dotted with stunted trees and bamboo clumps, and barely five hundred yards from the man's dwelling.

Only bulls in their prime possess the vitality of sustaining a vigorous and drawn out onslaught. A beast that has not arrived at this stage, could no more cope with the rigours of a hard struggle, than an old warrior could be expected to endure its physical strain.

However infectious or obstinately contested, fights seldom or never occur before or after the time of sexual excitement. When the period is over, bulls resume their normal composure and in spite of lurking resentment, they go about on good terms. But the approach of seasonal activity stirs their passions and they break the truce and become hostile, thirsting to renew their victories or to wipe off old scores, or as new aspirants to enter the lists.

The passion for fighting begins at an early age, for while yet quite young, bull calves indulge in playful encounters. These are often conducted with such good earnest, as to alarm the herd so that the parents run to punish their spirited offspring and with butts and prods cause them to disperse. On reaching the adult stage reckoned at the fourth year, young males awaken to the consciousness of strength, as the deciding factor in the battle of life, and begin to be eager to put their metal [sic] to the test. Accordingly, bouts are frequent among aspiring bulls, but at the best they are amateur performances lacking in sustained vigour. Between the ages of seven and eighteen, bulls are at the zenith of physical development, and the feature of the fights is the ferocity and endurance with which they are conducted. The closing stage covers the period of senility, when bulls lose their ardour for fighting, avoid companionship and seek quiet retreats.

These distinctive stages have marked influence on the growth of the horns. At the age of three and four, they are as unattractive as those of a cow and can do little injury. But onwards as the bulls become seasoned fighters, the horns expand laterally and attain the massive development that is so much sought after in a trophy. The growth tends more towards enlarging their sweep and thickness, than in protracting their length and curve, so that effectiveness is attained without discounting their ornamental value. As the outgrowth develops, the horny encasements begin to crack and fray at the tips exposing the core, and the openings are expanded by rubbing and pointing which sharpen the edges and add to proficiency. Bulls pay some attention to the work and utilise the bole of a tree or gravel bank to effect the improvements and then, test the points by plunging the horns into trunks with thick bark or hard earth. Stems ripped by gaur become conspicuous objects by the broad vertical cuts disfiguring their columns.

I met a young official just appointed to the service, who attributed these cuts to lightning striking the trees. In recounting

his experiences, he remarked on the number of sali stems he had seen split by the electric current and presumed the tree was a good conductor. Seeing me dubious, he volunteered to point out his discovery. I went with him next morning and at once saw his mistake and assured him of how the cuts were caused.

The lateral spread gives the horns of gaur the breadth for hooking the broad chest and shoulders; even so the weapons would make little or no impression on the hard and tough integument protecting those vitals, but with the points equipped for piercing, they become instruments of precision. The constant friction wears off the tips until horns of veteran bulls appear almost as straight stumps, with the cores protruding nearly a span out of the sheaths. The horns are now thick and blunted and the scutes very much jagged and torn, with their offensive power very considerably diminished.

I saw the head of an ancient bull reckoned to be twenty-five years old; it was shot by an Indian sportsman who was beating a solitary hill for sambar. The horns were worn to half their original length which shortened the bend and practically did away with the curvature. They did not count for much as offensive or defensive weapons, but lacked nothing in thickness and spread and in so far as appearances go, it was the finest gaur trophy that I have seen.

Aborigine shikaris tell the age of bulls by the ribbed bands developed at the base of the horns. Each ring counts for a year and the sum is increased by four that stands for the years comprised in the period of immaturity when no marks are formed. In this manner the ages of the oldest bulls with whose deaths I was in any way connected, were calculated to range from eighteen to twenty-five years.

During all my long acquaintance with gaur, I did not succeed in bagging a truly fine head. I came across them in all sorts of places and under all manner of conditions, they appealed to me as no other animal, in the matter of needing special protection. They appeared the finest ornaments among a multitude of settings with which forests are endowed, and the shooting of so grand a creature merely to add to the bag, struck me as folly. I seldom had the heart to fire and my butcher's bill is restricted to five bulls. The best specimen in my recollection was a bull on the Raja-Rani Mal plateau at the headwaters of the Jharkal river in Barwani State. It carried a magnificent trophy and though appearing lame, gave no

chance of a close shot during our long stalk. It was the only one of its kind in the locality and I never saw it again. I give the measurement of the two best heads that fell to my rifle: number one was within an inch of nineteen hands and is the bull of the fight described above, its age was reckoned at eighteen years; number two was a hand shorter with fourteen summers to its credit.

No. 1
1. From tip to tip, around the outer edge and acress the forehead: 5ft 10in.
2. Between tips: 1ft 10in.
3. Circumference of horn at base, well clear of forehead: 1ft 6in.
4. Across the sweep: 2ft 11 and one half in.

No. 2
1. From tip to tip, round the outer edge and across forehead: 6ft 0in.
2. Between tips: 1ft 9in.
3. Circumference of horn at base, well clear of forehead: 1ft 4in.
4. Across the sweep: 2ft 10in.

The adult age with cows is three years, their horns also, show the marking though less distinctly than those of bulls. The gestation occupies nine months and one calf is born; they calve almost every year. The cow withdraws from the herd when the time approaches and brings forth its young in a secluded spot, usually a depression in the ground. The young are nimble from birth and fit in a few days to accompany the parents on return to their groups. The newborn is at once adopted by the herd which becomes collectively concerned about its welfare. A herd's care for the young in the group is quite marked. When disturbed or alarmed, the creatures look to the calves being with them in their flight, regulating their pace with that of the little beasts. They are made to go in front or disposed between their guardians. An alarmed herd with young trailing up a slope or spur is a sight; it proceeds in Indian file and if the little ones loiter, they are urged forward gently by shoves from the heads of the grown-up beasts; if one is too young and weak to continue, it is allowed to rest while the parent stands by as guard. A cow with a calf is fierce and likely to attack if it is disturbed, and visibly distressed at losing its young.

Should the creature have been frightened into deserting the little beast, it will return to look, nosing the ground and turning about the head for a whiff of scent or least indication of sound that will direct it to its offspring. Gaur calves never survive in captivity and it is folly to capture them.

In an excursion to the Bhaisanand tract in the Asir forests of Betul, a calf got separated from its herd in a stampede caused by the men with me. We soon caught the little creature and urged it along some distance. It was a week or ten days old and could not go far; the men proposed carrying it to camp which was a long way off, but it looked very miserable and enlisted our pity, so we decided to set it free. We had come about five hundred yards from the place where it was captured and I told the men to carry it back, they assured me however, that the parent would come that far in search, and it was let go while we moved away. It immediately turned off the path on being released and went some paces and sat down in the tall grass.

Somehow I felt interested in the calf whose misfortune was due entirely to our intervention, and the possibility of its being deserted worked upon me; I was not pressed for time and felt I should wait and see whether the men were right in their belief. We therefore edged to a bank making allowances for wind, and sat in the cover of some rocks. After half an hour, the cow appeared along the path, and on coming near the spot where we had liberated the calf it became very excited, scampering through the long grass, lowing the while and snuffing the wind. In a few minutes the calf stood up and answered in the frog note that the young of cattle utter. The cow at once charged to it, but recoiled, owing no doubt to the human odour clinging to her offspring. It soon recovered from its fright and began licking the little beast and capering around it. Then they got on to the path and the cow started to trot back slowly with the calf hugging its side.

Gaur calves are not prompt in taking cover, like the young of deer and antelope, they are at sea when deserted and run aimlessly if pursued. On appearance of danger their parents do not leave them alone as do those of fawns, and unlike them calves have no conception of hiding in order to minimise chances of pursuit and capture.

Romps and games are not in the line of the tribe which is distinguished for its sedate bearing in contrast with other animals.

The beasts have strenuous work in getting about the rough country, and hard exercise is no inducement to be sportive. Calves do cut capers while the herd is feeding or marching and this is their only display in the way of play. They are sure-footed little creatures and in their graceful movements as attractive as fawns. To capture a calf three or four weeks old would need two men to exert their utmost speed.

Notwithstanding their formidable qualities, gaur are excessively timid and the failing reacts in opposite moods. Little incidents of common occurrence in the jungles, the origin of which the senses fail at the moment to divine the cause, are enough to make them lose their wits. In smelling and hearing on which the creature relies chiefly for protection, it will start at a whiff from a drove of pig or a strongly scented flower as easily, as at the chirp of a squirrel, the scurrying of a rat or the creaking of a branch swayed by the wind. There can be little doubt that the sensitiveness is the cause of the tribe being intolerant of other company, except where the character wins its confidence as a means of additional security. Moreover it affords the reason for inducing flight from imaginary as well as from real foes, or for driving them to fright at the least indication of the presence of an unwelcome visitor; even while he is a long way off. At the same time, if provoked to assault the beast proceeds to extremes, and the violence with which it treats the victim, would compare with the worst case of a tiger's attack.

The failing, or I may venture to call it 'fit of nervous demoralisation', is inherent more or less in all wild animals and supervenes the moment of tension. It is the cause of the extraordinary freaks of temper that afford so much speculation among sportsmen of experience, as to the why and wherefore of their origin. I find that it is engrained in gaur more than in other animals of my acquaintance.

The marked tendency of the tribe to aloofness and its unmistakable fear of human aggression, do not prevent it from living in close touch with the jungle folks. Gaur haunts are invariably occupied by a few huts or at most a single dwelling, whose owners although they are the most unobtrusive specimens of the backward communities, represent the finest woodmen with whom the tribe could reckon. They put up with the hardships of their secluded abodes to satisfy the roving instinct for which the remote settlements of their village folks fail to provide scope, and

so gaur and aborigine constantly meet during their wanderings. Instead therefore of disturbing the peace of the herds, the ties of propinquity foster friendly feelings between the man and the beast. In view of what has been said of the gaur, the association would at first sight appear a contradiction, but it is brought about by the wild mannerisms of the aborigine. These are his natural get-up, undivested of Nature's garb, his elusive movements, his reeking odour and so on, which, however repulsive to civilising senses, pass among wild beasts as the hall-mark of companionship. These crudities not only tend to familiarity with animals, but the men's constant association with them does away with the desire to pry into their doings, which wins their confidence.

Instances commonly occur of gaur lying up within stone's throw of a hamlet or browsing close by, indifferent to the drumming, shouting or singing going on. A lad's cries or a scare-crow dangling from a pole will often frighten the beast out of its wits, but it takes no notice of graziers or jungle folks going about their daily business whom it is constantly meeting. It invades the scattered sowings or passes through the lanes connecting the hamlets with as little concern, as if it were domesticated. Though avoiding contact, it browses with the folks' cattle and drinks at the same pool as they, and disports about the encampments without sacrificing an iota of its identity.

The antiquated weapons of the jungle people are unavailing against the giants and no attempt is made to molest them, so that other means are employed to kill them when the need arises, such as an eventful gathering for which roast beef is the bill of fare. As befitting the occasion, the hosts determine upon gaur flesh for the common menu and proceed to obtain it by trapping one of the mountain cattle. Their method is to secure a fall in a pit which is dug on a gaur track crossing a neck connecting favourite haunts. The excavation is concealed by a dunnage of light branches and leaves overlaid with gravel, giving the covering a natural appearance. A few men start early when the beasts will be returning to their haunts or leaving them to feed, and getting on the windward side of a herd, walk up coughing and expectorating, thereby guiding them towards the neck. On nearing the approach, they set up a din with shouts and whoops which stampedes the beasts, and in the pell-mell rush, one falls into the trap, and is attacked at close quarters and is killed by a motley collection of

weapons aided by stones. Game laws have long since put an end to such hunts.

The fellowship between gaur and elephant calls for some notice. My experience as regards the latter is limited for elephants had withdrawn before my time from the central parts where my work lay. However, there were opportunities of watching the solitary types at large, even then. It is true, they were said to be rogues escaped from captivity, but if so their prolonged freedom, covering a few decades had removed every trace of servility and as examples of study, were as good as wild elephants. Added to this, I had the benefit of hearing about them from veteran shikaris and elders who spoke from experience or had the information first hand from their seniors, and their accounts have helped me to form an opinion.

The fondness of the two beasts for each other is somewhat of a puzzle. They are so differently constituted and so widely separated in the order of classification that the natural conclusion would be to look to them as keeping apart. However, the case is quite the reverse, the ties drawing them together are, firstly, that they are both types of giants among the fauna and secondly, that their habits are very much alike. But besides these equalities, an important factor comes from the gaur being attracted by the commanding superiority of the bigger animal in the matter of self-defence which assures its companionship safe conduct against surprises.

Both tribes frequent dense cover and prefer the hills to low stretches of country and while the elephant cannot compare with the gaur in hazardous feats of mountaineering, it is nevertheless a surprisingly good climber, more so if we consider its enormous proportions which place those of its companion into the shade. They are excessively timid and apart from their own compact [sic] neither is tolerant of the society of other beasts. Their chief organ of detection is the nose and their principal food comprises the giant grasses growing luxuriantly in valleys among the foothills or on terraced slopes. The solitary elephants to which I have alluded, were also actuated by a desire for companionship in their friendship for the gaur. The beasts roamed with the herds and if they separated to retire, they were always together during excursions. The men said the two tribes associated just the same when elephant herds were about in the forests, where one went, the

other was sure to follow and the society was to their mutual advantage.

A notable example of familiarity was afforded between a bull elephant at large in the Asir and Bori forests and the gaur herds of the locality. The beast was absolutely wild and in the memory of the inhabitants, had been in the jungles for forty years or more. They had no doubt that it belonged to a herd and had got separated and wandered there from the Mandla forests where elephants were last in evidence. I came across it half- a-dozen times during inspections and shikar expeditions, and found it always with a retinue of gaur. From a distance, it appeared to merge in the big beasts gathered about it, and there was little to differentiate between its size and those of the large bulls standing near. It notified its presence if alone, by a few trumpet notes which had the effect of bringing the gaur to the spot. It went about freely among the others and took the lead in guiding activities. It looked to their wants, bending or pulling out bamboo stems and tearing down boughs of fodder trees to place within reach and with a fine sense of feeling, picked out tender shoots for the calves. It favoured the cows which thronged round it, while the bulls kept aside, and it lashed out with its trunk if they dared to hustle the cows to get to the fodder. It attacked the bulls and put them to flight if they attempted to fight in its presence. It had decidedly the acuter sense of the two, being the first to detect the approach of an intruder; its alarm was a shrill squeal and it headed the flight, the gaur keeping more or less closely on its tracks.

I had quite an experience with the beast one hot-weather day. I was inspecting the Bhaisanand forests and climbed the rise to gain a better idea of the growth, than could be obtained by going through the valley. A depression or disused tank, the relic of a nomadic settlement, existed over the elevation, and the pool formed in the rains contained water till the early months of the hot weather. The tract used to be the haunt of wild buffalo which gave the forest its name, but the beasts had been exterminated, or had left the locality shortly before my time.

To return to the adventure, on scaling the height my Gond guide detected the noise of splashing and we stopped to listen. We were in a belt of tall grass that grew around the pool, and could not see beyond where we stood which made us anxious as to the meaning that the churning of liquid betokened in that wilderness of silent

jungle. We moved cautiously to the edge of the curtain of reeds and looked out on the pond. There! - to our surprise was the elephant in the centre, seated in four or five feet of water enjoying a bath. It rolled from side to side squirting the muddy liquid over itself. On the opposite side to us; gaur sat in groups of three and four chewing the cud, or stood tearing and eating the grass, quite indifferent to their friend's exhibition of pleasure. The scene was a good instance of wild life that sportsmen accidentally come across in their wanderings after game, and rendered all the more attractive by the complete unconsciousness of the beasts to the proximity of danger. I watched as long as it was possible to stay, for camp was miles off.

The friendly feeling that the tribes evince towards each other in the wild state, does not keep the gaur from attacking a tame elephant employed in its pursuit. A brother official with a few years in the country wounded a bull and started to follow it up on his shikar elephant. They came upon it standing under bamboo cover and he fired and registered another hit; but nothing daunted, the wounded beast charged his mount and made it turn and flee, hanging on to its flanks and every now and again, plunging the horns into its sides. Being on a pad, my friend was severely jolted and it was as much as he could do to sprawl astride the seat and cling to the ropes. Under the circumstances, shooting was out of the question and the infuriated bull kept up the pursuit some distance. The bolting mount was too frightened to heed the efforts of its driver to stop, and it ran screaming long after the bull had left off pommelling it. It was severely bruised and unfit for use for days, and never quite recovered enough from the savage attack to be staunch in pursuit of big game. The bull was never found. I heard of a similar adventure occur to a party of young officials who were after gaur on elephants in the wilds of Chanda.

The wild buffalo is closely related to the Indian bison and yet, they will have nothing to do with each other. Again, wild buffalo and elephant are not close friends; they revel in water, but keep apart in feeding. There are jungles to which all three resort, but the beast keeps aloof from the gaur as much as it does from the elephant. In the case of the cousins, the separation can be explained by the choice of localities which they frequent, namely, the highlands for the gaur and the low lying tracts for the buffalo. The same distinction however, does not apply to the elephant

which if need be, is as much at home in the buffalo's haunts as it is in the hills. The objection to their company, at least on the part of the elephant, may be found in the surly character of the buffalo which makes it inclined to be quarrelsome, as compared with the complacent nature of the others. It is also more daring and vicious than the elephant or the gaur though in attack it lacks the élan that the others display.

My scant knowledge of the beast keeps me from pursuing the subject further, but jungle buffalo mix freely with tame herds taken out to graze and it is not at all unusual to find calves born of wild bulls. The union is encouraged by the owners who believe it infuses better blood into the offspring which is in consequence, healthier and stronger than young born of tame bulls. I heard of a group of villages lying on the outskirts of buffalo haunts, whose natives depended entirely on wild males serving their animals. The breed resulting from their union contained the best specimens of the domestic buffalo that my informant had seen.

Stalking gaur provides as good sport as following sambar. The beast though a very much heavier animal than the stag, is quite as quick in getting over difficult ground, its soft tread leaves faint traces on the hard gravel or stony soil of the country and makes pursuit very tiresome. The first weeks of the rains are the best time for the hunt because the spoors show distinctly in the sodden ground. Also, the gaur descend from the highlands to the lower reaches of its haunts where stalking is not quite the tiring work that it is on plateaus. The weather however, is not conducive to keeping out for any length of time. The heavy downpours on soil sun-baked for several months, make the jungle tracks teem with germs of sickness and occasion serious discomfort; incessant wet spreads damp which no improvised shelter can keep out; stagnant pools form and become breeding pits for malaria and cholera; the steaming atmosphere prevailing during the short breaks, soaks the unfortunate who happens to be out, in vapour baths that are most enervating; a variety of noxious insects flooded out of their shelters in crevices and cracks of the surface, swarm to wherever they can find lodgement and disturb what little peace remains. Few therefore have the courage to brave the risks of an expedition into the forests in the period. The only other time equally suitable as regards tracking though without the ills alluded to, occur during the brief spells of the winter or the hot weather showers. But the

sportsman must be close to the haunts to take full advantage of the brief opportunity, otherwise it is not worth his while to undertake the excursion owing to the long distance to be covered before he can get to the quarry. October and November come next in order of choice, but the months are pretty unhealthy and cover very thick; also it is the period of sexual activity and the beasts are restless and difficult to locate.

An early start is essential for success, and a good tracker is indispensable; an extra hand to relieve the sportsman of water bottle and bag of provisions, as well as, to aid in carrying the rifle which is nearly always a heavy weapon, spares him a good deal of discomfort and adds to the zest of the sport. The aim should be to strike for the main paths converging on feeding grounds or leading to coverts, as chances of meeting with gaur on their runs are greater, than in stalking through the areas or invading the retreats. Also, it is important from the start if practicable, to work up to the places against the wind. On reaching the spot, the party proceed slowly and cautiously, for there is no means of making certain whether the quarry is near, or how soon it may appear. The tracks will show if any have passed and their examination will tell the sex. Spoors of cows are smaller than bulls, very like footprints made by large sambar. It does not follow that the largest marks belong to veteran bulls; often beasts comparatively young leave big impressions. I know of cases where disappointment has resulted, when a long stalk showed the owner of particularly fine spoors to possess an undersized trophy. It is extremely difficult to gauge the quality of the prize from the footprints; the slightest tendency of spoors of frontal hoofs to increase towards a point comparatively, is an indication that the beast is a good specimen of its kind. But impressions of old bulls show traces of cleavage between the two toes of the hoofs, whereas those of mature beasts are set too compactly to disclose the marking.

These remarks presuppose clear prints in sodden or soft earth, while the trouble generally is to find the spoors in the hard ground or thick cover that obtains during the periods when stalks after gaur are usually undertaken. The alternative proofs to work upon in the absence of footprints, are the disjointed shreds of evidence shed by the beasts in their movements. Such are the mangled appearance of plants on which they fed, the lanes forced through cover in getting about and the bent and broken condition of herbs

and shrubs trodden over or forced apart by the animal's weight. A good tracker looks out for these signs of the beasts' presence and can tell at a glance whether they have been recently in the locality. It is quite an education to watch him work with these aids to discover the whereabouts of the quarry; he will pick up a twig and examine the wound in order to determine its freshness; explore the ground for the bits of chewed fodder dropped while feeding, to ascertain if they are moist or dry; stick his toe into the dung pats to test their warmth; carefully hold up the bent and broken foliage to see how they stood and from their drop fix the direction taken by the beasts; scrutinise the leaves and blades of herbs and grasses growing along tracks for signs of their having been brushed by the passage of heavy beasts; scan the trees to observe the heights reached by the creatures while browsing in order to gain an idea of the tallest animal; and so on. These trifles pieced together tell a tale and provide the index to work upon, and its accomplishment forms the badge of the craft. Briefly, they point to the time when the marks were made, to which direction they had gone and what to expect of the bull as regards its shootable worth.

Wind is the most disagreeable agent to contend against in tracking. The sportsman who is fortunate to be heading it all the time may consider half the battle won. Experienced men are prompt to take note of changes and shifts, and vary their movements accordingly. Often a successful track is spoilt by a sudden turn of the breeze when close upon the beast.

The sportsman who is in for luck may get very near his quarry. Many instances are on record of the short distances at which bulls have been bagged, and I got one within the space of a cricket pitch. The difficulty to the approach lies in the bull becoming suspicious that it is being followed which often causes it to disappear without giving the least warning of its nearness; if visible, its nervousness may be detected from its gestures as for instance, turning to look, jerking the head, sniffing the wind or hurrying its steps. The chances of getting even within reasonable distance to shoot, while the creature is nervy, are very few indeed. A possible means is by manoeuvring over a wide extent of ground. Sometimes too, it can be done by deceiving the beast; the pace is at once slowed and while the tracker and the bearer continue on the trail, the sportsman dodges out from between them and with the aid of cover makes a detour for the bull. A guide well acquainted with

the locality and its covers, will break off the pursuit, and then lead his master to encounter the beast in a distant quarter; the time involved in the diversion having restored the creature's confidence, it can be approached with renewed prospects of success. Very often the only thing to do is to come away and defer the shooting till a favourable opportunity occurs to get within effective range of fire.

I bagged a very suspicious bull in the manner last described. It had been stalked and fired at until it had developed cunning to elude its pursuers successfully. It haunted a plateau occupied by a few Bhils one of whom was a bhardwa who lived on a spur by himself. The bull was nothing very much as a trophy, so that its only attraction was its cunning whose defeat in my mind, acquired the same importance as the possession of a nobler prize; and I set about to circumvent it with the aid of a tracker from the plateau. We got on to its trail repeatedly for four days and saw it each time, only to lose it without obtaining a clue as to how or to where it disappeared. After a respite of two days, we tried again on the seventh which was a lucky number. Once more we were on its trail and chanced to pass the bhardwa's hut. Seeing us go by, he came out and inquired our business, and the tracker mentioned the object we were bound for. He at once volunteered to take us close to the bull and made a beeline for an adjacent domed hill, cut off from the main tableland by a low gorge. Heights of the kind are a feature of the country and form conspicuous landmarks among the hill ranges; they are almost impossible to climb owing to the upper faces being scarped and except for very pressing duties such as, to appease demons and spirits whose castles they are supposed to be, or as the abode of Jain shrines necessitating periodical visits, no one attempts to get up to the tops. I could not emulate the feats of my supple guides in raising and twisting my body into position in and out and over crevices and jutting rocks. But by sticking their spears into niches in the wall, they formed relays of steps up which I clambered. When we were on the top the bhardwa guided me across the few hundred spaces to the opposite bank and on nearing it, he stopped and told me to crawl up to the edge and look down, and I should see the bull. It turned out just as he said, for there, fifty feet below on a ledge from which the wall sprang, was the creature comfortably settled for the day under a dhak tree, and it did not take me long to bag the beast. I offered the man a money

reward for his assistance, but he would accept only a week's rations in grain and tobacco and a blanket of which he was sorely in need.

To safeguard against unpleasant developments, always possible in hunting dangerous game, it is as well to utilise any advantage the ground offers in the way of a commanding position to shoot from. Accidents with gaur are no doubt rare, nevertheless a wounded beast is dangerous to encounter and will not be withheld from charging should it resolve on reprisals. I have heard shikaris tell of unfortunate victims who were knocked about and cut up by horns and hoofs until all sign of life was extinct, and know two instances of its savage temper that will bear relating.

The Gond headman of Murdha in the Bhowergarh forests of Betul, was watching for game over a pool when a bull turned up to drink. Feeling sure his matchlock could kill the huge beast at the few paces within which it stood, he fired and succeeded only in wounding it; the bull charged the cover and pinned him through the right thigh. He struggled to extricate himself and was tossed forward, and very fortunately for him, got hurled over the bank into the pool. It was a small sheet of water a few feet deep, in the bed of a stream that ran dry during the hot weather when game resorted to it to drink. The bull could have easily waded the few paces from the bank to get at its victim, but with the natural aversion of the tribe for water, it left him alone and contented itself by watching on the bank. The man knew the temper of the beast he had to deal with and no sooner he was in the water, he got into the deepest part and sat down immersed up to the chin, so as to expose as little of himself as possible. The man's family disturbed by his absence, sent out the son in the morning with a search party who saw the bull standing by the pool. The men shouted to drive it off, but it turned upon them and they had to get up trees. Eventually, by yelling and firing off matchlocks they succeeded in scaring it away. The bull's behaviour made them anxious, and they hurried to the spot and found the man lying in the water, almost unconscious from pain and weakness caused by the broken limb. He recovered after a long illness, but lost the use of his limb. I knew the old Gond quite well and he gladly recounted the adventure for my benefit: its recollection always made him sad for he had been a great hunter in his day, and chafed under the enforced idleness. He was quite sure he owed his miraculous escape to being thrown into the pool as the wound had made the

bull very savage, and it spitefully kept watch through the night driving away animals that came to drink.

In the other instance a Bhil woman was the victim of an unprovoked assault. She was going to fetch water from a pool in the Sagbara defile in Barwani territory and arrived there at the same time as a bull coming from the opposite direction. Seeing the woman, it charged straight away, and in knocking her over, she was pitched into a cavity in the riverbed where she lay unconscious until rescued. She was only badly bruised, but being old and feeble the shock proved too much for her and she died after a few days.

I was once charged by a bull that I had hit fairly and squarely behind the right shoulder. It was coming towards me and I saw it before it knew of my presence, and stepped aside to take up a position in a depressed ledge on the steep bank of a nullah. It came on unconcernedly, quite unaware of the danger threatening its existence, and as soon as it walked into the zone of fire, it received the contents of my right barrel. Somehow, I omitted to press the butt of the heavy weapon well into the shoulder, so that the rifle reared up and got me on the neck and the concussion discharged the left barrel as well, resulting in another blow on the jaw. The stunning blows nearly sent me backwards into the nullah, and I stood up to balance myself on the slender footing that the ledge afforded. I was sure the bull had dropped, and was surprised to see it coming at a slow trot in my direction. With both barrels empty and shaky in trying to retain my foothold, I was in a plight as to what to do. It did not occur to me that being on the edge of a deep channel, the bull could not close on me without involving itself in the disaster of falling down the bank.

Something of the sort kept the beast from striking home, for when almost on me, it swerved off to a side, and went careering on till it charged into a bamboo clump whose twisted stems held the horns fast and the bull sat down by it to die. I heard the beast crashing about in its efforts to free itself, and could not make out the cause. Then, in half an hour all was quiet and allowing the same interval for the effects to cool, I started on its tracks and came upon it, scarcely two furlongs from the scene of fire, seated with its head embedded in the clump quite dead. On visiting the spot where the bull last stood, I saw that it had dropped on receiving the shot, but on rising it probably saw me struggling to keep my balance and was incited to charge.

It is not safe to flee from a charging bull; the beast rushes at a fast trot in spite of its bulky frame, and can outstrip the average runner over any distance. Jungle men if charged, dodge under cover or sling up branches and stems within reach, performances which few sportsmen can follow with success. Where precaution has been observed in occupying positions, the sportsman has only to keep still to avoid the bull's notice, and even should its attention be drawn to the spot by the sound of firing or sight of smoke, he will find that in ninety-nine cases out of a hundred, the beast will pass him in its mad rush when he can get in broadsides at very close range. Here, it is worthwhile recalling a brother officer's adventure.

My friend and his Mohammedan shikari stalked a bull at which he fired from behind a thorny thicket. The beast dropped and began to kick its heels; my friend was impatient to see the effect of his shot and stepped out of the cover in full view of the bull. It saw him and convulsed as it was by the mortal wound, it was quickly on its feet and making for him. Instead of turning into the cover to deliver a broadside, he fired at the oncoming beast and seeing no result, he started to follow his shikari with the bull close at their heels. He had not gone any distance before he tripped over a fallen branch which sent him sprawling. The bull being too near to pull up and fearing to stumble on the prostrate form suddenly pitched across its path, it bounded over him and fixed its attention on the shikari running in front. The man was maddened with fear at finding the bull gaining upon him and leapt into a zizyphus thicket that stood in his path, and disregarding the discomfort caused by the thorns, buried himself in its cover. In the meanwhile, my friend took advantage of the diversion to get up a tree, his cartridge belt was with the shikari and he had dropped his rifle and so was helpless to act. The bull moved round the thicket for a few minutes and then disappeared and was found dead some distance off. Two providential escapes in quick succession seems rather tall but I was told the story by the officer, with whom I worked in after years, when he was a reputed sportsman.

As a rule, a bull breaks into a short gallop when it is taken unawares and having increased the distance from the object of its alarm, it slows down and proceeds on its course at a leisurely walk. This is a brisk pace as fast if not faster, than the performance of a prize walker, and the beast keeps at the rate till arrived at a spot where it feels safe to sit or browse, as the case may be. Pursuit is

hampered more by the rough ground covered, than by the jogging walk at which the bull moves. It will single out a course in striking relation with its character, and according as it has been disturbed in a valley, at the foothills or on a summit, the flight will zigzag over a slope, follow the turns and twists of the ascending ridge or meander along the tortuous sides of indentations so distinctive of the plateau country. Consequently, the average sportsman is absolutely defeated if he tries to follow a retreating bull. A tracker acquainted with the habits and haunts of the particular bull, can save his employer a good deal of fatigue by heading him straight for its covert, or as with sambar, taking him to intercept its line of retreat. But without such a guide the sportsman is at sea and would be well advised to stop the pursuit no sooner he finds the quarry is on the alert. By doing so, he lets the beast gain assurance and improves his own chances of success on meeting with it again.

In common with dangerous animals, the importance of placing the shot in the right spot loses none of its prominence in the case of gaur, but on the contrary gains force owing to the protective shield with which the creature is fortified. The massive development of hide, muscle and bone renders the vitals impervious to wounds except from powerful weapons, and even then, unless aimed with due regard to the beast's anatomy, a crushing blow will do no more than produce an impression. A frontal shot is to be avoided, for both head and chest targets seldom avail to kill. In the one, the exceptionally thick bone covering the profile is not only hard to penetrate, but the head is presented at a provokingly oblique angle that deflects the shot. As for the chest the enormous thickness of hide, muscle and fleshy tissue successfully resist the missile. The marks to reach the vital organs without much difficulty are on the broadside, directly below the orifice of the ear, just over the middle of the neck, in the centre behind the left shoulder, and into the triangular pit above the hindquarters. They effect the brain, the throat and vertebrae, the heart, the liver and the kidney, offer the least resistance and the results are fatal and instantaneous.

Mr. Thompson, whose experience of death-dealing wounds was unrivalled, preferred the loin shot to any other for buffalo and gaur. He argued that the triangular pit was a ready and inviting target, easy to hit at the few score paces that the beasts were usually encountered, while the paralysing effect of the wound made the victim helpless, if not killing it outright.

A seriously wounded bull naturally seeks rest and will stop as soon as it feels safe from its pursuer, so that if the sportsman is at all certain of his aim, he may be sure that the beast will not go very far before calling a halt. Also, he may be sure that the longer it lies up free from disturbance, the less inclined it will be to get up and move on. Therefore, time is an asset in the chances of finding the quarry which must either succumb where it stopped, or become crippled by cramp and stiffness resulting from loss of blood. At first sight it seems cruel to withhold any immediate steps to put the beast out of pain; but the victim lying in silence taking in every whiff of scent or particle of sound, is much more likely to perceive the approach of its pursuer, than he is to detect its presence, and in the heat and excitement of the moment serious wounds count for very little with powerful beasts. Accordingly, the consequences are that the creature will either escape for good, lengthen out the pursuit or turn to attack, and whichever be the case, its agony is increased and prolonged. So there is nothing to be gained by the alternative; on the other hand, a few hours respite neither aggravates suffering, nor exposes the sportsman to the danger of a sudden attack.

Clever trackers often ask to be let alone to go ahead and reconnoitre the ground, and are usually successful in marking down the wounded beast without disturbing it. Enterprising men to whom permission has been declined, will even risk their employer's wrath and go off quietly to find the quarry. Being true woodsmen, they are as anxious as their sportsman to secure the bag and know better than he does what importance to set on the wound. The greater adepts they are at the art, the more they need to work alone, the presence of another hampers their movements and, unless they have confidence in him they lose their heads in an emergency, spoiling the chances of retrieving the beast. By themselves, they can obtain very useful information upon which the sportsman can base his plan of action. In my experience no seriously wounded gaur has ever escaped from their vigilance. Memories of incidents occur, when the men have defied me and gone off on their own quest, bringing back news that helped considerably towards retrieving tigers and panthers hidden in grassy banks where otherwise, only elephants could enter without fear of accident.

Gaur are occasionally shot in beats by unenterprising people in

quest of game who care less for the romance of sport and more for the means employed to attain the object; and so do not scruple to ignore the manly exercise and elect for the tame method of having the noblest quarry driven to them to shoot at their ease. It is a poor substitute which reflects on the prize, robbing the sport of half its pleasure.

Bulls are tenacious of life and will take a surprising quantity of metal when not hit in the right spot, even shots from powerful weapons aimed promiscuously make little difference in their vitality. Two young friends shooting in the Khandesh Dangs lost a bull into which they had emptied the contents of twenty barrels of a Martini and a twelve-bore rifle. Neither had seen a gaur before and on meeting the bull in their wanderings over the hills, they were struck by its monstrous size, and quite innocently supposed the best way to tackle the beast, was to fire volleys into its flanks as it kept receding. The first discharge caused it to go slow and in their youthful spirits, they kept up the chase firing whenever the beast turned a corner or showed through an opening. Done up at last, they stopped to rest and when ready again to renew the hunt, the bull had disappeared among the tangled hills. Another young fellow who was puzzling at the trail of a wounded bull when I met him, reckoned to have lodged fourteen shots into the beast with his magnum express. Still it was going strong and was never found.

These are the extreme instances of bad shooting that came to my knowledge, but there are others in which repeated right and left from heavy weapons failed to kill. The defeated bull I shot had several scars and search disclosed stumps of six bullets from a .500 express and two spherical shots from a twelve bore rifle. They were mostly embedded in cartilage close under the skin. Also, two spherical balls of large calibre were extracted from the chest of a bull shot in the Bori forests of Hoshangabad, while the wary creature whose downfall was brought about by a bhardwa, yielded five stumps of lead fired from .500, .450 and .303 expresses. Such examples appeal for the necessity of careful aim especially in the case of powerful beasts.

The first interview with a bull gaur is a thrilling experience and no one who has seen it emerge suddenly in an open bit of jungle or come upon it after an exciting stalk, can be blamed for being impatient to shoot, and everyone feels convinced of his aim on the grand target. But the exalted state of the feelings reacts on the

nerves to unsteady the aim and results in doubtful wounds, causing the creature intense suffering which the sportsman is most anxious to avoid. Therefore, the only remedy is to withhold the aim until control of the feelings has been regained. The antiquated methods of the aborigine at least made sure of the victim, but can the same be said of modern weapons handled by reckless shots? I fear not! Did means exist of obtaining facts and figures, the disparity in the proportions of animals bagged to the numbers that get away to die lingering deaths or recover after intervals of suffering, would form an unthinkable record and afford food for thought. The sporting fraternity has a grave responsibility in this respect, for the scant output of instructive literature on shooting. By this, it is not meant that there are not enough books on shikar, for they are more than plentiful, but what is needed are accounts dealing with the ethics of game shooting.

A very common reply vouchsafed nowadays to the sportsman in search after Indian bison is that the tribe frequented the locality within recent date of his visit, but since then had either greatly diminished, or left the haunts. The answer whether made in earnest or repeated haphazardly to satisfy the questioner's curiosity, is very true and the reason will be at once clear in view of what has been said. Ten years or so after leaving the district where I began work, a friend wrote asking for advice about gaur haunts as he was very anxious to shoot a bull. I wrote on his behalf to the officer then in charge of the forests whom I knew, suggesting certain tracts that had abounded with gaur during my early connection with the jungles. The man replied that since my departure, agricultural settlements had sprung up over some of the tracts while a railway was being built through the country, giving easy access to gaur haunts and owing to the causes, the herds had disappeared and not one remained in the localities I named. My correspondent was a fine sportsman and had no reason to overstate the case and I quite believed him. But a few words are needed to emphasise the point; the haunts were two score miles from the new line and the country hilly and unsuitable for good farming, so that neither should have influenced the cause of the decrease.

The rapid diminution of this handsome creature may be assigned to three causes - bad shooting, circumscription of haunts and spread of cattle disease. The former accounts for the large total of lost trophies, while the latter combine to a sure process of

extermination. The effects of defective aim has been gone into; as regards the others, the accepted policy to encourage the cultivator where and whither he chooses to settle, whets the appetite for land hunger among the nomadic members of the class. These unindustrious and short-sighted gentry are quick to seize opportunities to start operations over localities whose sole attraction lies in offering scope for wasteful methods, promising [a] few good harvests that are the inevitable preludes to erosion and subsequent abandonment of the sites. But the mischief in so far as it concerns game, rests in destroying their abodes and driving them from the neighbourhood, while the influx of animals owned by the settlers introduces cattle diseases among wild beasts brought into closer contact with their domestic cousins, and being unaccustomed to the rigors of illness, the jungle creatures die off rapidly. Even with birds, I have noticed peafowl and grey partridge that frequent hedges round about hamlets, develop the diseases of the domestic hen.

In the great cattle epidemics of 1899 - 1901, dead bodies of deer, antelope and gaur were met with pretty often during excursions into the forests, and signs showed that they had died of rinderpest. At one camp in Malgaon, word was brought of dead gaur having been seen in the adjacent ravine, I went out of curiosity and counted eight lying within a narrow space close to the path winding up the foothills to the Deogarh plateau. The herd had descended to drink at a pool in the Dholjur ravine which contained the only water obtainable within a radius of several miles, and was frequented by cattle of neighbouring villages. The disease was rife at the time and doubtless, the gaur caught it at the resort and being enfeebled, could not manage the re-ascent, and lay down by the path to die.

The remedies to lessen the evils, for it would be too much to look for complete immunity, are simple enough and such as would bear hardly on no one. The first is the concern of the shots themselves, and can be cured by due exercise of patience and forbearance while in the act of shooting. The remedy for the others is a matter of legislation that will disclaim against defective practices violating the existence of handsome beasts. Letting alone the attractive feature of the question which the pursuit of noble game inspires in developing manly virtues, there is the important claim of natural science. We know enough from its teachings of

losses incurred by the disappearance of valuable examples of life that can never be replaced not to play fast and loose with the existing forms. And finally, but which should really be foremost, is the question of the creatures' own right to live that is deserving of more attention, than is usually paid to the subject. Thus, sportsmen have a duty to advise on measures for arresting the decrease, and to be watchful that they do not lapse.

Promiscuous shooting often results in herds abandoning their haunts. Although gaur are disposed to be unsociable in their general relations with beasts among whom they live, as a tribe they are knit in the closest bonds of animal attachment. This has the effect of easily disconcerting the community on misfortune overtaking the individual. The removal of an odd bull of whose company the herd is unmindful owing to the scarcity of its visits, causes the others no misgivings. But it is very different, were a cow or bull forming the herd to suffer. Its absence would be immediately felt and animal instinct would connect the tragedy with the report of firearms or presence of the accoutred party - events which the herd witnessed and which the loss of their companion renders ominous. The creatures are stirred still further by the return of the wounded. Its restless and fretful disposition caused by pain and agony has a depressing influence, and animals unaccustomed to suffer are readily oppressed by the drooping spirits of the afflicted beast among them. They try to avoid it, while the victim looking for sympathy naturally keeps closer to its companions, so that the distressing sight disturbs and frightens them out of their wits. Consequently, the herd flees from the locality and abandons it for good.

It is a fallacy to suppose wounded animals seek seclusion and die in obscurity. It is perhaps the case with carnivora who have unmanageable tempers that preclude sympathy. But speaking in general, wounded beasts invariably rush in among their kind. Their distressing symptoms at first frighten and repel their companions, but in time they awaken pity and the others console with the unfortunate and lick their wounds, which is the healing balm of animal physic. The victims keep therefore with their friends as long as strength holds and when it begins to decline, they drop aside to die. The feeling of compassion is most in evidence with beasts that go about in pairs and many instances could be recorded of animals being encountered by the side of their dead

friend. Of those met with in my experience, a few will serve the purpose.

I shot a female panther over its kill and it vanished into long grass and died. The darkness prevented me from retrieving the creature and I had to come away without it. My shikari thinking he would steal a march, went off to find it before I was up in the morning, and hurried back to say another panther was near the dead one and growled and snarled and would not let him approach. I went with him; the grass was too tall to see to shoot and we had to shout to drive away the beast and then, got in. The idea occurred to the shikari that it might return, and he suggested that we should try and add it to the bag. So sending away the men with us, we sat behind some cover and true enough, no sooner they had gone, the beast returned and sat by its mate and was shot. It was the male and both were young and of equal age, belonging to the same litter.

In another incident, while watching over a waterhole at noon, I shot a buck four-horned antelope that came to drink, and kept in my position. A little later, the doe appeared and had her drink, then as it turned to leave, it saw the dead buck lying a few paces away. The doe started at the sight and ran to the shelter of the opposite bank quite near. Here it stood a minute or so and reassured by the prevailing silence, it went up to its mate, looked carefully and began licking the wound. After a few minutes it walked away looking mournful.

Once, when I was having a silent beat for a friend, a herd of cheetal walked out and he shot a young male, soon after the stag came trotting past and seeing its companion, stopped to sniff at it and was also bagged. Then again, a wounded black buck got away, and after some hours its tracks were discovered leading into a wheat field. In the distance, we saw a group of the creatures collected in a bunch and being curious to know what they were doing, we moved up and seeing us coming they dispersed. On reaching the spot, we found the wounded buck looking very sick and unable to move.

These examples may not be quite to the point, but they show that animals are compassionate towards the unfortunates of their kind. The monkey offers perhaps the best example of animal affection. I cannot speak from experience, but have heard from reliable sources that the female clings to its offspring long after it is

dead, and that a wounded monkey is always commiserated with by others of the pack.

A distinguished sportsman classified the utterances of gaur into three distinct cries, namely, the resounding bellow or call, the mooing or lowing like a cow to denote alarm or curiosity and the whistling snort emitted when frightened. These I have heard and agree as to the meanings they convey. I would add three more to the list - the sonorous snorts, metallic hisses and jumbled grumbling like that of a camel, expressive of anger and frenzy, uttered by bulls engaged in fighting. Also, I heard a dying bull close to me utter a whistling moan as it expired.

Gaur beef is distinctly gamey in flavour. In appearance it is rather like buffalo flesh without the latter's repelling tendency, nor as coarse-grained as the other meat. Fresh slices cut from the hump and fried are juicy, but require an unsparing use of condiment to make them appetising. Salted rump and brisket make a pleasant change in camp fare. Aborigines cut up the flesh into long strips and hang them on a bamboo pole or string stretched horizontally in the sun, and turn them about constantly till quite dry, after which the pieces are suspended to the roof of the cooking shed to smoke. The curing keeps the meat from spoiling and on high days and holidays, the strips are cut up into small pieces and stewed with vegetables as a savoury dish. The marrow bones make rich soup, it is strongly flavoured and needs to be seasoned with herbs and spices for epicurean palates.

The skin is much too thick and tough for ordinary use. It is excellent as covering for heavy cases and boxes where durability is desired, or for manufacture into trunks and leather articles put to hard use. A single hide can be turned into a canoe which will skim over water faster than any wooden or steel craft of the pattern I know of.

It is very useful for jheel shooting to rouse aquatic birds from shallow stretches of water, when heavier craft would be stranded in the sticky mud of the shoals or get stopped by the tangled growth of reeds and rushes. Jungle men utilize the hide for thongs by cutting it into thin strips and soaking in green oil till they are as supple as cords for binding. They also use the skin to cover floors, and in days of strife that preceded British rule, their braves fought with shields prepared from the skin.

It seems incredible that an immensely powerful animal as the

gaur can fall a prey to the tiger, the feat is nevertheless a fact that speaks for the brute's courage, daring and skill; it however, shrinks from the job, and instances of victims being overpowered and killed are rare. Mr. Sanderson has described how a tiger manoeuvres in grass to invite an attack by gaur and then, turns the encounter to its own advantage. He had got the account from his men, but the aborigines of the parts where I worked, could give me nothing in corroboration. The stratagem would not be beyond the tiger's cunning and a parallel is to be found in the skilful way, I was told, it dealt with the porcupine by skirmishing to induce the prickly beast to loose off its hurtful quills before attacking it.

There were opportunities of judging the tiger's relations with its formidable neighbour, in my many excursions into gaur haunts conducted over a period of nearly two decades. The opinion I came to was that the tiger shrank from tackling its powerful neighbour and deliberately avoided it when out in search of a victim. I have seen fresh tiger pugs on animal paths sodden by the overnight's rain, stop short as the brute turned off into the jungle to avoid a bull coming from the opposite direction. The spoors overlapped the pugs, as the beast passed on its way without heeding the tiger's presence. It was very evident that the tiger surrendered the path to the gaur; had it intended business there would have been signs of a struggle or a hurried flight; their absence showed the gaur was allowed to proceed undisturbed. Then again, tiger pugs have been seen close to spots where herds with calves rested or fed, but no marks of a disturbance; the brute was hungering to bag a calf and feared to tackle it because of the protection of its parent and companions. The settlers in these remote haunts who shared in the spoils of the tiger's hunts, declared that it very rarely killed a gaur, and the event was so uncommon that it was regarded by them as extremely sportive; they said moreover, that the victim was nearly always a cow or young bull. The conclusion would be, the tiger fears to tackle the beast and attempts the feat more as a test of its powers, and less for choice or necessity; the same applies to its dealings with other powerful game.

During my long sojourn in the forests, I only once came upon a gaur killed by a tiger. It was a heifer about to calve and had separated from its herd for the purpose. Except for the opening in the abdomen, it was lying whole on a bed of bent and crushed

grass in a depression where it was attacked and killed with little trouble, for there were no signs of a hard struggle. My guide fixed the time of the occurrence about eighteen hours, so that it met its fate on the afternoon preceding our discovery. The tiger had gone away with the fetus which accounted for the carcass being intact, as the unborn was ample meal for the time. There was every reason to suppose that it would return, and glad of the opportunity for a shot, I at once arranged to sit up and watch for the brute. But apparently, it had detected our presence as it never came to the kill, though we heard it moving in the long grass near-by. The tiger had either stalked the heifer to the spot where it lay, or had come upon it while seated on its bed, and taking it unawares easily killed it. The creature's condition would also unfit it for a struggle and make the tiger's task easier.

The ruins of ancient fortifications dotted about the summits, occasionally became resorts of gaur. Built purely as strongholds for itinerant warfare, they are difficult of access and seldom or never visited by people in the countryside. Their long neglect has made them a prey to the demolishing influences of jungle growth and many forts are buried under its folds. Their walled spaces afford the very kind of quiet and shelter that the monarchs of the mountains seek in their retreats, and not infrequently they resort to them for rest during the day. The Asirgarh and Saonligarh ruins in Betul and the Ramgarh fort in Barwani were utilized as such haunts, and I have started gaur from their precincts during visits of curiosity. In the latter, I also surprised a bear resting in what must have been the sleeping apartment of the chieftain of the fort.

The Bhils and subordinates of the neighbourhood described a visit of a party of young hunters to this fort before the forests came under control. The men who were the guests of the State, were taken to see the extensive view of the surrounding country, that is to be obtained from the summit. On entering the enclosure of the walls they were surprised by the presence of a herd of gaur. The creatures disturbed by the sounds were crowding into the gateway just as the men appeared, seeing whom they ran back. There being no other way of escape, the herd rushed about the ruins while the hunters manned the entrance wall, and the followers worked round to drive the beasts out. Whereupon. the herd made for the gateway and were easily shot down, only two escaping out of eleven; also the bag contained one shootable bull. Uncommon as

the incident is, it shows how thoughtless acts are committed by those who should know better.

In the rains when cover is very thick, bulls now and then stray far from their haunts in search of new pastures, and sometimes the excursions are continued beyond the limits of their range of movements. The maze of tangled hills and valleys overgrown with rank vegetation obscures their vision, causing them to lose their bearings and wander into unlikely places. Thus, the sudden appearance of a bull in the centre of an inhabited tract creates no little stir among the rustics who often have not heard of the tribe's existence. The bull's size and actions are exaggerated by youths employed to watch fields who are usually the first to make its acquaintance, and the people turn out to drive off the marauder, supposed to be eating up their crops. Their antiquated weapons avail them nothing and the beast is driven from pillar to post by a cavalcade of the young bloods with their dogs.

A bull that strayed from its domains into the Jobat and Jhabua forests had an unfortunate experience. it was driven about by the people till it ended its life by eating excessively of young castor oil plants that upset its gastric organs. No doubt it was quite unfamiliar with the plant, which is not to be found in wild localities. It could have come only from the Barwanit or the Khandesh hills, over sixty miles in a beeline from the scene of its visitation. the bull seized the imagination of the folks to the extend that its horns were cut off and preserved as relics by the two principal shikaris.

On another occasion, a bull strayed over seventy miles from its haunts and tarried in the locality until the close of winter, when all cover was burnt and cleared. It could no longer escape the watchful eyes of the rustics and became the object of sport for the young bloods. To seek sympathy, it tried to gain admittance among the grazier's cattle, but a fierce bull buffalo dreaded alike by men and beasts, drove it out of the herd and chased it into a distant belt of scrub jungle. The buffalo's triumph was however, short lived, for no sooner they reached the woods, the bull gaur turned on its pursuer and inflicted such severe punishment that the creature returned crestfallen and died soon after from the wounds. The bull eventually left the locality and nothing more was seen or heard of it, so that very probably it got back to its hills by forced marches under cover of night.

These are instances of long excursions which are exceptions, rather than the rule with the tribe; moreover, they are undertaken only by bulls that have become detached from their herds and wandered astray, even so their journeys never extend beyond the sub-hilly tracts.

Chapter XVI

Miscellaneous Incidents

The reader who has done me the honour of following so far will know that an outdoor life in the jungles is inseparable from little incidents which at the time draw scant notice and are soon forgotten. And yet, they illuminate diverse elements that become interesting on being pieced together. It may be useful to mention some of those noted either during personal observations or from hearing tell of them by people who had the information first-hand.

Most groves of large trees reserved for camping grounds have their colonies of monkeys. In the frequented resorts, they have acquired the sense of boldness to be troublesome and are often a veritable nuisance to travellers seeking shelter and repose under the inviting foliage. But, off the beaten tracks where camping grounds are occupied only during the occasional visits of district officials, monkeys are shy and attractive and a source of interest and amusement to the silent watcher from under the folds of his tent. I am speaking of the Langur or black-faced baboon and the brown monkey which abound in the forests of the central parts. It is safe to say that no other genus of the tribe combines intelligence and mischief to the same extent as the sacred Langu,r who appears as the deified Hanuman of native legends that credit it with all sorts of feats in the adventures of Indian heroes.

We find scientists claiming connection between man and monkey, but apart from technical evidence, it will be admitted by those who have witnessed our Simian ancestor in his haunts, that he acquits himself admirably as man's representative in the animal kingdom. I have often beguiled leisure hours watching the baboon under all kinds of conditions and could not help comparing its superior intelligence with animals among whom it lives. It would add to the store of knowledge if we knew what the beasts think of their versatile companion. Judging from appearances the probability is that they regard it as a prodigy of their race. Certainly, animals submit to the monkey's pranks with good humour while the flights of daring in which it can indulge in its arboreal domain, fill them with a sense of awe; they will stop short in their wanderings to gaze at its antics, or stampede with fear at its alarming note betokening the approach of some dangerous beast.

The belief that monkeys are timid creatures will not pass muster. I have had an encounter with dog-baboons and seen and heard of their daring which do the tribe credit. A pack with a few dog-monkeys may show the white feather, but when six or more get together, the tendency is to be aggressive and they will put up a defence or if need be take the offensive even against an inveterate foe as the panther.

To tell of my own experience, I was camped in a lonely spot infested with baboons; at noon the men dispersed as usual on various jobs and errands, leaving the camp more or less quiet. I occupied the time in reading on a deck chair and dropped off to sleep. I was startled by a crashing of pots and pans and thinking the cook might be in difficulties, I ran to the kitchen tent some paces away in order to investigate. To my surprise however, I was confronted by a number of monkeys occupied in an inventory of the cooking utensils. The timid ones scattered on my arrival, but the big baboons showed defiance swearing in monkey jargon and with grimaces and gestures daring me to approach. I took up a tent peg lying near to hurl at them, but nothing daunted they made a combined attack and I had to withdraw rather precipitately to get my hunting crop from the tent. Seeing me return with the weapon did not disturb them and they came for me again and though I hit out with the whip, they persisted in their attacks but took care to keep out of its reach. Obliged once more to beat an undignified retreat, I got my gun and fired a shot, which sent them scampering off to the neighbouring trees. Their menacing attitude showed plainly they were intent on mischief had I remained to dispute their occupation.

Elsewhere I have mentioned a scene showing baboons in pursuit of a panther that was making off with a victim monkey. A somewhat similar experience befell a Gond shikari who was watching for game over a water hole in the dry bed of a stream. He said that a pair of wild dogs rushed down the bank to seize a solitary monkey coming to the spring for a drink. The pack of baboons playing on the opposite bank saw the attack and charged down to the rescue of their companion. They at once formed a cordon round the dogs so that they could not get away. For some minutes they opposed each other using a tumult of threatening language until the dogs fled after a mauling, with the monkeys in pursuit.

My bull-terrier bitch had an unpleasant encounter with baboons. She was in the habit of giving me the slip during a march and running after them. One day I heard yells of distress and rode up to investigate, and found her being worried by the big baboons while others of the pack sat and stood about chattering approval. I daresay my timely intervention saved her from being killed, as it was she was badly torn and had to be treated for days before she recovered from the wounds.

I have heard tales of baboons playing pranks on tigers by pelting them with fruit or broken twigs when the beast passed under trees occupied by monkeys or was discovered by them during its slumbers. I have known them approach very near the lairs of tigers, and in beats for tiger or panther, they invariably turn out, sometimes separated only by a few paces from these fierce beasts. If we except tiger and panther, baboons show no fear of wild animals, and instances are related of their jumping on the backs of deer and cattle through pure devilry.

During a halt at Rampura in the Bhowergarh forests of Betul, a baboon took an Indian baby of about a month old up a mahua tree. The event took place close to camp and my men and I were the first to reach the scene on hearing the cries of the bereaved parents. The mother had placed the child in a basket at the foot of the tree and gone to the assistance of her husband who was ploughing within a stone's throw of the spot. The monkey managed the removal very quietly for the parents knew only on hearing the infant's cries from among the branches. The howls they set up on making the discovery attracted everyone and might have resulted in an untimely end for the child had not the old kotwal or watchman come up also and cautioned them to be quiet and told the crowd to disperse. The people saw the sense of his advice and left the monkey alone and as he had foretold, it came down the tree after a while and restored the babe to its cradle. The baboon's action may be interpreted as an impulsive prompting of maternal feeling combined with monkey curiosity. It sat on a fork among the upper branches paying little or no heed to the shouts and cries of the crowd, and hugging the infant who stopped crying after some minutes. In discussing the incident with the kotwal who spoke from experience, I learnt that the incident had occurred before, and once owing to the disturbance, the monkey dropped the infant and the fall killed it.

At a camp in a forest village, I saw monkeys join the village children in games of hide and seek. They kept aloof from the youngsters, but mimicked them in taking cover and running from place to place.

I had a pet baboon presented to me while it was quite a mite and my Mohammedan orderly took care of it. It became very attached to him and obeyed him implicitly; the creature would sit for hours in a corner at his bidding and do some queer things trying to imitate the servants. The way it set about to tie on a turban was very funny; it could never keep the folds in position, so that they came undone no sooner wound. A great game was to leap on the backs of my dogs and pony and frighten them; once too the scamp tried it on an Indian gentleman who was on a visit. In taking leave he was stepping from the verandah, and it sprang off a pillar when its presence was not suspected, and settled on my friend's shoulder. The contretemps of having a large baboon suddenly alight on his body, put the gentleman into a trembling fit so that he had to come in again and rest himself before leaving. The creature could not bear the report of a gun, being terrified out of its wits on hearing a shot fired. Moreover, it would get very agitated if it saw dead game brought into camp, and whimpered and remained mournful for long afterwards.

The way monkeys swing themselves about among branches is little short of marvellous. A full-grown baboon is a fair weight of five or six stone, still it negotiates the flimsiest supports in its aerial flights. Such feats may only be practicable by a very supple development, rendering the system amenable to every shift of motion. I have measured distances of leaps between branches, in one case it extended over so much as forty-two feet of horizontal space and fifty-nine feet of extension by the incline course marking the actual flight. A place is shown on the marble rocks near Jubbulpur, by the gorge through which the Nerbudda river flows, as the spot from where baboons used to leap across to the opposite bank. The chasm looks very forbidding with a width of at least eighty feet, nevertheless the belief had firm hold on the people's imagination. The only way to account for it was that once trees stood on the sides overhanging the gorge and so lessened the gap, as well as provided support for monkeys to hold in getting over. If we consider how monkeys are forever bounding from branch to branch, it is surprising how very rarely one sees or hears of

accidents. Natives declare that when such an event occurs, it results in the unfortunate being either killed outright or hooted out of the pack should it survive the fall. A baboon that fell off a tamarind tree in my compound died, but I had no opportunity of confirming the latter part of the statement.

Monkeys kill snakes in a way quite their own, though it must often involve their own lives. They avoid them like other animals and it is only when they come upon them unawares while playing about hollow trees, and the monkey has no choice between avoiding the snake and getting bitten that it tackles its foe. Cobras more than other snakes have a fancy for tree-hollows and are moreover aggressive, consequently monkeys have little chance of escaping if it is a case of coming to grips.

I was once called out to see a baboon that had hold of a cobra. The monkey seized the snake firmly by the neck and with angry gestures kept rubbing the head against the branch on which it sat, while the reptile coiled about its body, turning and twisting to be free. Other monkeys of the pack sat apart remonstrating with their companion on its foolhardiness. The head was nearly rubbed away before the baboon stopped and freeing itself from the coils, let the snake drop to the ground. The cobra was of fair size and had already bitten the baboon which never moved from its seat and after a few minutes fell dead all in a heap. The natives assured me baboons always resorted to this method of killing a snake.

It is not unusual to see monkeys playing on trees covered with beehives, and yet, they are never bitten by these fiery little creatures. But, let another shake a branch with a comb however slightly, and the bees will instantly swarm out to the attack. I have known of cases in which disturbed bees have without discrimination set upon human beings and animals that happened to be near, and bitten and chased them for distances, while monkeys occupying the very tree with the hives were left unmolested. It is difficult to account for this exclusiveness. An aborigine explained the monkeys' immunity as the result of a friendly pact between the monkey tribe and the bee family arising out of the following incident: a queen bee got caught in a jungle spider's web and despite every effort of its followers, could not get extricated. Whereupon the escort went in search of assistance to rescue their queen and found a sambar which was turned by their entreaties to go with them. But the web was high and although the

stag stood up on its haunches and swayed its antlers, it could not reach the net and had to give up the attempt. The bees then met a bear whom also they persuaded to come to their aid. The bear climbed into the branches to try to get at the web from above, but it was suspended in space and could not be dislodged. Lastly, they called a monkey and the resourceful creature sprung through the web tearing it and freeing the queen. In token of gratitude for this service, the bees swore to always respect the monkey and moreover, to leave honey in the combs just sufficient for the monkeys' use on emigrating from their hives.

It is amusing to see monkeys on cold mornings crowd together round a heap of dry sticks imagining they were warming themselves over a fire. They keep huddled together so closely that the warmth from their bodies produces the heat which they suppose is given out by the sticks. I have seen both jungle and town monkeys do this, so that it is not easy to say whether the habit is natural or merely in imitation of what they have seen natives do.

Monkeys have some sense of prudence, evidence of this came to me unexpectedly while fishing in a pool of the Machna river near Kantawari on a hot-weather day. We, that is my native assistant, Gond shikari and I, were seated in a depression of the bank watching for a bite when my attention was drawn by the latter to what appeared strange proceedings among monkeys assembled on the opposite bank. They seemed unaware of our presence and were busily occupied scratching up the loose sandy soil in various places and burying something in the burrows. The shikari who spoke from experience, told me what they were doing, but I was curious to see for myself and after the monkeys departed we went across to look. On opening the cavities, we found their contents comprised agglutinated lumps of the size of large marbles, placed in little heaps of ten or twelve between layers of fresh temru leaves. They were edible balls prepared from the pulp of temru and chironji fruits, the juicy capsules of mahua and bhilama flowers and various gums. They had been stored in these surface cellars for use during the damp cold days that follow the hot season. According to my informant, the preparations were an antidote against sudden chills that are so liable during the rains when the monkeys would take them out to eat. It is common knowledge that the ingredients utilized in the composition are believed by the people to have stimulating properties that fortify the digestive

organs against disorders due to chills. As a matter of fact, aborigines will always lay up a reserve of mahua for use during days of inclement weather. But the incident shows that monkeys are sensible to the needs of bad times. Years later in another province, a Bhil brought identical balls to show me for curiosity and as evidence of the baboon's ingenuity and foresight.

In every pack there is a monkey more knowing and cunning than the rest who leads them in games and is the imp of mischief. The old monkeys are more or less reserved and will not join the escapades in which the adults of the pack indulge.

My native assistant gave me an account of a squint-eyed baboon in the sacred city of Brindaban, who assumed disguises to frighten women and children. It was a great rogue, and played tricks with impunity on unsuspecting travellers who made pilgrimages to the place. It would snatch their food and articles of wear, and suspend the latter on impossible supports, as from slender branches of trees or high lofts and balconies of native houses. Also, it would creep up softly while they slept and exchange their belongings causing unpleasantness between parties, elsewise dispose of them in houses creating trouble between pilgrims and residents. He assured me that the monkey's doings led to a police case owing to a traveller accusing his host under the awning of whose roof he had slept, of taking his goods. During the investigation the lost property was found in an upper room of the dwelling which inclined the issue in the complainant's favour. The baboon, however, was soon afterwards discovered on a tree in the accused's courtyard, and its thieving propensities were so well known that the case was dropped.

The prejudice shown by the natives towards persons who have had the misfortune to lose an eye or to possess a squint-eye is really astonishing, and they will exclude him from their councils. The mere suspicion of the unfortunate being in any way connected with an undertaking is looked upon as spoiling the good chances reasonably expected from the enterprise. They will take care that he keeps out of the business and should this be unavoidable, resource [sic] will be had to various formalities in order to remove the evil eye he is supposed to have cast on the matter in hand.

I had a squint-eyed orderly whom I was advised to dispense with, but he was good at his work and remained on in spite of the aspersions cast on his character. For some time I failed to find out

the cause of his unpopularity. Eventually I noticed that on starting out for a shoot the sweeper who is the lowest of menial servants, constantly put himself forward without any apparent reason. It was provoking that of all men, he should be the last to fix my attention as I left camp. One day I angrily inquired the meaning of his repeated intrusions and learnt that he had been ordered by my men to make himself obtrusive as a set off to the orderly's evil eye. The men verily believed he brought me bad luck and since I declined to get rid of him, nothing less than the sweeper's presence would remove the infection. And strange as it may seem, in looking through the record of shoots, and adjusting dates with the sweeper's visits, it surprised me to find how closely successes and failures corresponded with the days on which he was or was not in evidence. The men were equally prejudiced against a Brahmin's appearance on the occasion, especially if he were swarthy.

Speaking of defects makes one think how seldom one sees or hears of them among wild animals. Such a thing as a maimed or halt creature from birth is a rarity. I have shot a tiger with a stump for a tail and a panther with one eye. Neither bore traces of injuries received after birth and still, I would not like to be positive on the point for it is possible the animals might have come by them while very young and so lost all signs of the accidents.

Freaks, which are of a separate nature of faults, are as rare as cases of malformations. Taking discolouration, I have seen white antelope, barking deer and squirrel. Also, in a beat, an animal looking very like a white panther passed some distance from me and the stops who were close to it, made certain that it was white.

Shikaris maintain that young of animals born with defects are either destroyed by the parents or die of neglect, and it is only very rarely that one escapes to grow up. The explanation is quite probable. Obviously a defective creature would be handicapped in the struggle for existence and so instinctively, parents destroy their malformed offspring.

A hermaphrodite among animals is even rarer than a case of defect or freak. I shot a blue bull that united the properties of both sexes. It had horns and throat tuft like the male as well as the colouring of the female; the genital organs combined those of male and female without either being developed. The beast was in the prime of life, well set up and in better condition physically than bulls generally are. It was bruised with scars and festering sores

inflicted by a pointed weapon, such as a horn, showing that the beast was an unwelcome companion among the bulls of its tribe. Moreover, I came across it in a very unlikely place for blue bull, while looking for bear below the scarps of the Ramgarh hill in Barwani. It stood, a brown mass, silhouetted against the cliff and I mistook it for a hind sambar and had no intention of shooting when my Bhil espied the horns, and taking it for a strange animal I fired. In spite of a fatal wound, the beast gave us a long chase over very rough ground and was not run down until the following morning. I had the head set up for curiosity.

Blue bulls are ungainly beasts that haunt the outskirts of forests and are therefore, not a jungle animal in the real sense of the word. They are seen occasionally inside forests, but that is when they have been disturbed, or else which is more common, in cases of solitary bulls that seek the seclusion of the forest to be free from interruption. Blue bull are regarded by sportsmen as tame beats, that is they can be bagged with little trouble; on a clever pony it is easy to run down and spear them. At the best they offer poor trophies, hardly worth preserving; they become easy prey to tigers and wild dogs. In their own fights they show the tenacity of the bovine race. Encounters are continued for long intervals and to escape from its pursuer, the defeated bull very often gets among village cattle. I was told of a fight in which the bulls were so occupied in goading each other, that a Gond shikari stole up without being noticed and speared one of the fighters.

The blue bull's companion is the chinkara or Indian gazelle. Like its big cousin, this pretty creature haunts the fringes and patches of stunted wood and scrub that are a feature of the open country. It is a sight to see a pursued gazelle bound over bushes and obstacles that abound the ground it haunts.

Chinkara shooting is fascinating sport and means dodging in and out between covers of bushes, mounds, depressions and watercourses. Its peculiar note of alarm not unlike a human sneeze, often deceives the inexperienced stalker; this is very likely responsible for its local name, as the Hindustani equivalent for "to sneeze" is "chinkna". Chinkara are wary creatures and swift of flight and very seldom get taken by preying animals.

The only "forest" antelope is the little four-horned beast whose habits resemble those of the barking deer. It is very timid and shy and its bark is easily mistaken for the deer's. Its peculiar jerky

stride in walking betrays its movements, and but for its diminutive size and the plentiful cover in its haunts the probability is that the creature would have been exterminated by its enemies. Four horned antelope stamp the forefeet like deer to indicate danger.

The victim to one of the strangest fatalities in my experience was a four-horned antelope. The incident occurred at a water hole in the Jhiripani reserve of Nimanpur. The cavity lay in the dry bed of a stream whose wall-like banks rose up twenty feet or so lined with stunted trees, smothered in the folds of climbing plants that formed dense cover providing favourite resorts for animals and birds. Its secluded position was rendered more attractive by the presence of a large number of fruit trees, as the wild fig and mahua. During the long hot-weather days, creatures from far around gathered to feast on the tempting harvest of fruit and flowers, and having had their fill and visited the water, they retired into the shelters to escape the scorching heat of the middle of the day. It was an ideal place to watch the fauna, and my Bhil shikari knowing the interest I took in this form of diversion, had erected a shelter where we could wait unseen and witness all that went on.

It was during one of our watches here that we saw a four-horned antelope come up the stream along the foot of the opposite bank. It was making for the water on the side we were sitting and had still a short way to come when it collapsed with an agonising cry in the coils of a python.

Quite unknown to us, the reptile lay on a ledge of the bank and as the little beast drew near below, it darted off its seat over the antelope's head, enclosing the neck as a quoit rings a pig. Instantly the shoulders were pinned by the tightening coils and the creature fell headlong. The uncanny sight put me into a quiver and filled me with a sickly feeling. The Bhil urged me to shoot; stupidly I fired and cut short the reptile's career, and so lost a rare opportunity of witnessing the sequel to a unique occurrence. The express bullet raked the struggling mass, passing through the coils twice within three feet of each wound. When we came up, the snake was nearly dead, but the antelope, although fatally disabled by the python as well as the shot, still struggled and had to be put out of pain. Even when dead, the reptile was so firmly twisted round the creature that the coils had to be hacked off to free the body; we then found that the fore-legs and ribs of the little beast were forced in and broken. The antelope was a young male and the

python taped a trifle over nine and a half feet, with a girth of fifteen inches at the thickest part. I preserved the skulls for the museum started at the Anand High School in Dhar.

My native assistant who was in camp at the time related an adventure he and his forest officer had with a python while touring in the wilds of Mandla in the Central Provinces. On the occasion, they were seated on an elephant inspecting a coppice. Their mount started a young hind sambar which trotted in front. It had gone a short distance when a python leapt out on its back and rapidly fastened round the body, and the hind fell with a yell of pain. His boss shot the reptile, but in the few minutes that elapsed it had crushed and broken the back and ribs of its victim. He could not say for certain from where the snake appeared, he thought it sprang up from the ground.

I was telling a Bhil headman my experience and he mentioned that a local woodsman had been attacked by a python in the previous year. The man was sent for and repeated that in searching for honey among the cliffs overlooking his village, a python hiding in a crevice of the rocks, got on to him and instantly coiled round his loins pinning him to the spot. He felt its tightening grip on his body increase every moment and with difficulty managed to extricate himself by hacking at it with his scythe. He was sure that the weapon saved his life for without it, he could not have freed himself.

I heard from another headman that some of his villagers released a sow from the toils of a python. They were going on an errand and the path lay by a clump of elephant grass. On nearing it they heard a pig squealing in distress and thinking it was gripped by a tiger or panther, they shouted and threw stones to frighten away the beast. When they ventured inside the patch they found the sow struggling in the coils of a huge reptile. They soon put an end to both with their bows and arrows and appropriated the pig for their dinner.

The Bhil's fondness for the dog is founded on an episode in folklore telling of a Bhil's adventure with a python. It is a eulogy on the animal's fidelity and attachment in supplying its master with the means of rescue from a horrible death. The man was attacked by the reptile while sleeping in his field, and was in the act of being swallowed piecemeal, when his dog fetched a knife with which he ripped up the snake and freed himself.

These few instances will show that the python makes little or no discrimination in its choice of victim. Moreover, it springs to the attack either in a coil like a rope, to ring the prey, or lashes out its prehensile body like a whip, to bind the victim. In this latter respect, jungle men say that in making the sweep, it anchors itself to the ground by the horny protuberance at the root of its tail.

I once came upon a struggle between a whip snake and an eagle hawk. Apparently the bird saw the snake lying at the root of a sapling and swooped down and seized it about the middle of the body. But before the hawk could get away, the snake managed to wind round the bird and at the same time, to coil its tail around the stem of the sapling, so that the hawk was tied to the plant. When we arrived on the scene the bird was flapping its wings, making frantic efforts to fly, and tearing at the snake all the while. After twenty minutes or so, the snake began to loosen its hold as it gradually succumbed under the attacks of the bird's sharp claws and strong beak, and freeing itself the hawk flew to the closest tree. It looked very fatigued after the tussle and I shot it to examine its injuries. No bones seemed broken but the feathers were ruffled and a broad purple ring where the snake had coiled round the body showed how tightly the bird had been held. The snake was a good specimen of over eight feet.

The partiality snakes have for milk is common knowledge, but it has given currency to many tales among the people. They say that in its thirst for milk, the snake will tie the hind feet of milch animals with its coils and suck from the udder, but the teat used invariably becomes barren.

I am reminded of an incident that occurred while staying with friends. Every night the nurse put out the child's milk on the verandah to keep it from curdling as very often happens in the warm atmosphere of rooms in India. The bowl of milk protected by a wire gauze covering stood on a tripod, but every night the quantity diminished mysteriously without the cover being disturbed. The nurse imagined the thief was a clever cat which tilted the cover and after drinking the milk let it fall back in position. One morning she was earlier than usual and went out to fetch in the bowl, but was intensely frightened at seeing a large black snake withdraw its head from under the cover and make off in the garden. She raised an alarm and before anyone could come, the snake had disappeared. Some weeks after the event, I shot a

large black cobra in the mendhi hedge where the nurse had last seen her snake and it answered to the description. The cobra was no doubt the culprit and yet for days the child had shared in the milk with a poisonous reptile without being any the worse for the experience.

To a sportsman who wanders about jungles infested with poisonous snakes it is a marvel how seldom or never he comes across a dead animal whose death can be traced to snake-bite, notwithstanding wild beasts move about in just the sort of covers which harbour snakes. In many cases their tough hides are some protection, but it does not altogether explain the immunity, for bitten cattle often die. It is to be sought in their fine sense of scent which enables them to avoid shelter harbouring the reptile. On two separate occasions I have seen a badger and a wild cat turn off suddenly from the covers for which they were making, and on going up to investigate the cause, I both times found a Russel's viper coiled up underneath.

I have only once seen a wild animal killed by snakebite. It was a barking deer that had come to drink at a pool above which my camp was pitched. The fatality occurred in the early morning and my syce, who saw the incident, said the snake was a Russel's Viper. The deer lived only a few minutes after being bitten and was brought to me soon after it expired. It had a dark blue stain on the left fore-leg where the fangs had been inserted.

Snakes make a peculiar chirping noise when they go about. It rather resembles the cry of a bird in distress. All the sounds I have heard were alike, excepting that some were more shrill than others. The natives attribute this difference to sex, as they say the male's note is louder than the female's.

I was shown a clutch of snake's eggs that were obtained from a crow's nest. They were smaller than those of a cobra and the man who brought them assured me that they belonged to a tree snake. Snakes are very destructive to eggs and young of birds and I have watched them during the nesting season hunt systematically among branches for nests. Jungle men declare that snakes locate them by scent.

Bull frogs devour small snakes. They also seize and swallow small birds. I saw frogs catch their winged prey through my office window which overlooked a cistern where water was collected for the garden. The situation encouraged a thick growth of vegetation

round the pool, and birds visited it on hot days to bathe and drink. Also, the damp and cover tempted a pair of bull frogs to live by the water and their amphibious habits made it simple for them to seize and drown little birds that came there. The modus operandi was to lie low in the herbage and when a batch of sparrows for example, collected at the cistern's edge and began to bespatter in the water, the frogs leapt one after the other among them, seizing one or two with their mouths and carrying them into the pool. The little birds being drenched and crowded together were not quick enough in avoiding the frogs and one or two of their number nearly always became prey to the amphibia.

I was mentioning the incident to a friend who related that while going over a golf course, he saw a myna - a bird the size of a thrush - fluttering in a puddle-hole. He went up to look and found a large frog holding on to its feet and trying to drag it down. The frog was submerged under the slime and the bird struggled on the surface. He could not account for its strange situation until he poked the spot with a stick when the frog jumped away releasing the bird.

Aborigine shikaris pay great attention to the calls of birds and any noticeable change in their behaviour fills them with curiosity. Often and often I have found the forecast founded upon strange calls or actions of certain birds come true. In fact, forest tribes place so much reliance on them that it is an accepted principle to seek for signs and portents from particular birds before embarking on errands or undertakings. Their folklore contains interesting tales about birds of which certain kinds and their doings are taken as guides by the men to suit their own actions.

Here is one tale that I heard relative to the colour of eyes in the matter of seeing. It told of a bet between the vulture and the pigeon to determine which of them possessed the greater power of vision, for the pre-eminence among feathered tribes was held by the former and the latter was not even regarded as a competitor. On the occasion the vultures were circling down from the sky to feed on the carcass of an ox lying hidden in a thicket and meeting a pigeon it became inquisitive to know the nature of its companion's mission. The bird replied that it was bound on the same business which was taking its friend. The answer however, did not satisfy the vulture who puzzled to find out how a dead body which was moreover concealed from prying eyes, could interest a grain-feeding and least ostensible [sic] bird, as the pigeon. It therefore

challenged its companion to prove its words. On alighting on the spot, the pigeon pointed to the grains of corn wedged in one of the hooves of the defunct animal. Accordingly the vulture surrendered its privilege and instead, the bird tribes accorded the pigeon precedence over its famed opponent. The incident is said to account for the harmless pigeon having the milky eyes of a bird of prey, and is also applied as a truism to persons with grey eyes. It is believed that white or grey pupils serve to penetrate the mist of long distances enabling their owner to be far-sighted.

Among the tales allusion is made to a large bird called Hansraj, whose appearance corresponds to a swan, only it is as much a bird of the woods as of the water. The creature is said to be always accompanied by its mate; their visits are few and far between and they are more or less invisible, but this is because they appear only at nights, disappearing into impenetrable woods or marshes during the day. Great virtues are claimed for the bird; the mere cast of its shadow is alleged to be propitious and those who are fortunate enough to come under its influence, have their prospects immediately improved. A romantic tale about this mysterious bird was as follows:

A king had three daughters of whom the youngest possessed all the amiable qualities of her sex and was the darling of her parents. But her loving nature excited the envy and hatred of the other sisters so much so that the maiden's endeavours to win their affection was met with scorn and derision. They were resolved upon injuring her, but every attempt to raise trouble seemed only to prove her merits and endear her the more to the parents. Therefore, they consulted to do their sister bodily harm and planned to line her bed with splintered glass, so that when she lay down, the sharp fragments would penetrate the linen sheeting and enter the body. The fact of the maiden wearing glass ornaments, would cause their overt act to pass as an accident moreover, her good nature in readily assuming blame would stifle suspicion. They put their evil design into practice and the unconscious maiden was groaning with pain no sooner she had laid down, owing to the sharp fractures working into her body. The stricken parents did all they could for their daughter; the best physicians could no more afford relief, than divine the real cause of the trouble, and the patient lay convulsing in agony between life and death. Wherefore the King decreed that whoever cured the

Princess would receive her hand in marriage and become the second man in the kingdom.

Now, a youth of good family in poor circumstances was passing through the country and retired to sleep for the night under a tree by the wayside. He was disturbed at midnight by hearing sounds of voices near him and woke to find, they were the colloquy between two birds in the branches overhead. Listening attentively, he heard the hen bird ask its mate if it knew of the calamity that had befallen the beautiful princess of the land. Hansraj said he did, and the only means of saving her life rested in someone forthcoming wise enough to apply their excretions as hot fomentations over the afflicted parts of the maiden's body. Natives have a firm belief in the infallibility of such excretive products as a means of relieving pains arising from the appearance of foreign matter in the body. This disclosure made the young man impatient to act, and with the coming dawn he collected the droppings in a bag and set off for the palace. On arrival he made known his errand and was instantly ushered into the king's presence where he begged to be allowed to test the virtue of his remedy. The request was at once granted and the youth followed the prescription that had been so opportunely made known to him. The application caused immediate relief and the princess fell into deep slumber during which the pieces of glass began to show at the points of the sore parts, and were without difficulty picked out with a pair of tweezers. The patient recovered rapidly and the youth was honoured and fêted. In due course, the event was celebrated amid great rejoicings by the marriage of the princess to the hero who became the adopted heir.

The story of the vulture guiding the faithful Lachman in his quest for Sita will be familiar to readers of the great Epic of the Hindus. But I heard a curious tale of the kuranj or damosel crane, showing the earliest invaders the approach into the fertile plains of India. Strangely enough it was told me by an ancient Bhil whose race is classed among the aborigines of India. He verily believed that his race was an offshoot of the great Central Asian family and took precedence over the Aryans in entering India. I was resting in a forest clearance after a long stalk one hot day in March with my two Bhil guides near me, and hearing the familiar call of the kuranj we looked up to see a long string of the birds flighting high overhead. It drew some remarks on their habits when my friend

ventured to relate the story. According to him, the ancestors of the Bhils lived among lofty hills and plateaux beyond the snow-line bordering Northern India. The lakes and marshes of these hills were the home of the kuranj, but the birds migrated during the season of stress and were back again with the return of spring improved in condition, making it evident that the lands they visited were fertile. In the course of ages their mountains were denuded of forest growth and rendered sterile, so that the race found it difficult to obtain a livelihood. The leaders therefore marked the migratory flight of the kuranj by relays of outposts and discovered that it crossed the snow barrier by negotiable passes. Emissaries were sent to spy out the land, who returned and gave a glowing account of its fertility. So the race of Bhils emigrated en masse and occupied the plains of the great rivers from which they were ousted and driven into the hills of the Midlands by Aryan invaders.

The familiar birds of every native homestead are the crow, raven and kite; the cunning and daring they acquire by living in close proximity with human dwellings render them a perfect nuisance to the inmates. They prey on whatever excites their fancy; food and poultry come in for the most attention, it is a miracle that chickens are reared. Full-grown fowls and ducks are often molested and killed and even, newborn kittens and pups isolated from the parents, become their sport. The raven is by far the most daring of the fraternity and being exceptionally strong on the wing, can pursue and overtake most birds; a swift creature as the pigeon is chased and killed. A common sight of bazars is to see kites swoop down and snatch food from the hands of persons, and cases occur of children's faces being lacerated by their sharp talons.

I watched a raven do a smart piece of work. One of my men had hardly sat down to a meal of cakes and meat curry when he had to leave in answer to an urgent summons, so covering the plate with a handkerchief he departed to obey. He was gone but a few paces when a raven swooped down from the tree under which the food was left, removed the cloth and in half a dozen short flights transferred the contents of the curry dish into a hole at the foot of the trunk, and covered it with a few stones. Then taking a cake, it flew up among the branches. The man was back again after a few minutes and seeing his food diminished and my terrier playing a short distance off, concluded at once that the dog was the thief and

set up a quarrel with the sweeper for letting it come to the plates. I was anxious to see what the bird would do and kept silent. The man of course, emptied out whatever was left in the dishes, for Hindus will not eat food of which a dog has fed. When he had gone and quiet restored, the raven came down, put aside the stones and set to enjoy the meal at its leisure.

The mischievous trio have a decided partiality for bright objects, and during the nesting season various knick-knacks and coloured fabrics are lodged in their nests. Rats and squirrels that live in and about dwellings, and birds generally, are equally fastidious in the choice of nesting material. But the trio named more than others I know, show marked preference for appropriating articles in domestic use. It may be that close contact with domestic life breeds a desire to share in the good things in which human nature is apt to indulge.

A silver cup belonging to an old egg-stand that I prized was retrieved from a crow's nest. The scullion had laid out the parts to clean on a mat in the verandah and the cup vanished mysteriously in the few minutes he went indoors to fetch other plate. There was no possibility of suspecting the real culprit, everything pointed to the scullion being the thief so he was given ample time to repent and then was made over to the law. About a fortnight after the event, the sweeper who looked after the poultry decided to demolish the crow's nest in the compound, as the parent birds harried the chickens. So his boy climbed the tree to get the nest down and on reaching it found the cup inside with the young birds. I felt sorry for the servant who was immediately released from custody and reinstated.

An interesting inventory could be compiled if means existed of getting together lists of things recovered from birds' nests. I know of quite a variety taken out on occasions. It comprised coloured handkerchiefs, soft collars, neckties, woollen scarves, coloured socks, pieces of ribbon, lace, reel of thread, skeins of wool, cloth and leather purses, bead necklaces, a pair of scissors, glass bead bangles, glass stopper of a scent bottle, a tortoise shell penknife, a silver egg cup, teaspoons, a pioneer brand tobacco tin, a brass nut and twisted brass and copper filings.

It is interesting to watch birds building nests. The work absorbs their whole attention and energy, the one object being to get the nursery ready as quickly as possible. With some, as in the case of

tailor and weaverbirds, the nests are works of skill, and no other mortal could piece together the shreds into the models adopted by the birds. With others, as in those of the woodpecker and the coppersmith, they show an insight into woodcraft because the tissue must be past a certain stage of vitality before it will yield to the birds' chisels. On the other hand, most ground birds provide the merest apology for nurseries, depending on the concealing colouration of the surroundings to protect the brood from their numerous enemies.

I was seated reading on an arm-chair in the verandah of my bungalow one morning and glancing off the paper, saw a pair of tailor birds very busy among the foliage of a croton plant that stood in a pot at the entrance into the portico. The pot was barely six feet away and I could see the tiny creatures were making frantic efforts to get together two of the large new leaves, but they resisted their attempts to be bent in the position the birds wanted them. When they departed, I examined the leaves and found their edges perforated with minute holes filled in with little wisps of fibre, cotton wool and spiders' web. The leaves hung on stiff to the stem and it seemed to me, could not be made to join without tremendous exertion for such tiny birds. It was evident, they had selected the two leaves to form the envelope of their nest, but had so far failed to get them close enough to join up the insertions at the edges. The following morning, the birds renewed their efforts and again met with no success, and on re-examination I found that the wisps had been slightly increased in length. To save the birds further trouble, I pinned the leaves placing them as near one another as possible without exciting suspicion. In the third attempt the birds had little difficulty in attaching the leaves and the nest was soon built. The tiny creatures would have succeeded eventually no doubt, in getting the leaves to join. Being unequal to the resistance, they contrived the alternative of lengthening the wisps which would give the necessary stretch to reduce the strain. I watched the work proceed and saw the birds make the connection by intertwining contiguous wisps till the leaves were gradually drawn into position. This was a discovery, for until then I was under the impression that the leaves were stitched as with a cobbler's awl.

A pair of bulbuls - a bird bigger than a sparrow - had a nest in a myrtle bush at the entrance to my bedroom. The nest is a tiny cup-shaped structure with not enough room for the hen bird. But this

one contained a brood of three young, tightly squeezed inside the hollow. I looked into the nest while getting in and out of my room to see how the birds progressed. For a week they continued in the cramped space; I noticed however, that one of the little birds appeared starved in comparison with its companions and I supposed the cause lay in its having hatched out last. Then, I missed it and peering into the bushes saw it dangling in a fork lower down. Thinking it had been pushed out by the others, I replaced it in the nest. But on my next visit, it was again out of the nest and I restored it as before. Later on, while at my toilet I looked through the window pane, and saw the hen bird hold the sickly chick by the neck in its beak and fly out of the nest and drop it a few paces away. This plainly showed that it was not wanted in the nest and moreover, explained its poor condition. The first thought would be to look upon the action as cruel and unnatural. The bird must have had strong motive though to sacrifice its young and on considering the matter the reason was simple. The nursery could not hold more than two young, so one must sooner or later have dropped out of itself. Furthermore, the parent birds were unable to keep pace with the increasing appetites of three little mouths and rather than that all should suffer by being fed less and grow up weak, they chose the lesser of two evils in neglecting and casting out one of the brood. I rescued the cast-off, but it had been too ill used to survive.

It was amusing to watch the expedients adopted by the parent birds in order to divert attention from the bush. A favourite device was to sham being wounded and sprawl about the ground as if helpless. This dodge was practised to dupe birds and animals equally as men, for example a crow, a dog or a person approaching the bush would be treated to the same diversion, and if any of them went up to the bird to catch it, it would suddenly fly away.

I have seen jungle fowl and grey partridge with chicks behave like the bulbuls to deceive hawks and cats. Again, I have known mynas and jays get taken in defence of their offspring by sparrow hawks, depending on their size and strength to effect escape when the bird of prey's attention was turned away off the young.

Some birds, such as the hoopoe and barbet, puff themselves out to an abnormal size should they see a snake near their nests, while they utter a mournful note to attract the reptile. I remember the start it gave me to see a hoopoe assume the guise; with feathers

ruffled and standing erect and the tail cocked up like a fan, it might have been taken for a woolly ball instead of a bird. I wondered what it was up to when the Bhil with me, pointed to a cobra making for a hollow in the tree which contained the bird's nest.

I saw a pair of horned owls perform a series of tumbles in order to engage a panther's attention. They had a nest in a cornice of a ruined gateway marking the entrance to an old fort. The beast over whose kill I was watching, instead of coming by the jungle path in front, chose to manoeuvre the ground before tackling its meal and climbing the gateway, sat just over the nest to survey the spot where the kill lay, some paces beyond the ruin. Except for a glance, it took no notice of the birds' gambols and when it got down I shot it.

Small birds have a great many enemies to contend with, and they maintain the struggle for existence owing to Nature's protective concealments of which they are instinctively conscious and make a full use in difficulties. Not only do preying animals and birds take heavy toll of the little lives, but many insects are highly injurious to incubating eggs and nestlings. Of these the fierce black and brown ants that infest trees are the most destructive. I have come upon cases where they were in the act of devouring the young of pigeon, dove, parrot and robin. It becomes impossible for a bird to rear a brood among branches or hollows of trees on which the ants appear.

I was once walking through a coppice wood and hearing the excited twit, twit, of sun birds overhead, looked up and saw one of their young struggling in a web. Apparently the little creature had quite recently quitted its nest and flown into the trap of the large wood-spider which spins about the strongest web I know of, the thread having the yellow gloss of silk. The spider is identified by its active habits and deep yellow-brown colouring. The parent birds darted about twitting in and out of the web, but the spider kept at its post by the victim enclosing it rapidly in a network of cemented thread. I rescued it but it was covered with sticky excretion and could not fly and the feathers had to be carefully wiped before it could get away. The insect did not seem disturbed by the size of its victim nor by the attacks of the sunbirds, although the birds hunt small spiders.

The beginning of the hot weather which coincides with the spring in Europe, marks the period of general excitement among feathered tribes. It is the season when birds don their nuptial

plumage and are eager to display their merits. This excites rivalry and creates friction resulting in disputes which end in pitched battles by the warrior males. The violence and persistency of these attacks culminate in those of the raven, the crow and the kite and woe! to the unfortunate that is down, for unless it can escape by faster flight, it is soon set upon by a host of its kind that may have had nothing whatever to do with the quarrel, and pecked to pieces.

In these fights, birds are often so taken up with their quarrel as to lose all sense of danger, and can be easily caught by their enemies. With a stick, I have knocked over crow, myna and sparrow that were too absorbed in fighting to notice my approach, and have seen hawks and cats effect captures. One of my long-dogs seized a grey partridge while engaged in a duel, and I saw a panther pounce upon two jungle cocks in the middle of a stiff fight, and nab both.

Bird nature makes no allowance for the weak and vanquished. Wounded birds or those in difficulties, whether caught in snares or lucklessly entangled in matting of branches or weeds, are set upon by their companions without compunction and mercilessly treated, if not killed outright.

There is no mistaking the distress notes of birds, they are so ominous of trouble as to be distinguishable even to a tyro. Jungle men hearing them rush to the spot indicated and often retrieve game from animals and birds of prey. I was once superintending fellings when we heard the piercing shreak [sic] of a peafowl. Two of the lads instantly charged off and brought back a cock they had rescued from an eagle hawk. On another occasion a hare was recovered in the same way.

I have heard shikaris declare that peacocks attired in full plumage abstain from fighting out of respect for their appearance being chary to risk spoiling their adornments, and moreover, that juvenile cocks willingly retire before the elder birds and so avoid a breach of the peace. Certainly, I have never seen a fight between two of these handsome birds fully decked in their bright colours, though fights among young males that have not arrived at the same stage of plumage, are common enough.

A common forest scene but one which few have opportunities to witness, is a peacock dance. Imagine in the midst of jungle, a small opening with a level stretch of ground clear of undergrowth, by a shaded pool or water-course, soon after sunrise or before sunset

Part of the frontage of Jehaz Mahal, Mandu, 1904

Hindola Mahal, Mandu (front view) showing restoration work in progress, 1904

Jehaz Mahal, The "Ship Palace", Mandu, 1906

Hoshang's tomb before restoration, Dharamsala, Mandu, 1904

Nahar Jharolea,
Mandu, 1905

Dharamsala, Hoshang's tomb, Mandu, 1904

"Thirteen Years Among the Wild Beasts of India" - Sanderson's book, whilst not directly linked to J.D. St Joseph's work, is a highly relevant read on a closely similar subject.

with the sun's rays playing through the foliage and the dhak, amaltas, kachnar and karanj trees in full bloom. Here, the birds will gather after a drink. Then, a brief courtship begins and a cock will begin strutting around its spouse, its feathers unfolding and expanding with each revolution till it gets the measure of its steps and sets its gorgeous spread to advantage. Now, it will pace the floor in a series of short rushes, slow steps and hops describing various diagrams and with every change of motion vibrating its feathers that give out a ringing note like a sharp clank of tinselled attire. More cocks join in and they pass and repass each other with precision, alternating their steps to suit the actions in the diverse parts of the dance.

A theatrical scene as I have attempted to describe, is either an accidental discovery or the reward for patient watchings. I have seen monkey, deer and antelope stop short in their wanderings and gaze at the sight as if entranced. Even birds gambolling among the branches become still for the time being. The cocks of many bird species dance for the benefit of their spouses, and some of the wren family present as pretty a picture as any dancer. But for gorgeous display, subtle grace and striking deportment, the performance of the peacock is surely matchless. Peacocks frequently dance in captivity, but it does not seem quite the same thing as the exhibition in the seclusion of a jungle haunt, the absence of which robs the spectacle of its spell. The peacock is a born dancer and male chicks begin to disport [themselves] soon after they are hatched and so make it easy to distinguish them from the hen chicks. I have seen women of the dancing profession try to copy the peacock's movements in their public performances, but at best it is a miserable attempt.

I witnessed a funny exhibition of dancing by a saras crane while fishing among reeds on the bank of a tank [a small lake]. It kept moving in a turn and turn about swing, lifting and depressing its long legs alternately, with wings flapping to suit the action, and every few minutes uttering a hoarse note of pleasure. Being at a loss to account for its comic display, I went up to the spot to look, and almost walked over the hen bird sitting on a brood of newly hatched chicks. So it was evident the flourish was the cock's way of welcoming its new family. The saras is regarded more or less as a sacred bird in the countryside, and is mentioned in sayings as a model to strive after in connubial affection.

Amongst the bird dancers I know of, the florican's performance is very curious. It shoots up ten to fifteen feet, uttering a croaking note not unlike that of a frog. It can be approached on a camel, close enough - for it frequents long grass - to watch its dance. The start is an imitation of the opening stage in the peacock's dance, then, using its wings as elbows, or sails above the body, it springs up in successive beats. As far as can be ascertained, the bird's display marks the periods of courtship and incubation of the eggs. A popular belief, however, is that it rises to seize the cantharides beetle which swarm in the rains, when the florican also appears. But the theory will not bear admission by those who have watched the bird's performance closely.

There is no comprehending what birds eat. The palates of some are discriminating to a nicety, others are promiscuous feeders. But apart from these extremes, particular birds make certain foods exclusively their own. Such is the florican who feeds on the cantharides beetle, which no other birds that I know of will touch. Or, again, the sun bird which eats the little poisonous nesting spider which other birds avoid.

In abnormal times birds, like animals, resort to foods that they otherwise eschew, so that during a time of stress it is not uncommon to find grain feeders living on insects, and vice versa. In the great drought when water over wide stretches of forest country failed outright, I often wondered how the jungle fowl in these tracts managed to exist. But the aborigines informed me that they eat minute particles of quartz which diminished their craving for water. I therefore cut open some fowl, as well as partridge and dove shot within the areas, and found their stomachs contain an abnormal quantity of grit. Incredible as the explanation may seem, there must be some truth in the assertion, and to me there seems no other way of accounting for the forced abstention. At the same time there is no gainsaying that their vitality was greatly diminished, making them easy victims to preying animals and birds. However, this does not lessen the fact that the birds kept from drinking for long intervals.

The feathered tribe contains a variety of mocking birds which, though a class by themselves, include representatives from several orders. Like the rest of the mimicking fraternity, they are conscious of their power to create panic and will practise it as readily to frighten the solitary timid bird as to dismay and scatter an

assembly. Perhaps the greatest offender in this respect is the species of green barbet, somewhat bigger than a sparrow. The mimicking vocabulary of this little creature comprises a marvellous assortment of notes of both animals and birds, especially those of prey. I have watched it spread fear among birds disporting peacefully on banks of streams or branches of shade and fruit-bearers, moreover, its performance is so clever that I have heard the calls answered by beasts, such as the jungle cat and fox, whose cries it was imitating. Once, also, while waiting in a machan for a panther's return to its kill, two doves frightened out of their wits by what they imagined to be a falcon's cry, darted onto my leafy bower for refuge, too alarmed to resist capture. It deceived me quite as much as the birds, until finding the cries had come near, I peered through the enclosure and saw the impostor hopping among the branches of a neighbouring tree.

Many of us are familiar with tales about the butcher-bird pinning insects to spines of thorny plants, but most birds of prey maintain larders. At the beginning of my service, I had the craze for bird-nesting and made it a point to keep eggs collected only by myself, and it surprised me, how often in exploring nests of hawks, kites, vultures, owls and even in those of storks, herons and egrets, I came across pieces of meat, bone, game and fish in various stages of decay lining the outskirts of their abodes. Vultures and the large hawks and owls occasionally utilise old nests for larders, building new ones near by in which to rear the young. The atmosphere about these tenements is as foul as that near a rotting carcass. An unusual find I made was a dead kitten of the jungle cat in the larder of an eagle hawk.

I have often rescued victims from birds of prey and at one time my poultry contained a number of such foundlings. In the compound of the bungalow, there were some clumps of the giant bamboo whose dense cover was a favourite resort for numerous birds. At sunset, the grove became alive with the hum and bustle of bird life. It was a sight to watch them flighting in twos and threes or in small groups and flocks to their nightly retreat, and then for half an hour, they would indulge in vespers in which the different strains would mingle in a deafening orchestra.

As may be expected, the grove was frequented by hawks not merely for preying, as they seldom caught the birds once they had gained the protection of the bamboo stems, but as a retreat to

devour young poultry seized from the yards of Indian dwellings. The distress cries of the victims gave warning of the harrier's approach and in a minute I was in the grove with my pellet bow, then, as the bird would settle down to kill its quarry, a pebble rattled through the leaves and twigs startling it into letting go the victim which fell to the ground, and was caught and tended. Sometimes on getting over the surprise, the hawk would swoop down to recover the quarry, and I have had my hands scratched in the bird's attempt to snatch the prey out of my hold. As a rule, hawks grasp at a vital spot, such as the heart, liver or lung; in order to embed the talons into the organ and so put an end to the victim's struggle. In seizing birds on the wing, hawks invariably take an upward turn which seems to fetch the victim within closer grip of its spoiler, enabling it to dig the claws well into the body.

Hawks often hunt in pairs, but preferably in the breeding season when they have need to make sure of their prey, and will occasionally seize and kill weaker members of the tribe. I have seen kestrel, harrier, merlin and sparrow hawk fall victims to falcons and shikra. If taken young, hawks are easily tamed, though to train them, especially to fetch the quarry to the hunter, is a matter of patience and skill in handling the birds. Most species are daring and will not be deterred by the size of the quarry on which they are set. I had a shikra that would without the least hesitation, dart off to seize jungle fowl, demoiselle crane and brahminy duck - birds twice and thrice its size and weight. But if it caught them readily enough, it could not retain the quarry which would free itself and escape, so that one had to be prepared to run up and secure the prize. I noticed that in dealing with large birds, the hawk set about ripping open the victim's throat or neck with its beak. The reason is clear, the size of the quarry would place the vital spot beyond the reach of its claws and then, the neck would be most vulnerable to the hawk's method of killing.

I had a curious experience with two missionaries recently out from home. I was camping on the Khamla plateau in Betul and the brethren stationed in the locality called on me. I received them in my tent and we talked on various subjects relative to the country. Then, on rising to leave, one of them asked that as they could not speak the vernacular, if I would oblige them by taking their servant to task for insisting on refusing to cook a turkey which they had shot. The announcement took me by surprise and I exclaimed that

there were no wild turkeys in the country. But they said the man with the bird was outside. I therefore went out of the tent and was not a little amused to see the man standing under a tree with a dead king vulture lying at his feet and my servants gaping around and pestering the unfortunate with questions, for to them the sight of a man with so foul a bird was a matter for ridicule. On going up to him, the man appealed to me to put the sahibs right as to the unclean habits of the bird which even the lowest class of natives would not use for food. But the brethren seriously believed their bag was an Indian form of the turkey and pointed to the features about the vulture's neck and head as strongly resembling those of that bird.

Dogs are a great companion in a nomadic existence and I was never without them. A cross breed of terriers bigger in the limbs, than the variety we know by the name, serves the best all round purpose and a pack of three or four will tackle almost anything. In coursing after jackal and fox I preferred them to long-dogs; owing to their shorter reach the pursuit covered some extent of country and the horseman could keep abreast all the time and enjoy the ride, whereas with long-dogs the chase ended all too soon and over rough ground the mount had no look in at the finish. Terriers are nippy in attack and will escape mauling when a bigger dog would suffer badly. Also they are good in all weathers and require little care. My pack of three was very useful in hampering or pulling down wounded beasts attempting to escape.

For a time, I had a couple of long-dogs, offspring of imported parents - kangaroo hounds - crossed with an indigenous breed - Rampur hounds - which fitted them for the climate. They were excellent coursers, and all for killing, and no jackal or fox had a chance of escape unless by going to earth before the dogs were near. They ran down chinkara, a feat that says a good deal for their fleetness, considering what a swift little creature the gazelle is. They would readily tackle wolf and hyena, but avoided panther and bear, whereas the latter always afforded great sport to the terriers.

Like most of the breed, my terriers were excellent ratters; also, they would hold up a poisonous snake, such as the cobra, if they saw one, keeping it a prisoner by circling and barking around it but avoiding the reach of its fangs, until someone arrived to kill it. They were the cause of hunting down a good many reptiles in the

compound. An amusement was to slaughter locusts. They would rush into a crowd that had settled, grabbing the while with their mouths but dropping them as quickly after a feeble crunch, so that in few minutes, their paths would be strewn with hundreds of dead and dying insects.

The country is occasionally visited by swarms of locusts that do considerable damage. In normal times, flights occur once or twice in a decade, but in the cycle of short rainfalls culminating with the great famine, it was not uncommon to have two or three in one year. The visitations are looked upon as a dispensation of Providence for scourging the wickedness into which the people have lapsed, and with true Eastern resignation to Fate the people are averse to undertaking measures that aim at destroying or checking the multiplication. Accordingly, the insects leave vast areas sown with eggs which in a dry year hatch out millions of voracious feeders, so that the evil they provide for is greater than that committed by the flights.

Some of the wild tribes roast and eat locust and curiously enough, I came across families who treated it with honey as a delicacy because they said its saltish flavour went well with the sweet, thus recalling the incident of the wilderness in the great Preacher's life. In some parts, village folks extract oil from the insect, which is believed to possess healing properties in cases of pains due to chills.

An experiment was carried out in a neighbouring province to spread disease among the swarms by infecting specimens with parasitic germs. To give some idea of its success, I came upon many thousands of dead locusts reduced to skeletons, and on breaking open a few I found the abdomens lodged with thread-like growths entwined in minute reels that undoubtedly were the cause of death. At the time I did not know of the experiment and supposed it to be a larva that had effected an entrance when the creature was settled, and tried to identify so efficacious a malady. A Bhil seeing me interested, ventured the suggestion that the disease was due to spider infection since locusts must come in contact with that insect which would naturally sting them. I daresay he founded his statement on the resemblance of the woolly growth to a whisk of spider web.

Speaking of spiders recalls incidents with the tarantula which is a common visitor to tent dwellers on hot weather nights. It is an

active rapacious creature and will soon clear the spot about the lamp table of insects attracted by the light. Moreover, it is daring to a fault and will not be deterred by the size or character of an insect. A pastime during the dull hours was to place a tarantula with a scorpion under a glass finger bowl and watch them fight. The former usually succumbed first and the latter soon after. The fight resembled a wrestling match in which their strong mandibles did more execution than bites of stings. Once, too, I saw the spider rush at a large tiger beetle, but it had underestimated the other's mettle, for with little effort the formidable creature cut the tarantula in halves and went on its march none the worse for the encounter.

Another evil born of the great drought was a plague of rats which appeared between the years 1901 and 1902. They were entirely field vermin and seemed to spring up in thousands everywhere. Fortunately, they came after the kharif [spring crop] - the staple crop of the country - had been harvested, otherwise their ravages must have imposed famine conditions. As it was, they ate up everything of value remaining in the fields and then attacked the buds and tender shoots of forest plants. They became almost as obtrusive by day as by night, and a common sight was to see them foraging at all hours of sunlight. Their appearance brought on the scene numerous birds of prey: land harriers, kestrels and merlins were constantly skimming over the fields or scanning the ground for their victims. The rats acquired such boldness as to bite the hands and feet of sleeping people, and on two or three occasions I was shown infants whose toes were eaten into while the parents were absent and too far away to hear their cries. The oldest inhabitants had no prior recollection of a plague of the kind and the rats disappeared as suddenly as they had come.

Those who have not explored the granaries of field rats would find it hard to credit the quantities stored by a single family. I have been present at the openings of several bins, and the following are a few figures of the weights of grain recovered:-

No.1 bin in wheat field yielded 23 lbs. of threshed corn.

No.2 bin in confines of maize and millet field yielded 9 and 18 lbs. of grains.

No.3 bin in dal field yielded 14 lbs. of pulse.

No.4 bin in potato field yielded 22 lbs. of potatoes.

These are the highest figures I obtained. Even so, they throw some light on the loss caused by rats in the grain output of the

country. In some places the poorer classes turn in after the crops have been removed and search the fields for these cellars to dig out the grain.

In parts of the country cultivators contrive to exterminate the vermin by simple means. Field rats have a tendency to form colonies and select a raised site, such as a bank, a hedge surface, a heap or a piece of gravel for their settlement. Each family has its separate nest, but the runs communicate by subterranean channels. Consequently, when a farmer finds a colony he blocks the exits, leaving one open for his scheme. This is enlarged to contain the mouth of a ghara [an earthenware, narrow-necked pot], filled with combustibles that will smoke profusely, such as leaves and cowdung pats. It is buried up to the neck and sealed to the ground with puddled clay, and a hole pierced in its bottom through which a piece of live coal is inserted and kept alive by blowing with the mouth until the stuffing is ignited. The hole is now closed and opened every few minutes to admit air and to fan the fire, driving the smoke into the subterranean passages where the inmates, deprived of the outlets of escape, are suffocated. I have seen thirteen couples, large and small, killed in this way in a colony.

Rats sometimes resort to a clever expedient for robbing eggs. The usual method is to roll them into the cellar, but apparently, if the entrance is so steep as to cause the eggs to get out of control and break they carry it down in a sort of conveyance. This is managed by a rat clutching the egg tightly to its body with the four paws and letting its mates drag it into the chamber. As a rule they eat the egg when it has rotted and set. Also, they have a curious way of tasting fluids of whose nature there would appear to be some doubt in the rat's mind. The tail is inserted in the liquid and then licked. I have watched a rat do this over an open castor oil lamp and gather, from what I have heard, that it will do the same with all liquids other than water.

Appendix A

Relationships with the forest tribes called for great sensitivity and care at all times and in every project. In these excerpts we see something of St. Joseph's respect for and understanding of the Bhils and his interest in their character and way of life. The co-operation of the headmen of the tribe was essential to success and simplified its achievement. **D.M.St.J**

Working with the Bhils: relevant reports and letters

The headmen supplied the information that led to the detection of offenders: their goodwill prevented malignant or illicit acts: their regard for the official checked negligent practices: their affection for him caused them to rally from distances without summons, to put down conflagration, capture bands of thieves, or impound herds of semi-wild cattle let loose to graze in the reserves at nights. They furnished information about the marketable values of products in whose collection and removal they were the chief agents. Their intimate knowledge of the forests aided considerably in carrying through operations without undue delay. It will be obvious that such ready means of practical co-operation meant a good deal to the official who naturally wanted good results, but had not the wherewithal to aid him.

It was usual to make the most of the men's crude knowledge to compensate for the needful appliances that were not forthcoming even for the rough and ready works of forest exploitation. Thus, in aligning roads and paths their keen sense of topography dispensed with the use of surveying requisites, while useful bridges would be thrown across deep fissures at vantage points without going to the expense of time and labour in determining the positions by scientific means. Similarly, channels would be graduated purely by the eye and compared with those laid out by mathematical instruments, as also substantial quarters would be built without trained supervision. Then too, logs and poles were hewn and fashioned with the axe into marketable sizes that had all the appearances of having been sawn and axed. In the rocky country, road construction was continually coming upon massive stone and defied [refused] to yield to the implements available, and heating would be substituted for blasting. It consisted in piling over the

obstacle a load of fuel with which the forest was littered, and burning the stack until the rock got well heated; then a few buckets of water would be thrown on the stone causing it to crack all over when the fragments were easily dislodged with a pickaxe or a stake and the obstruction removed.

Forest tribes are clever at manipulating the axe and can usually convert the most uninviting timber in the rough into attractive sizes for marketable purposes to command ready sale. Of the jungle races with whom I was acquainted, the Korku tribe excelled in the skill of wood-paring. A keen eye to the structural qualities of wood enabled them to work the axe with a polish that displayed the grains to advantage, at the same time sizing the piece to trade requirements, so that a little carpentry could put it to use at once. They devoted some time and attention to the craft and were always assured of good prices.

In a dry and hilly country, we were often confronted with the problem of finding water. The first time the matter forced itself on my notice was in connection with a forest village whose people had been wanting to abandon the site because in the hot months they had to go long distances to obtain even a bare supply. But the village's retention was important as being the only one of consequence in furnishing workers for forest operations. Therefore, a good deal had been expended in boring for water, but the basalt rock comprising the surface was one of the worst formations in which to look for a yield and so far the attempts had proved costly failures. I happened to mention the case to a cultivator who was accounted to be a good judge of rocks and soils, and he suggested digging through an established white-ant heap as the means most likely to strike at a supply since the termites needed water for their colony. The advice was put into practice on my next visit to the locality, a busy hive of the insects being chosen for the experiment. According to the memory of the elders it had existed for over half-a-century. It was barely a hundred yards from the village among a mound of rocks which if anything looked as unpromising a spot as could be wished to make the attempt. But evidently, there was a fissure in the rocky crust leading to an impermeable sub-stratum, and boring disclosed a permanent spring with a copious flow. Great rejoicings marked the discovery of the water and a day was set apart for feasting and doing sacrifice and pooja at the site. Subsequently to the further delight of the village folks, a masonry well replaced the excavation.

It may be remarked that the colony contained over a score of separate nests and about thirty queen-ants in various stages of development were obtained in the diggings, a good few being as big as a sausage. Some jungle tribes eat the queen-ant which is believed to possess properties that invigorate the system.

In the rains or during floating operations, it often became necessary to negotiate swollen streams. Such things as boats and cables were unknown in jungle regions and journeys had to be made in dugouts or astride inflated skins which, though uninviting objects, were as safe in the hands of the fisher folks as the best of water crafts. The former were rudely hewn out of floatable timber, especially of the semal or wood-cotton tree which is easily worked and is moreover a good swimmer. A dugout carried three or four passengers besides the fisherman and was plied by a bamboo pole or paddling with the hands.

The other called senai was a contrivance formed of a cattle or sambar skin made supple and pumped with air until it resembled a carcass. Its merit lay in the skin being removed off the animal in the sack. This was essential for its stability and it was surprising how well the skinning was managed, as with the exception of the natural openings and the cuts to sever the hoofs, the hide remained intact like when it covered the carcass. Deer skin was preferred owing to its softer texture and greater flexibility as compared with that of cattle. A large senai could carry two passengers seated crosswise at the ends, while the ferryman stretched himself athwart the middle with feet and hands dangling in the water at the sides to paddle and guide the float. Its lightness rendered propulsion easy, so that the feet's strokes made it skim the surface with the rapidity of a racing boat. The men worked it cleverly in shooting rapids that are a feature of most hill streams. They could guide the craft through narrow falls flanked with rocks and boulders where the least mistake would have ripped the frail thing open.

Once my wife joined me in a ride on a float over a mountain stream that emerged out of a gorge with tremendous velocity. At first the men demurred to take a lady because of the perils on the journey, but a stalwart plucked up courage to volunteer for the honour and we started with misgivings marked on the men's features, my ranger insisting in riding on the path along the river's bank and keeping us in view. Our destination was about a dozen miles down the river to our camp and the man paddled the craft into mid-stream and let it

float with the current, taking care to keep it in the centre. It swept along like a cork, leaving the horseman behind in spite of his efforts to keep abreast. There were half-a-dozen rapids to get through and I confess, I had secret fears as to the wisdom of taking my wife on the excursion, but the man knew his business and guided the craft safely over the falls much to her enjoyment.

My native assistant had an unfortunate experience in crossing a swollen rivulet. The stream flowed through a slimy trough of flint rendering foothold slippery and precarious. We were warned by the guide to dismount and cross on foot, and seeing the wisdom of his advice, I got off my pony and waded across. The subordinate who rode a camel was sure the beast's pad would negotiate the bed and urged it into the water. Before he had got to the brink, the mount began to display uneasiness and was forced in by a free application of the stick. In the middle it reeled about like a tree struck by a storm, trying to keep its footing and lurched to one side and fell, plunging its riders into the water. But the scene was comical indeed. Imagine a tall creature powerless to control its lanky limbs, in an element least agreeable to its nature and indulging in loud oaths peculiar to the tribe at the risk to which it had been exposed, while, quite helpless on his high perch, the rider with his son clasped to his waist making frantic efforts to steady the mount, then the collapse with a great splash and the men emerging from the water dripping with wet and slime. It seemed a fitting judgement on the unnecessary chastisement inflicted on a dumb creature.

Forest Department
19-7-05
Bhopawar Agency C.I.   27-7-05

My dear St. Joseph

Your duties take you so much amongst the Bhils that you must have fairly good insight into their characters etc.

I have before me the question of the maintenance of the Malwa Bhil Corps and shall be glad if you will kindly give me the benefit of your knowledge on the subject.

The ostensible object of the corps was to provide a means of livelihood to Bhils and by the discipline etc. to extend civilizing influences amongst the tribe.

How do the Bhils view the idea and does the liberty to enlist appeal to them generally? Has this enlistment caused civilizing influences to extend? Is it looked upon as an honourable means of livelihood readily availed of?

Why do the Bhils show signs of unrest if a detachment of their own brothers is sent into the country?

There are doubtless many other points connected with Bhil character in general and which you can give me valuable information upon.

Suppose it was decided to disband the corps, what would be the result? Or suppose it was decided to remove the corps and place it in another part of India how would the general population of Bhils view the results and how would it affect the men removed? Are true Bhils enlisted or is it only the raff and Bhilalas and Naiks etc. who enlist?

27 July
Yours sincerely
F.G. Bevill
Dhar

29-vii-05

Dear Major Beville

Herewith the information called for in your letter of the 27th inst.

Most of the men recruited for the M.B.C. (Malwa Bhil Corps) are from outside the Agency, chiefly from the Panch Mahal district of Guzerath. Among those who enlist locally, I think, the greater number are from Jhabua and then from Jobat and Ali-Rajpur. The corps does not appeal to the local Bhils and if the cases of those who enlist are sifted, it will be found that most of them have joined owing to outside influence e.g.: a) enticement held out about pay and prospects in the corps, b) advice to parents by the P.A.'s, superintendents, Dewans or other high officials to make the young and unruly bloods join or c) advice by a member of the corps who has married into the family and risen in rank.

The enlistment has not caused civilising influences nor is it looked upon as an honourable means of livelihood; firstly, it is considered as curtailing freedom about which every Bhil is very zealous, secondly, as leading to habitual drunkenness for, though as a rule Bhils are fond of liquor, excepting on high days and

holidays and the cases of the few who are addicted to it, they drink little or nothing and many are practically abstainers; thirdly as loosening morality among men and women alike; fourthly as engendering habits of sloth and ease. In the matter of the last three points, I have heard complaints from relatives and friends myself. Again, about two years ago during Holi (the spring festival), there was a fracas between the local Bhils and the detachment Bhils, posted at Silavad when the former ridiculed the accoutrement of the latter, telling them to throw them away and come and fight them (local Bhils) with their ancestral weapons.

The cause of unrest is that the posting of a detachment is looked upon as synonymous to putting down a rising or for the purpose of subduing the wilder spirits or conflicting with their freedom. Thus on arrival of a detachment, especially if it is the first occasion, rumours are set afloat, that the Sirkar wishes to exterminate them or to seize their young men for service elsewhere or to subdue the wilder spirits or for guarding their monuments.

I do not think disbanding the corps would affect the country in any way. The corps men would soon settle down among their people and take to their original pursuits. As regards the removal of the corps elsewhere, the population in general would view the matter indifferently, but the men themselves and their relatives would doubtless clamour against the change.

In my opinion the Bhils do not enlist, most of the young men joining are those who have come under civilizing influences. There are a few scions of good, influential families in the corps, but it will be found their enlistment originally was due to pressure on outside influence. I think the men who mostly enlist are naiks, the predatory class among the Bhils, who are often found living on the outskirts of towns and large villages. There are few if any mankars, the lowest type of Bhils or Turvees Patlias etc. etc., the best of the Bhil classes.

The Bhils as a rule are a shy, restless people dwelling in rude erections of wood, bamboos and grass, and ready to vacate at the first sign of provocation, discontentment, sickness or disease. In such instances they more often than not remove to a more sequestered spot in the neighbourhood. They are very lightly clad, a piece of cloth which passes between their legs and fastens to a thick thread round the waist and similarly another piece around the head which exposes the crown, is usually all they wear. They

either go bare-footed or wear sandals, consisting of a piece of leather for a sole, fastened to the foot with string, or bark. It will be observed, therefore, how repugnant the dress adopted by the Bhil corps men must be to their feelings. They love sport and cover great distances walking or running. A quiet and unannounced visit into the precincts of the village will often reveal the men and boys hunting hare, pigs, foxes and even cats. I have known them to run down sambar, blue-bull and bear.

They are truthful and do not easily forget an injury. On the other hand they are grateful for the slightest kindness shown. They are worst under the influence of drink, when any wrongs suffered in the past are remembered and magnified so much that they are only too ready to wreak vengeance; they are especially resentful of slights cast on wives and mothers.

They dislike manual labour and rather than work as coolies, they will do without food or live on the coarsest substance, such as leaves or flower buds of plants. If not otherwise engaged, they will roam over the forests in search of edible and other products for home consumption or barter or sale.

Should they like a person they will admit him to their homes and give him of their best; the women (wives) too will come and bend their heads at the feet as a mark of submission, while the unmarried girls will chat and laugh around. They will consult him as an oracle and take his advice as regards naming of children, marriages, and other household matters.

On the other hand they resent intrusion by those whom they do not like or of whose character and institutions they have doubts; in such cases the women will keep aloof.

Their sense of hearing and seeing are highly developed and in the forests they fear nothing. In the town or outside their country they are apt to be cowards and will allow themselves to be bullied by the smallest youngsters.

Yours sincerely,
J.D. St. Joseph

THE PIONEER (1)
Monday 16th December 1901

CENTRAL INDIA
From a correspondent at BARWANI 10th December

The Honorable Mr. Bayley, Agent to the Governor-General in Central India, whose visit was looked forward to with great enthusiasm by the people, arrived in Talwara on the 4th instant by the new road Thikri-Talwara, constructed as a famine relief work. He was accompanied by the Political Agent, Captain Barnes and his Assistant Mr. Gabriel C.S. After visiting wells and baories (2) and reading some of the old inscriptions in them, and after ascertaining the extent of the impending distress, he came to Anjar on the 5th instant, where he examined and distributed prizes to the boys' and girls' school and inspected the new dispensary, thana (3) and the ginning (4) factory. The following day he reached the capital town of the State under a salute of 13 guns. The whole of the afternoon was occupied in the prize distribution, the laying of the foundation stone, presentation of the Kaiser-I-Hind medals, and holding a Durbar of State officials."

In his address to the large assembly Mr. Bayley said that he was very pleased to have the opportunity of visiting Barwani, but regretted that it was impossible for the Rana Sahib to be present, engaged as he was in pursuing his studies at the Daly College, in preparation for his life as ruler of the State. Meanwhile, continued Mr. Bayley, much excellent work had been done during the young Chief's minority, under the wise guidance of Mr. Barnes, by local officials all of whom were to be congratulated on the result of their labours. His Excellency the Viceroy had therefore been pleased to bestow on two of the officials of the State silver medals of the Kaiser-I-Hind decoration, an award instituted by Queen Victoria to reward services rendered to the people of her Indian Empire.

Mr. Bayley added that he had hoped to present these medals at a special Durbar to be held for the purpose; but owing to Her Majesty's lamented death this was impossible. He was however very glad to have the opportunity of presenting them that day in the presence, as he hoped, of some of those who had benefitted by the labours of the recipients.

Turning to Mr. St. Joseph, Mr. Bayley said: "It gives me very

great pleasure to hand you this medal. Your service to the Barwani State began nearly four years ago when you came here from the Central Provinces as Chief Forest Officer. Your management of the State Forests has been eminently successful and your tact and consideration in dealing with the officials of the State and with the wild jungle tribes, who are persons principally affected by the new forest rules, have been very marked. During the famine of 1899-1900 you organised relief measures with excellent results, the Bhils and other jungle tribes being employed at grass cutting and similar occupations in all respects congenial to them.

Some Rs 27,000 were expended on these and 5,000,000 units were relieved, while the State realised no less than Rs 38,000, or a profit of Rs 1,000, by the sale of grass and other jungle produce. I am glad to think that a wider sphere of utility has now been opened to you owing to your appointment as Forest Officer to the Dhar and Ali-Rajpur State, as well as to Barwani and I sincerely trust that your efforts to restore the valuable forest property of these States to its proper level will be crowned with success."

(1) A well-known newspaper
(2) Wall enclosed wells
(3) Police Station
(4) Cotton or spinning factory.

Letters

14 March 1902 to Captain Barnes: Mr. Bayley was pleased to notice when on tour in Barwani and Ali Rajpur the keen interest which St. Joseph took in his important duties, and the excellent terms on which he appeared to be with the Bhils.

1903 from Captain Barnes to J.D. St. Joseph, Chief Forest Officer of the Bhopawar Agency: The Hon'ble the Agent to the Governor General fully concurs in the high opinion expressed by me of the work done by you and he notes with pleasure the commendation bestowed by you on your subordinates, especially Mr. Chaju-Ram.

9th September 1905 from Captain Barnes to the First Assistant to the Agent to the Governor General in Central India: I have pleasure to bring to notice the names of officials especially mentioned by Mr.

St. Joseph in his report, as also the services of Mr. St. Joseph himself, whose perseverance and tact in dealing with the Bhil population has so greatly conduced to the results achieved.

Mr. Bayley, Agent to the Governor General from 1900-1905 wrote, on his retirement, a very kind letter from the Residency in Hyderabad.

My Dear St. Joseph
I was so busy at the end of the time at Indore that letter writing was very difficult, but I must not delay any longer to wish you goodbye, and, if you will allow me to do so, to tell you how very fully I appreciate the excellent work which you have been doing in the Bhopawar Agency during the time that I was Governor General's Agent. Forest work among a destructive and shy people like the Bhils is by no means easy, but you were wonderfully successful both in winning their confidence and in checking their habit of burning the hillsides. You also rendered very useful service in other respects to the Dhar Durbar, and I must not omit to mention the good influence which you exercised some years ago on the Rana of Ali-Rajpur at a critical point in his career. Every Political Agent under whom you worked spoke of you to me, deservedly, in the highest terms and I am very glad to think that the Bhopawar States are likely to have the benefit of your services for many years to come.
With every good wish for your future career
I remain
Yours sincerely
signed Chs. S. Bayley

From Major F.G. Beville. 1905
Bhopawwar Agency
Central India
To J.D. St. J.: Very many thanks for your very interesting work on the Bhils which will be most useful to me. It is most good of you to have taken so much trouble in preparing it.

October 22 1905
From Capt. C.E. Luard, Superintendent of Ethnography for Central India to the Political Agent in Bhopawar: Please convey

thanks to Mr. St. Joseph for his note on Bhils. It is very good of him to have taken so much trouble with all his own work to do also, and I am very grateful to him for it.

Appendix B

A Bhil Legend, chosen from J.D. St.J's collection

About the ancestry of the Barwani Chiefs related by Gamhira Naik of Borkheri, and, regarding his connection with the ruling family. The old Naik is now over 70 years of age.

Some centuries before the advent of the British, his ancestor, Kalia Naik, emigrated from Ekalbara, a village close to Pulsood and now included in the Sendhwa district of Indore. As a youth, the Naik (Kalia) was in charge of the goats in his village. One morning while grazing them in the scrub jungle adjoining the village, the Mandloi's son came up and caught one of the goats by the ear and insisted in dragging it away. The Bhil remonstrated with the young man, but he would not let go of the goat and instead hit the Bhil a clout with his stick. This incensed him so much, that he strung his bow and shot the Nandlio's son who fell down. The Bhil, terrified at the result of his action, fled from the place and hid in the khodra (deep nala) [ditch] on the outskirts of the village. In the afternoon his wife came there to fetch water and, seeing him hiding, enquired the reason, when he mentioned the occurrence, stating the advisability of fleeing from the place in consequence. The wife insisted on accompanying him, and went and fetched food and clothing for their journey. They started as soon as it was dark and after several days of wanderings in the Satpura Mountains which were then occupied by extensive forests, they arrived at Borkheri. (The village is on the Nerbudda, 16 miles due West of Barwani, and about 40 miles from Ekalbara.) At the time, Borkheri was inhabited by a race of Gujars and was the seat of a Rajput Chieftain, called Dharmi Raja. News of the Bhil's arrival was soon carried to the Chief who sent for him and inquired into his antecedents. On hearing his story, he took him in service, appointing him to supply the stables with grass.

Kalia Naik, accordingly, set about his work and started with a daranta (scythe) to cut grass on the slopes of the hill known as Baba Bhurha or Jhirmal deo. The instrument being blunt would not cut with ease, so he picked up a stone and began sharpening it, this not only gave it an edge, but converted it into gold and silver (half and half). Kalia had no idea about the value of metals and could not distinguish one from the other and so took no account of the prize

in his possession. On returning, he handed over the implement with the load of grass to the stable servants who took it to the officer. He was surprised at seeing the transformation and took it and showed it to the Chief who ordered that another larger scythe should be supplied to the Naik on the following day. This, too, would not cut easily and Kalia began to sharpen it as before, with the result that it also changed into gold and silver. Like the other, it was handed in at the stable after the day's work and eventually shown to the Chief who sent for the Naik and enquired the cause of the difference, when he related what he had done. He was told to fetch the stone the next time and he brought it and made it over to the Chief. Other implements were now tested with the stone, when it was discovered that on applying it on iron, the friction would change the iron into gold and silver. Consequently, all the iron implements and things in the Chief's possession were rubbed and transformed into the precious metals. The Chief now ordered that, in future, instead of collecting the land revenue in cash or kind, it should be paid in the form of iron implements. Thus, as these were received, they were converted into the precious metals.

In course of time, the Chief's wealth increased so much that it was spread abroad far and wide. It reached the ears of Rum Jum Padshah who ruled at a great distance away in the North. He was piqued to hear that there should be another ruler competing with him in fame for wealth. He therefore ordered two tumbas full of regiments to get ready to march on Dharmi Raja. Accordingly, they started for the South to attack the Raja. In the meanwhile, Ragat Rori Mata (a local deity at the entrance of the pass into Borkheri) appeared before the Raja in a dream and apprised him of his danger. The Raja was not only surprised to hear the account, but expressed his inability to cope with the forces sent out against him, and invoked the deity for assistance. The Mata promised to guard the principal pass (into Borkheri) and summoned 900 Bhairons (deified heroes) to take up positions on her right and 900 Joguns (deified wizards and witches) to stand on her left while Bhil archers led by Kalia Naik kept in reserve at the back. The troops of Rum Jum Padshah now arrived at the pass and encountered the mixed bands of Bhairons, Joguns and Bhils and a fierce battle ensued. The Joguns worked their witchcraft and caused the arms of the enemies to become powerless to strike, while the Bhairons and Bhils slew them in numbers till one tumba full of regiment lay dead at the

pass. The remaining troops withdrew from the scene and returned to their country where they extolled the deeds of miracle and valour performed by the forces of Dharmi Raja.

The news incensed the Padshah more than ever and made him determined to reduce the Chief. Fresh levies, sufficient in numbers to fill three tumbas were ordered to get ready to march South against the Raja. The commanders on this occasion however, divided their forces and leaving two tumbas of regiment to attack the pass, the third tumba made a diversion of several miles and descended on Borkheri by way of Nalti which was unguarded. The Raja was completely surprised and prepared to flee, so taking his principal Rani and a few faithful followers and the stone, he escaped into the interior of the Pachham Pahars. A band of the victorious troops pursued him closely. At the mouth of the Sagbara defile, there stood an enormous Sag (Teak) tree, which observing the Raja's plight, decided to aid him. Consequently, when the Raja with his retinue passed through under it, the tree fell across the opening with a great crash barring the passage through the defile, so that the pursuers finding themselves discomfited, gave up the chase and returned and joined the rest of the troops.

The Raja went by way of the Jharkal ravine to the Toranmal plateau (in Khandesh) where he rested and meditated on his struggles and, attributing them to the stone, he cast it into the lake on the plateau, in order to safeguard himself against further annoyance. After a short stay at the lake, he started to wander over the hills in search of a site for a new abode and eventually fixed on the Ramgarh plateau (in Barwani) as his future residence. A fort was built and a city soon sprang up all around. Kalia Naik now headed a deputation and prayed the Raja to return to Borkheri, the home of his ancestor. The Chief demurred at first, but was got to consent and left the new city. When he came to Borkheri, he became disheartened at seeing the devastation caused by his enemies and declined to stay there. Consequently, he crossed the Nerbudda and occupied a new site, some miles distant. Here, he built a fort, and a city soon sprang up which he called Dharam-Rai after himself. He restored the worship of the local shrines and passed his days in meditation and prayer doing charitable acts by dispensing largesses lavishly on the poor and needy. His actions pleased the gods who conferred on him the power of transmigration.

One night in his sleep, Dharmi Raja dreamt that a ship was

becalmed in the ocean and in urgent need of his assistance to enable it to continue its voyage. Consequently, transforming himself into a spirit, he went to her aid and having started the vessel, returned to his bed wet and slimy, owing to his passage through the ocean. The Rani finding the bed damp and slimy, got up and awoke him, and insisted on knowing the cause of his being in that condition. The Raja tried to pacify her, but she would brook no excuse, and he had to promise to tell her in the morning. At daybreak the Rani reminded him of the promise; whereupon he asked her to prepare an offering of rice, coconut and red paint and accompany him to the Nerbudda where he would disclose the secret. Accordingly, they both went to the river and at the spot now known as Haranphal, they offered prayers to the river goddess. The ceremony over, Dharmi Raja took some of the offerings in his hand and standing in the Nerbudda implored his wife not to question him about the secret if she desired him to remain with her. But as she would not desist, he told her, and immediately after, the Nerbudda enveloped him in her folds, so that he disappeared from earth. To perpetuate his memory the Rani had temples erected over his footprints on the rocks on which he stood, while in the river bed and the temples still stand at the sites.

On the Raja's disappearance, the Rani with her two sons, Padam Singh and Lal Singh, returned to Borkheri village where the sons of Kalia Naik, Balia and Salia, formed a guard for her protection. On one occasion, she undertook a journey to Bijasen (a village 8 miles from Borkheri) on business to the Patel (headman) accompanied by an escort of the Bhil brothers. At night she was warned by the Patlan (Patel's wife) that her husband had conspired to keep her a prisoner in the house. The Rani, therefore, left immediately to return to Borkheri. On the way, the Bhils questioned her regarding her precipitate departure and after some demur, she told them the cause of her leaving so suddenly. This angered the Bhil brothers who having escorted her in safety, returned to attack the Patel for daring to conspire against the Rani. The Patel, having been warned of their intentions, dug a moat round his house, covering it with grass and mud to hide the ditch so as to deceive the assailants while he himself remained ensconced in a niche. The Bhil brothers soon arrived and on going over the covering, the eldest, Balia, fell into the moat and was immediately cut down by the Patel, whereupon the younger, Salia, shot his arrow and killed the Patel

and returned with his head to the Rani. The Rani was, however, very much distressed at the death of her faithful servant and decided to retire from life. Consequently, having assigned Borkheri and Murkutta villages in jagir to the two brothers and their descendants, she left with her eldest son, Padam Singh, for Ramgarh. The younger, Lal Singh, stayed on and founded the fort of Rajgarh on the Goi River close to Borkheri. Here, he stayed and administered the country along the Nerbudda for his brother. Their descendants are the present rulers of Barwani.

The Naiks continued in the enjoyment of the revenues from the two villages till the Mutiny (1857) when owing to risings among the Bhil tribes the State was taken under British management. Old sanads and grants were now called in by Lieutenant Cadell, the administrator, for verification. The Naik, however, could not produce the copper plate granted to his ancestors by the Rani, as it had been mislaid owing to family dissensions. But, on the strength of oral evidence, the jagir over one of the villages, Murkatta, was confirmed on the Naik's family, while the other, Borkheri, escheated to the State. The jagir of Murkatta continued with the Naik's till 1903 or 1904, when it was also resumed by the Revenue officer on some excuse. Thus, the family are now reduced to the sukree (grain doles per plough) paid him by the people of the village, Borkheri.

Note 1: The allusion in the above to tumba which is the shell of the pepo or fruit of the gourd (Lagenaria vulgaris) indicating the strength of the regiments, denotes the numerical entity of the forces. It signifies the numbers of soldiers that it would take to fill the shell of the pepo with the dust set up by the march of soldiers through the main gateway of the citadel, where the shell would be suspended for the purpose of collecting the dust.

Note 2: The lineage of the Barwani Chiefs goes back to the 9th century, when tradition has it, the ancestors emigrated from Chitor in Mewar.

Note 3: Borkheri is now a Bhil settlement, but it shows signs of having once been strongly fortified. It lies almost in a hollow flanked by steep slopes, except on the East, where the entrance is by a gorge through a chain of low hills and, here, is the shrine of Ragat Rori Mata.

Note 4: At Haranphal are the rapids of the Nerbudda where the river forces an entrance through the Satpuras. In descending

through the gorge, the river forks out into three or four tongues or currents, 15 to 30 feet wide, between which intervene the rocks on which are built little temples. Tradition has it, that once an antelope (black buck) hunted by dogs from the opposite side crossed the river by bounding over the rocks and, hence, the name Haranphal, temples being erected over the hoof marks embedded on the rocks. The Naik's legend, however, attributes the presence of the temples to a different cause, as has been noticed above.

Appendix C

The Barwani State Forests
From St Joseph's Work Records

In the Bhopawar Agency the Barwani State is bounded on the north by the Nerbudda River, on the south and west by the British district of Khandesh, and on the east by the State of Holkar. The forests occupy the hill ranges and detached spurs of the Satpuras enclosing in the centre the confused mass of hills and valleys under cultivation. The climate is dry and cold during the winter from November to February, very hot and dry from March till June, warm and steamy during the rains from July to October.

Generally speaking the inhabitants of the state are a fairly well to do class of agriculturists, labourers and cattle farmers. The census of 1901 shows that 50% are Hindus, 5% Mohammedans and 45% Animists. In the towns and villages they are mostly of Aryan stock, but within the forests the villages are almost exclusively occupied by aboriginal tribes of Bhil origin, many of whom have shown an aptitude for agriculture and settled down as good cultivators. Most of them, however, are content with reaping a meagre harvest, supplementing their scanty earnings by trading in forest produce.

The dwellings in the State are of four distinct types. Those belonging to patels, headmen of Aryan stock or members of trading and literary classes, consist often of a two-storied block on one side of a quadrangle, the other three sides being closed in by living rooms, granaries and stabling all built mostly of teak. The main entrance to the courtyard, wide enough to admit a cart, is closed by massive doors of teak, bound and studded with iron. The building is roofed with tiles, laid on split or whole bamboos tied or nailed across rafters. The value of the timber used is about 500 rupees.

In the second type of habitation the main building consists of one storey, the walls being encased in a timber framework, sometimes hollow, to be utilised as bins for storing grain. The roof is lightly tiled, the tiles resting on bamboos laid across roughly dressed rafters. Sometimes a courtyard is enclosed by a mud wall with supported roofing of thatch or tile providing a shelter for cattle. Cattle pens of graziers and inferior castes are left open to the

sky. The whole woodwork costs from 75-200 rupees and lasts for 30 to 40 years.

The aboriginal dwellings are made of wood, bamboo and grass. The walls are of wattle or bamboo matting, daubed with a thick plaster of cow dung and mud, fixed between rails and stout posts 4 to 6 feet apart, on which rest the transoms supporting the long rafters from the ridge pole. The roof is of grass thatch, laid over brushwood spread over a light trellis. To prevent the roof being blown off, poles of heavy wood like sali are placed over the thatch and firmly tied at the ends. A few paces in front of the dwelling is the cattle pen. Grain is stored in large bamboo baskets, daubed with cow dung and mud plaster and placed within or alongside the main dwelling. The whole construction is firmly hedged all round with thorns and bamboos, with a wicket opening into the space in front. The cost of wood and other produce used in these houses varies from 20 to 100 rupees.

The last type of dwelling is a rude one-roomed thatched hut, with walls of wattle, plastered over with cow dung and mud, the thatch laid on brushwood spread over a light bamboo trellis. The wood of such huts costs a few rupees and needs renewal after 5 years or so.

Agricultural implements used are of the primitive type: the hal or plough, tephun or drill, khakar a combination of harrow and rake, and the kopla or bullock hoe. To watch their fields while the crops are ripening, cultivators usually erect machans, temporary sheds raised above the surface on posts stuck in the ground. On ceremonial occasions of marriages, births or deaths it is customary to build an awning of grass under which the feast is held. Aboriginal tribes erect monoliths of stone or teak called gatta to perpetuate the memory of the dead.

During the six months preceding the rainy season the majority of the aboriginal population maintain themselves on jungle products. Fruits, flowers, bulbs, roots and tubers are collected and eaten either alone or with cereals.

The two principal types of forest in Barwani are those where teak predominates or where the anjan is the dominant tree; the one requiring a well drained, moist soil and the other dry, hard ground pervious to roots. The country in the Nerbudda and Goi basins is par excellence the home of the anjan. Teak on the other hand thrives best in the country included in the hills south of the Goi valley.

Mixed forest with anjan covers about four fifths of the area. Besides anjan, the principal constituent species are dhaora, khair, sali, karin, kakar-seja, rohin, moein, kalan, gurar, chichola, palas and bhutakas. Teak, tinas and sadar are found at the bottom of slopes and deep ravines but never in any quantity and seldom attaining large dimensions. The anjan never exceeds 100 feet in height while its girth varies from 4 to 12 feet. The spread of cultivation and consequent population have proved disastrous to the tree's existence. Not only are its leaves prized for fodder but the bark from saplings is extensively used for cordage. Sali predominates on the higher slopes: mahua, charoli, tendu and bahera are usually seen on terraced slopes; kalan is plentiful on the outlying spurs, isolated hills and ridges bordering the Nerbudda.

In mixed forest with teak, occupying the hill ranges included in the southern chain of the Satpuras, this tree is markedly predominant. Its chief companions are tinals and sadar with shisham and bhea on the higher ranges. Other associated species are dhaora, kaim, haldar, guran, sali, dhaman, aonla and khairbora. The wild plantain ran-kela grows luxuriantly on shaded aspects of the higher ranges or in damp ravines.

The principal woods from the point of view of the exploiter are teak, shisham, bhea, sadar, haldar and tinas which attain large dimensions; the average stature of teak is about 50 feet, but trees 65-70 feet high are not uncommon. Their girth, averaging 5 feet, can be 8-10 feet. Ring countings show that teak takes 120-150 years to attain a girth of 5 feet. The best sadar is found on concave surfaces, a girth of 12 feet often being reached.

As regards the condition of the forests, the absence of any conservation until within the last 10 years (i.e. 1896-1906) has resulted in all timber being exploited from accessible tracts; while unregulated grazing of the past has interfered with the healthy development of young growth. The chief sources of injury to the trees are fire, grazing, night frosts, lopping, barking for fibre, unregulated nomadic cultivation and insects, of which the most harm is done by the teak defoliator (hyblae puera). Its ravages usually commence at the end of the rains and last for two months or so.

The first semblance of management began with the appointment of a Forest Officer in October 1894. Prior to this, no conservation worth the name existed, forests being looked upon as

sylvan wastes that needed no conserving. Shifting patch cultivation, known to the Bhils as Butli or Joomti prevailed unchecked; unregulated fellings were carried on without let or hindrance and lopping of shisham, anjan, tinas and sadar was customary among graziers with large herds of cattle. Similarly, pollarding teak leaves for thatching and barking anjan saplings for fibre, were extensively practised.

Exports of timber began to be taxed about 1870. The revenue this collected averaged about 13,000 rupees for the next five years. To prevent illicit exports and promiscuous cuttings an ingenious method was adopted whereby the Bhils were allowed during one month of the year to cut and remove for sale whatever they pleased from wherever they liked.

The staff was augmented about 1890 and at the beginning of 1891 consisted of 27 members all told, costing 2,516 rupees per annum; there was the daroga (who drew 30 rupees a month) a naib, or assistant, 6 daffadars, 18 forest guards and one clerk (the lowest paid guard drawing 5 rupees a month.

Work undertaken for the benefit and management of the forests has had various aims: to assure their protection from fire, to plan departmental fellings and thinnings, cultural operations, building of quarters for the establishment, the construction and restoration of wells (baoris and bunds) and silvicultural experiments. One characteristic of the Barwani forests is that the best species of tree have always been the most maltreated, whilst inferior species, except in the vicinity of cultivated land, have been allowed to flourish.

In past years different woods have been marketed for building purposes or to meet agricultural needs (such as carts, wheels, ploughs, yokes, axe handles, clod crushers, goading rods); bamboos were needed for manufactured articles like baskets, sieves, trellis work, fish snares, bows and arrows, fishing rods, brooms, walking sticks; teak, gurar, semal and gular were needed to make boats and canoes, baikal and arni for tobacco pipes. Other trees met other needs such as bed frames and legs, furniture, combs and toys and troughs for watering cattle.

As for fuel all woods were needed for lime burning; khair and dhaora for cooking on charcoal; special charcoal from mahua and khair for blacksmiths and goldsmiths.

The forest also supplied oil for cooking and lighting from the

mahua fruit, the flower being used for making spirits. Rosia and kanji oil, honey, musli and amaltas to name only a few were used for medicine.

The chief export lines were the Agra-Bombay road through Mhow, others joining that road ran from Barwani to Thikri, from Rajpur to Shaida. Water transport by the Nerbudda would have afforded easy acces to Broach on the Bombay-Baroda Central India Railway had it not been for the succession of numerous rapids encountered after Murkutta whereby the passage is rendered both dangerous and costly, not to be attempted on any account.

Quite one half of the produce finds its way to the British district of Khandesh, to Kuksi and Nisarpur in the Native States, in the Barwani State itself to Rajpur, Pansemal and Khetia. In the former days when teak, bhea and shisham timbers were procurable, Indore and Mhow, distant 104 and 90 miles respectively, used to be important markets, but as the supply of large trees became exhausted exports to these places ceased. Anjan logs still (1906) find their way to Dhar and Sirdarpur, distant 80 and 55 miles respectively.

Produce is removed either in carts, by head loads or on pack animals. Dragging is employed for heavy logs or where there are no cart tracks to reach the roads. Logs for fuel used to be rolled down hill sides but this is now forbidden. The daily wages for unskilled labour is 3-4 annas per man 1-2 annas per woman and 1 anna per child.

Light fellings only are now required in the teak area under a 15 year rotation. Fruit trees such as mahua, temru, charoli and edible fig, unless aged and useless should be spared to prevent erosion. All trees for reservation should be marked with a chest high ring of paint.

Management and conservation issues

An attempt must be made to give an idea of the practical measures bearing on the work of forest conservancy as they confronted the head executive before the advent of scientific methods.

Forest boundaries in the early stages of afforestation were laid out haphazardly; not only did they challenge the configuration of a hilly country but trespassed unnecessarily on village lands and even invaded the environs of the habitations themselves. On the

other hand they sometimes receded simply to exclude valuable growth. Such was an excellent sample of the work done by low paid subordinates whom it was impossible to supervise. An undermanned department could not keep up with the surveyors in the task of providing cleared belts, or pillars to set down the bare outline of future boundaries. Before the landmarks could be provided, lines were shifted with a view to encroachments, and later on became fruitful causes of dispute.

In my capacity of Working Plans Assistant in Betul and Hoshangabad forests the work of boundary revision formed part of my duties. Like all work carelessly performed, it entailed more trouble and labour than would have resulted from relaying new boundaries. On one occasion I was seated outside with maps lying all about me when the watchman turned up to take me out for an afternoon stalk. He became interested in the pictures, as he called the drawings, and inquired about them. After listening attentively he pointed out the original lines so as to save me the vexation of toiling on the revisions. He showed me the first demarcation, which had long since been obliterated, putting me in possession of the facts, first hand. The man's uninvited intervention taught me to make use in future of this source of information, so that whenever there was cause for suspecting the removal of old lines, I took care to enlist the goodwill of the watchman and got through the work swimmingly.

Departmentalism fetters an official with set rules difficult to override without inviting displeasure. This is not unnatural, considering the time and labour expended by the brains of the Service in drawing up the rules and getting them passed into law. Some heads of departments encourage initiative among their men, others are unsympathetic towards those contemplating a new plan; but rules may be relaxed as well as tightened in their scope. In latter days belief in the infallibility of fire protection has been shaken. Enormous sums were expended on the prevention or control of forest fires. No means were left untried to impress upon the staff the gravity of the offence if rules were disobeyed. So much so that the fire season became a nightmare, disturbing everyone's peace of mind. I remember how, on my first assuming office, the official whom I was relieving described the various protective measures then in force with a serious insistence that was awe-inspiring.

The jungles included in the charge were strictly preserved and wherever I went, evidence of the importance of fire protection dominated everything else connected with forestry. In the early years of my career, being an eye-witness with little or no experience, I was second to none in carrying out orders relating to fire rules. In the course of time, however, observation made me modify my view.

On an excessively dry and hard surface, impenetrable to the tended roots of germinating plants, seasonal fires were welcome, as they cracked and blistered the crust, preparing it for the reception of the seed. Looking back to the decades when the existing forests grew up, it was apparent that they had had no special protection from fire; their growth had been secured by the absence in any numbers of human beings and cattle. To me it seemed that man was upsetting the provisions of nature by the application of rules which involved much expenditure, (and only met with partial success).

Accordingly, when free to act independently, I tried to make the fire measures suit the conditions of plant life, in order to blend the issues for and against fire protection. The results were as satisfactory as might be expected with untrained staff whose low pay rendered them inattentive to duties and so often spoiled or delayed promising efforts.

Wherever good regrowth existed fires were kept out for three or four years, when burning, following the rains, quickly rid the area of superfluous growth by lessening cover, so that the plants restarted with fresh vigour while the ground was prepared for the germination of new seedlings. On the other hand areas, where reproduction was more or less absent, were treated annually to partial burning, letting fires pass through during the early months when the undergrowth was still green, and then concentrating efforts to safeguard them during the hot period that followed.

In arid country, the raising of plants by artificial means was impracticable owing to expense and uncertainty of results, but various attempts were made nevertheless to encourage reproduction. The expedient that met with most success was a copy of the primitive mode of cultivation with axe and fire. It consisted in clearing plots, burning the rubbish over the area and raking up the soil when suitable seed would be sown broadcast over the patches. These operations were repeated for two or three years, after which the areas were strictly preserved from fire and grazing.

Once an accident led to a useful discovery. In a corner of a little nursery used for experimental purposes, a quantity of teak seed was laid out to dry. A fence of dry grass and thorns caught fire and spread to the layer and was reported to have reduced the seed to cinders. A month or so later another report followed mentioning that the piece of ground which had been occupied by the seeds had been transformed into a germination bed of teak seedlings. This was interesting news and I took the earliest opportunity to pay the place a visit. Truly the spot was carpeted with young plants struggling to keep abreast of each other. Evidently, the fire had rapidly passed through the layer, cracking or partially burning the strong shells and so setting fire to the kernels which burst into activity as soon as the soil was moistened with rain. It was apparent that seeds with hard shells needed some such treatment in order to expedite germination. So then, seeds possessing thick envelopes, like those of teak, harra, bahera, chironji, were subjected to a roasting process before being sown. At first this was done in ovens or pans and the seed kept until opportunities to sow occurred. It was subsequently found that a much higher percentage germinated if the treatment was effected over the sowing beds, and sprinklings of light combustibles such as dry leaves and twigs were spread over the seed and fired. These operations were most successful if carried out at the beginning of the rains.

There were precise rules about leaving no stumps in coppice fellings, and dressing the stools level with the ground. The treatment answered well in moist localities but not on dry, hard areas because the close cutting caused deep, wide cracks in the wood which exposed and killed the adventitious buds, impairing regrowth of shoots. Softwoods were affected less than hard as they were well supplied with sap to withstand the scorching heat. It was noticed that the raised stools outside coppice areas were the better for being felled high, as the injury was not as serious as with the close cuts. Consequently future fellings were made with raised stools and there was no reason to regret the change.

In growing new woods one of the aims was to grow tinas with teak. Both were highly valuable species, the former serving as an excellent underwood in a high forest of teak. The difficulty lay in how to make the combination successful. For a long time we were at our wits' end to discover a means of blending the needs of the two species in order to bring them into useful association.

It so happened that during the prolonged drought numerous fields bordering on reserves had gone out of cultivation; many of them contained teak preserved by the former owners because of their value. Seeds from the tinas standing inside the reserves were blown out into the fields and sown broadcast so that, when the drought ended and the work of reclaiming the lands began, young self-sown tinas were already established. After ploughing these threw up abundant root suckers to replace the parent stems. Here was an answer to the problem we had been trying to solve. Superfluous species were killed, the ground, burnt, raked and sown, produced after three years a large crop of promising sucker shoots. Success seemed assured but before the plants could attain any size the site had to be sacrificed to the land hunger of the people.

The great drought played havoc with vegetable life generally, and for years a feature of the forests was the sorry spectacle presented by trees in various stages of decline. Attempts were made to arrest their mortality by removing dying stems so that new shoots might replace them, but it was found that their vitality had been too severely tested by the complete and prolonged withdrawal of moisture from the surface. Owing perhaps to the fact that young growth in favourable localities is more susceptible to hardship than if used to severe conditions, so in contrast with the dry, baked slopes, the mortality of trees in valleys is infinitely greater. This proved beyond doubt that the ratio of moisture maintained in the neighbourhood of growth is higher than in open spaces. The position of strata may influence the presence of moisture. I have known springs to increase their flow in a period of drought when water all round had ceased to be obtainable.

Part of the forests in which my work lay was the home of that delicate and valuable species, the anjan or ironwood tree. It seems a misnomer to call this tree delicate, for it flourishes on the driest of stony slopes imaginable and yet the word is suitable if one considers how successfully the species has resisted attempts at artificial reproduction. A man from home will easily see in young trees their close resemblance to the birch, but older trunks are too massive to be comparable.

Apart from its commercial uses, anjan has an aesthetic value quite its own. The wood has tremendous vertical strength and can support almost any weight. Where the tree abounds it is not

uncommon to see a log used as a post for the converging arches of bastions or towers in old forts, supporting several tons of masonry. In some cases, the uprights have supported the fortifications for centuries and still retain their strength, as in the old fort at Bhabra in the Ali-Rajpur State.

The anjan provides highly prized fodder for cattle, especially needed to keep up a supply of milk when animals are run down. Its fibre has strength and durability and is employed by forest tribes as substitute for hemp or coir string or ropes. It produces leaves at the height of the hot weather and no one who has travelled over the baked tracts where the anjan grows can have failed to notice the refreshing breezes generated by the new foliage which has a thrilling effect on the sunbeaten traveller.

A belief that gained support with regard to the raising of forests, was the close association of teak and bamboo as the ideal crop of the future. As I believed in the idea, many plots of teak and bamboo were started under my own supervision. Little did I realize how the two species had become associated.

The only method of cultivation practised was by axe and fire, so that from time immemorial the forests had been cut and burnt and grown up again. The tribes, however, carefully discriminated between useful species and those of no use, and so valuable woods such as teak, shisham and tinas were preserved.

During my first visit of inspection during which I hoped to consult tribal headmen about introducing conservancy measures, I came upon an extensive area where cuttings had recently been concentrated. It was charred and burnt and there remained only trees profitable for edible production or prized for their timber. The men said the last crop of cereals had been gathered and that now the site would be left to recuperate. A few bamboos occurred on banks and nullahs and in ravines, but outside the area. I learned that a bamboo seed year occurs once in twenty-five or thirty years. On my next visit, a year later, the ground was covered with bamboo seedlings. Within a decade the tract had become the type of teak-cum-bamboo forest with which we were familiar. The teak now towered over the bamboo. Subsequent search showed that most of the teak had disappeared, the few remaining being sickly specimens. It was evident that the two could not grow together as an even aged crop, however well they might flourish if there was a difference of a good few years between them.

It was clear that a light demanding species like the teak could not possibly pass long years under the thick cover of bamboo growth. It was also plain that the bamboo, flowering and dying every twenty-five to thirty years, was undoubtedly younger than the teak with which they associated. Moreover the dry heated atmosphere surrounding bamboo growth is inimical to other young plants like the shisham and tinas as I realized when I noticed the absence of re-germination close to their clumps.

I had an amusing experience some years after the forests came under my charge. The tract abounded with jungli fowl and I invited a brother officer to join me in a week's shoot. As soon as he saw the crop of teak and bamboos - the latter had now after seven to ten years attained almost their full height - he went into raptures on how they grew together. He could hardly believe that the phenomenon had come about since the forests were under my charge.

My experience of bamboos is chiefly confined to the dendroclamus strictus which changes in appearance according to whether it grows on rock or in soil; it is at its best where teak has intruded, comparing favourably with the giant bamboo; on crystalline formation the stems tend to be dwarfed and solid yielding the much prized shaft for hog-spears.

Vernacular and Systematic names of some of the 196 trees, shrubs, annuals mentioned, commonly occurring in the Barwani State.

Indian name	Scientific name
Anjan	Hardwickia finata
Aonla	Phyllanthus Emblica
Babul	Acacia arabica
Bahera	Terminalia belerica
Bhea	Pterocarpus marsupiu
Bhutakas	Eloeodendron glaucum
Bor	Zizyphus Jujuba
Bur	Ficus bengalensis
Charoli	Buchanania latifolia
Chhind	Phoenic sylvestris
Chichola	Albizzia Lebbeck
Chitanvel	Plumbago zeylanica
Dhaori, dhawai	Woodfordia Floribunda
Digamali	Gardenia gummifera
Ghatbor	Zizyphus xylopyra
Gurar	Albizzia procera
Haldar	Adina cordifolia
Imli	Tamarindus indica
Jambu	Eugenia jambolana
Jhakur	Acacia lenticulasia
Kalak	Arundinaria spp
Kalan	Anogeissus pendula
Katarsa	Amaranthus spinosus
Khair	Acacia Catechu
Lsora, moti-gondi	Cordia mixa

Indian name	Scientific name
Mahua	Bassia latifolia
Mohin, moein	Odina Wodior
Nim	Melia indica
Ohala	Ficus palmata
Padal	Sterospormum suaveolens
Papri	Gardenia lucida
Pipul	Ficus religiosa
Raini	Mallotus philippenensis
Ran-bor	Zizyphus vulgaris
Ran-kela	Musa ornata
Rohin	Soyinida febrifuga
Sag	Tectone grandis
Sali	Boswellia serrat
Shisham	Dalbergia latifolia
Teak	
Tendu, temru	Diospyros Melanoxylon
Tinas	Ougeinia dalbergioides
Tokar, bans	Dendrocalamus strictus
Ukli	Salix tetrasperma
Zarkali	Amaranthus gangeticus

Appendix D

St. Joseph's preoccupations went far beyond the call of forestry management. He was interested in the medicinal properties of the plants to be found amongst the trees and how they might best be developed. These extracts from his letters show his own concerns and attention to detail in attempting to make local knowledge available to a wider audience. The letters are followed by a glossary of plants and trees. **D.M. St.J.**

To the Imperial Forest Botanist,
Forest Research Institute,
Dehra Dun,
Camp Barwani, 18-III-10

Sir

I am sending in a separate parcel a specimen of a milky creeper belonging apparently to the *Euphorbiaceae** order. It grows on rocky cliffs spreading in all directions along the perpendicular faces by means of adventitious roots which spring out at the nodes and bind it to the rock. It is locally known as Bhura Bela and is highly valued for curing Rheumatic pains and scorbutic complaints.

I have not seen it in flower or fruit. I shall feel obliged if you will get it identified.

I have the honour to be,
Sir
Your most obedient servant
J.D. St. Joseph.

*On the 10th April 1913 R.S. Hole sent three specimens of *Euphorbiaceae* to Kew for naming.

From R.S. Hole, Esq., I.F.S., F.C.H., F.L.S., F.R.S. - Imperial Forest Botanist.
To The Chief Forest Officer, Bhopawar Agency, Camp Barwani,
Dehra Dun, the 6th April 1910.

Sir,

I have the honour to regret that I cannot identify the specimens sent with your No.362 dated 18th March 1910 without specimens of

the flowers or fruit. Kindly send flowers and fruit if possible.
I have the honour to be,
Sir
Your most obedient servant
R.S. Hole, Imperial Forest Botanist

Nirdarpur
15.IV.10

Dear Mr. Dewar Chand
During my camp at Borkheri we came across a creeper growing on rocky cliffs. Mr. Zakiruddin obtained a specimen which was sent for identification, but the Forest Botanist writes to say he cannot identify it without flower or fruit. Will you please therefore order Zakiruddin to obtain a specimen with flower or fruit and send to me without delay.
Yours truly,
J.D. St. Joseph.

Forest Office Barwani
The 7th December 1910

My Dear Sir,
Please refer to your Demi Official letter No.490 of the 15th April 1910. I beg to state that endeavours were made to obtain the fruit and flower of the creeper in question, but all in vain.

The local people also say that they too have never seen the species either in flower or fruit.
Yours most obediently,
D. Chand

Camp Ajandu,
28-I-11

Dear Mr. Dewar Chand,
Please refer to your D.O. No.334 of 7/12/10. Bhura Bela has been identified as *Sarcostemma intermedium* and the plant is known to flower and fruit so that the statement of the local people you support is erroneous. I shall be obliged if you will obtain specimens in flower and fruit.

The specimen I obtained was near Borkheri, and if you will explain to the Forest Bharti and Kalu Patel of Borkheri, they will doubtless be able to get the specimens in flower and fruit.
Yours truly,
J.D. St. Joseph

To R.S. Hole Esq., F.C.H. Imperial Forest Botanist, Dehra Dun, Camp via Mhow, C.I. the 20.X.12

Sir,

I have the honour to forward specimens, mostly annuals, for identification. A descriptive list giving the local names as well as the uses to which they are put are attached. Please return the specimens when done with.
I have the honour to be
Sir
Your most obedient servant
J. St. Joseph

From R.S. Hole Esq. I.F.S., F.C.H., F.L.S., F.R.S., Forest Botanist To The Chief Forest Officer, Bhopawar Agency, Mhow.

Dehra Dun the 29th October 1912
Sir,

I have the honour to acknowledge receipt of the 41 specimens of herbs sent with your letter dated 20th October 1912 and to point out that one of the principal objects of carrying out identification work at Dehra Dun is that of extending our own botanical collections and herbarium and it is impossible for me to spend a considerable time on the identification of specimens which we are not allowed to keep here for future reference. Kindly let me know whether in the light of these remarks you wish for the return of your specimens.
I have the honour to be,
Sir
Your most obedient servant
R.S. Hole Forest Botanist

To R.S. Hole Esq. F.C.H., F.L.S., etc. Imperial Forest Botanist, Dehra Dun Camp Mhow, the 1-XI-12

Sir

In reply to your letter of 29 10/12 I have the honour to state that the specimens may be kept in the Herbarium as desired. The collector omitted to press duplicates and, as it was thought you would probably have them in your collection, their return was accordingly requested. I shall however thank you to supply the scientific names if they can be identified.
I have the honour to be
Sir
Your most obedient servant
J. St. Joseph

Some of the medicinal plants, relevant to the letters, collected in Ninkhera State C.I.

Poptia - Phaseolus aconitifolius - a creeper. The root is rubbed and mixed with water and given to patients suffering from smallpox. Said to have a soothing effect.
Dudhi - Euphorbiaceae. Its milk is applied to the nose of a patient suffering from a bad cold to grant relief in breathing.
Tulsi - Ocimum sanctum. Utilised in offerings to gods.
Chirmi - Solanum nigrum. A piece of root, washed and given to patients afflicted with toothache to hold inside the mouth, will reduce pain.
Chara - Crotolaria Orixensis. Its root is efficacious in case of snake bites, if rubbed, mixed in water and given to patients to drink.
Lepria - Anotis monosperma - a creeper. The root is rubbed, mixed with water and given to infants suffering from Badal-ke-bimari (pneumonia).
Pila-dhatura - Argemone mexicana. The leaves are ground, made into a paste and applied to wounds of horses suffering from sore backs.
Burra-agiya - Colossocardia linearifolia. The leaves are mixed with tobacco and smoked by patients suffering from severe neuralgia.
Chota-agiya - striga lutea. The root, rubbed, made into paste, is applied to burns.
Lohung - Indigofera hirsuta. The root is rubbed, mixed with cows

milk and given to patients suffering from Guzrati bemari: pleurisy or pneumonia.

Kumbhi - Leucas cephalotes. The branches are crushed and put into a steaming pot. When the vapour is inhaled it is said to cure severe headache.

Trees occurring in the Dhar State forests and their uses.

Baikal - Celastrus senegalensis. The leaves pounded on a stone are applied to wounds of various kinds and considered to possess very healing properties. They are also burnt and used in the same manner. A juice is extracted from the bark and used internally for urinary diseases. The seeds are considered very effective for lung diseases especially consumption.

Chicola - Albizzea Lebbek. The seeds are used as tonic and purifier of the human blood. A snuff is prepared to cure brain diseases but is used in very little quantity. The wood is used for certain parts in the cartwheel and in making furniture. Some think the wood inauspicious and do not like to use it in house building.

Gamar - Choclospermum gossypium. The wood is of very inferior sort and is not even liked as fuel. When an epidemic prevails among tame hens, the jungle tribes of this country use the wood as a preventive; a small pit is made in a piece of wood, filled with water for the hens to drink.

Mohin - Odina Wodior. The juice of the bark is applied on eruptions and also on obstinate ulcers. The gum is given internally for asthma. Wood is used in making juras (yokes for agricultural purposes.

Mokha - Schrebera swicteniodes. During the last great famine of 1897 the Bhil tribes used the tender leaves as a vegetable and the bark was pounded into flour and eaten.

Nigur - Vitex Negundo. The leaves are often used for swellings of the joints due to rheumatism. They are heated on a fire and applied to the affected parts by means of a bandage; this is done repeatedly for 3 or 4 nights or until the patient recovers. The green leaves are also kept in the sleeping room to shun the mosquitoes.

Pendra - Gardinia turgida. The Bhils and other jungle tribes of this part of the country use the raw fruits in place of soap for washing clothes. The unripe fruit was boiled and eaten during the last famine; but when it ripens it gets rather poisonous.

Rinj - Acacia lenophloea. The gum yielded by this plant is locally

used for medicines. The woody eruptions on the stem, taken off and rubbed on a stone into a paste and applied on the glands are said to cure scrofula. The bark grounded into powder and mixed with flour is eaten in time of famine and scarcity.

Rohan - Soymida febrifuga. The deep red bark is very commonly used for the purpose of dyeing clothes. The wood is also much liked for building houses and wells.

Shiwan - Gmelina arborea. The root is used as an article of medicine for various diseases. The wood is much prized and sought after by the natives of this place for making drums, tablas (small Indian hand drum) and other instruments of music.

To R.S. Hole Esq're F.C.H. etc.
Dehra Dun Camp via Mhow the 18-XI-12

Sir

I have the honour to forward some more specimens collected in Jobat and Ratanmal States in this Agency. They are mostly of annuals put to economic uses by the forest tribes inhabiting those tracts. The description list is attached. I shall be glad if you will furnish me with the botanical names of the plants.

I feel I should apologize for some of the specimens, they have been mostly collected by untrained men and hence the poor quality.

I have the honour to be
Sir
Your most obedient servant
J. St. Joseph

Collected in the Jobat State, C.I.

Warni - Vernonia cinerea. The juice of leaves is extracted by boiling and applied to infants suffering from Ratwa (nettle rash).

Phangia - Lindenbergia abyssinica. The juice extracted by boiling is applied to cure swellings on the body.

Ati-jhara - Achyranthes aspera. Young plants are dried and burnt, the ashes mixed in water nd the vessel with the concoction set over a fire, to boil till the water evaporates and the residue settles as salt. This is considered efficacious in cases of severe stomach pains and indigestion.

Collected in Ratanmal State, C.I.

Karwi-nai - Enicosteme Littorale. In cases of fever, the leaves are pounded and tied on to the wrist or arm of the patient, believed to absorb the heat and lessen the temperature.
Gharia. The fruit is tied to the ears of patients suffering from severe toothache to lessen the pain.
Kali-dudhi - Hemidesmus indicus (creeper). Its root is rubbed, mixed in water and given to drink in cases of snake bite.
Rareri - Thespasia Lampas. Its root is boiled in water and given to patients suffering from jaundice.
Hatia-munjara. Its root is rubbed and made into a paste and applied to ulcers in the mouth.

By the 18th May 1913 R.S. Hole had retired and been succeeded as Forest Botanist at Dehra Dun by R.N. Parker, F.C.H.

**To The Forest Boatanist, Research Institute, Dehra Dun,
Mhow the 16-V-13.**
    Sir, I have the honour to send herewith under registered cover, IOI specimens of medicinal plants collected in the Jhabua State in this Agency, for identification. A description list mentioning their uses is also sent.
**I have the honour to be
Sir
Your most obedient servant,
J. St. Joseph.**

A shortened list of these, most now identified by R.H. Parker.

Kabri-dudhi (a creeper) - *Cryptolopis elegans.* It is utilised in warding off attacks from large bees (Apis dorsata) by individuals collecting honey. The roots are ground in water, the paste rubbed over the body, while a piece of the root is chewed and held between the teeth. Thus equipped, he approaches the hive, the scent preventing the bees from settling and stinging the offender.
Rajgari - Gloriosa superba. A deadly poison. A tola weight of the root pounded and mixed with flour and given to a human being or any animal will cause death almost instantaneously.
Jangli-Kikeri. The root ground in water and the paste applied to

severe wounds, will cause them to heal in five or seven days.

Chrpota - Physalis minima. Four leaves with two of Bor (Zizyphus jujuba) are eaten at early dawn on a Sunday by a patient suffering from persistent attacks of fever that will not succumb to other cures; said to be efficacious if taken on Sunday mornings only.

Lilvi - Evolvulus alsinoides. When cases of smallpox take a bad turn, the patient is exposed to the fumes of smoke from the roots which checks complications.

Jangli-nim. Individuals becoming prematurely grey, apply the leaves, ground very fine into a paste, to their hair which has the effect of changing it to its natural colour, black, in about three hours.

Kuli-jung - Celosia cristata. Its root is rubbed in water and the mixture sprinkled constantly for two days on the body of a person bitten by a Russell's viper; while the part bitten is also constantly daubed with the mixture. This is said to remove the poisonous effects of the bite.

Jangli-mogra - Kunonia cinerea. Persons under the influence of witch craft, are rubbed with paste made from the roots ground in water for two or three days, when the influence is removed.

Chandloi - Amarantus Blitum. Four tolas weight of the juice extracted from the leaves and drunk by patients suffering from anaemia, for seven days, will effect cure.

Thecheni - Rhyncosia minima, a creeper. The root is rubbed in water and the mixture given in the early morning for two or three days, to patients suffering from dysentery.

Dhola-mogra - Aeru scandens. Patients whose joints have become stiff owing to rheumatism, are made to drink the mixture obtained by rubbing the root in water, for seven or eight days, at early dawn while the juice from the leaves is well rubbed over the body. the treatment said to cause relief.

Jangli-gobi - Sonchus oleraceus. Roots and leaves are ground, made with water and a little salt into a poultice which is then heated over fire and applied hot on the throat of patients suffering from diphtheria. A cure is said to be effected in three or four days.

Dhamai - Phaseolus aconitifolius. Used to cure persons bitten by the poisonous Goira (Iguana). A piece of root to be rubbed in water to which is added a little ghee and given to the patient to drink.

Beria - Anisomeles ovata. About two tolas weight of seeds, ground fine, mixed in water and drunk, is said to cure rabies.

Gulab-gota - Leonotis nepetaefolia. Used to neutralize effects of alkaloid poisoning. Leaves to be ground find, mixed in water and given to patients who have swallowed opium or other poisonous drugs.

To the Forest Botanist, Research Institute, Dehra Dun
Mhow, the 22-V-13.
Sir,
I have the honour to send, under registered cover, specimens of economic and medicinal plants collected in the Barwani, Ali-Rajpur, Kathiawara and Ratanmal States in this Agency. Descriptive lists mentioning their uses are herewith attached.
I have the honour to be
Sir
Your most obedient servant,
J. St. Joseph.

12 of the 50 specimens collected in the Barwani State

Bane - Herpestis monniera Used to cure bronchitis in children.
Jangli-san - Crotalaria juncea. Bark used for manufacturing ropes.
Hati-sila - Achyranthes aspera Stalks used as toothbrush to strengthen the gums.
Unt-Kantasla - Echinops echinatus. Used to remedy smallpox cases.
Goma - Leucas cephalotis - a creeper. The flowers are used to cure sever coughs.
Rajgiri - Corchorus capoularis. The seeds are given to be eaten by patients bitten by poisonous snakes.
Rajan - Corchorus olitorius. Used in cases of snake bite. Also the leaves are eaten as a vegetable.
Dhera - Cleome monophyllas. The juice extracted from the leaves is dropped into the ears of fever patients to give relief.
Musli - Cuculigo. The bulb is used as a tonic.
Kumbhi - Leucas cephalotis. The flowers are used to cure neuraigic headache.
Jangli-gulab Anisochilus carnosus. The juice of the plant is dropped into the ear to cure earache.
Nine examples are given of plants that can be eaten as spinach, other vegetables, fruit or rice.

4 of the 11 specimens collected in Ali-Rajpur State

Chivard - Cassia Absus. The seeds ground in water and the paste applied over the eyes, when painful, will cause relief.
Phuli - Canscora diffusa. The ash obtained from burning one leaf is mixed with a little honey and the paste given to infants suffering from infantile fever.
Jangli-mircha - Spilanthes Acmela. The flower is ground and made into pills in the juice extracted from the leaves of the same plant and the pill given to patients suffering from intermittent fever.
Chancheria - Pupalia lappacea. The root is rubbed in water and the paste applied over nettle rash for cure.

4 of 20 from Kathiwara State

Dugria - Indigofera hirsuta. In years of scarcity the seeds are ground into flour and prepared into cakes and eaten.
Suneri - Vicoa auriculata. The root is pounded, made into a mixture with water and given to horses suffering from colic.
Rajhal - Adiantum iunulatum. A fern. The leaves crushed are applied to bites from the sloth bear.
Bho-Aouli - Polygala chinensis. The juice extrcted from the leaves is used as smelling salts by patients suffering from sever cold.

5 of 10 from Ratanmal State

Marchi - Centratherum molle. The root is rubbed in water and the paste applied to wounds.
Undri. Equal portions in weight of the root and beetle [betel] nut are ground together, mixed with little gur, made into 5 pills and one given daily to patients suffering from epileptic fits, said to cure after the fifth dose.
Bhoran - Anisomeles ovata. The root is rubbed in water and the paste applied over the body of a patient who has had sun or heat stroke.
Chivel - Barleria Gibsoni - a creeper. The root rubbed in water and applied to scorpion stings will remove the pain.
Ateri - Helicteros Isora. The root ground in water, made into a mixture and given to cholera patients will stop the disease and cure in two or three days.

From R.N. Parker, Esq. F.C.H. Forest Botanist, Dehra Dun, U.P.
To J.D. St. Joseph, Esq/.
Chief Forest Officer,
Bhopawar Agency, Mhow.

Dehra Dun the 19th July 1913

Sir,
   In reply to your No. 578 dated 12th July 1913 I have the honour to inform you that the two plants you sent appear to be stages of one species, one fruiting and the other in leaf. I am planting these plants in order to keep them under observation. The plant is I think *Synantherias sylvatica* but I will examine it again if it flowers here next spring and let you know the result.
I have the honour to be
Sir
Your most obedient servant
R.N. Parker
FOREST BOTANIST

Parker's next letter, if written, has not survived.

In the spring of 1914 John Daniel became seriously ill and left for England at the beginning of August.

Appendix E

The main source of the following short histories is the East India Gazetteer, quotations from which have been edited. It was published in 1825, sixty-six years before St. Joseph embarked on his career in forestry. It is interesting to compare his account with the earlier records concerning the Bhils, particularly in the light of the present controversies regarding the Nerbudda/Narmada Dam, and the whole question of the position of 'tribals' and aborigines in India; all the more so too in relation to the current plight of Patna and Bihar, now one of the poorest regions of the world with a reputation for corruption and crime, and the scene of much social unrest and political violence.

St. Joseph visited and photographed some of the following places in the early nineteen hundreds: Benares, Bhopal, Dewas, Dhar, Indore, Khandesh, Malwa, Mhow, Monghyr, Nerbudda/Narmada, Patna, Rajpur, the Satpura Mountains, the Tuptee (Tapti) River, the Vindhya Mountains.

No mention is made in the Gazetteer of Jobat, Amkhut or Barwani; in 1825 they were probably minor settlements, as was also Naini Tal, 50 miles from the Nepal border. Fortunate people now escape there during the hottest months or to Dehra Dun, 100 miles from the Chinese border, now the home of the Forest Research Institute, the Wildlife Institute of India, the India Military Academy, the Survey of India Office and many schools.

Benares is one of the oldest cities in the world. An important Hindu site, it was sacked by Muslims who occupied it from the 12th to the 16th centuries. A Hindu ruled again in 1738 and the city was ceded to the British in 1775.

From the East India Gazetteer:

The Sanskrit name of this place is Varanashi, from the streams Vara and Nashi. On the Ganges, where the river makes a fine sweep of about four miles in length, on the convex side of the curve which is the most elevated, stands the holy city of Benares. The margin is covered with houses to the water's edge.

The streets are extremely narrow and difficult to penetrate even on horseback. Some of the 12,000 stone and brick houses, from one to six stories high, are fantastically painted with mythological figures from the Hindoo pantheon, with very small windows to prevent glare and inspection. The opposite sides of some streets are

so close as to be united by galleries. The number of mud houses exceeds 16,000 besides garden houses. The population estimated in 1803 at 582,000 has now increased by 50,000. One in ten is supposed to be a Mahommedan. Natives from all parts of India, Turks, Tartars, Persians, Armenians and even Europeans are found in Benares. The European houses are handsome but look naked for want of trees; but this bareness is requisite in India on account of the myriads of mosquitoes and other winged and unwinged insects which their foliage would harbour.

To mortify the Hindoos a mosque was founded on the sacred spot of a Hindoo temple, destroyed to make room for the Mussulman edifice.

Mendicants are numerous; many natives are actively engaged as bankers and diamond merchants, Europeans as indigo planters, lawyers or medical men. Lawsuits are unceasing as the natives are constitutionally litigious respecting their property.

In 1801 besides the public college of Hindoo literature there were private teachers of Hindoo and Mahommedan law receiving nothing from their schools, trusting to donations from pilgrims of rank and regular salaries from Hindoo princes.

A legend informs us that Benares was originally built of gold but because of people's sins turned to stone, and has now, owing to increasing wickedness degenerated into thatch and clay.

Brahmins occupy about 8,000 houses. They admit that even the beef-eating English who die at Benares or who become firm believers in Gunga (the Ganges) may go to heaven.

The surrounding country is extensively cultivated, the most valuable produce being sugar cane, opium, tobacco, betel leaf and indigo.

This celebrated town has enjoyed the most undisturbed tranquility since it came under the direct government of the British nation by the expulsion of Cheit Singh in 1781.

Bhopal (Bopaul 1825) is the capital of a small independent Mahomedan principality in the province of Malwa. The districts of Sindia and Kotah lie to the north, Sindia to the east, Sindia and Holcar to the west, the Nerbudda river to the south. The surrounding country is an uneven jungly tract, but fertile and well watered.

In 1723 it was ruled by an Afghan adventurer. His death was followed by the usual mixture of usurpation, assassination and other irregularities inherent to all native dynasties. His successor

having made a long and effective defence of Bopaul against the forces of Sindia and the Nagpoor Raja, appealed for help from the British government but a deaf ear was turned to his supplications. In 1816, on the eve of being subdued, he died. Interference was unavoidable, and the state was taken under the protection of the British and its territories greatly augmented.

Dewas is a town in the province of Malwa. In 1820 it contained 1187 inhabited houses, and about 5930 persons. For thirty years prior to 1817 the Puars of Dewas suffered the extreme of misery, having been so incessantly plundered and oppressed by Sindia, Holcar and every Pindarry (marauder) and freebooter of the day that their being in existence or possessing an inhabited village appears almost a miracle. A pleasing contrast was presented in 1821 when, having been almost deserted, it became a populous town with 141 villages repeopled.

Dhar. An ancient city in the province of Malwa. The Dhar territory comprehends about 400 square miles and when properly cultivated yields almost every tropical production, amongst others opium. It contains 179 villages 25 of which are in the wild and hilly tracts and inhabited by Bheels. In 1820 the number of inhabited houses was 7,573 for the population of about 37,865 souls, in the proportion of one Mahommedan to sixteen Hindoos.

The city of Dhar appears at one period to have covered a great extent of ground. It is surrounded by a mud wall, the interior containing some good buildings, and is well watered by eight large and two small tanks (lakes, ponds). The fort is entirely detached from the city and stands about 40 feet above the plain, with walls 30 feet high fortified with round and square towers.

In 1817 when British troops entered Malwa and took over Dhar it was the only possession that remained to its twelve-year-old ruler after all the robberies committed by Sindia and Holcar.

Indore. A city in the province of Malwa. The capital of the Old Indore State having been destroyed by fire during the war between Sindia and Holcar in 1801, the present (1828) city is almost entirely modern. Some of the streets are tolerably spacious but it does not contain a single structure worth looking at. After its capture by the British and the Treaty of 1818 M.R. Holcar, a boy of about twelve years of age, accompanied by his principal chiefs came into the British camp, and a Prime Minister was invested with the management of affairs.

At present (1828) the reserved territories of Holcar consist of 1,800 sq. miles extending along the southern bank of the Nerbudda; 4,800 sq. miles extending along the north bank of the Nerbudda; 4,500 sq. miles in different detached portions. (The latter probably accounts for the number of separate areas of Indore in the 1895 map of the Central Provinces on page 2).

The young prince abandoned the former custom of always residing in camp and fixed his residence at Indore which under the Prime Minister's able management rapidly increased in extent, wealth and population. 'Holcar' was remembered and the name used by St. Joseph.

Khandesh (Candeish, Khandesa). A province of the Deccan. A large proportion of Khandesh is remarkably fertile, being watered by copious streams, on many of which expensive embankments have been constructed. In 1820 some portions of land remained in good cultivation, others, recently abandoned, conveyed a high notion of their ancient fruitfulness and capability of renovation. But a large proportion of the surface at that date was covered with jungle, swarming with tigers among the ruins of the former villages. The natural beauties are much enhanced by the number of limpid rivulets, hardly ever dry, that flow down from the table land and fall into the Tuptee (Tapti).

The decline of Khandesh may be dated from 1802 when it was ravaged by the Holcar and the following year depopulated by famine.

The Bheels now withdrew to their fastnesses and made predatory incursions and the Pindarries (mounted marauders) annually devastated the plains. Some order was installed by the British conquest of 1818 but the Bheels of the Satpura Range (which although not more than 1500 feet high have a difficult access and pestilential climate) continued to give much trouble and were only brought under by cutting off their supplies and pensioning the rulers to restrain the excesses of their subjects. The same plan was followed with the Bheels of the Chandore Range and with the Bheels and Coolies of Baglam.

It will require a long period of time to restore to prosperity a territory that has been so thoroughly depopulated. The existing villages are for the most part built of mud and protected by a miserable wall and fort of the same material without ditch or outwork.

The chief rivers are the Nerbudda and Tuptee. Among the hills and along the courses of these rivers many Bheel Bhilla tribes are to be found whose chiefs formerly commanded most of these passes. It is in the wild tract stretching along the left bank of the Nerbudda that they have been least disturbed and it is here that we may expect to find their peculiar usages in the purest preservation. They are a jungle people differing from the other inhabitants in manners and appearance. Towards the west in Gujerat they meet the Coolies and towards the southeast they come in contact with the Gonds but the discrepancies that distinguish those tribes from each other have never been clearly ascertained.

The Bheels and Gonds inhabit the interior where they cultivate little, being naturally averse to agriculture and addicted to hunting and rapine; the Coolies are found mostly on or near the seacoast as fishers and pirates but on the whole are more civilised than the two other tribes. Their common points seem to be an aversion to regular industry and a proneness to thieving and robbery, in which they are so expert that they were formerly employed by the native chiefs to desolate the lands of their adversaries.

In person the Bheels are small, dark complexioned men, nearly in a state of nakedness, constantly armed with a bow and arrow. They are subdivided into an endless variety of tribes and families, each living under its own Naik. In religion they are said to be Hindoos of Brahminical persuasion - yet they bury their dead, a marked distinction; and in their feeding are addicted to many impure practices for they eat beef and pork and drink spirits of every description. From a census taken in 1820 of the Bheel population of the Vindhya Range there did not appear to be more than six to a square mile.

That the District of Khandesh is capable of great improvement is evident from the dilapidated remains of more than one hundred substantially built dams and aqueducts, constructed for irrigation, which at a small expense might be again rendered available.

It never recovered from the devastation of Holcar troops in 1802-3, the subsequent famine of 1803-4, the destructive farming system incursions of the Pindarries and ravages of the Bheels. To these causes of ruin may be added the number of tigers with which the country absolutely swarmed, sixty having been killed in one month, and the epidemic of 1821 which swept off thousands.

When, in 1819, the district was finally in British possession, a

vast extent of unreclaimed jungle was discovered, and nearly one half of the villages, deserted and abandoned to the beasts of the forest.

In 1820 the agricultural classes were decribed as peaceable and inoffensive, but timid and helpless, ground to the earth by the multiplied calamities they had experienced.

Malwa A large province of Hindostan, estimated at 220 miles in length by 150 the average breadth. A traveller proceeding from Jeypoor to Indore, a city 1998 feet above the level of the sea, has to thread several defiles and occasionally cross a low ridge and is only made sensible of the increasing elevation by the decreasing temperature.

The descent towards the north from the Vindhya mountains is marked by the course of the numerous streams which have their source in that chain whence they flow due north until they join the Chumbal and ultimately the Jumna and the Ganges.

The seasons are those common to Western India: the rainy, the cold and the hot. The fall of rain during the months of June, July, August and September has been estimated at about 50 inches.

The soil of Malwa is noted for its fertility. Among the principal grains are wheat, gram, peas, jowary, bajary, moong and Indian corn. Rice is only raised in small quantities for home consumption but a surplus remains of sugar cane, tobacco, linseed, garlic, turmeric and ginger. Indigo also in small quantities, also the morinda citrifolia, a red dye plant. But of all the vegetable production opium is the most important, the soil and climate being singularly well adapted to the cultivation of the poppy. Malwa opium is particularly esteemed by the Chinese who assert that it contains two-sevenths more of pure opium than an equal of the Patna and Benares drug. The Malwa tobacco is by far the best in India and much sought after by the votaries of the hookah.

In this province the savage tribe of Bheels are found in considerable numbers, especially in the mountains contiguous to the Nerbudda.

The designation of Pindarry was at first applied to a body of roving cavalry which accompanied local armies. The Pindarries were principally wholly the leaders of the Mahommedan religion but all castes were allowed to associate with them. They constituted a nucleus round which might assemble all that was vagabond and disaffected, all that was incapable of honest industry

and peaceful occupation. In 1814 the total of all these marauding bands was estimated at 31,000 horse.

In about 1819 the proportion of Mahommedans to Hindoos was as one to twenty-one.

Mandu (Mandow). Now (1825) the ruins of an ancient town in the province of Malwa. In the 15th century this once celebrated city was called Shadrabad, City of Joy. It is situated 2000 feet above sea level at the edge of the Malwa plateau on the summit of a mountain in the Vindhyan chain, and separated by a vast chasm from the adjacent territory. During the rains this chasm is obstructed by water, and the approach to the town, apparently the only one, is by a broad causeway along the bottom of the ravine then winding up the mural face of the rock. The city's natural defences are reinforced by the massive walls, over twenty miles long, of a historic fort dominated first by Hindoos then provincial Muslim dynasties, and a scene of constant siege and battle. The area within the walls has been estimated at 12,654 English acres.

From 1405 to 1434 it was the capital of the Mahommedan Kingdom of Malwa under Hoshang Shah Gori.

Inside the battlements which have ten gates there are mosques, very large tombs and palaces, the style of architecture being mostly Afghan. The most remarkable and longest standing of the remains are the Palace of Baz Bahauder, strikingly placed on an eminence, the Jehaz Ka Mahal standing on a sort of isthmus between two spacious tanks, the elegant 'Ship Palace' so called because it overhangs three lakes, and the Jumma Musjid, by far the finest specimen of Afghan mosque to be seen in India, and the mausoleum of Hussein Shah (Hoshang Shah's tomb) a massive structure composed entirely of white marble from the banks of the Nerbudda and forerunner of the Taj Mahal.

Around 1575 Baz Bahauder (Bahadur) became ruler of Malwa. He has long been remembered for his skill in music and romantic attachment to the beautiful singer of Sarangpur, Rupmati.

During the monsoon season a fine mist shrouds the palaces. The lakes around which the city is built are planted with masses of lotus.

Prior to the military occupation of Malwa province Mandu seems to have been abandoned to the tigers and to such parties of Bheel robbers as occasionally sought shelter and concealment in its halls and fastnesses.

Mhow. A town in the province of Malwa 10 miles south of Indore, 2,019 feet above the level of the sea, resting on a background of mountains which extend to the Nerbudda river.

In 1820 the large force at this place was not regularly housed and the mixture of tents with temporary huts and small bungalows gave the scene a very animated and military character. In 1822 the barracks were completed and a considerable fortress erected.

As a military cantonment Mhow is of great importance and is supplied with stores from Broach; all heavy substance can be carried more than half-way by water.

Monghyr. A celebrated town and fortress situated n the South side of the Ganges which here in the rainy season presents a prodigious expanse of fresh water.

The fort is large and surrounded by a deep ditch and has probably been a place of note from the remotest antiquity. Since the expansion of the British dominions beyond Delhi, it has been suffered to go to decay and is now degraded to an invalid station and a lunatic asylum.

The town of Monghyr consists of sixteen different market places scattered over a space about a mile and a half long and a mile wide. Between the river and the northern gate of the fort is a suburb, mostly built on the sand of the Ganges which renders it necessary every year to remove many of the houses during the flood. The number of houses may be estimated at 5,000, six persons allowed to a house.

Both Hindoos and Mahommedans make frequent offerings at a shared place of worship.

The gardeners of Monghyr are noted throughout Bengal, and the tailors are not of less celebrity. Much of the army clothing is made here, and shoes of both native and European fashion. Here also are workmen who make European furniture, palanquins and carriages. The blacksmiths occupy about 40 houses and make goods after the European fashion, coarse when compared with English articles but useful and cheap as will be seen by the following prices:

Double barrelled guns 32 rupees, rifles 30 rupees, muskets 8 rupees, pistols 10 rupees, table knives and forks per dozen 6 rupees.

Nerbudda, (Narmada) from narma = pleasure, da = she who bestows. The source of this river does not yet (1825) appear to have

been explored by any European. According to native testimony it rises in a pool or well 2,463 feet above the level of the sea, close to the source of the Sone. From hence its course is due west, with fewer curvatures than most Indian rivers until after about 700 miles it falls into the sea below Broach. During its passage it is much obstructed by rocks, islands, shallows and rapids which renders its navigation in most parts difficult or impracticable. With respect to its breadth there is much variation. At Sacur to the West of Jubbulpoor it is about 600 yards in breadth, at Mandleysir 1200 and above and below Broach where there are several islands it extends sometimes to the breadth of 3 miles.

The name of Deccan was formerly applied by Hindoo geographers to the whole of the countries situated to the South of the Nerbudda.

By Ptolemy, the Nerbudda, properly Narmada, is designated the Namadus.

Patna -Padmavati - a large city, capital of the province of Bahar (Bihar) situated on the south side of the Ganges which is here five miles wide in the rainy season.

It is difficult to settle the exact boundaries of Patna, for to exclude all beyond the walls would reduce it to a trifle, while the suburbs are built in a very straggling, ill defined manner. It comprehends an extent of 9 miles along the banks of the Ganges.

Within the walls Patna is rather more than one mile from East to West, and three-fourths of a mile from North to South, the whole exceedingly closely built. Many houses are of brick, others of mud with tiled roofs, few are thatched. During the heats of spring the dust is beyond idea, and in the rains every place is covered with mud.

Notwithstanding that Patna is one of the chief European settlements of India, with a court of appeal, a circuit, a city judge, magistrate, collector, commercial resident, opium agent and provincial battalion, the number of European houses and settlers is surprisingly few.

Patna was formerly fortified after the Hindostani manner with a wall and small ditch but these are now in the last stage of decay and the gates tottering to their base.

Many years ago the Company [Honourable East India Company HEIC] erected here a depôt to contain rice, consisting of a brick building in the shape of a beehive with two winding

staircases on the outside, which have been ascended on horseback. By means of these stairs it was intended that the grain should be poured in at the top, there being a small door at the bottom to let it out. The walls at the bottom, although 21 feet thick have given way, a circumstance of very little consequence, as were it filled (which it never was) it would not contain one day's consumption for the province. It is now used as a depôt for military stores and visited by strangers on account of the echo which is remarkably perfect.

Patna's enlargement and prosperity in the 18th century were owing to the European commercial factories belonging to the English, Dutch, French and Danes who traded to a great extent especially in cotton cloth. This trade has greatly declined although those of opium, nitre and indigo have increased.

In the middle of the city the Catholics have a church, in 1811 the best looking in the place although the flock only consisted of about 20 families of native Portuguese.

There are many mosques here, but none large. Some are now let by their owners as warehouses; although the proprietor has thus debased his mosque, he persevered strenuously in calling the faithful to prayer. In this vicinity and near Dinapoor potatoes are cultivated to a large extent. Most of the European vegetables thrive uncommonly well and are now eaten by Mahommedans and the Hindoo castes that use garlic and onions, but all Brahmins reject them as impure.

Such are the vicissitudes of Indian cities that Patna may now claim precedence of Delhi and Agra as to size and population. In 1811 it was reckoned to contain 52,000 houses of which 22,188 were mud walled huts covered with tiles or thatch; six persons may with safety be allowed to each house which would give a population of 312,000 besides which there is a considerable floating population of sepoys, camp followers, boatmen etc.

In 1813 the police of Patna were reported to be in a very inefficient state, the large islands in the vicinity, covered with jungle, affording a secure asylum for robbers. A proper watch maintained in the great street would prevent nocturnal depredations to any great extent unless collusion took place on the part of the native police officers.

Rajpur. A town in the province of Malwa, eighteen miles from Kooksee (Kuksi). It stands on the high road from Malwa to Gujerat and is surrounded by a thick jungle, cultivated in some spots by the Bheelala tribe.

Satpura Mountains. An extreme range of hills in the Deccan - situated between the Nerbudda and Tuptee rivers, and almost wholly occupied by the Bheel tribes. In appearance they differ from the Vindhyan mountains having bold, romantic outlines, rising into lofty peaks, but in geological structure they are similar. The highest peak is about 2,500 feet above the level of the sea.

Vindhya Mountains. On the summit of the northern range is a table land of great extent. In the south the chain extends east and west along the valley of the Nerbudda river, and may be termed the southern wall or buttress of the elevated plateau of Malwa. It is only in a few detached spots that it attains a greater height than 2,000 feet, but the Shaizghur, the highest peak in the Mandoo range rises to 2,628 feet above the level of the sea.

The city of Indore is at 1998 feet, and the descent to the valley of the Nerbudda by the Jaumghaut, about 30 miles to southward, is steep and abrupt, but the ascent from the north is much more gradual.

A good description of the Vindhyan Mountains with all their spurs and ramifications is much needed.

The Vindhyan Range is the Ouindion of Ptolemy. It covers an area only a little smaller than England and is formed of massive sandstone.

Source material

1. Draft of **Work and Sport in the Wilds of Central India** (Published as: **Life in the Wilds of Central India**)
2. Notes – Original. Miscellaneous. On the Bhil Clan
3. Monograph No. II The Jungle Tribes of Malva
4. Monograph No. III Jihantia Brahmans – Central India
5. Monograph No. IV Tribes of Barwani
6. Notes and letters on Ethnography
7. Correspondence regarding Ethnography of Bhils in Bhopawar Agency
8. Collection of Medicinal Plants and subsequent correspondence between Imperial Forest Botanist Dehra Dun, U.P. Oude 1) R.S. Hole 2) R.N. Parker and the Chief Forest Officer, Bhopawar Agency, J.D. St. Joseph, Camp Barwani.
9. Working Plans for the Forests of Barwani State
10. Report on the Forest Administration 1906-1907 in States under Bhopawar Agency
11. Report on the Forest Administration 1910-1911 in States under Bhopawar Agency
12. Report on the Forest Administration 1911-1912 in States under Bhopawar Agency
13. Report on the Forests of Gwalior State 1904

Glossary A

Indian words explained by the author

balhar	broad bean
baori	masonry well with steps leading to water
bhat	bard
bhardwa	witch doctor
bhumka	disease doctor
bhut	ghost
buth	shifting patch cultivations
charpoy	native cot
chatty	basket
chela	disciple
chowdri	village agent
daranta	scythe
Dhemars	fishing class
Diwan	chief minister in Indian princely state
durri	tent carpet
gatta	monolith in memory of the dead
ghara	earthenware narrow-necked pot
ghee	clarified butter
ginning	cotton spinning
gur	Indian sugar
gurn	religious preceptor
hal	plough
haq	sanctioned prerequisite
Holi	spring festival
Jheel	a breed of duck
Jogun	deified wizard, witch
jolaha	weaver
joomti	shifting patch cultivation
jura	yoke
kachhu	a breed of horse

kalal	liquid vendor
Kalidas	a great Sanskrit poet and dramatist; a popular author
kanungo	revenue employee
kathas	lectures by people versed in classics
khakar	harrow, rake
kharif	spring or monsoon crop
khodra	deep ditch, canal
kilki	shrill human note
kopla	bullock hoe
kotwal	village watchman
ladus	balls of grain
lagan	consummatiion
lamjhana	service to a family by a future son-in-law
littee	native cake
lota	brass vessel
mandroa	wooden platform supported by poles
makkar	lowest type of Bhil
maund	82lb weight
mohur	gold coin of an early mintage
munshi	reader
Naik	leader
nazur	senior orderly
nilgai	blue-bull
palea	someone born feet-first
pardhee	professional game catcher
patwara	a scriber
pindarry	a mounted warrior
pori	little girl
Punchayat	council of elders
ratwa	nettle rash
senai	a 'boat' made of inflated skin
ser punch	village headman or president in council
sirvee	class of famed agriculturalists

Life in the Wilds of Central India

sowar	mounted orderly
sukree	grain doles per plough
tabla	small hand drum
tank	small lake
Tees mar Khan	victor in thirty deeds
tephun	a drill
thana	police station
thuggi	attackers who strangled travellers
tumba	shell of the pepo or fruit of the gourd, indicating the strength of a regiment
tumrea	a pumpkin
turvee	village watchman

Glossary B

Indian words undefined by the author

amaltas	laburnum
bajary	millet
bast	flexible fibrous bark
bhang	Indian hemp used as a narcotic and intoxicant
bharti	official
bismullah	"In the name of Allah", an Islamic prayer
bund	a well
buria	money lender
coign	place of advantage, affording a good view
coupe	stretch of forest to be felled
dacoit	class of gang robbers
daffadar	petty officer in police
dak bungalow	simple resthouse
daroga	chief officer in excise or police
dhak	tree with brilliant flowers, or mail, post
dhobi	washerman
diaphoretic	causing perspiration
durbar	formal reception
fakir	religious devotee
halal	meat prepared the Islamic way
howda	seat with canopy on elephant
jagir	title deed
jowary	millet
long dog	greyhound
machan	hideout in a tree
mahout	elephant driver
moong	lentil

Life in the Wilds of Central India

naib	deputy governor, assistant
nullah, nala	ditch
padshah	emperor
patel	headman
peon	attendant, orderly
pir	Mushin holy man
pooja, puja	Hindi religious devotions
pundit	Brahmin lawyer
raff	common run of people
ryot	farmer
sadhu	a holy man
sanad	deed, warrant
shikar	hunter
shikari	hunting
sircar, sirkar	government
tamasha	function or entertainment
tola	measure of weight
tope	grove
vakil	attorney, advocate
vedas	the most ancient Hindi scriptures
vedic	apertaining to the vedas
waler	breed of horse imported from Australia
yakshi	evil spirit
zamindar	feudal landowner

British people mentioned in the text

BAKER Sir Samuel 1821-1893
Traveller and sportsman. Visited Ceylon 1846, 1848. Travelled in Africa 1861-1865. Gold Medal of the Royal Geographical Society. Vigourously opposed slave trade. Continued to travel occasionally in many parts of the world for the purpose of hunting big game.

CORBETT Edward James (Jim) 1875-1955
Destroyer of man-eating tigers, naturalist and author. Born and educated in Naini Tal; served with Bengal and N.W. Railway; took Kumaon Force to France 1917-18; became expert photographer of big game; granted Freedom of Forests in India; moved to Kenya 1947; wrote "The Man-Eaters of Kumaon" (1946), "The Man-Eating Leopard of Rudraprayag" (1948) and "The Temple Tiger" (1954).

FORSYTH Sir Thomas 1827-1886.
Indian civilian educated at Haileybury and Calcutta. Rendered valuable service at Umballa, 1857. Created CB for his conduct in the Mutiny. Commissioner of the Punjab 1860-1872. K.C.S.I. Promoted trade with Turkestan. Envoy to Kashgar, 1873.

KIPLING Rudyard 1865-1936
Born Bombay. Educated United Services College, Westward Ho! Joined staff of Lahore Civil and Military Gazette, 1882. First book, Stalky & Co, published 1899. Wrote especially of the Empire doing justice and upholding law. Settled in London 1889. Two Jungle Books written 1894-5. Awarded Nobel Prize for Literature, 1907. Refused Laureateship 1895 and O.M. three times.

MARRIS Sir William 1873-1945
Indian Civil Servant. Contemporary and friend of Rutherford at Canterbury College, New Zealand. After Oxford went out in 1896 to North West Provinces and Oudh. In 1921 made K.C.S.I and Governor of Assam. Governor of United Provinces 1922-1927. Principal of Armstrong College, Newcastle-upon-tyne 1929-37. Vice chancellor of Durham University for two years. Translated Horace, Catullus and Homer into English verse. Vice Chancellor of Durham University.

MEADOWS-TAYLOR Colonel Philip 1809-1876
Indian officer and novelist. Arrived India 1824. In service of Nizam of Hyderabad in military and then civilian capacity. By 1827 was Assistant Superintendent of Police. Investigated mysterious murders in that region. Returned to England 1837. Back in India 1840. Special Correspondent of The Times 1840-1853. On outbreak of Mutiny kept district of Booldana quiet. Author of "Confessions of a Thug" 1839 and five other novels relating to Indian history, also "Story of My Life" (edited by his daughter 1877).

PICKERING Carol (née Titus)
Daughter of American missionary parents. Born and brought up in the United Provinces, now Uttar Pradesh. Educated at Woodstock School in Landour, Mussoorie, in the Himalayas and for one year at a women's college of Lucknow University before going to the United States for further education. Returned to India 1946 to marry D.P. Hardy, of the Indian Civil Service, United Provinces cadre. They retired from India at the time of Independence, 1947, and went to the Gold coast, now Ghana, where D.P.H. worked in the Colonial Administrative Service. Returned to England 1955. D.P.H. was ordained as an Anglican priest in 1956. He died in 1977. Subsequently C.E.P. married W.S.F. Pickering.

POLLOCK Field Marshal Sir George 1786-1872
Entered East India Company 1803. Took part in campaign against Holkar 1804-5. Served in Nepal 1814. 1st Burmese War 1824-26. Major-General 1838. Kabul 1842. Created G.C.B. Returned to England 1846. Senior Government Director in East India Company, 1854. Field Marshal 1870. Baronet 1872.

RUTHERFORD Baron R of Nelson 1871-1937
Born Nelson, New Zealand. 1st Class Honours Mathematics and Physics, Canterbury College, New Zealand. Worked under Sir J.J. Thomson, Cambridge Professor of Physics, Manchester, 1907. Developed nuclear theory of atoms, 1906-1914. Cavendish Professor of Experimental Physics, Cambridge University 1919-1937. Directly inspired many of the spectacular discoveries after 1933. F.R.S. President 1925-30. Nobel Prize 1908. Knighted 1914. O.M. 1925. Buried Westminster Abbey.

SANDERSON George c. 1846-

Landed in Madras fresh from school, 1864. Proceeded to station in Mysore. Controlled 150 miles of river-drawn irrigation channels, 716 miles in 1868. H.Q. Mysore. 1873 appointed to catch elephants. 1875 in charge of Bengal Elephant Catching Establishment. 1877 returned to England on 15 months furlough on medical certificate. Wrote "Thirteen Years among the Wild Beasts of India." 7th edition published Edinburgh 1912.

SLEEMAN Sir William 1788-1856

Indian administrator born Cornwall. In 1809 nominated to an infantry cadetship in Bengal Army, went to India. Gazetted ensign 1810, lieutenant 1814, served in Nepal War 1814-16 in 12th Bengal Infantry. In 1802 appointed junior assistant to Governor General's agency in Nerbudda Territory. Henceforth employed in civil and political posts, retaining military right to promotion. Captain 1825, Colonel 1853, Major-General 1854. Served as magistrate and district officer in Central Provinces 1825-35. His most remarkable achievement was an exposure of the practices of the Thugs, an organised fraternity of professional murderers. 1835-1841 superintended suppression of Thuggi and dacoity. His revelations were a basis for Meadows-Taylor's "Confessions of a Thug" published 1830. 1843-1849 political resident in Gwalior. Offered residency at Lucknow by Lord Dalhousie 1848. In 1854 was compelled by ill-health to leave for the hills, then ordered home. Died on homeward voyage off Ceylon 1856. K.C.B. conferred on him four days before his death, on recommendation of Lord Dalhousie.

THOMPSON Richard Horatio Ely (From India List 1901)

Late Forest Department Central Provinces. 1855 Joined the service as overseer of Government tea plantation, Gorwhal. Assistant superintendent Kumaon forests 1860. Assistant conservator of forests 1864. Transferred to Central Provinces 1871 as Department Conservator. Services lent to Government of Ceylon 1887. Conservator 1892. Floreat 1890-1900's.

FINALE

It has often occurred to me that the Forest service is deserving of a motto to which its members could point as the motive of their aim. The omission is the more striking if we consider that this fine profession controls the destiny of the vegetable kingdom which furnishes the essence in the industrial life of the world and so, in no small degree, provides for the welfare of future generations.

When I was entrusted with the independent charge of the Southern States' forests in Central India and unfettered with departmentalism, I set about to search for a suitable device and adopted a line from Virgil contained in the words 'si dare vis silvae plus tibi culta feret', which seemed to me most appropriate for this purpose. It would be difficult to compose one that would more forcibly express the truth of what forest work means and I suggest it for the consideration of the heads of the service.

Also, it seems a slur that so important a service should be without an order of its own to confer upon deserving members who have worked to advance the knowledge of one or other of its various sciences. There are institutions claiming the privilege that appear small, as compared with the vast domain of research embodied in forest management. A more simple and expressive title than that comprised in the words "Knight of the Forest" could not be easily found.

The pride and affection I feel for the noble cause of Forestry prompts me into putting forward these proposals. Their adequacy will not be dented, but their advocacy savours of obstructive sentiments which are excusable in view of the purpose served. This is shown by their being assigned the closing lines in these memoirs.

JD St J

CW01310803